Education for Values

Education for Values: Morals, Ethics and Citizenship in Contemporary Teaching

Edited by Roy Gardner,
Jo Cairns
and Denis Lawton

KOGAN
PAGE

First published 2000

Kogan Page Limited
120 Pentonville Road
London
N1 9JN
UK

Stylus Publishing Inc.
22883 Quicksilver Drive
Sterling
VA 20166-2012
USA

British Library Cataloguing in Publication Data

A CIP record for this book is available from the British Library.

ISBN 0 7494 3065 6

Typeset by Kogan Page Limited
Printed and bound in Great Britain by Biddles Ltd, Guildford and King's Lynn

Contents

The Contributors and Editors   *ix*

Introduction   **1**

1. **Morals, Ethics and Citizenship in Contemporary
    Teaching**
    Jo Cairns   6

PART I: APPROACHES TO TEACHING VALUES

2. **What Scope Is There for Teaching Moral Reasoning?**
    Graham Haydon   27

3. **Three Approaches to Moral Education**
    Colin Wringe   38

4. **Philosophy for Children: How Philosophical Enquiry
    Can Foster Values Education in Schools**
    Robert Fisher   50

5. **Sharing Values with a Selfish Gene**
    Philip Goggin   67

PART II: ISSUES IN EDUCATION IN VALUES

6. **Legitimating the Moral Curriculum**
    Paul Yates   79

7. **The Contribution of Special Education to Our
    Understanding of Values, Schooling and the Curriculum**
    Brahm Norwich and Jenny Corbett   96

8. Citizenship Studies, Community Service Learning
and Higher Education
John Annette 109

PART III: TEACHER EDUCATION AND VALUES

9. The Moralization of Teaching: A Relational
Approach as an Ethical Framework in the
Professional Preparation and Formation of Teachers
Michael Totterdell 127

10. A Code of the Ethical Principles Underlying Teaching
as a Professional Activity
John Tomlinson and Vivienne Little 147

11 The TTA Consultation Documents on ITT: What, No
Values?
Stuart Ainsworth and Andrew Johnson 158

12. Communities in Search of Values: Articulating Shared
Principles in Initial Teacher Education
Val Fraser and Mick Saunders 186

PART IV: RESEARCH FOR EDUCATION IN VALUES

13. Valued Educational Research: Reconceptualizations
of the Curriculum
David Scott 203

14. Education for Integrity: Values, Educational Research
and the Use of the Life History Method
Paul Armstrong 218

15. Representation in Research: Whose Values Are We
Representing?
Jane Erricker 230

PART V: COMPARATIVE STUDIES

16. **Ethics (Re)placed: Considerations for Educating Citizens in Post-Apartheid South Africa**
    Robert Balfour   **249**

17. **Researching Values in Cross-cultural Contexts**
    Elwyn Thomas   **257**

18. **Can Those Children Become 'Good Cats'? Dilemmas in Curriculum Reform in the Schools of Beijing, China**
    Xiaopeng Li   **273**

19. **Valuing Studies of Society and Environment**
    Gavin Faichney   **285**

20. **In Search of a Vision of the Good: Values Education and the Postmodern Condition**
    Hanan Alexander   **300**

21. **In Search of Common Values: Ethnic Schema, Ethnic Conflict and National Reconciliation in Fiji**
    Steven Ratuva   **311**

22. **A Canadian Experience: Transcending Pluralism**
    Donald Santor   **323**

Index   *336*

The Contributors and Editors

Stuart Ainsworth is Co-Director of the Equality and Discrimination Centre, University of Strathclyde, Glasgow.

Prof Hanan Alexander is Vice President for Academic Affairs at the University of Judaism, California.

Prof John Annette is Assistant Dean in the School of Social Sciences, Middlesex University, UK.

Paul Armstrong is Lecturer in Adult and Continuing Education at Birkbeck College, University of London.

Robert Balfour was formerly Lecturer at the University of Natal and Rhodes University, Grahamstown, South Africa.

Jo Cairns is a Senior Lecturer in Education at the Institute of Education, University of London.

Dr Jenny Corbett is Senior Lecturer in Special and Inclusive Education at the Institute of Education, University of London.

Jane Erricker is Senior Lecturer in Science Education and Education at King Alfred's College, Winchester, UK.

Gavin Faichney is Lecturer in Social Education at Deakin University, Victoria, Australia.

Robert Fisher is Director of the Centre for Research in Teaching Thinking, Brunel University, UK.

Val Fraser is a Lecturer and researcher in the School of Education at the University of Nottingham, UK.

Dr Roy Gardner is a Senior Lecturer in Education at the Institute of Education, University of London.

Philip Goggin is Continuing Professional Development Framework Manager at the Manchester Metropolitan University Institute of Education, Crewe and Alsager Faculty, UK.

Graham Haydon is a Senior Lecturer in Education at the Institute of Education, University of London.

Andrew Johnson is Co-Director of the Equality and Discrimination Centre, University of Strathclyde, Glasgow.

Denis Lawton is Professor of Education at the Institute of Education, University of London.

Xiaopeng Li is a Member of the Institute of Sociology at the Chinese Academy of Social Sciences, Beijing.

Vivienne Little is Lecturer in Education at the Institute of Education, University of Warwick, UK.

Brahm Norwich is Professor of Educational Psychology and Special Needs at the University of Exeter, UK.

Steven Ratuva is Lecturer at the University of the South Pacific, Suva.

Dr Donald Santor is Lecturer in Values Education, University of Western Ontario, Canada. Formerly, he was Education Officer for moral and religious education, Ontario Ministry of Education.

Mick Saunders is Director of the PGCE Programme at the University of Nottingham, UK.

Dr David Scott is a Senior Lecturer at the Open University, UK.

Dr Elwyn Thomas is a Lecturer in Education at the Institute of Education, University of London.

Prof John Tomlinson was formerly Director of the Institute of Education at the University of Warwick, UK.

Michael Totterdell is a Lecturer and Assistant to the Dean at the Institute of Education, University of London.

Dr Colin Wringe is Reader in Education at Keele University, UK.

Rev Dr Paul Yates is a Lecturer in the Graduate Centre, University of Sussex, UK.

Introduction

Jo Cairns

The publication and adoption of the revised curriculum for 2000, the Dearing Report, *Higher Education in the Learning Society* and *Learning to Succeed* have set a challenging agenda for compulsory, post-compulsory and higher education in the next century. Each seeks to articulate and further the contribution of education to a democratic, civilized and inclusive society. This volume sets out to respond to the challenges positively and imaginatively by bringing together the experiences, reflections and insights of its diverse and distinguished authors.

First, the volume delineates a number of approaches to teaching values and the issues that arise in educating values. It then seeks to illuminate these approaches and issues through reflective studies on the nature and practice of teacher development and educational research in and for values education. The final section of comparative studies brings together a variety of approaches and concerns to the worldwide urgency to work with values for education, for as our final contributor, Donald Santor (Chapter 22), reminds us, 'It is impossible to teach children anything and not engage them directly or indirectly in values education; values education simply "comes with the territory"' (Purpel and Ryan, 1976).

To borrow a sentence from a fellow contributor, John Annette (Chapter 8), 'If we are to move beyond sound bites or empty phrases... it is now central for both educators in schools and in higher education to openly debate the issues of education for morals, ethics and citizenship in the community and their place in the curriculum.'

This volume aims to contribute significantly to that debate by encouraging all those involved with values for education to participate through discussion, reflection, teaching and research.

All of our contributors set, and make reference to, the diversity of values to be found in our pluralist society. Some choose to include lists and categories of values that have formed the basis for varying approaches to values in education. The Schools Curriculum and Assessment Authority (SCAA) adopted a similar mechanism in the recommendations that followed its National Values Forum. None would disagree that values are not free-floating entities, there to be captured, made curriculum-friendly and taught with competence to previously value-free learners, with the resulting pedagogical success measured by badge-wearing learners subscribing voicelessly to their teachers' value system. John Tomlinson and Vivienne Little(Chapter 10) prefer to speak of principles that they define as values-in-action. Like them, other contributors anchor their understanding of the nature and articulation of values for education in the purpose and complexities of education itself, or in valued attributes of human beings participating in education and the community.

For Hanan Alexander (Chapter 20) we require nothing less than 'renewed ways of feeling intelligently, thinking morally and living thoughtfully'. The challenge for him of values education in an emancipated post-modern age is to promote only those putative ethical visions that embrace the conditions of moral agency and are therefore at home in open societies. He argues that all communities within a society must share a common commitment to 'preserve, protect and defend the status of all human beings as intelligent, empowered and fallible moral agents'. Another contributor, Elwyn Thomas (Chapter 17), refers us urgently back to research that enables us to experience the intimate sensitivities that abound at *the level of the individual* (my italics), which are so crucial to our understanding of what human values are all about in whatever cultural context.

The demand for a sensitive appraisal of the place of formal education in defining present and future directions in society as well as in shaping the values and identities of individual learners is a strong underlying theme throughout this volume. For example, Graham Haydon, in the section 'Approaches to Teaching Values', proposes introducing pupils to moral reasoning. Although such an approach would rid education (and society) of the charge of 'out-and-out anything goes subjectivism', it would also engage each learner with the processes by which he or she can come reasonably to individually satisfying decision-making. In the same section Colin Wringe outlines two approaches to moral education that can currently be found, namely the 'social utility view' and the 'group values view'. Both approaches, he argues, are unsatisfactory, indeed morally illegitimate, for they are concerned with controlling the young for the convenience and comfort of adults. He defines the prime purpose of moral education as 'to enable members of the younger generation themselves to live satisfactory lives together in a world constructed in accordance with their own aspirations and understanding'.

Such approaches to the place of values in education and education in values highlight aspects of the values agenda set by the present government. Although aspirations are couched in familiar and inclusive language, our mapping of the territory is as yet imprecise, with the result that short-term curriculum solutions in this field should only be evaluated against larger, medium- and long-term objectives. To this end Jo Cairns (Chapter 1) points to important work being undertaken within the area of school cultures and school–community links. She asks, 'How do we promote individual school cultures that take seriously and encourage the development of certain knowledge, attitudes and values in individual pupils?'

Two further questions raised by Jo Cairns must be addressed at both national policy and individual school levels. In the first she draws attention to the increasingly important voice of the learners in setting the agenda for their learning. She asks, 'How do we enable pupils to take responsibility for their own self-development and that of the school community?' The second underlines the key role of individual teachers in the process of defining values, for she asks, 'How do we enable teachers to be the "ultimate change-agents" in developing and promoting values for education?'

How policy is developed and decisions are taken about schooling and the curriculum is discussed by Brahm Norwich and Jenny Corbett in the section 'Issues in Education in Values'. They set out cogently the diversity of values to be examined there and argue that the values encompass individual and social aims. Aims for individuals can include realizing each and every individual's potential; intrinsic appreciation of knowledge, understanding, moral and aesthetic experience; developing a sense of self-worth for all and becoming an active and responsible citizen. Aims for society can include community participation; social cohesiveness; equalizing opportunities; maintaining and raising standards; reconstructing society and preserving the best of past traditions. This multiplicity of values can be seen as an expression of the diversity of voices in society. They argue that these voices need to be recognized and integrated in a balanced way. Brahm Norwich and Jenny Corbett also argue that the issues that arise in educating those with disabilities and difficulties underline the multiple nature of values and highlight the tensions this generates in policy making about schooling and the curriculum generally. They consider special education to be a 'connective specialism' and through its connective features it can thereby make a wider contribution to education.

In the same section John Annette examines the challenges set specifically by the revival of the concept of citizenship in contemporary political discourse. Further, its study in the Academy has led to fundamental questions being asked about the nature and purpose of education, including higher education. His concern is that the very real difficulty of defining citizenship and therefore its context leads to a very limited development of citizenship education. He then argues for a strong link between citizenship education and experiential learning. He traces the development for active citizenship, which is seen as including education in critical thinking, political literacy, moral values, spiritual values and emotional literacy through to an equal emphasis on the principles of experiential learning. Annette concludes that Community Service Learning can be established generically across a university but a major challenge facing universities will be to encourage disciplinary and multi-disciplinary community service learning in the subject-based curriculum.

The warning signals are clear, not only to universities, but also to schools currently settling in to the new curriculum. Do the aims of education, spelt out in the Secretary of State's introduction to the revised curriculum and by Dearing in his *Enquiry into Higher Education*, demand a more radical reform of the curriculum within all compulsory education than the current tinkering with subject-based approaches permits?

At such a complex time for compulsory education the role of the teacher and the nature of the teaching profession is crucial. As the intermediaries between national policy and the individual learners and their communities, teachers hold a privileged position. Annette reminds us of Arnot and Ivinson's study of 375 trainee secondary teachers in England and Wales, which found that less than 10 per cent of them felt comfortable teaching education for citizenship. Many felt that citizenship was a value-laden and inappropriate concept to impose on multicultural classrooms.

The section on 'Teacher Education and Values' focuses therefore on the increasing emphasis on ethics in the teacher's role. Michael Totterdell (Chapter 9) argues that teachers stand as gatekeepers to increasingly powerful forms of knowledge, and the powers of discrimination required to use them wisely and for the good of others will demand a strong focus on ethics in the teacher's work. This ethical ethos among teachers will both shape and be shaped by the nature and purpose of curricular activity. Its outcomes will include the cultivation of a shared sense of collective purpose, communal solidarity and participatory ethos by which any public morality can alone be sustained. It will also contribute to teachers becoming what John Wilson (1990) describes as morally educated persons in the sense of having the ability to make both worthwhile attachments and judgements of merit.

In the same section John Tomlinson and Vivienne Little (Chapter 10) propose that the ethical principles that inform teaching derive from epistemological authority and from professional purpose. They suggest that these inhere in three dispositions essential to teaching: the disposition to rationality, the disposition to promote the interests of those taught and the disposition to humility in relation to the provisionality of knowledge, the fallibility of those who claim to know and the partnerships of learners in the process of education. Tomlinson and Little go on to enunciate helpfully 11 principles for teaching, which include having intellectual courage, having vocational integrity, showing moral courage and exercising human insight and humility.

As the outcomes of educational endeavour are increasingly judged by the presentation of appropriate evidence to stakeholders, including learners, parents, government, Ofsted, QAA and employers, the section on 'Research for Education in Values' is timely and helpful. David Scott (Chapter 13) argues that values are central to the activity of research, that is both the values of the researcher and the values of those being researched. Research is therefore inevitably a 'fusion of horizons' (Gadamer, 1975) in which different sets of values fuse to produce new knowledge. These values are located within historical contexts or 'traditions of knowledge' (MacIntyre, 1982). The production of knowledge has a close relationship with the way society organizes itself.

David Scott's chapter provides an insightful context for us as teachers to evaluate our tasks within values for education. Elwyn Thomas, in the section 'Comparative Studies', reminds us that 'planning a curriculum which aims to reflect both universal as well as relativistic cultural values, that may assist a pluralistic society to exist in harmony, will be a strong challenge whatever the circumstances'. How we plan the next strategic stages within the changing curriculum contexts we share cannot rely wholly on already accumulated knowledge and evidence. It is hoped that this volume will encourage all engaged in the enterprise to continue to question their aims and purposes; to examine success and failure very specifically within their individual learning and teaching contexts; and finally, to seek continuously to share their policies and good practice with the wider community of their profession and their local community. The knowledge that we continue to seek about how best to articulate and harness values for education will, as Scott reminds us, have a close relationship with the way society chooses to organize itself. Current educational research is in a state of flux about the nature of values and their place in the curriculum. That, however, must not limit the possibilities for exploring best practice in contemporary teaching in and for values because that is *our* territory.

Chapter 1

Morals, Ethics and Citizenship in Contemporary Teaching

Jo Cairns

Introduction

> The task of schools, in partnership with the home, is to furnish pupils with the knowledge and ability to question and reason which will enable them to develop their own value systems and to make responsible decisions on such matter. (NCC, 1993: 5)

> … but may I remind you that the problem facing teachers is a very serious and deep one. Unless the society in which they live and work gives some coherent account of what it considers important in human life then teachers have no real framework in which to operate… (Sutherland in Sacks and Sutherland, 1996: 48–49)

An unresolved dilemma for teachers since 1944 has been the definition of their role in relation to the developing values of their pupils. In the White Paper (1943) preceding the 1944 Education Act, schools and religious education had been charged with 'reviving the personal and spiritual values of the nation'. The Education Reform Act 1988 called upon the whole curriculum to promote the spiritual, moral, social and cultural development of pupils and of society. In 1992 the National Curriculum Council reminded schools that their 'values lie at the heart of the school's vision of itself and itself as a community'. While in 1998, teachers were told in the Green Paper that 'pupils will need education for a world of rapid change in which both flexible attitudes and enduring values will have a part to play' (DfEE, 1998: 12).

The need for education to promote both individuals and a society equipped to compete in globally challenging markets has led to the present Government's current rationale for change in educational purpose and activity. The consequences of such change are the subject of the following analysis by Morley and Rassool (1999):

> Educators have had to negotiate a litany of changes: new managerialism; new forms of assessment; new partnerships eg with school governors, employers and parents. Teachers are held responsible for alleged falling education standards, plus a range of social ills such as youth crime, violence, young people's alienation and disaffection. Paradoxically teachers are being burdened with enormous social responsibility, while simultaneously being constructed as professionally wanting. (p 5)

Against this background of unrelenting change, biting criticism and the ever-expanding fields of knowledge and technical developments that comprise the teacher's tool-kit, those concerned with the core business of schools, namely the learning of the pupils, demand a clarity of role and responsibilities. To assist in this process the Institute of Education, University of London, held a conference to discuss a major component of this process, values and the curriculum. The theme of this book was central to the deliberations of the conference and most of its chapters began life as papers there. Our purpose is to present possible networks of concepts, arguments and processes which will lead to intellectually and emotionally challenging foundations for the consideration, articulation and implementation of values teaching and acquisition in and through the curriculum of our schools in 2000 and beyond.

The Education Reform Act of 1988 and the National Curriculum which it introduced for England and Wales ushered in an era of curriculum change and evaluation. Before the ERA the curriculum of the primary phase was left in trust to the schools themselves and it contained approximately the same mix of subjects as exists now in the National Curriculum. The secondary system was guided and directed by the examination boards but again the programme of subjects offered differed little from that offered today.

There was a general professional consensus, with some notable exceptions in professional practice, of the nature of the school provision. It was an academic focused course of study which might be best represented by Young's (1999) view of curriculum as fact. This is a curriculum based on knowledge which appeared to have an existence of its own and to which the learner had to relate in order to be judged educated and successful. Young (1971) had long argued that knowledge should be seen as a cultural construct which should be viewed within the cultural context in which it was taught and acquired. Knowledge, therefore, could not have universal features that could lead to the assessment of its quality transnationally. The quality of learning and its knowledge base needed to be assessed in the light of the community in which the individuals lived and could be expected to continue to do so.

Such a view of knowledge opens important questions of what should be taught in schools in England and Wales but these were not explored in the development of the National Curriculum which in adopting a subject-based pattern reflected the inherited structure of the school's timetable and basis of professional practice in the schools. The opportunity was missed to devise new and innovative approaches to curriculum design in favour of the tried and tested curriculum which had been devised in the 19th century as a reflection of academic life at the university. Within this design there were many opportunities to emphasize measurable outcomes in terms of pupil achievement through pass rates, examination successes and progression to higher levels of education. What was missing was an overt statement of the potential impact on the growth and development of the pupils as individuals with all their varying characteristics, personalities and foibles. As Lawton (1996) has argued when considering the nature of young people's learning about the nature of society:

> England is a complex society with a very elaborate political and social structure. But most people leave school almost entirely ignorant of the socio-political system... England is a democratic society with a high rate of social mobility, but schools tend to divide the young socially, academically and culturally, rather than to encourage co-operation, social harmony and a common culture. (p 33)

So no statement on outcomes has appeared which related to the nature of the graduand of the education system as an individual in his/her own right, as a member of the community of the school, of the family, of the community at large nor of his/her awareness of the rights and obligations of the individual within a modern society.

Curriculum guidelines issued since 1988 have placed emphasis on the provision of Personal and Social Education and on Spiritual, Moral, Social and Cultural development. Instructions for inspections carried out on behalf of OFSTED have also required there to be assessments of the school's provision for the development of broader aspects of education provided. The Crick Report (1998) stressed the need for education for Citizenship and in particular included the teaching of democracy within its remit. Most significantly, as part of the revision process of the National Curriculum, the Qualifications and Curriculum Authority (QCA) declared that 'there is a need to develop a much clearer statement about the aims and priorities of the school curriculum as a necessary preliminary to any review' (QCA, 1997: 1). The publication of the Consultation Material May–June 1999 of the national curriculum saw the revised curriculum as having four key functions:

- establishing an entitlement;
- establishing standards;
- promoting continuity and coherence;
- promoting public understanding.

Issues about the nature and scope of the existing curriculum were not therefore addressed. Rather the status quo was maintained, with only limited opportunities for a slimmed-down curriculum and opportunities for curriculum innovation in Education Action Zones etc. A thorough-going review of the content of the curriculum and its processes in relation to the newly stated aims, namely, 'to provide opportunities for all pupils to learn and to achieve' and 'to prepare all pupils for the opportunities, responsibilities and experiences of life' is significantly missing.

In short, the revised curriculum mainly sets about the task of:

1. defining more sharply the processes in which schools and pupils must participate if all pupils are to receive their entitlement to achieve their best;
2. establishing a flexible and coherent framework which can most readily and quickly meet the needs of all pupils.

Both processes are important. On the one hand the present curriculum has failed both ends of the ability spectrum, with 8 per cent of pupils leaving school with no qualifications and no commitment to an ongoing learning agenda, while at the same time special classes and summer schools are organized for the gifted pupils. Nor has the present curriculum provided a comfortable home for the embedding of the Code of Practice or sometimes for those pupils and teachers from minority cultures.

A curriculum for learning or a curriculum to be learnt?

Colleagues in the field of Special Educational Needs have argued cogently that the legislated curriculum is the chief deliverer of the matching of learning experiences to the individual learning needs of the pupil; see, for example, Carpenter *et al*, 1996. As a result, at this time of revision of the national curriculum it is crucial that the values underpinning its aims, content, implementation and practice must be addressed and moreover be open to public scrutiny and comment. Indeed the need for public vigilance in overseeing and subscribing to the purpose and framework of a revised curriculum is particularly significant at a time when:

- one of the greatest education crises of the post-modern age has arisen, namely the collapse of the common school – a school tied to its community and having a clear sense of the social and moral values it should instil;
- the cafeteria curriculum of widened choice, an attempt to accommodate the more diverse needs of a broader secondary school population with increased diversity, brought with it only chronic incoherence in curricular experience and the decline of any sense of community or common purpose in the bureaucratic, fragmented world that secondary schools have become (Hargreaves, 1994, p 57).

The pupils' voices at this time can also be heard demanding change. Reviewing the data they had collected, Rudduck *et al* (1996) reflected:

> Pupils are urging us to review some of the assumptions and expectations that serve to hold habitual ways of teaching in place – we have to take seriously young pupils' accounts, and evaluations of teachers and learning and schooling. (pp 177–78)

Mary Marsh, head teacher of Holland Park School when speaking on the publication of *Opening Minds* (RSA, 1999) has also commented, 'I think it is very welcome that someone is asking some radical questions about the way our children are taught. Far too much of what has happened in schools has been incremental and built on what was there already' (*The Guardian*, education section, 15 June 1999).

What the consultation materials offer by way of change are two overarching aims for the curriculum by which all pupils' standards of attainment are to be raised. Thus the school curriculum should aim to:

- provide opportunities for all pupils to learn and to achieve;
- prepare all pupils for the opportunities, responsibilities and experiences of life (p 5).

Learning for life is thereby equated with learning for achievement. There is nothing inherently problematic about this. As Rutter (1979) found, pupils are most likely to achieve when there is strong emphasis on success. The context however of the learning remains the traditional curriculum; a curriculum which has been fiercely contested, not least in its effectiveness in the preparation of young people for adult life (Lawton, 1999). A curriculum for 2000 and beyond must surely incorporate a more radical overhaul than this one, which has simply been topped and tailed, with aims precariously tacked on to old material. For the curriculum demands the integration of the young into the existing adult world which is fast expanding its knowledge-base, is global and ever-changing. There has rarely been a time when the need to consider, reflect and pilot the values and processes underlying a child's learning was more crucial. We might again here agree with Lawton (1996: 120–21) when he commends Ranson's (1994) more ambitious plans for a future 'learning society':

> In periods of social transition, education becomes central to our future well-being. Only if learning is placed at the centre of our experience can individuals continue to develop their capacities, institutions be enabled to respond openly and imaginatively to periods of change and the different communities become a source of reflective understanding. The challenge for policy makers is to promote the conditions for such a learning society – preoccupations with the issues of purpose and organization should then result in extensive public dialogue about reform.

The current proposals for revision of the national curriculum are indeed evidence of the Government's commitment to 'education, education, education'. Further, the revised curriculum forms a part of the Government's determination to establish a learning society, underpinned by a lifelong learning agenda. There are concerns, however, about the Government's ability to deliver without an exploration of first, the reasons and circumstances which encourage individuals to participate in learning and second, somewhat restricted understandings at present about the nature of learning. At the moment rhetoric abounds as in the speech by Henry McLeish, Scotland's new Minister for enterprise and lifelong learning:

> We need to make learning so attractive and people so aware of its value, that life-long learning as a part of adulthood becomes the norm rather than the exception. (THES, 18 June 1999)

Perhaps a start might have been made by defining the characteristics of an educated individual in social terms. Learning might then have been framed by Jean Lave's understanding of it as 'participation in a "community of practice"' for at present the fundamental social process underlying successful learning is glaringly absent:

> The concept of community and hence of 'knowledge' and its 'location' in the lived-in world, is both crucial and subtle… A community of practice is a set of relations among persons, activity and the world, over time and in relation with other tangential and overlapping communities of practices. A community of practice is an intrinsic condition for the existence of knowledge, not least because it provides the interpretative support necessary for making sense of its heritage. Thus participation in the cultural practice in which any knowledge

exists is an epistemological principle of learning. The social structure of this practice, its power relation, and its conditions for legitimacy define for possibilities for learning. (Lave and Wenger, 1999, p 25)

Michael Young (1999) notes that:

The failure of schools to give a high priority to the condition for learning is not just a problem of school improvement. It can only be overcome in a learning *society* which privileges learning relationships in all spheres and sections of society. (pp 169–70)

If we are to remain a society in which learning is recognized for its contribution to that society's well-being and social harmony, then considerations of curriculum change for this society must put at their centre explorations of the possibilities of being human and a functioning citizen, rather than as appendages at the edges.

A schooling in values or values in schooling?

Gus John (1998) reminds us there has always been a debate about the role of schooling and education in promoting social cohesion and furthering the democratic ideas of the state. In most western societies schooling has been projected as an ideologically neutral activity in which promoting democratic participation and active citizenship is equated with promoting conformity and transmitting the dominant values and outlook of ruling élites on the 'majority' community. He then argues that this view of schooling has been rightly contested by those who believe that such a view implicitly requires the school to act as a shock absorber for many of the ills that beset children and families.

In 1993, in Access and Achievement in Urban Education, HMI reminded us that since schools lack the capacity to carry out programmes for change unaided, underlying issues of poverty, unemployment, poor housing, inadequate health care and the frequent break-up of families remain formally outside of the school's territory. Mortimore (1998) has commented that for the individual child this can mean: poor housing, diet and health; proximity to pollution; crime and drugs; more frequent disruption and accidents; the necessity for part-time work; fewer books, IT facilities, outings and holidays; the shame of poverty and for some the stress of racism. In turn disadvantage can thus impact on a child's educational opportunities physically, emotionally and psychologically.

Formal education cannot ignore such challenges when entitlement and standards lie at its heart. On the one hand then, the revised curriculum could assert the need for equal opportunities policies and declare itself satisfied when a policy is produced to meet an inspection checklist. On the other, those elements of poverty and social inequality might be ordered out of view by some school effectiveness models which distance themselves from the differences in social and economic backgrounds of pupils. The curriculum in this mode would possibly seek to achieve Foucault's 'factories of order', predictable and controllable. Far better though that such inequalities remind us of Paulo Freire's principles (in Freire and Macedo, 1999):

1. That there is no education without the ethical. Education is cognitive, it has directivity. It is directed towards possibility. It has beauty and it is ethical. It has to do with values.
2. That learning can only come about through an increased awareness of one's life situation that results from action upon it.

In our revised curriculum do we have the potential for delivering learning for individuals, their schools and communities which is transformative? Can knowledge and ways of knowing touch young people in such a way as to transform their attitudes, values and beliefs? A curriculum thus achieving would need to be organized so that the learning is relevant to the experiences and expectations of the learner. Rose (1995) critically reflects on this that, if 'we determine success primarily in terms of test scores, then we ignore the social, moral and aesthetic dimensions of teaching and learning and as well, we'll miss those considerable intellectual achievements which are not easily quantifiable' (p 3). The social backgrounds and identities of our pupils must not be ignored for as Stoll and Fink (1996) point out, 'there is a direct connection between how pupils feel about themselves and their achievement in schools' (p 129). Set against the background of the present input/output model of education, such a purposeful curriculum model would have to compete against the odds. As MacBeath (1999) has commented:

> The inherent weakness of the input/output model is widely recognized among school effectiveness researchers but it has provided such a powerful tool... that matters of values and attitudes are simply excluded because they do not fit the model. (p 15)

In brief will the revised curriculum provide the appropriate setting for Gus John's vision (1998) of a democratic school whereby we can negotiate learning with children in a context of a respect for rights:

- a respect and valuing of culture;
- an understanding of the social dislocation that characterizes many children's lives;

- respect for every individual as a human being with dignity and with a divine essence that drives instinct for freedom and human liberties (pp 11–12)?

Joined-up thinking between revised curriculum proposals and a values-based model of schooling

In the earlier green paper, *Teachers Meeting the Challenge of Change* (1998) under the heading of 'the Imperative of Modernization', the Government sets out its agenda for 'a world class education service for all our children… Pupils will need education for a world of rapid change in which both flexible attitudes and enduring values have a part to play' (p 11).

Very rapidly in the green paper the agenda becomes one of creating mechanisms for management of teaching competence and the teaching profession. We see that neither the consultation document nor the revised curriculum nor the green paper spend time unpacking the context, processes or learning outcomes of compulsory education, apart from 'achievement' measured by national testing and competence league tables of results, both national and international. The context as we have already seen is complex and yet the processes are not articulated. Ambiguity is thus written into the revision of schooling for the next century. For Turner this would not be a surprise. He argues (1990) that the very essence of Weber's view of modernity is ambiguity. He goes on:

> Modernization brings with it the erosion of meaning, the endless conflict of polytheistic values and the threat of the iron cage of bureaucracy. Rationalization makes the world orderly and reliable but it cannot make the world meaningful. (note 6, pp 6–7)

Perhaps we educators should make a start on joining-up and making meaningful the present Government's explicit statements and aims with the present knowledge-based curriculum. First, what should be the content of the learning and experiences of compulsory schooling? Gardner (1991) argues that a knowledge-based curriculum is essential since human beings move to new experiences as a result of past ways of knowing:

> Organized subject matter represents the ripe fruitage of experiences… it does not represent perfection or infallible vision; but it is the best at command to further new experiences. (p 198)

On the other hand the RSA (1999) argues for a competence-led curriculum, where competence is defined as 'the ability to understand and to do'. The five broad competencies are: for learning; for citizenship; for relating to people; for managing situations; and for managing information (pp 18–19). The RSA project workers describe the genesis of their thinking as:

> People come out of education and find that what happens to them in the outside world is a bit of a shock. We felt that we should be addressing why that is, and how education should better prepare people. (*The Guardian*, 15 June 1999)

Pring (1995) has already presented us with a values-based model which integrates more closely the post-school experience of work and choices with the school curriculum:

> So long as there are thoughts to be developed, relationships to be formed, activities to be engaged in, feelings to be refined, then there is room for education... And that requires bringing the educational ideal to the vocational interests of the young people, educating them through their perception of relevance, helping them to make sense of their social and economic context, enabling them to be intelligent and questioning in their preparation for the world of work. (p 190)

A current joined-up approach to the choice of appropriate knowledge and experiences for schooling of the next century might usefully balance the following criteria:

- Connectivity of the knowledge and experiences with the pupils' and teachers' present and future life-contexts as citizens, people in relationships, parents and knowledge-makers.
- Potential impact of the knowledge in transforming the pupils' understanding of their conversations with their physical, personal and moral worlds (see Pring, 1996: 113). He argues that such a context 'embraces not just those people with whom one interrelates on an immediate and personal level but also institutions'. Further, some of the social context includes 'the products of the deliberations of others long since dead – in books, film, art and ritual'.
- Knowledge and experiences organized in ways which encourage collaborative learning.
- New knowledge can be created.

In short, at the heart of schooling focused on the learning needs of the individual learner, their school community and their wider (global) situation, we might well consider its core business to be the development and application of knowledge, rather than the handing on of former knowing and other people's knowledge. All knowledge would then be personal but acquired within the social context of the school with its networks of relationships. Making sense in complex situations with the use of simple and complex knowledge would be at the root of curriculum purpose and content. To illustrate we might turn here to the **model of knowledge creation** offered by Nonaka and Takeuchi (1995), and considered by Hargreaves (1998: 30) in relation to teachers' own knowledge-creation (Figure 1.1). It is clearly, as well, valuable in guiding our route from the current knowledge-based curriculum to one guided by the aims of education offered in the consultation documents for the future learning of pupils. This model focuses on the interaction of explicit and tacit knowledge as the key to new knowledge. The aim of teachers would be to make explicit with pupils those experiences and understandings which the pupil holds tacitly or unknowingly and which are related to the explicit knowledge and ways of knowing under exploration within the curriculum. The pupils would then explore modes or processes of assimilation of implicit and new knowledge as they work on common questions and problems. At its heart is the purposeful sharing of knowledge and experience with others where the exchange of knowledge demands reflection by all to discover what is already known to them and what new knowledge arises when called upon to be articulated or applied to learning-in-action situations.

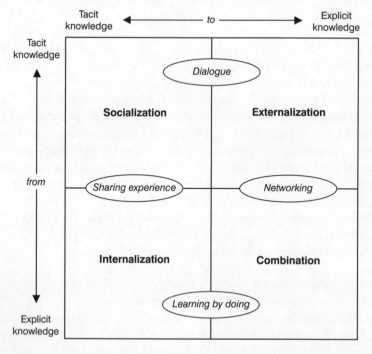

Figure 1.1   *The Nonaka and Takeuchi (1995) model of knowledge creation*

We might usefully conclude this part of the process of joining-up the 'framework' couched in ambiguity offered by current government proposals with a values-based model of schooling by looking at John White's (1998) own conclusion to his discussion about generating educational aims:

> All this gives only a partial picture of the knowledge and understanding which children will need. A fuller account would map this more systematically. It would also say more about the logical hierarchies among knowledge which now come into view, for example the dependence of knowledge about society on some grasp of science and technology; the key role of literacy in the acquisition of so much else. (p 34)

Our present discussion, by focusing on the values underpinning the purpose and content of the curriculum, does not attempt to map fully the curriculum content needed to deliver a purposeful revised curriculum. Nevertheless our contributors attempt to look at specificities in that map.

Next we must examine the second ingredient in the process of joining-up policies which might lead to a values-based model of schooling; namely the school itself. Rigsby *et al* (1995) argue:

> A further way to think about schools, is to see them as structures that are intimately and irrevocably woven into others, all of which serve political, economic, cultural, religious and social aims. The interrelated nature of such institutions makes it almost impossible to plan and implement change in one without affecting the others. (p 7)

From his study of school-community connections in New Haven, Comer (1987) concludes that it is unwise to separate the academic from the social and emotional development in children and that there is a pressing need to incorporate all the resources of a school (including parents and the community) into a common blend of care and education. It is more consonant with reality to reflect, too, on the 'culture to be constantly constructed and reconstituted by the school community' through the nature of the partnerships between the head teacher, the teachers, students and parents described by Bates (1986).

The present proposals for the review of the curriculum (QCA, 1999a, 1999b) do little to bridge the considerable distance between a developing rationale for a curriculum which itself 'cannot remain static [but] must be responsive to changes in society and the economy, and changes in the nature of schooling itself. Teachers have to reappraise their teaching in response to the changing needs of their pupils and the attitudes and ideas of society and economic forces' (QCA, 1999a: 4) and 'restricting changes to the national curriculum to the essential minimum' (QCA, 1999b: 1). Key changes, the QCA argues, will develop from:

- identification of a broad set of values which underpin the work of the school and the wider school curriculum;
- schools working in collaboration with families and the local community (p 4).

The values selected are 'valuing ourselves, our families, our relationships and the wider group to which we belong, together with justice, truthfulness and a sense of duty' (p 4). A framework is then discussed as the basis for personal, social and health education (PSHE) and citizenship at key stages 1 to 4. This framework is to be non-statutory for PSHE and citizenship at key stages 1 and 2 and a Statutory Order is to be introduced for a foundation subject in citizenship at key stages 3 and 4. All revisions in the national curriculum, including those relating to PSHE and citizenship, are included in a framework within which schools can develop their own approaches.

The school and its individual teachers and pupils now therefore constitute the catalyst for the real work of developing and practising values and citizenship education. Will the values framework offered in the consultation document provide an adequate and viable compass for the schools to find their bearings? Is not the Government, in setting out its own statement of values, mistakenly assuming that the same set will be accepted, interpreted and implemented as school policy across all schools, despite their diverse and often plural contexts? Despite the work of the National Values Forum and the subsequent research by the SCAA and QCA into how schools plan their values education, we can still agree with Taylor (1996) that 'little is known of the process by which schools agree to core values which are acceptable to all' (pp 125–26).

If we then accept as a useful working definition Halstead's description of values as 'principles, fundamental convictions, ideals, standards or life-stances which act as general guides to behaviour... and which are closely tied to personal integrity and personal identity' (1996: 5), we may assume two pre-suppositions. These are both closely connected to the professional lives and private values of teachers:

1. All teachers share a professional identity that recognizes and submits to a specific form of personal integrity.
2. Compatible standards of behaviour and valuing will be found across all schools.

It is tempting, following the above analysis, to presume that the Government's suggested framework with its heavy reliance upon each school to formulate its individual approach to values education, is dependent upon the market forces currently at work in our schools for the success of its approach. Halstead (in Halstead and Taylor, 1996: 7–8) points to Elliott (1994) who recognizes that 'market forces within schools enable a pragmatic solution to the problem of value pluralism to be effected' (p 415ff). Elliott suggests that the market provides the context for the negotiation of values between providers and customers. In order to thrive the school cannot uphold values which diverge significantly from those of the community it serves.

Thus our fundamental questions must be:

- How do we promote individual school cultures in which each takes seriously and encourages the development of certain knowledge, attitudes and values in individual pupils?
- How do we bring teachers into this debate 'for they are the ultimate change agents' (Bruner, 1996: 84)?
- How do we enable pupils to take responsibility for their own self-development and that of the school community?

The evidence in Taylor's research (1996: 125) has shown that pupils' self reports reveal moral and cultural awareness and a sense of fair play. Priestley, speaking at the fifth annual conference on Education, Spirituality and the Whole Child in July 1998 at Roehampton Institute, London (report forthcoming), has recalled a time when the emphasis in teaching was on the whole child as a person rather than as today when the emphasis from the TTA and the DfEE is on the teaching process and learning. There is a need for a reconsideration of the notion of child-centredness because teaching has become more of an applied science. As Priestley argues, ethical categories have been removed by current trends in teacher professionalization and concentration is now on the 'stuff' of teaching rather than the human beings concerned. Yet Taylor (ibid: 135) has shown that pupils discern the qualities of teachers through the use of ethical categories. For example, she tells of the Head of Year 9 who was universally respected and liked by pupils, one of whom said, 'I would go to Mr J. He's a safe teacher, he is. He's brilliant. He's funny. He's fair. He listens to your questions and problems.' The central roles of teachers and pupils in the formal and informal curriculum processes of values education should not be underestimated. At the very least their experiences of sharing sometimes passionate, sometimes humorous, sometimes profound conversations about their developing values and changing perspectives on the world they share should lie at the heart of individual school development planning and the national debate about values and citizenship education.

Therefore part of our response to the three fundamental questions must lie in the way we describe and define the work within each school culture for we know that each school or institution develops its own culture. Bryk (1996) has reminded us that we 'live through our institutions' (p 39). Pupils, teachers, parents and governors each share in the life of and grow through the schools in which they learn, teach and share responsibilities. Stoll's definition (in Stoll and Fink, 1996, reprinted 1999) of culture is particularly helpful here:

> Culture describes how things are... In essence, it defines reality for those within a social organization, gives them support and identity and creates a framework for occupational learning. Each school has a different reality or mindset of school life. (pp 82–83)

We must therefore in our joining-up process facilitate the continuous movement between the general policy statements which encompass educational vision and policies and the individual school's members' understanding of the culture and function of their school. How then to move from a general statement, exemplified by this example from the New York State Council on Curriculum and Assessment (1997)?

> The schools we envision are exciting places: thoughtful, reflective, engaging and engaged. They are places where meaning is made... Their teachers function more like mentors, wise advisors than information transmitters or gate-keepers. They create a bridge between challenging learning goals and students' unique needs. They are continually learning because these are schools where everyone would be glad to be a student, or a teacher – where everyone would want to be – and could be – both. (Cited in *Leading Edge*, **1** (3), 1997)

Lawton (1996: 114) suggests that in talking of the culture of schools we rather carelessly speak of 'beliefs, values, attitudes and expectations, etc' as though they all imply the same level of commitment. Instead he proposes three categories in ascending order, 'Beliefs, Attitudes and values and Behaviour'. Thus in matching these three categories of culture with aspects of school management and planning, he proposes the following alignment:

Beliefs	Vision (of educational ideal)
Attitudes and values	Mission (statement of aims, goals, purposes)
Behaviour	Implementation/School Development Place (a choice of strategies to achieve mission)

A school that takes the role of all its members seriously will devise means of involving all its members both in mapping the values of the school and in ongoing monitoring of the application and impact of those values in:

- describing the educated pupil and worthwhile learning;
- establishing processes to explore, share, argue about and evaluate the values of all members of the school community;
- evaluating the place of the school and its formal curriculum in promoting and developing agreed values among all its members.

The task for schools is great but those already working energetically in this area speak of its enormous benefits. We might look, for example, to the conference reports which emanate from the Living Values Programme, which is supported by UNESCO, UNICEF and the Brahma Kumaris World Spirituality University. The research of Bryk *et al* (1993) highlighted the importance of the school as a communal organization (in McLaughlin, O'Keefe and O'Keeffe, 1996). He reports that the focused academic programmes in the Catholic schools they investigated are embedded in a larger social organization of the school as a community. This communal structure is centred around three core features:

- an extensive array of school activities which provide shared interactions and experiences among adults and students;
- a set of formal organizational features which enable the community. Teachers are not just subject matter specialists but mature persons who encounter students in hallways, the neighbourhood and the playing fields;
- a set of shared beliefs about what students should learn.

The research yielded evidence that 'in schools with a strong communal organization there were fewer problems with classroom disruption, absenteeism, class-cutting and dropping out. Thus the basic social organization of the high school as community has substantial social and personal consequences for both teachers and students' (p 29).

The plea by Bryk (1996) for a lack of fragmentation in the way we structure and use schools by paying close attention to the values we profess and share is perhaps the most hopeful and challenging conclusion we might bring to our discussion about the possibility of joining up a vision and purpose for the revised curriculum with the existing subject dominated national curriculum. A final challenge must however be addressed. How in our present world, characterized by Sutherland as one of 'upheaval, disruption and uncertainty in its deepest social and intellectual foundations' and exhibiting 'cultural pluralism, the fragmentation of knowledge and moral atomization' (Bryk, 1996: 5–6), do we ensure that pupils and teachers alike engage with the articulation and practice of values which the aims of the curriculum demand? Since we might easily characterize our present culture as one of indifference, particularly moral indifference, what chance for an intellectually and emotionally challenging and worthwhile values and citizenship education?

References

Bates, R (1986) *The Management of a Culture of Knowledge*, Deakin University Press, Melbourne

Bruner, J (1996) *The Culture of Education*, Harvard University Press, Cambridge, MA

Bryk, A S, Lee, V E and Holland, P B (1993) *Catholic Schools and the Common Good*, Harvard University Press, Cambridge, MA

Bryk, A S (1996) Lessons from Catholic high schools on renewing our educational institutions, in *The Contemporary Catholic School*, ed T McLaughlin, J O'Keefe and B O'Keeffe, Falmer, London

Carpenter, B, Ashdown, R and Bouvair, K (eds) (1996) *Enabling Access: Effective teaching and learning for pupils with learning difficulties*, David Fulton, London

Comer, J P (1987) New Haven's school–community connections, *Educational Leadership*, **44** (6), pp 13–16

Crick Report/QCA (1998) *Education for Citizenship and the Teaching of Democracy in Schools*, QCA, London

Department for Education and Employment (1998) *Teachers Meeting the Challenge of Change*, The Stationery Office, London

Elliott, J (1994) Clarifying values in schools, *Cambridge Journal of Education*, **24** (3), pp 413–22

Freire, P and Macedo, D P (1999) Pedagogy, culture, language and race: a dialogue, in *Learners and Pedagogy*, ed J Leach and B Moon, Open University, Milton Keynes

Gardner, H (1991) *The Unschooled Mind*, Basic Books, New York

Halstead, J M and Taylor, M J (eds) (1996) *Values in Education and Education in Values*, Falmer, London

Hargreaves, A (1994) *Changing Teachers, Changing Times*, Cassell, London

Hargreaves, D (1998) *Creative Professionalism: The role of teachers in the knowledge society*, Demos, London

HMI (1993) *Access and Achievement in Urban Education*, HMI, London

John, G (1998) Taking SMSC forward, in *Summary Report of SMSC Made Easy*, November, Living Values, Nuneham Courtenay, Oxford

Lave, J and Wenger, E (1999) Learning and pedagogic communities of practice, in *Learners and Pedagogy*, ed J Leach and B Moon, Open University and Paul Chapman, London

Lawton, D (1996) *Beyond the National Curriculum*, Hodder and Stoughton, London

Lawton, D (1999) *Values and the Curriculum: A curriculum for the 21st century*, Woburn Press, London

Macbeath, J (1999) *Schools must Speak for Themselves*, Routledge, London

McLaughlin, T, O'Keefe, J and O'Keefe, B (eds) *The Contemporary Catholic School*, Falmer, London

Marsh, M (1999) London, *The Guardian*, 15 June

Morley, L and Rassool, N (1999) *School Effectiveness: Fracturing the discourse*, Falmer, London

Mortimore, P (1998) School improvement, *Leading Edge*, **2** (2), September, Institute of Education, London

National Curriculum Council (1993) *Spiritual and Moral Development – A discussion paper*, NCC, York

New York State Council on Curriculum and Assessment (1997) New compact for learning, in *The Right to Learn*, ed L Darling-Hammond, Jossey-Bass, San Francisco

Nonaka, I and Takeuchi, H (1995) *The Knowledge-Creating Company*, OUP, Oxford

Pring, R (1995) *Closing the Gap: Liberal education and vocational preparation*, Hodder and Stoughton, London

Pring, R (1996) Values and education policy, in *Values in Education and Education in Values*, ed J M Halstead and M Taylor, Falmer Press, London

QCA (1997) *Aims for the School Curriculum 5–16*, QCA, London

QCA (1999a) *The Review of the National Curriculum in England: The consultation materials*, QCA, London

QCA (1999b) *The Review of the National Curriculum in England: The Secretary of State's proposals*, QCA, London

Ranson, S (1994) *Towards the Learning Society*, Cassell, London

Rigsby, L, Reynolds, M G and Wang, M C (eds) (1995) *School-Community Connection: Exploring issues for research and practice*, Jossey-Bass, San Francisco

Rose, M (1995) *Possible Lives – The promise of public education in America*, Penguin Books, New York

RSA (1999) *Opening Minds*, Royal Society of Arts, London

Rudduck, J, Chaplain, R and Wallace, G (1996) *School Improvement: What can pupils tell us?*, David Fulton, London

Rutter, M *et al* (1979) *Fifteen Thousand Hours: Schools and their effects on children*, Open Books, London

Sacks, J and Sutherland, S (1996) *Education, Values and Religion in the Victor Cook Memorial Lectures*, Centre for Philosophy, University of St Andrews

Stoll, L and Fink, D (1996) *Changing our Schools: Linking school effectiveness with school improvement*, Open University Press, Buckingham

Taylor, M (1996) Voicing their values: pupils' moral and cultural experience, in *Values in Education and Education in Values*, ed J M Halstead and M Taylor, Falmer, London

Turner, B S (1990) Periodization and politics in the post modern, in *Theories of Modernity and Postmodernization*, ed B S Turner, Sage, London

White, J (1998) New aims for a new national curriculum, in *The National Curriculum Beyond 2000: The QCA and the aims of education*, R Aldrich and J White, Institute of Education, University of London

Young, M (ed) (1971) *Knowledge and Control: New directions for the sociology of education*, Collier Macmillan, London

Young, M (1999) *The Curriculum of the Teacher*, Falmer, London

PART ONE

APPROACHES TO TEACHING VALUES

Chapter 2

What Scope Is There for Teaching Moral Reasoning?

Graham Haydon

Introduction

When I first began to study moral philosophy, and to think about moral education, I frequently encountered the assumption that there is a certain way in which people ought to think about moral questions, and hence the idea that moral education should involve teaching pupils – or at least in various non-didactic ways enabling or encouraging pupils – to think in the appropriate way. In recent years these ideas seem to have become deeply unfashionable. To put the theme of this chapter concisely, I believe these ideas are well worth resuscitating.

You might interpret the title of this chapter as asking whether it is possible to teach moral reasoning. Actually, I think that question is fairly easy to answer: it *is* possible. It is not too difficult to come up with something like a set of guidelines for moral reasoning, and there is no reason to think that teaching pupils to apply such guidelines is any more difficult than teaching them to think in the ways appropriate to, say, doing history or chemistry (I am not, by the way, saying that this is easy). The more difficult question is whether schools *should* be trying to teach moral reasoning, given various objections that have come to the fore in recent years. So I hope here to devote just a little space to arguing that it is possible, and much more space to asking whether it should be done.

How does one show that it is possible to teach moral reasoning? One way is to produce a model of moral reasoning and then to find evidence, from current practice or if necessary from new studies, that reasoning according to this model can be taught. Since I have no findings from research studies to report here, I shall merely rely on an appeal to plausibility: if we can have a clear and simple enough sketch of moral reasoning, there will be no reason to think, in advance, that it's not teachable.

The best way to show that it is possible to have a set of guidelines for moral reasoning is to produce one. To show that this is not too difficult, I'll do it at the beginning of the chapter. No doubt, and quite rightly, all sorts of questions will come to mind when you read these guidelines – these will be the kinds of questions, if I can anticipate them, that I need to address in the rest of the chapter. But it will be more productive to address the questions if we have in front of us an example of what a set of guidelines for moral reasoning might look like; so here is just such an example (deliberately expressed in non-technical language).

Be aware of the ways in which what you are doing is going to affect other people. Think about this if it's not obvious.

Try to think yourself into the position of other people affected by what you are doing; try to see what it is like to be in their shoes.

Think whether they would be likely to agree to what you are doing. Sometimes, the appropriate way of doing this will be to ask them. If that's not possible, you can still ask yourself 'if I were in their position, would I agree to be on the receiving end of the kind of thing which I, now, am thinking of doing?' (For example, if you have in mind to do something which involves deceiving another person, ask yourself whether you could agree to be deceived in a situation like this.)

Having seen what it would be like to be in the position of each of the people affected – seeing it, if you can, as if it were happening to you – ask yourself whether you think it is all right for people, in the sort of situation you're in now, to do the kind of thing you are thinking of doing.

Where does that model come from? There are many influences behind it. So far as philosophical writing about morality goes, it has something in it both of Kant and of the rival tradition of utilitarianism; it is closest probably to the ideas of the Oxford moral philosopher Richard Hare; but I can also recognize an influence in my thinking of the German social theorist Jurgen Habermas, and of the American psychological researcher Lawrence Kohlberg.[1] But outside of academic writing there is in it something of the everyday question 'what if everyone did that?'; and that carries in turn echoes of a tradition stretching back to the Golden Rule of the Bible 'do unto others what you would have them do unto you', while something similar is found in many other traditions.[2]

I have set out a model of moral reasoning, to show that it can be done. I am not suggesting that this model should be taken up just as it stands. If there are to be attempts to teach moral reasoning, then either this will be done on the initiative of individual schools, according to their own understanding of moral reasoning; or, if there were to be a national model, and appropriate teacher training to back it up, then presumably some sort of working group would have to agree on the model to be used. But my guess is that any model which would be likely to attract sufficient agreement would have to say something about considering the effects of one's actions on others, and it would have to have an affinity with the 'what if everyone did that?' question; and so it would not look totally different from the version above.

So let me turn to what, at least for this chapter, is the more substantial question. Is there any good reason for not teaching moral reasoning? I want to look at a number of possible objections and to try to draw the sting from them. In fact, in some cases I shall concede a lot of the substance of the objection but still argue that there remains a good case for teaching moral reasoning; replying to the objections will help in bringing out the positive case. At the end I shall summarize what I take the positive case to be. So let me look first at four broad kinds of objection:

1. a suspicion of the very idea that it is desirable for people to think about what is right and wrong;
2. a disbelief that there could be such a thing as a *right* way of moral reasoning;
3. the idea that the kind of model I've suggested is biased or over-narrow and misses a lot that is important in the way people think about and evaluate what they are doing;
4. the possibility that moral reasoning will have little effect on how people actually behave.

There will be overlaps between these objections, but this will serve as a way of categorizing various negative reactions to what I have in mind.

First, then, some people are suspicious of the very idea of people thinking about what is right and wrong. They want people to follow the old certainties; once people begin to think for themselves, the only certainty (on this view) is that they will go off the rails.

So far as education is concerned, there is even a curious brand of anti-intellectualism around when the topic is one of right and wrong. People who are concerned about educational standards will usually believe that there are appropriate ways of thinking in particular areas of the curriculum, so that when pupils are thinking about a problem in, say, maths or physics it does not follow, just from the fact that they are doing their own thinking, that there is no limit to what they can reasonably come up with. Yet where questions of right and wrong are concerned, these same people seem to believe that if pupils think for themselves they might come up with anything at all – at which point we begin to get invocations of Friedrich Nietzsche, relativism, and various other bogies. This actually suggests that these critics themselves subscribe to a kind of irrationalism about morality, believing that morality does not rest on any rational basis, and therefore that there is no such thing as a right way of thinking about moral matters. If they believed there were a rational basis for morality, why would they be so worried that other people, doing their own thinking, would come to the kind of answers which they (the critics) think are wrong? If they believe there are right answers in morality, why should they be so sceptical about ordinary people's capacity to see what these answers are?

What I am saying here, of course, does assume that moral reasoning will at least sometimes – but not necessarily always – lead to a definite conclusion. I think it is not too difficult to see that this is so – given a particular model of moral reasoning.

Suppose the question is 'Would it be all right to beat up this old man for fun?' Remember that the kind of thinking I've suggested involves putting yourself in the other person's position, and asking whether he could agree to what you are doing. Is there any doubt that someone thinking in the way I've sketched will have to reject the idea that it is all right to beat people up for fun?

This particular example, of course, does not lead to any moral conclusion that you, the reader, don't already accept (I think I am fairly safe in assuming that). My point is that, when you think of some kind of behaviour which you take to be quite clearly wrong, the idea that people *thinking* about right and wrong may lead them to different answers should be the least of your worries. Surely what lies behind such behaviour, when it happens, is more likely to be sheer thoughtlessness than serious moral thinking which has come to different conclusions from yours? But what, after all, of the bogey of relativism? Isn't the worry that once people begin to think about whether there really are any moral standards which they should adhere to, they will come to the conclusion that it is all relative and anything goes? This may be the first kind of position people come to once they begin to think seriously about matters of right and wrong (there was some evidence for this in Kohlberg's (1981) research); a bit more thought shows how difficult it is consistently to hold a relativist position.[3] The answer to worries about relativism is not less thinking but more and better thinking (and how could anyone with a serious concern for education think otherwise?).

The next kind of objection is more likely to come from those who *have* subscribed to some form of relativism. It is that there cannot be a single correct kind of moral thinking. There are simply different ways, and we cannot prove that one is better than another; or alternatively, while there may be a limit to what we could sensibly count as moral thinking, there is nothing to say that we have to engage in moral thinking at all. At least for the sake of argument, I am prepared to concede this objection. (Others who agree with me in the general thrust of this chapter might take a different line on this point.) To claim some kind of Platonic validity for a particular model of moral thinking is probably to make the task of persuading people to adopt it more difficult. Educators can and should make a more modest claim: that this is a way of thinking which has shown itself to be useful and also quite widely, even if not universally, acceptable (what I mean by calling this way of thinking 'useful' will become clearer near the end). We should be able to say 'this is a way of moral thinking which is worth teaching' without having to claim that it is laid up in heaven or handed down on tablets of stone.

To my mind a more serious objection than the ones I've considered so far is the idea that the kind of model I've suggested is biased or over-narrow and misses a lot that is important in the way people think about and evaluate what they do in their lives. Moral philosophers in recent years have often been sceptical of what appear as unduly rationalistic accounts of morality. We are told that morality, or an ethical life, is not a matter just of making decisions from time to time about particular moral questions; it is a matter of how one lives one's whole life from day to day and year to year. And we are told that what is most important is that people have the appropriate dispositions – qualities of character involving their motivation and feeling, not just their intellectual capacities. Sometimes the idea is that when people have the appropriate dispositions then, by and large, they will see what to do without having to work it out by following any particular process of reasoning. Thus, many moral philosophers and writers on moral education in recent years have revived a model of moral virtues taken originally from Aristotle. There have been influences tending in the same direction from empirical researchers, particularly stemming from Carol Gilligan's (1982) response to Kohlberg's model of moral reasoning. The notion of an ethic of caring – for the concrete other in the concrete situation – is proposed as complementary to and often as superior to an ethic of abstract and general principles of justice.

My response to this is: a) to agree with almost everything in it; b) to argue that none of it makes the idea of moral reasoning dispensable; and c) to argue that the points the critics make about the need to respond to the concrete situation rather than applying abstract principles are quite compatible with the kind of moral reasoning I have in mind.

First, there is certainly more to morality than thinking from time to time about what one should do. But we can hardly deny that this is part of it – not because we hold one conception or another of the nature of morality, but because of the nature of life in the modern world. (It's possible to imagine a way of life in which people can get by without ever stopping to think about what they should do, but it's unlikely to be a life that any of us or our students or pupils will lead.) People do find themselves in situations which they themselves see to be difficult, where it is not at all clear what is the best thing – morally – to do. They also find themselves in situations where, if they don't think, they may act in ways which they or others will certainly regret later, but where if they had stopped to think things would have turned out better for all concerned. But in fact none of the theorists of virtue or proponents of an ethic of care, from Aristotle to Gilligan and Noddings (1984), have denied the need for moral thinking; what is in dispute, rather, is the form that moral thinking should take.

The major objection has been to a model of moral reasoning which consists in starting from a general rule or principle, seeing that a particular case falls under that general rule or principle, and hence deducing what one should do in the particular case. Thus, for a simple example:

One should not tell lies.
Saying this to X would be telling a lie.
Therefore I should not say this to X.

It should be clear that the model of moral reasoning that I proposed above is nothing like this. In fact there is nothing about rules or principles in the model I suggested – unless you want to describe the whole model as setting out rules for thinking. But there is an important difference between procedural rules for thinking, and substantive rules for behaviour, which tell you 'do things of this kind' or 'don't do things of that kind'.

Some people may think that I have not left sufficient place for rules or principles telling people what they should or should not do. They may want to say, in effect: 'let people follow their own moral reasoning, so long as they adhere to such and such rules'. In responding to this I want to make a distinction between rules and principles. This distinction is not consistently marked in ordinary language, but there is precedent for it in some philosophical writing about morality, and it seems to me a distinction worth marking.

Rules, then, as I am using the term here, are relatively specific prescriptions for conduct, such as 'don't tell lies' or 'don't hit people'. One way of treating such rules is to see them as requiring no thought in their application at all; but that would be to make of morality a mindless procedure. If there is to be careful thought about what we ought to do, then there are the possibilities both of recognizing sometimes that what a rule requires is indeterminate, and of recognizing sometimes that it is better to make an exception to the rule. Only thinking can tell us when we should make an exception. We have to consider whether, in the particular kind of case before us, it can be right (for anyone in just this kind of case) to act in a way that involves, say, not telling the truth. But notice that the same form of reasoning which could tell us in a particular kind of case that it would be right not to tell the truth, would also tell us in many other cases that it would be wrong to tell a lie. The conclusion is that the rule is not really necessary; moral reasoning, if it is working well, will tell us when to tell the truth and when not to.

Now this might sound dangerous. People feel that recognizing a rule gives some security, whereas if people are to think things through for themselves on every occasion, they will be liable to get it wrong. There is something in this; we don't always have time to think things through, and sometimes our thinking may go wrong.[4] Also, we are more able to rely on other people's actions if we know what rules they are likely to be following. So there is some point in having general rules. But we shouldn't think of the rules as prior to the thinking. If anything can justify the rules in the first place, as well as justifying exceptions to them, it can only be moral reasoning.

The case with principles is rather different. As I propose to use the term here, a principle is a more general consideration which is to be treated as relevant in any moral thinking.[5] Examples of principles in this sense are 'respect for persons', 'fairness' and 'consideration of interests'. Clearly these are not rules in the sense of specific prescriptions for action. How, then, could they function? Recall that the model of moral reasoning I proposed above began: *Be aware of the ways in which what you are doing is going to affect other people. Think about this if it's not obvious.*

In thinking about how one's conduct will affect others, one needs some basis by which to count the effects on others as relevant or irrelevant, good or bad. After all, some effects on people may simply not matter. If I keep in mind such considerations as fairness and respect, then I have an idea of what I am looking for. Does this mean that an awareness of principles is essential to moral reasoning? Not quite, because if people are treated in a hurtful way, or unfairly, or disrespectfully, then (on certain assumptions which I needn't go into here) they are treated in ways in which they would prefer not to be treated. So at least theoretically it is possible, as Hare (1981) has argued, to carry through a whole piece of moral reasoning in terms of how far people's preferences are satisfied – the preferences, that is, of all who are or who might be affected by one's action. But general principles do provide something a little more substantial to work with, especially when one has no direct access to other people's preferences; and also, which is important, reference to general principles may facilitate the teaching of moral reasoning.

This stage of my argument began as a response to the objections to a deductive model of moral reasoning, in which a specific answer is deduced from something general. That model might be true of the reasoning that consists in straightforwardly applying a moral rule, but I have given rather a small role to that kind of reasoning. I've suggested a larger role for principles, but taking principles into account is not a matter of deducing a determinate conclusion from a principle. Having in mind that one should try to be fair and to respect people and not to hurt them does not detract at all, so far as I can see, from the concreteness of thinking about what to do in a particular situation. Much moral reasoning *is* a matter of attending to the actual situation, seeing how people will be affected in this situation, seeing whether these people in this situation could agree to what you are proposing to do – actually asking them and talking it through when possible – and in all of this paying attention to how people will feel, whether they may be hurt, and so on. This is the sort of contextualized thinking that writers such as Noddings or Gilligan have in mind. In that kind of thinking, as they conceive of it, implicit principles seem to be operating, even if unacknowledged; if these writers do not want to refer to principles that is perhaps because they associate principles purely with a deductive model of reasoning from the general to the particular.

The kind of reasoning I am talking about is very far from an algorithm. It will not always lead an individual to a resolution of a problem in which they can feel confident; and it will not guarantee that different people thinking about the same situation will come to the same answer. It would be a mistake to conclude from that that it can be dispensed with.

What, finally, about the question of whether thinking translates into action? It would be quite implausible to suppose that people who engage in moral reasoning will always behave better as a result. This is true even when 'better' is defined in terms of the outcome of people's own moral thinking, for notoriously people don't always do what they think they ought to do (cf Straughan, 1982). On the other hand, if one thought that moral reasoning would make no difference to what people did, then of course there would be much less reason for being concerned about moral reasoning within education.

However, either extreme position here looks less plausible than something between. All we need to believe, for moral reasoning to have a legitimate place in education, is that people sometimes do what they think they ought to do, and that sometimes they come to a belief about what they ought to do as a result of doing some moral reasoning. I have not said that the teaching of moral reasoning should ever be the whole of moral education. Any overall programme of moral education has to address affective and motivational aspects as well as cognitive.[6] But it would make no more sense to neglect cognitive aspects than to neglect motivation. It is sometimes suggested, for instance, that schools should try to develop altruism (cf White, 1990, chapter 3). But if by altruism we mean a motivating concern for the good of others, this motivation in itself will not tell one what is in others' interests. Sometimes, no doubt, that will be obvious, but there will be times when, even given altruism, serious thought is needed to see what to do.

Besides, it would be a mistake to think that the only kind of situation in which moral reasoning is appropriate is when an individual has to think about what he or she is to do. There are situations in which people need to talk together about what they collectively are to do – many professional contexts, for instance, are like that – and in such cases a shared sense of how moral reasoning is to proceed provides a shared language in which the discussion can go on. And then again, there are moral issues of public concern – such as many frequently arising concerning health care and advances in the biological sciences – on which every citizen has the right and arguably the responsibility to form an opinion and take part in debate. So the public role of an agreed form of moral reasoning would be at least as important as its personal role.

While it is important, then, not to expect too much from moral reasoning, it's also important not to expect too little from it. We should certainly not expect that it will give us – either collectively or individually – determinate resolutions to all the problems that may worry us. But at the same time, we should not suppose that there won't be many cases where it will give a pretty clear answer. And this is surely an important lesson that education should be getting across to people. If the question can be raised – as it can, for how could education rule out in advance the raising of certain questions? – of whether it is all right to lie and cheat and disregard people's interests, then it is important that educators can show that there is a way of reasoning that – at least in many cases – will lead pretty clearly to the answer that it is not all right. It is not, of course, enough just to assert that there is such a way of reasoning. It has to be determinate enough to be actually teachable, so that people can do the reasoning and see for themselves that they come to these conclusions. We cannot ensure that they will do it, at least outside the context of the classroom (this was one of the criticisms Mary Warnock (1977, Chapter 4) made against John Wilson). But even for people to see that it can be done is an important step away from an out-and-out, 'anything goes', subjectivism.

I have said nothing here about *how* moral reasoning might be taught. There is as much scope here as in any part of the curriculum for imaginative materials and approaches. I'll only mention one here as being particularly worth exploring further: the role of discussion. Part of the form of reasoning I set out was:

- Try to think yourself into the position of other people affected by what you are doing; try to see what it is like to be in their shoes.
- Think whether they would be likely to agree to what you are doing. Sometimes, the appropriate way of doing this will be to ask them.

This is already enough to show that moral reasoning should not be (to use the terms Habermas (1990) uses in his critique of Kant) purely *monologic*, but should often be *dialogic*. Classroom discussion will itself sometimes be moral reasoning in progress. And there is a possibility too that an awareness of the nature of moral reasoning – which is an awareness of a kind of thinking that the vulnerable and interdependent condition of human beings calls for – may emerge for individuals out of their experience of trying, in dialogue with others, to come to an agreed decision about what is to be done on matters which affect them all.[7]

Notes

1. All writers referred to were, or are, prolific authors, but for typical or central accounts see Kant (1785), Hare (1981), Habermas (1990), Kohlberg (1981).
2. I must also make a special reference to the work of the Oxford educationalist philosopher John Wilson, who for many years has argued for something not far removed from what I'm arguing for here. See, eg, Wilson (1990). Perhaps after about three decades his time has come.
3. What I am referring to here is a relativist position about *everything* in matters of right and wrong. Denying relativism in this sense does not at all commit one to denying that in many respects different people have different values, and it certainly doesn't commit one to trying to impose the same values on everyone.
4. A similar case is argued by Hare (1981), Chapter 2.
5. Cf Peters (1981), Chapter 4.
6. I have said more about motivational aspects in Haydon (1998).
7. I have said more about the role of discussion in Haydon (1997) and in a forthcoming chapter 'Discussion of values and the value of discussion' in a volume on Values, Diversity and Education, edited by Mal Leicester, Celia Modgil and Sohan Modgil, to be published by Falmer.

References

Gilligan, C (1982) *In a Different Voice: Psychological theory and women's development*, Harvard University Press, Cambridge, MA

Habermas, J (1990) *Moral Consciousness and Communicative Action*, Polity Press, Cambridge

Hare, R M (1981) *Moral Thinking*, Oxford University Press, Oxford

Haydon, G (1997) *Teaching about Values: A new approach*, Cassell, London

Haydon, G (1998) Behaving morally as a point of principle: a proper aim of moral education?, in *Education in Morality*, ed J M Halstead and T McLaughlin, Routledge, London

Kant, I (1785) Groundwork of the metaphysic of morals, in *The Moral Law*, (1948) H J Paton, Hutchinson, London

Kohlberg, L (1981) *The Philosophy of Moral Development*, Harper & Row, San Francisco

Noddings, N (1984) *Caring: A feminine approach to ethics and moral education*, University of California Press, Berkeley, CA

Peters, R (1981) *Moral Development and Moral Education*, Allen & Unwin, London

Straughan, R (1982) *'I Ought to But...': Philosophical approach to the problem of weakness of will in education,* NFER-Nelson, Windsor

Warnock, M (1977) *Schools of Thought,* Faber, London

White, J (1990) *Education and the Good Life,* Kogan Page, London

Wilson, J (1990) *A New Introduction to Moral Education,* Cassell, London

Chapter 3

Three Approaches to Moral Education

Colin Wringe

Introduction

Two kinds of moral motivation

Talk of moral education commonly conceals a distinction between two rather different sets of goals, their rationales and appropriate modes of achieving them. I shall refer to these as:

- the social utility view;
- the group values view.

While recognizing that in any educational situation, endeavours correspond-ing to both views may be taking place, I shall explore the distinction between them, arguing that failure to recognize this distinction and to be clear about our aims on particular occasions may not only impair the success of our efforts but compromise our credibility in the eyes of both the young people we seek to educate and adults, parents, colleagues and the public at large, upon whose support we are bound to rely. Subsequently, it will be argued that neither of these conceptions of moral education meets the needs of our present predicament, either separately or in combination, and a third possible approach will be tentatively proposed.

A *social utility view* of moral education is taken when people become inter-ested in the topic because of concern with such things as the incidence of mostly rather petty delinquency among the young, such as individual acts of violence, burglary, car-crime, vandalism and the like as well as intoxication, drug taking and sexual licence undermining the established order of family life. Classroom disruption destructive of a satisfactory learning environment for others may also be included. This kind of concern and the consequent interest in moral education may from time to time be heightened by spectacular acts of violence or, at a different social level, cases of business fraud or political corruption which add to the impression that society as a whole is in a parlous moral state.

To be contrasted with this is the *group values view* according to which certain kinds of conduct, commitment and belief are promoted not primarily because they are convenient to the respectable adult world but because they form part of a valued way of life with a particular system of beliefs, practices and relationships. The way of life may be that of a religious group. Quaker, Catholic, Muslim and other religious communities are characterized almost as sharply by their moral priorities as by their theological tenets. But equally it may be largely or wholly secular. Aristocratic codes of honour, the rules of polite society in recent centuries which defined the conduct to be expected of a gentleman, or a lady, the respectable materialism of the aspiring lower middle classes, would all be cases in point, each with their formal or informal modes of moral education. On such a view, untruthfulness, theft or intoxication are often condemned, not so much because of the inconvenience they cause to others but because truthfulness, honesty or abstinence are seen as important values in themselves.

On the social utility view, as the term implies, moral education is undertaken because of the inconvenience, disturbance, injury or expense caused by delinquent or irresponsible behaviour. The emphasis of such an approach is upon the behaviour itself, upon securing acceptable, or rather avoiding unacceptable, behaviour. The actual reasons why someone refrains from mugging, burglary or drunken and disorderly conduct are relatively unimportant and the educational methods used relatively immaterial. Habituation, negative reinforcement, deterrence through the fear of tough sanctions, the persistent, unreflective inculcation of rules, codes and moral certainties may be interchangeable with methods involving critical discussion and the development of such moral reasoning as will lead to the internalization of desirable principles like truth-telling, non-violence and respect for others. One mode of control may be substituted for another according to time, place and judgement as to the likely response of the young people concerned. The overriding criterion is effectiveness in diminishing the incidence of socially undesired behaviour, though the varying moral legitimacy of these methods may be a matter of concern to some.

On a group values view, the undesirability of intoxication, pilfering or lying stems not so much from the inconvenience or harm inflicted upon others. The indignation or, as it will often be, the sorrow caused by these acts arises rather from the evidence they provide of the state of the offender's character or soul. The offender has proved herself 'unworthy' of her family, her school, her religion, her class, or whatever. The individual has let himself down, fallen from grace, demonstrated that he is not a gentleman, revealed himself in his true colours, and is not a suitable pupil for a school of this kind. The deviant act is less important for its consequences than as the outward evidence of the offender's true nature.

In the case of the social utility view, the purpose of moral education is instrumental from the point of view of the adult world. Young people are being brought up, often quite unashamedly, in the interests of that adult world. On the group values view, by contrast, the aim will often be represented as benefiting the young people themselves. The purpose of moral education is seen as developing in its recipients, qualities that are valuable to the recipients themselves as well as to others, for various reasons: because they will gain favour in the eyes of the divinity, prospective suitors, influential persons in society; or because those qualities may contribute to the individuals' well-being by enabling them to lead a more worthy and worthwhile life, contribute to their moral development, or assist the realization of their potential. If the group sees itself as having a certain elite status, socially, morally, racially, the moral education received by the young is a key part of the extended initiation into adult membership of the group.

Further practical consequences flow from this difference of emphasis between our two approaches to moral education. If conduct is important as evidence of inward states, these states themselves are not negligible. The why of appropriate behaviour is at least as important as the what. The rationale of the desired behaviour, be this genuine or spurious, must be communicated and absorbed. This may be done explicitly or informally by example and commentary upon real or fictional persons and events. In contrast to the social utility approach, the construct of a 'good' pupil, a good citizen, a worthy member of society or representative of the school will be an important element in the moral educator's armoury. Commitment to an all-embracing ideology, belief system or religion will provide the essential rationale for the desired behaviour and once this is achieved, shaming, which is inconceivable on the social utility view, becomes a powerful sanction.

This is not to say that moral education in a group values tradition may not sometimes be accompanied by ferocious physical punishments, as many who have enjoyed a religious education of various kinds will confirm. This apparent paradox may no doubt be accounted for by the fact that the misdemeanour is not taken at face value and met with a sanction of proportionate severity, but is seen as an offence either against the highest of all authorities or against some absolute value, to threaten which strikes at the very heart and *raison d'être* of the community. The offence not only has to be prevented from recurring with inconvenient frequency in the future, but utterly purged and expiated. Punishment is no mere instrument of deterrence but an attempt to re-establish the moral equilibrium of the universe (see Foucault's 1975 distinction). The fact that it may be seen as being for the recipient's benefit may also lessen the obligation to be moderate. The harsher the chastisement, the clearer the expression of love.

It may be thought that in a pluralistic, liberal society of the kind that many people would regard as desirable today, social utility rather than group values is the more desirable foundation of moral education, for the latter requires not only conformity but conviction which it may only be possible to maintain in a fairly stable, monocultural context where the values of family, school and wider society are in accord. Criticism and reasoning beyond a certain range of permitted or prescribed themes are unlikely to flourish in such a situation and in the modern world such a community may feel the need to remain closed and protect itself artificially. Schools may need to be segregated by sex, religion or class. Surveillance needs to be close, addressing word and thought as well as overt deeds, and such education may only be undertaken in good conscience by believing and committed members of the religion, caste or community themselves, whose lives as well as their professional practice may be pressed into the service of the educational goal. They must serve as an example to their charges (Carr, 1991) and are obliged to suffer the constraints of an exemplary life, or practice discretion and hypocrisy.

Despite its instrumental treatment of the young, moral education directed towards social utility at least has the advantage that it does not, or does not necessarily, attempt to impose beliefs. Provided one keeps one's nose clean, one's soul remains one's own. One is subject to coercion, for the sake of the freedoms and rights of others but, in principle, one remains free to disobey and take the consequences. Though constrained and coerced, the young person is not required to subordinate him or herself to a higher authority but just keep his hands off the persons and property of others, or suffer some proportionate unpleasantness. There is no shame, humiliation or naivety in this, even if one eventually becomes habituated to act honestly when one is no longer being observed. To act so as to avoid unpleasantness to oneself is the mark of prudence and rationality, and is consistent with freedom and dignity.

The downside of a moral regime that concentrates on overt behaviour and does not presume to interfere with the internal belief system and values orientation of the individual is precisely that. It may reduce the incidence of mugging, theft and drug addiction and produce the sort of person who stays out of jail, doesn't give himself airs and is generally prepared to live and let live but it is unlikely to produce the character who will go to the stake for justice and truth or knowingly risk life and limb for queen and country. This requires the internalization of an aggressive super-ego, a commitment to perfection before which any falling short is intolerable, rather than mere satisfeasance and the avoidance of sanctions. Such a frame of mind presupposes positive values typically generated by groups possessing and transmitting to each generation ever more heightened forms of their moral certainties, capable of producing heroes and martyrs, or bigoted fanatics.

Some problems

It will by now be clear why failure to discriminate between these two approaches to moral education undermines both effectiveness and credibility and also why neither approach is entirely satisfactory in the modern world.

The group values approach can only be used successfully in the kind of monocultural community in which the relevant values are held and can therefore give consistent and solid support to the educational institution, and receive equally uncritical support from it. A few such communities, notably religious groups possessing their own schools, continue to exist. But for better or for worse – and many perfectly honourable and moral individuals would unequivocally say for better – they contain only a minority of the population in countries such as our own. In a secular context few groups of educators would be unanimous in their support of any particular set of group values and many would regard any such uncritical support as inconsistent with the educator's duty.

Being conscientiously unable to support, or even bound to oppose, the severe line taken by some of their colleagues over, say, mild sexual interest, minor pilfering or diplomatic classroom untruthfulness ('Did you speak, Michael?', 'No, Sir.') would inevitably be seen as undermining sound moral standards. On the other hand, concentration on the external manifestations of behaviour, and then only when these were likely to cause problems, would seem shallow and inadequate if not downright cynical to those for whom moral education was about commitment and the development of a positively virtuous character. The tendency to modify sanctions to the gravity of the harm done or the offender's particular deterrence needs rather than to the misdemeanour may also be offensive to those committed to group values according to which certain moral imperatives may be absolutes and, as it may be, prescribed sanctions may be seen as an obligation.

In a non-monocultural school, pupils as well as teachers will come from differing traditions with regard to the distinction we have discussed above. Those accustomed from home to severe punishments or, failing that, severe expressions of disapproval from authority figures, are likely to be unimpressed by the more relaxed atmosphere of the secular institution which seems largely concerned with expediency and even not to care about lax behaviour that does no one a great deal of harm. Those, on the other hand, whose concept of morality is of a more consequentialist nature are less likely to take seriously injunctions based on values to which neither they nor their perfectly law-abiding and considerate friends and families attach great importance or even regard as positively misguided.

There is the further consideration that more frequently than in the past, children move out of their closed communities and may become critical of the more explicit moral certainties they have acquired, either at home or at school. This is a further cause of conflict and confusion. To premise moral imperatives upon such certainties, and more especially upon substantive religious beliefs, means that when those certainties or beliefs are jettisoned, the rest of morality may go with them, whereas the attempt to give morality a more critical foundation at school may undermine the very certainties upon which others might have relied satisfactorily throughout their lives.

From the above, it will be apparent that attempts to compromise between the two approaches to moral education we have identified so far are bound to be unsatisfactory, if not actually counterproductive. The expedients that immediately suggest themselves, however, are likely to be even more problematic. One possibility might seem to be that we should have separate kinds of institutions allowing different approaches to moral education to be pursued without being contaminated by each other. In that way the moral message would not be weakened by alternative views. This would certainly appeal to the advocates of educational separation on the basis of religion or distinctive philosophies. But as events in other parts of the world (Bosnia, Northern Ireland, the Middle East) have shown, such a policy would be politically, indeed morally disastrous. One can think of no surer recipe for hatred, strife and, ultimately, bloodshed than groups of citizens exclusively educated in contempt for the moral basis of each other's lives. In the light of earlier comments it will be unnecessary to add that the remaining alternative of promoting one of these approaches while suppressing the other would be unacceptable to a large part of the population, and therefore inappropriate and inefficacious in the education of their children.

It should be stressed that the problem is not one of diversity of values in an obvious or superficial sense. It comes as no surprise that the SCAA forum of adults of different persuasions has been able to agree in identifying four key areas of moral concern,: namely self, relationships, society and the environment (School Curriculum and Assessment Authority, 1996b). As far as moral education is concerned, the problem lies not in agreeing on what those areas are, or even on some of the things we should do about them. It lies not in the matter but in the manner of our value judgements, how we hold them, what we conceive the rationale for them to be. On this point the SCAA document explicitly declines to commit itself, suggesting two sources of values, God and human nature, both of which would be unsatisfactory to many moralists in either religious or secular traditions. (For many Christians, for example, God approves of love because it is good; it is not good simply because God, for reasons best known to himself, happens to like it. The precise features of human nature are essentially controversial, and some aspects of it require to be constrained and certainly cannot be taken as a guide for conduct.)

The two possible approaches to moral education we have considered so far are also unsatisfactory, not only in combination as we have seen, but also individually. Both are concerned with controlling the young for the convenience and comfort of adults, either in relation to their material interests, or in order not to disturb the world view and pattern of relationships in the light of which they have lived their lives and made important sacrifices in some cases, but which may not be appropriate to the lives of their children, or the world in which those lives will be lived. Many, but perhaps not all, people would agree that such an attempt to subordinate the interests of one generation to those of another is morally illegitimate except, perhaps, in a very stable society in which the young will come in their turn to enjoy the benefits now enjoyed by the older generation. It is no fit basis for a programme of moral education in a rapidly changing world in which this is no longer the case. It is also unlikely to be effective, unless pursued with a degree of ruthless determination we should all abhor, heightening in our brightest and most independent-minded, as well as our most truculent and difficult young people, the kind of rebellion, disaffection, disenchantment and cynicism with which we are already familiar. Even where apparently successful, it is calculated to produce a kind of moral infantilism in the young, rendering them incapable of shouldering those responsibilities and taking those opportunities in adult life for which, it has been suggested, we should prepare them.

Just what those responsibilities and opportunities will be is a matter for debate. They are, however, not something upon which the present adult generation is in a position to pronounce authoritatively, for they will be exercised and enjoyed in a world to which the practices and conceptions developed to cope with the events and conditions of our generation's lifetime will no longer precisely apply. Earlier writers concerned with moral education (Kohlberg, 1976; Wilson, 1972; Straughan, 1982) believed this meant we should strive to develop moral reasoning in young people involving very general moral principles which could be applied to diverse situations in a multifarious and changing world. More recently it has come to seem possible, to put it no more strongly, that reliance on such principles in itself may have been a measure of our immaturity (Foucault, 1984) or have simply served as instruments in the exercise of power (Foucault, 1973). If there is any truth in this view, those who think the principal dragon to be slain in the field of moral education is that of relativism (School Curriculum and Assessment Authority, 1996a) will need to think again. The task to be accomplished is less easy than slaying a beast, though this simplistic response may be suggested by the more primitive side of our nature. Learning to live morally in a world without absolutes, as perhaps our children must, is more difficult to conceive, and may require a measure of intellectual flexibility, which the younger generation will hopefully be able to attain more easily than ourselves.

Moral maturity, the ability to cope with the moral responsibilities of adult life, can certainly not be a matter of tutelage to a dead father figure, natural or supernatural, or subjection to the injunctions of a bygone generation, but of finding ways of living together satisfactorily in a world more varied and less certain than our own or previous generations have known.

An alternative possibility

Only a megalomaniac or true prophet would attempt at this juncture to offer a positive programme to solve all our problems in the field of moral education. What follows are therefore modest and hopefully uncontroversial proposals attempting to define and, above all, limit the scope of our aims and expectations in this field.

We may begin by identifying two aspects of youthful behaviour that are commonly thought to lie within the field of moral education but, strictly speaking, fall outside it. First, for whatever reason, adolescents and young adults, especially young males, do appear to go through a period when they are boisterous, moody, irresponsible and rebellious. This results in various incidents of undesired behaviour ranging from classroom disorder in and around the age of 14 to petty larceny and occasional serious and sometimes tragic acts of violence. Few people acquainted with young people of this age regard them as fundamentally bad or inveterately committed to criminality. Indeed, it is a cliché of one educational tradition that those who are most impatient of authority in youth often make sterling citizens in later life. As this phase is usually left behind with the natural passing of the years the appropriate response would seem to be not moral education but containment. The wise course would seem to be to minimize conflict by allowing the phenomenon room to express itself, but within defined limits. No doubt these limits need to be clear and backed by non-damaging but effective sanctions. From the point of view of moral development, however, the chief requirements would seem to be the negative ones that containment should be adequate to prevent young people from committing major misdemeanours that lead to their being permanently stigmatized and excluded from continuing their socialization into normal adult life, and that sanctions should not be so severe or so arbitrarily applied as to leave the victim permanently embittered or hostile or bring him/her into contact with older offenders, ie with criminals properly so-called.

A second phenomenon falling outside the strict ambit of mainstream moral education is that of the small number of permanently and deeply malevolent young people for whom the only option is special treatment, be this in the form of severe, punitive sanctions, therapy or long-term confinement. These cases are less matters of moral education than public policy, though teachers, like others who come into contact with young people, may be involved in its administration in both cases.

Turning to the domain of moral education proper, it is here suggested, perhaps surprisingly, that this should not be predominately prescriptive or concerned with behaviour at all. It is assumed that rational behaviour is motivated by being seen as either advantageous or worthy of admiration in the eyes of the agent and his/her reference group: in Weber's terms, it is either *zweckrationell* or *wertrationell* (Aron, 1967). On this view, one motive for unacceptable behaviour is that it pays off, either in material or symbolic terms. This is the obvious way to account for the behaviour of adult fraudsters, corrupt politicians or the barons of organized crime, not to mention opportunist acts of larceny or criminal bravado committed for the sake of admiration by the offender's peers.

If the perception is widespread that the most successful and esteemed members of the older generation behave badly and not only get away with it but owe it some of their success and the esteem in which they are held, it is not surprising if our moral injunctions are derided, and those who follow them are thought of as dupes and fools. An important part of the task of moral education, therefore, must be to convince the young that it is simply not the case that the most successful and highly esteemed members of the older generation have become so by unworthy means, or that those who have behaved well, worked hard all their lives or whatever, like our pupils' parents and relatives perhaps, are likely to end up in obscurity and destitution.

If there were any truth in this picture we should be in something of a dilemma. We could scarcely be expected to lie to the younger generation for this would be an unsound basis for moral education and some of our pupils would see through us. If adult society were actually corrupt and current concern with moral education were simply an attempt to dupe the majority of future citizens for the benefit of others, honourable educators could have no part in it but would then, at least, have no reason to blame themselves for their failure to morally educate the young. If we were truly concerned with morality under those circumstances we should need to direct our efforts towards our own generation and ourselves rather than the young. In this as in other respects, education cannot be expected to compensate for the shortcomings of society.

If conduct is indeed rational as we have suggested, a second possible cause of bad behaviour would be when the agent sees nothing, or nothing she wants, or wants urgently, to be gained by behaving well. In more stable times, those who behaved well ended up enjoying the things their elders had: wealth, status or some lesser honour deemed appropriate to their station. In these changing and more competitive times, even these rewards are no longer assured. Those who simply perform faithfully the tasks that God and tradition set before them are likely to end up unemployed, impoverished, derided and pitied by more prosperous members of society. It is no surprise if the young do not wish to imitate them. More importantly, however, these rewards themselves, wealth, status and material contentment, are rejected by many young people, which is a further dilemma for the moral educator. Should he counter this tendency, or be gratified by it? The recent SCAA document (School Curriculum and Assessment Authority, 1996b) is strangely silent on this key issue but, historically, the cult of Mammon has often been disparaged by our moral traditions.

If bad behaviour is perceived as more attractive than good, it is helpful to ask what are the rewards that bad behaviour offers and good behaviour does not. If one possible cause of bad behaviour is sheer frustration with one's prospects and situation, deviancy and crime may seem the only option that is challenging, requires courage, skill and nerve, represents achievement and brings the admiration of peers.

On this view a second goal of moral education would be to convince the young that there are opportunities for challenging and rewarding activity and a life satisfying in their terms that is within the bounds of moral and social acceptability. Successful performance in this aspect of moral education would be a matter of showing the young, convincingly, how such opportunities are to be attained, of instilling the necessary motivation and self-confidence, of, to use a current phrase, 'empowering' them to eventually change unsatisfactory aspects of their lives in socially acceptable ways. In this sense life skills would have an important contribution to make to moral education, and not vice versa (Hyland, 1995).

If there are in fact no such opportunities for most pupils, the moral educator would once again be faced with a problem. To put it bluntly, if the problem was that given the nature of our society, there was no chance of most young people finding a life satisfying to themselves within the bounds of acceptable conduct, attempts at moral education would be a singularly inadequate solution. The expedient options open to us would be the indoctrination of false beliefs ('We can all achieve a satisfying life if we behave well and work hard'), repression ('Your life may be grim but step out of line and it will be a jolly sight grimmer' – the 'get tough with young thugs' approach) or to recast moral education in terms of the hope and aspiration for social change.

This last proposition may seem somewhat startling and it is certainly not suggested that the moral educator should preach revolution or foment mayhem on the streets. It will, however, be recalled that one of the shortcomings of the social utility approach was its inherent inability to provide inspiration for the idealism of the young, while the group values approach was so often premised upon ideals and aspirations that no longer had credibility in their eyes. It is also arguable that part of the disenchantment of the young with the whole notion of values stems from the sheer tediousness of adult treatment of the topic, from our over-scrupulousness – our fear of official disapproval perhaps – in avoiding controversial issues. It is precisely by controversy that moral commitment is generated. Genuine moral issues are necessarily controversial, for they inevitably touch upon the important interests of powerful people.

It is also evident that to restrict moral education to the realm of individual and personal conduct excluding wider moral, ie political and social, issues of the day is arbitrarily to curtail the scope of young people's moral awareness and full development as human beings. For the most conspicuously immoral aspects of modern life concern not individual acts of robust physicality, light-fingeredness or prevarication but the gross acts of inhumanity and ongoing situations of injustice condoned or supported by the adult world at a political level. In a democracy, moral education must necessarily include political education, unless we believe that individual views are without influence upon political outcomes. Including issues at this level has the great advantage of harnessing in a positive way for moral education, some of the commitment and the enthusiasm of young people and sympathy for the unfortunate, in a way that is difficult to imagine in the context of other approaches.

Some may question whether such a general approach to the task of raising young people's awareness of values has much relevance to the problems of youthful delinquency which currently cause public concern. Doubtless this remains to be seen, but it is not obvious that those who have been encouraged to think about the plight of the old and the poor or the destruction of the environment by commercial interests would find it quite so natural to mug old-age pensioners and rob them of their savings or even vandalize plants and trees in their local park.

Suggestions in the final section of this chapter have been premised on the notion of helping the young to gain a realistic understanding of the world in all its complexity, impermanence and imperfection in order to be in a position to cope with it and forge their own version of a satisfactory way of living together after our generation's practices and preconceptions have become inapplicable and passed into oblivion. The prime requirement here is not prescription but that young people should come to understand society and the mechanisms by which it operates. To do this honestly may entail acknowl-edging that the way our generation does things may be capable of improve-ment from a moral point of view. To suggest, even by omission, that nothing is to be done is to consolidate despair. To hint at the possibility of improve-ment and to indicate that there are ways in which it may be brought about is not only to encourage hope but to offer a challenge and an incentive and, inci-dentally, to provide a small example of selflessness and trust, for in contrast to the approaches to moral education criticized earlier our concern is not to en-able us and our generation to live out the remainder of our lives undisturbed by the alien ways of the young, but to enable members of the younger genera-tion themselves to live satisfactory lives together in a world constructed in ac-cordance with their own aspirations and understandings.

References

Aron, R (1967) *Main Currents in Sociological Thought 2*, Penguin, Harmondsworth

Carr, D (1991) *Educating the Virtues*, Routledge, London

Foucault, M (1973) *Naissance de la Clinique; une Archéologie du Regard Médical*, Presses Universitaires de France, Paris

Foucault, M (1975) *Surveiller et Punir: Naissance de la Prison*, Gallimard, Paris

Foucault, M (1984) What is enlightenment?, in *The Foucault Reader*, ed P Rabinow, Pen-guin, Harmondsworth

Hyland, T (1995) Morality, work and employment: towards a values dimension in voca-tional education and training, *Journal of Moral Education*, **24** (4), pp 445–56

Kohlberg, L (1976) Moral stages and moralization, in *Moral Development and Behaviour*, ed T Likona, Holt Rinehart and Winstone, New York

School Curriculum and Assessment Authority (1996a) *Education for Adult Life: The spiritual and moral development of young people*, School Curriculum and Assessment Authority, London

School Curriculum and Assessment Authority (1996b) *Consultation on Values in Education and the Community*, School Curriculum and Assessment Authority, London

Straughan, R (1982) *Can We Teach Children to be Good?*, Allen & Unwin, London

Wilson, J (1972) *Practical Methods of Moral Education*, Heinemann, London

Chapter 4

Philosophy for Children: How Philosophical Enquiry Can Foster Values Education in Schools

Robert Fisher

What matters at this stage is the construction of local forms of community within which ci-vility and the intellectual and moral life can be sustained.

Alisdair MacIntyre (1984, p 224)

Sometimes you're afraid to say things, but in philosophy lessons you can say what you really think and sometimes you change your mind.

Michelle, aged 10

Introduction

This chapter explores the way philosophical enquiry with children can support moral and social education in schools. It draws on the author's research into the use of philosophy for children in primary and secondary schools, and argues that genuine values are best created and tested through a structured process of reflection and sustained discussion. The nature of a community is explored, and links between moral education and reasoning are illustrated from research in schools. A community of philosophical enquiry not only provides students with the opportunity to apply critical thinking to beliefs and values, it also offers them a model of values in action. This model is shown to be a powerful means of moral education because values are embedded in the very procedures and moral routines of shared enquiry. The chapter ends with a discussion of ways of evaluating a moral culture developed through philosophical enquiry.

There is growing concern in many countries about the problem of teaching values. In this country hardly a week passes without some public agonizing over a fresh example of lack of moral judgement. The important role that education can play, at home and school, in the moral development of children hardly needs emphasizing. Recent discussion papers and the setting up of the National Forum for Values in Education and the Community highlight the challenge schools face in educating for democracy, and in core values such as respect for self, respect for others and respect for the environment (SCAA, 1995, 1996, 1997). It would be difficult to find fault with these values or with the call for pupils to develop the ability to make judgements on moral issues by applying moral principles, insights and reasoning. The problem emerges when the question is raised about how moral judgement is to be taught.

The simple answer is that schools should teach what is 'right' and 'wrong'. On this view teaching consists in upholding certain core values, such as truth-telling, care for others and following socially prescribed rules. But moral education must be more than teaching these core values, no matter how commendable these values may be. Values taught didactically may not be internalized, may not become part of the beliefs and values of individual children. The point is that children need to learn that all moral acts have reasons, and they need the skills that will help them to deal with the moral conflicts that they will face in an uncertain world. As one eight-year-old put it: 'The trouble is people are telling you to do different things, and sometimes your mind tells you to do different things too!'

Children are characterized by conflicting natural tendencies – to be generous and to be selfish, to be competitive and to be co-operative, to love and hate and so on. In trying to teach our pupils to be thoughtful and reasonable persons, with the capacity for resolving conflicts in themselves and in society, we must see that the school environment, and classroom practice, is thoughtful and reasonable. Moral education, as opposed to moral indoctrination, cannot be conducted without treating children as rational beings capable of reasoning about conduct. One way to do this is to create a community of enquiry in the classroom that embodies the social forms of reasoning and of respect for others. Through participating in a community of enquiry children learn how to reason and can cultivate the social habits required for good moral conduct.

Philosophy undertaken in a community of enquiry can make a contribution to values education programmes as well as developing language and thinking skills. It can help children develop the skills and dispositions that will enable them to play their full part in a pluralistic society. It can boost their self-esteem and intellectual confidence. It does this by creating a caring classroom community where children learn to:

- explore issues of personal concern such as love, friendship, death, bullying and fairness, and more general philosophical issues such as personal identity, change, truth and time;
- develop their own views, explore and challenge the views of others;
- be clear in their thinking, making thoughtful judgements based on reasons;
- listen to and respect each other;
- experience quiet moments of thinking and reflection.

Philosophical enquiry initiates children into public discussion about meanings and values. It encourages them to think what it means to be reasonable and to make moral judgements. Such discussions are not just 'talking shops' but help to create a moral culture, a way of thinking and acting together that cultivates virtues of conduct such as respect for others, sincerity and open-mindedness. In a community of enquiry children are encouraged to find their own path to meaning via discussion with others.

As educators we cannot control what children will think or their response to the dangers and temptations they will face on the streets and in their private lives. We can, however, try to establish a safe place in which to share what they think, feel and experience, and in which their thoughts will be heard. A community of philosophical enquiry is a group willing to discuss matters of importance that relate to the concerns of children in their daily lives. It provides a safe space for thinking, and a creative context for ethical enquiry with children of all ages and abilities.

The concept of a community of enquiry is not new, nor is it unique to philosophy for children. Various forms of 'circle time' have been developed to create a supportive environment in which to explore feelings and build self-esteem. A community of enquiry offers a circle time approach aimed at improving the quality of thinking as well as the expression of feeling. But in what sense is it a 'community', and how does this community foster moral development?

What is a community?

The concept of 'community' has been the focus of lively political and philosophical debate in recent years. One strand of this is reflected in Hegel's notion that communities emerge out of conflict-filled situations, as a synthesis emerges out of opposing theses. In philosophical terms this reflects a difference of view about the role of argument in the formation of communities. Should a community (or a relationship) always seek to establish a shared viewpoint, or should it recognize and allow different viewpoints? Should the guiding principle of a community be to seek to resolve conflicts of argument through consensus and a synthesis of views, or should there be a recognition that differences of opinion and varied viewpoints are inevitable?

There has been much interest recently in the notions of 'community' and communitarian theory. These echo Hegel's ideas of the ideal community which is rationally organized and founded on individual freedom. For Hegel, critical thought and reflection is the key to developing freedom within an organic community. This concept of free enquiry as a constituent of community began with Socrates, as recorded in the Platonic dialogues. Typically Socrates would engage in dialogue with some worthy Athenian who thinks he knows what it is to be good and just. This 'knowledge' turns out to be merely the ability to echo some customary concept of morality. Socrates through questioning this view has no difficulty in showing that this received view cannot be the full story. For example, against the common idea that justice consists in giving to each what is owed to him, Socrates suggests the case of a friend who has lent you a weapon but has since become deranged. Should you return him the weapon? The questions raised by Socrates lead his audience to reflect on the conventional morality that they have uncritically accepted. This critical reflection pursued in a spirit of free enquiry makes reason, not social custom, the arbiter of right and wrong. The unconsidered acceptance of received wisdom cannot for Socrates be true wisdom.

This Socratic view that a community should be founded on principles of freedom of expression and recourse to reason has its problems. What happens, for example, when there is a conflict of interest between the needs of individuals and the democratically expressed interests of the community? Socrates was after all condemned to death by democratic Athens. One way of overcoming this problem of clash of interests is for the relationship between individuals and community to be organic and reciprocal. Hegel argued that communities must be organic in the sense of having their conventions open and adaptable to reason. Communities should develop through adapting to the individual needs of its members. Hegel believed that all communities are, and should be, in a state of evolution. In Hegelian terms what is constitutive of the moral order in a community, such as a classroom or a family, should always be open to review and reason. Liberal theory provides a means for ensuring this openness to change in response to the needs of individuals through the process of democracy, embodying the rights of all to a voice and a vote.

The elements of community identified so far are that it:

- embodies as a principle the freedom of expression of individuals;
- makes critical reasoning, not convention, the arbiter of moral judgement;

- is organic in the sense that its working procedures and values are open to adaptation;
- is democratic in ensuring that all its members have a right to a voice and a vote.

When two or more people come together, they not only respond to the institutional and social order they find themselves in, but are also in a sense co-constructors of that order. They are involved in the process of socialization into a specific way of life that constitutes the community. This process is made possible by the symbolic resources provided by language and the shared meanings provided by communication. We learn standards of normative behaviour, whether expressed in talk or action, by observing how others respond to us, anticipating responses and developing our own repertoire of responses. This process is not only crucial to the development of our ability to communicate in groups, but also to the development of self-esteem and socialization. Nor does it end once the child is socialized to the norms of a community. For the child as participant also becomes constitutive of the community, developing continuing awareness through interaction with others and influencing the response of others, and thereby the nature of the community, by their interactions.

Discussion plays a central role in the development of a community, because it requires symbolically the speaker to put oneself in another's place in order to know how to model one's information (syntactically, semantically and pragmatically) so as to be comprehensible to others. This ritualization of speaking through a shared discussion, involving practice in 'speaking for another to understand', can be seen as part of an interactive process that creates both a linguistic and moral relationship, and the blending in a sense of the self into the community.

What then is the difference between any community and a community of enquiry?

The 19th-century sociologist Ferdinand Tonnies made a useful and much-cited distinction between natural and artificial communities – *Gemeinschaft* and *Gesellschaft* . A natural community is one united by a common knowledge and shared experience, whereas an artificial community is an association created for a common goal such as a factory or school. A natural community has a voluntary nature, it is characterized by a self-discipline, by 'unwritten rules' and by purposes that are intrinsically meaningful. A family can be regarded as a natural community intermediary between the individual and the state. An artificial association is one that is bound by rules and by purposes that are extrinsic to its members. A community of enquiry aspires to the condition of a natural community, united by the following characteristics:

- shared experience;
- voluntary communication;
- a shared understanding of meanings.

What differentiates any learning community from a community of enquiry is the notion of shared enquiry. The 19th-century philosopher Peirce is generally credited with coining the phrase 'community of enquiry', which he used to characterize the ideal of scientific research. It was a community in the sense of having shared procedures and common interests. In this sense every subject area or discipline has the characteristics of shared enquiry. Dewey linked the notion of democracy to enquiry and applied it to educational theory. Classroom enquiry for Dewey should be related to real experience, and to authentic questions and problems. Matthew Lipman applied this Peirce/Dewey methodology to philosophical discussion in the classroom to create the Philosophy for Children programme in the United States (Lipman, 1991). This methodology is now in use in classrooms in more than 30 countries around the world, and a growing range of materials are being developed to facilitate philosophical discussion in schools. What unites this practice is a particular kind of moral order created in the classroom. So what is a community of enquiry, and how is it created in a classroom?

What is a community of enquiry in the classroom?

A community of enquiry can be said to have been achieved when any group of people act co-operatively in the search for understanding. Not only does each member benefit from the ideas and experience of everyone else, each person feels a valued part of the whole community. This structure shares characteristics of effective thinking groups, from political 'think tanks' to university research groups, from industrial research teams to school staffs, from families at home to classes in school. This sense of community has a dual aspect: a **rational structure** for effective thinking and shared ideas, and a **moral structure** of mutual respect and shared democratic values. A community of philosophical enquiry can become the context for a particular and powerful kind of moral conversation.

The philosopher Habermas argues that moral judgement is best developed through a kind of idealized conversation (Habermas, 1990). He claims that the distinctive idea of moral discourse is not to find universal laws but a general law that will be agreed to be a universal norm. In this way it is possible to escape from mindless acceptance of given rules and from mindless relativism which suggests there are no moral norms at all. 'The only norms that can claim to be valid,' says Habermas, 'are those that meet (or could meet) with the approval of all affected in their capacity as participants in a practical discourse' (Habermas, 1996, p 66).

Habermas is here referring to an idealized conversation through which moral agreement is reached. It is this idealized conversation through which a group discussing contestable and problematical matters of real concern comes to better judgements and (sometimes) a consensus which is the ultimate aim of a community of enquiry. There are problems with this Habermas/Lipman view of dialogical consensus. Some of the questions we need to consider include:

- Does consensus equate with moral goodness? What is the relationship between moral consensus and moral autonomy?
- What is moral development, and is there a link between this kind of moral discourse and moral development?
- How is moral discourse to be taught?
- Does moral judgement move to action? Can it help to build an ethical school, or an ethical community?

Habermas sees Kohlberg's stage theory of moral development as a possible means of assessment of the growing competence of students in moral discourse. What this competence in moral discourse entails for Habermas is the capacity to exercise reason in making moral judgements. Such moral reasoning must be undertaken in social contexts, through participative discourse and argument, since judgements will result in generalizable and interpersonal principles adopted by each 'for all and for all by each'. But why should such participative moral reasoning be better than the moral musings of a lone thinker?

One of the notions that underpins the idea of community of enquiry is that of distributed intelligence (Perkins, 1992). Schools have traditionally treated students as solo learners who do most of the intellectual work of learning inside their own heads.

Those that value the notion of distributed intelligence (Perkins, 1992) or the more modest notion of 'distributed cognition' argue that human cognition is at its richest when it occurs in ways that are socially, physically and symbolically distributed. People think and remember through interaction with other people, with all sorts of physical aids and socially shared symbolic systems. This is what Perkins (1992) calls a 'person-plus' concept of intelligence. Defenders of the classic notion of intelligence would complain that real intelligence is what is inside people's heads. Those who argue that we should educate for and through a 'person-plus' view of intelligence say that intelligence is accessed not only through introspection (knowledge in the head) but also knowledge represented and readily retrieved through social, physical and symbolic resources.

Three of the ways of distributing intelligence or cognition can be summarized as:

- *social distribution of intelligence* – co-operative group learning and collaboration, pair problem solving, Socratic teaching and Communities of Enquiry;
- *physical distribution of intelligence* – notes, journals, portfolios, computers, video, etc;
- *symbolic distribution of intelligence* – verbal and visual forms including talk, texts such as stories, lists, concept maps, charts, tables, taxonomies and diagrams, etc.

Children's thinking develops in co-operative situations through talk, and with the help of a range of artefacts from pencil and paper to computers. Co-operative learning is often used to achieve a variety of ends, including socialization, but if it is to achieve cognitive and curriculum objectives then it needs careful design. Research into group work shows that the teacher has a vital role to play in structuring the social and cognitive context of learning. Teachers have to exercise the executive control, or mediation of group learning experiences. Similarly, if students are to benefit from the social distribution of intelligence involved in a community of enquiry they need help in recognizing opportunities, in managing the cognitive burden and in maintaining motivation. They also need an experienced manager to mediate the process, so that eventually they can themselves take over the executive function and become autonomous in the social learning situation. So how is this achieved?

Children and their teacher sit in a circle and share some reading and listening. The children take some thinking time to devise their own questions and to discuss them. The group meets regularly. The questions get deeper and more thoughtful. The pupils' discussions get more disciplined and focused, and yet also more imaginative. The topics for discussion are chosen by the children themselves, and they cover a range of personal, social, moral and cultural concerns. The process by which this is achieved is called a community of enquiry. This chapter describes what a community of philosophical enquiry is, and how it can contribute to the moral and social development of children in primary and secondary schools.

The following summarizes the elements of the Philosophy for Children approach to developing a community of enquiry through whole class discussion in the classroom:

- *community setting*: sit so all can see and hear each other, teacher as part of the group;
- *agreed rules:* for example – 'Only one speaks at a time', 'Everyone listens to the speaker';
- *shared reading*: each has a turn to read, and the option not to read, a chosen text;
- *time to think*: time is given to think about what is read, what others say, and what I think;
- *time to question*: a forum is provided for raising questions, problems and ideas;
- *time to discuss*: each has a right and opportunity to express their own opinions and feelings;
- *listening to others*: each must listen to others, and consider different views and ideas;
- *communicating*: developing skills of self-expression through talking, listening, reading or writing;
- *extending thinking*: through activities and exercises that apply and extend leading ideas.

A community of enquiry has both a cognitive and a moral dimension. Learning to listen to and respect the opinions of others is part of the caring for others that is central to the values of many schools. But how is caring achieved, and is it a sufficient basis for moral education?

Moral education – is morality taught or caught?

> For our discussion is no trifling matter but on the right way to conduct our lives.
>
> (Plato, *Republic*, V111 352d)

There is a Russian proverb: 'It takes a whole village to educate a child.' Much of moral education is indirect and depends on the influence of external models in the culture or community, and on what has been internalized as the norms of ethical behaviour. There is widespread agreement that young people must first be taught appropriate behaviour by conforming to rules and conventions – and that the reasons for abiding by certain rules should be clearly articulated. But if morality is essentially the product of a way of life, is it possible to teach moral autonomy?

Aristotle thought that moral philosophy was not for the young, for two key reasons – their inexperience and their lack of rational principles. Piaget and Kohlberg argue that it is the egocentricity of young children that prevents moral development before seven or eight years. But although young children have little reflective understanding of moral knowledge there is a growing body of evidence that even young children of four and five years can answer questions about moral rules and can consider the consequences for others. Young children have a keen sense of fairness and this can be developed through discussion stories and real-life situations. Even young children, within the limitations of their experience and of their powers of reasoning, can become engaged in imaginative and provocative moral thought. Gareth Matthews gives an example of this – Ian, aged six, one of three children, when his parents' friends monopolized the choice of television programme, asked in frustration: 'Why is it better for three people to be selfish than one?' (Matthews, 1980). Young children face many dilemmas in their lives, and these can often provide the yeast for moral discussion, as illustrated in the following example:

Should animals be killed?[1]

Extract from a discussion with six-year-olds:

Child: I don't think animals should be killed.
RF: Why not?
Child: Animals haven't done anything to us, why should we kill them?
RF: Sometimes animals are killed because people want to eat them, like cows or rabbits.
Child: We shouldn't kill cows… they give us milk and that's good for you.
Child: If we kill animals we shouldn't eat them. You wouldn't want to be eaten would you?
Child: It's not fair to kill animals to eat them. There are plenty of other things to eat.
RF: Some animals are killed and eaten because they taste nice.
Child: That's not fair.
Child: Sometimes you have to kill animals when they are very ill.
Child: Or if it's hurt, in an accident or something.
Teacher: Some wild animals kill people, should animals be killed if they are dangerous?
Child: Like tigers – they can kill people.
Child: I think we should only kill animals when they have killed six people or more.
Teacher: Should an animal be killed if it has only killed one person?
Child: No, because it doesn't know what it is doing.

The argument for moral education through philosophical enquiry can be summarized as follows:

1. Democratic ideals require educational practices that avoid indoctrination and promote the ability of people to judge for themselves.
2. Therefore in moral education we should avoid moral instruction and concentrate on developing children's reflective moral judgement.
3. Developing children's reflective moral judgement requires a programme of moral education through which children come to think critically and responsibly about moral issues.
4. Philosophy through a community of enquiry is the best discipline for promoting thinking in education.
5. Therefore moral education should include a form of classroom community of philosophical enquiry.

Democracy involves the belief that mutual understanding among diverse interests can only be achieved through genuine dialogue and discussion. Since the time of Aristotle, ethics has been seen as a public concern, a kind of practical knowledge fostered through critical discourse in a self-governing community. But what form should this self-governing community take?

Philosophy with children involves an imaginative reasoning out of problems together. Whatever the topic, children can learn to build a community of enquiry whereby all participants are encouraged to use each other's ideas as building blocks to increase understanding. Philosophy is ideal for children's personal and social education as through it they can learn to discuss logically and creatively such fundamental moral issues as freedom, fairness and friendship, and social issues like law and order and the nature of government.

What is government for?

The philosopher David Hume was asked: 'What do you consider the object of government?'

Unhesitatingly he said: 'The greatest good for the greatest number.'

'And what is the greatest number?'

'Number one.'

The following is part of a discussion on the same question with nine-year-olds:

> Child: Governments exist to provide things like roads and schools.
> Teacher: What happens if governments don't provide them?
> Child: If they don't provide them you choose a new government.
> Child: Governments are there to do things you couldn't do by yourself, like defend yourself against enemies and crooks. That's what the police are for.
> Child: Yes but the police aren't the government. That's parliament. Parliament controls the police… I think.
> Teacher: OK. So, what's the most important job that a government has got?
> Child: To protect people. From burglars and suchlike…
> Child: They're there to look after you…
> Child: …when you can't look after yourself.

Teachers of philosophy in the classroom might differ in their answers to moral or political questions but agree that discussion in a community of enquiry can encourage and support children in the search for values by which to live, and can promote both the search for individual identity and a sense of community. One of the keys to understanding is good communication. Common to the theory and practice of philosophy in the classroom is the aim to develop the skills of speaking and listening. But also it is a means of promoting the curiosity, the inclination to question and the exercise of imagination which are vital for the motivation to learn. There is a close connection between the nourishment of the moral dimension and the development of reason. For children, and for us all, it is not just the question of knowing what is good that is important, but the ability to answer the question 'Why should I be, or do what is, good?' Any moral renaissance will be best served by the cultivation of careful thinking in communities of enquiry, and by careful evaluation of the moral culture that is being developed.

Evaluating moral development

There are problems in trying to evaluate the development of any moral culture. Certain indicators such as levels of bullying, disruption or theft might be available. Other observable features would include the evidence of reciprocity in the behaviour of individuals and groups. Reciprocity is shown in the 'give-and-take' of discussion, in the co-operative nature of a community of enquiry. These reciprocal relations link our self-directed thoughts, feelings and actions with the thoughts, feelings and actions of others. Moral development means enabling children to develop a set of values that are both personal, relating to self-interest, and public, relating to the interests of others.

Self

One of the key elements of ethical living is autonomy. Autonomy is the capacity for self-government. It is indicated by evidence of children thinking for themselves, for example in taking a minority viewpoint, or in challenging the viewpoint of others. It shows itself in a developing sense of self-esteem, and in the willingness of children to take responsibility for how their lives should be lived. Autonomy can be exemplified in questions such as:

- What do I really think?
- What do I feel about myself (or about the situation)?
- What sort of life do I want to lead?
- What sort of person do I want to be?
- What are my values and my priorities?
- Comments from teachers that indicate a growing sense of autonomy in children include:

  'That is the first time I have heard Jasbir volunteer her own opinion.'
  'Kirsty showed she was able to self-correct when she changed her mind and corrected her earlier opinion about what it means to be a friend.'
  'Paul really showed confidence when he stuck out for his opinion against the others.'

Others

Another sign of reciprocity is empathy, that is the state of being emotionally and cognitively 'in tune' with another person, in particular understanding what their situation is like for them. We show who we are through our sense of self (autonomy) and through our relationships with others (connectedness). The paradox of human life is that we are both separate as individuals yet connected as part of a culture. Individuals find fulfilment in living relations. Who we are is partly made up of the context that we are in and the relationships we have formed. This dichotomy between self and others is reflected in two views of democracy, one identifying democracy with the freedom of the individual to pursue self-interest, the other seeing individuals essentially as creators of communities. In any community there is a tension between the right to freedom and the responsibility towards others. In a community of enquiry the right to freedom is shown in two ways: one is freedom of expression (even when you are wrong); the other is the right to silence, to pass, to listen and not to comment. Responsibility to others is shown through caring behaviour.

Caring or empathy requires the exercise of moral imagination, that is the ability to create and rehearse possible situations, to make 'thought experiments' such as putting oneself in the place of another. This sense of interconnectedness, in which children realize they are one among many with interests and desires like others, is a necessary foil to prejudice and to thinking of people as stereotypes. The kinds of questions that exemplify empathy include:

- How would you (or that other person) feel?
- How would I feel if it happened to me (or to you)?
- What would it be like (or would you think) if you were the other person?
- Have I ensured (are we ensuring) equal opportunities for all?
- How do I show others I respect and value them?
- Examples of teachers noting evidence of caring behaviour in discussion include:
  'Saeed did well to insist that everyone should have a turn to speak.'
  'An example of the way Karen shows empathy was when she said, "Imagine what it would be like to be that person...".'
  'What was significant was the way everyone listened attentively to what others had to say.'

Society and beyond

A third related element is the ability to 'decentre' from the self, to look at a situation as it were from above, what Mead calls 'the generalized other', what Singer calls 'the point of view of the universe' or what might be called 'transcendence' (Fisher, 1998: 18). This refers to the ability to transcend individual or group interest to think what would be right for anyone in a given situation. Transcendence relates to the awareness of the concept of justice and to principles of fairness. For some moral theorists, such as Kant and Kohlberg, the highest form of moral reasoning lies in the formulation of universal principles or duties. For others transcendence lies in seeking what is good, right or fair for people in a particular situation.

Transcendence points to an awareness of rights and values that transcend individual interests and desires. Transcendence looks beyond the self-interest of individuals or groups such as friends and family, to include the wider society and ultimately a world-view. It is to be conscious of the relationship of human beings not only to each other but to nature, and to understand our duties to other species. The kinds of questions that exemplify a set of transcending values include:

- What would be the consequences of acting this way?
- What are the implications of behaving (or believing) that way?
- What is the right thing to do?
- Would it be right in every circumstance?
- What principle, value or moral is involved?
- Examples of evidence of awareness of universal moral values include:
  'Anne referring to the principle of doing to others as you would have them do to you.'
  'I liked the way Kerry said if the rule was right for you it was right for everyone.'
  'Paul did not just say it was not fair, he gave a reason why it was a fair rule and in what circumstances it should apply.'

The elements of ethical living can be summarized as follows:

Qualities of a moral person	Principles of moral education	Key question
Autonomy	Thinking for oneself	What is right for me?
Empathy	Showing care for others	What is right for others?
Transcendence	Upholding principles of justice	What is right for all?

The link between creative thinking and moral thinking is summed up in the need to encourage imaginative reasoning. As one child said during a discussion: 'Without an imagination you can't draw, you can't read... without imagination you can't do anything.' The use of imaginative reasoning is necessary if children are to come to see themselves not only in relation to others in the present world, but also in the world that could be. With the help of others a community of enquiry can help children to transcend the present, to construct an understanding not only of what is but what could be. Participation in a community of enquiry aims to give children the tools they need to question their situation and to begin the search for constructive ways to change or transform it. As one child put it: 'We can make a better world... the question is "Where do we begin?"'

A community of philosophical enquiry is a group willing to discuss matters of importance, matters that relate to how they live and learn in their daily lives. During the process, signs of change occur. Children learn how to object to unsupported claims and weak reasoning, they learn how to build on and develop the ideas of others, and they learn how to generate alternative world-views that challenge and extend their thinking. Because it is a philosophical enquiry there is a focus on the underlying concepts of daily experience such as time, space, truth and beauty. As children probe these concepts they learn how to ask relevant questions, detect assumptions, recognize faulty reasoning and gain a sense of competency in their ability to make sense of the world.

As children begin to internalize the procedures of enquiry with the help of a good model they begin to take over responsibility for running and evaluating the sessions. The teacher's role becomes that of coach and participant rather than leader. In evaluating their own sessions, in developing rules for running the session and criteria for judging the session, children develop the capacity for self-correction and self-management. A community of enquiry thus provides a living model of a moral community in action (Fisher, 1990, 1996, 1998).

Evaluating progress in a community of philosophical enquiry

A teacher evaluates the progress of her philosophy class of six- and seven-year-olds:

Although it is impossible to separate the growth and maturation that has taken place in response to their work in other lessons I feel the children have responded positively to these sessions in a number of ways:

- Their general behaviour in the sessions improved.
- Their readiness to listen to and engage with other children's thoughts increased.
- They seem more willing to take risks with their thinking, and to share their thoughts.
- They have more sophisticated opinions which they express more clearly.
- Several quiet or shy children have offered valuable contributions.
- An increasing number of original thoughts were expressed in sessions.
- The children seemed to become more in tune with each other as persons.

Over the year I have become more and more convinced that philosophy for children would make a truly great impact if it were adopted as a whole school approach. In this way all the advantages I saw emerging in Green Class could be extended and multiplied.

Genuine values, like all moral points of view, are best created and tested through reflection and sustained enquiry. The community of enquiry provides a model of values in action as well as an opportunity to subject values to critical enquiry. It becomes a powerful means of moral education because values are embedded in the very procedures and moral routines of the enquiry. These are the rational passions or dispositions of critical thinking without which a community of enquiry cannot successfully function. Children in a community of enquiry learn as much through the act of participation as they do from what they say. As one child remembering his participation in enquiry the previous year put it: 'I remember how we talked and asked questions, and had to give everybody a turn and think about what people had to say in the philosophy class, but I can't remember now what was said.'

Note

1. The quotations from teachers and children in this chapter are taken from the Philosophy in Primary Schools Project undertaken by the author in London schools 1993–96. For more information on the use of philosophical enquiry in the classroom see Fisher, R (1998) *Teaching Thinking: Philosophical enquiry in the classroom*, Cassell, London.

References

Fisher, R (1990) *Teaching Children to Think*, Blackwell, Oxford
Fisher, R (1996) *Stories for Thinking*, Nash Pollock, Oxford
Fisher, R (1998) *Teaching Thinking: Philosophical enquiry in the classroom*, Cassell, London
Habermas, J (1990) *Moral Consciousness and Communicative Action*, MIT Press, Cambridge, MA
Habermas, J (1996) *On the Cognitive Content of Morality*, Meeting of the Aristotelian Society, London, June
Lipman, M (1991) *Thinking in Education*, Cambridge University Press, Cambridge
MacIntyre, A (1984) *After Virtue*, Duckworth, London
Matthews, G (1980) *Philosophy and the Young Child*, Harvard University Press, Cambridge, MA
Perkins, D N (1992) *Smart Schools: From training memories to educating minds*, Macmillan, New York
School Curriculum and Assessment Authority (SCAA) (1995) *Spiritual and Moral Development*, SCAA, London
School Curriculum and Assessment Authority (SCAA) (1996) *Education for Adult Life: The spiritual and moral development of young people*, SCAA, London
School Curriculum and Assessment Authority (SCAA) (1997) *National Forum for Values in Education and the Community: The values*, SCAA, London

Chapter 5

Sharing Values with a Selfish Gene

Philip Goggin

Introduction

The suggestion of this chapter is that the logic and power of self-interest should be harnessed to achieve a consensus among young people about a broad set of principles and values. Such a set of values may be thoroughly secular in derivation, but in no way excludes an ethic of duty or religious obligation. Further, even a morality based on self-interest quickly moves to other regarding principles, as will be shown. Thus, self-interest is far from being an enemy of a more conventional way of thinking morally.

An obvious feature of our own times is the instrumental view of market transactions. Egocentricism – some might bluntly speak of selfishness – is seemingly evident at all levels of public and private life, ranging from 'lottery fever' to the lapses of politicians.

It is not necessary to argue that egocentricism is more prevalent than, say, 50 years ago, in order to show that it is an important aspect of the human psyche. Self-interest has always had a strong appeal.

The argument that follows is that we should be more explicit about personal advantage. There *is* a convincing story to be told about the personal advantages of many shared consensus values, and how personal advantage can nudge an individual towards a wider set of considerations.

Schools have, in many cases, switched the emphasis from sanctions to rewards and have developed a system of social and material prizes for appropriate behaviour. But these rewards may only operate successfully in a contrived environment. Once outside that environment the rewards may appear to melt away. Young people may find themselves in situations where they are thrown back on a code that seems to offer little more than a series of old-fashioned oughts with talk of unselfishness or even self-sacrifice. It is all too easily dismissed, without reflection, as irrelevant or childish or impossibly idealistic or simply barmy. In contrast, the language of prudential considerations and rewards may have more impact and be used to encourage a range of behaviour well beyond the school's direct control.

Moralists may despairingly wring their hands at the apparent prospect of the collapse of the duty ethic. But what right have they to assume that duty is the only starting point for morality? What of our knowledge of how children's thinking about morality develops, moving through prudential considerations to recognizably moral aspects?

Values which can be derived from self-interest

While we may be interested in finding prudential justification for morality, we are haunted by the difficulty of demonstrating that it is always in a person's interest to act justly, and outraged by the spectre of a just man or woman acting purely out of self-interest. But are these objections fatal?

The argument can start by pointing to the likely link between honesty, justice, compassion, etc and human well-being *generally*. Indeed, what would be the point of morality if it did not connect at some point with human interests? But what of the individual who sees no reason why he or she should not cheat on the system to gain personal advantage?

Plato tried to show that justice was equated with what we would now call psychic health. It may not always be possible to demonstrate that behaving justly is always going to bring about a result which is in the agent's interest, but perhaps it can be shown that a just person is happier in the long run given what we know of human nature. We might speak of such a person as having an integrated personality, perhaps. Where greed or passion upset the natural balance in public (and so inevitably in private) life, Plato would argue justice is destroyed and with it human happiness.

Aristotle extended these arguments with the Doctrine of the Mean: crudely, the view that our emotional life should have a logic and proportionality to circumstance.

Now, of course, this talk about what constitutes human nature is notoriously open to special pleading or cultural distortion. But it does resonate with some of the things we know about the human condition: the need for security, a sense of belonging, self-esteem, for example. It also points to a wider notion of self-interest than mere self-preservation. It suggests the desirability of a range of qualities and aspirations which individuals may associate with their own well-being. At the very least it suggests a model against which an individual might compare him or herself. The individual can ask: what sort of person do I wish to be, how do I wish to solve problems and overcome obstacles, how do I wish others to think of me, what sort of friends do I wish to attract, etc? Answers to such questions may flesh out particular requirements – but are unlikely to call into question fundamental psycho-social insights. From these individual decisions about lifestyle, chosen against a model of human well-being, it is likely that a range of principles such as fairness, consideration for others, thoughtfulness towards the environment would emerge. Of course, someone could choose principles like cruelty, or callousness, though it would be difficult to show how such principles sustained well-being – even as defined by the subject.

A similar conclusion emerges when we consider what it is to be a person. However much Western culture might emphasize individualism, we are inevitably social creatures caught up in a web of interactive entanglements. Psychologists have seriously challenged the 'nativist' view of development, which pictured the emergence of the person as an unfolding of an innate potential, comparable to the seed growing into a flower. Once, then, we recognize our interdependence as individuals the distinction between individual interests and collective interests becomes ever harder to draw.

It is true, of course, that the boundaries of our interest group may be quite tightly drawn. Pre-adolescent children, for example, commonly seem to go through a stage of gang loyalty where the interests of a small number of peers override the interests of others. But the logic impels towards an ever-widening reference group, and one necessarily learns first about those closest to one before relating to others.

So, again, an individual must consider the principles that sustain the social group if he or she is to address individual interests.

How does an individual maintain the ability to make choices in life, assuming most people wish to make their own choices rather than have them made by others? The last thing anyone would want is to be trapped in a predetermined set of values. Arguably, on purely prudential/egotistical grounds it is worth cultivating dispositions (with associated values) not unlike those identified by Aristotle – courage, sympathy, magnanimity – since they serve to keep one open to new possibilities and change.

Thus, we can go a lot further than Plato or Aristotle, who saw a just society as a prerequisite for those whose reasoning was weak. Following Mackie (1977) and Poole (1991) we can argue that a social system based on respect for persons is an intrinsic element of personal well-being.

Here we begin to see how self-interest opens into a much less instrumental view of human affairs, and arguably moves the subject to reason more 'morally' as conventionally understood.

I only come to an awareness of myself as a centre of consciousness as I recognize others as centres of consciousness. As a social being I recognize that my own desires are intersubjective in that I must interact with others who are free to choose to interact. This recognition cannot be purely instrumental as to view others in this way would be to destroy the very substance of my concept of myself as an independent person. I would undermine my own personhood.

We can make the argument more immediate. If we regard our friends as instruments to our own purposes, we destroy friendship itself. We can, of course, act in friendly ways in order to complete business or professional transactions and we may indeed make real friends in the process. But this only serves to underline the point: true friendship goes beyond purely instrumental purposes; and while arguably we all need friendship for our well-being we cannot force others to be our friends or buy their friendship (though it is possible that money may be a catalyst in establishing a friendship).

A similar pattern emerges with a self-interested virtue like 'stickability', for example. Persistence is a feature of a person's life, not something which can be turned on and off to suit the occasion. As such it is always likely to pull within its orbit an ever-widening set of circumstances and interests. Thus, if I am to be reliable as a supporter of a particular institution I am likely to be drawn into a range of person-centred issues to do with the welfare of the members of that institution. I cannot simply switch off my support for the institution at the point at which I start getting involved in others' interests.

Following Wilson (1990) we might suggest to a child that if he or she wants something, that something is wanted *for a reason*. These reasons might be soundly or unsoundly based. Part of what would contribute a sound reason is that the good in question is *justified*, as distinct from something that an animal-like creature may be instinctively drawn towards.

The egoist is thus drawn into a public mode of justification. Even to claim that it is a sufficient reason for having something if I happen to want it would make no sense unless I could 'represent myself as one case of a general principle' (Wilson, 1990: 99).

Prudential consideration can lead to wider considerations in another way. Following Baier (1958) we might show that if two egoists had a conflict of interest over a limited good (such as the custody of a child, or a particular house) there would be no way of resolving the issue, nor even limiting the methods which might be used by either party to attain their goal. Thus, self-interest narrowly defined is bankrupt as a social system.

Of course, the egoist may still be unmoved by these considerations or perhaps he or she may use the form of the argument in a devious way to serve further egotistic goals. The key point, however, is that the egoism cannot rest easy. It is a philosophy that points beyond itself. In the hands of a skilled teacher, these pointers can be exploited.

Even if it were argued that that immediate prudential advantage will nearly always seem more attractive to most young people than any more general social advantage, there is a case for taking seriously these starting points.

Thus, it can be suggested that what has been called 'variable rationality' (Griffiths, 1984: 226) should be taken seriously as part of the process of generally developing rationality. This variable rationality will vary depending on emotion and feeling, but will have rational features within those limits. Starting where children are – a major plank of constructivist learning theory – is likely to be more fruitful than imposing a strange conceptual system. Moreover, whether as children or adults, we need to learn to reason on moral questions in ways which take account of our feelings. As Smith (1985) argues:

> morally we learn in part by truly experiencing our feelings, by attending to them and reflecting on them, on their conflicts and ambivalences, and by living among others who do the same. (p 58)

White (1984) wrote of 'the practical wisdom which learns to manage, control and direct the emotion in an intelligent way as part of the larger project of promoting one's own and other's well-being' (p 236).

Our knowledge of child development suggests stages of moral reasoning in which prudential consideration play a significant part. Piaget's seminal work of 1932 suggests a clear developmental progression in which later stages are dependent upon the successful completion of earlier stages. Thus, the child at the Reciprocal Stage (which develops out of an Authoritarian Stage where rules were unquestioned) sees rules as worthy of respect because all in a given society/community will benefit from this implementation. A potent question to a child at this stage would be: how would you feel if you suffered because someone had broken a particular rule? Experience of working through this social reciprocity leads on to the Equity Stage where altruism becomes the guiding principle in the way rules are devised and applied.

The important point to note for our purposes is that without the experience of working through rules at the Reciprocal Stage, altruism would never gain a purchase on the rules. Further, it is worth recording that reciprocity continues to be a factor in moral reasoning. In other words, prudential considerations operate alongside altruistic ones. (Other commentators have also noted the way altruism is reinforced by personal satisfaction. Peck and Havinghurst (1960) noted that pleasure in observing the happiness of others as a result of an altruistic action motivates and sustains the altruistic conduct.)

Moral reasoning must mesh with how people decide to act. Thus Straughan (1989) in comparing *justificatory* reasons with *motivational* reasons for acting in certain ways is prepared to recognize motivational reasons as (in part) constituting the justificatory reasons.

To fail to trace the implications of considering actual motivational factors could be disastrous. Carr (1991) has argued that if we base our morality on an ethic of obligation:

> morality is to be regarded as no more than a disagreeable constraint, and personal fulfilment is to be sought elsewhere than in a life of aspiration towards the moral virtues. It is to a life of indolence, self-indulgence, vanity, acquisitiveness and cynical exploitation that they turn (and claim as their right) and the moral conceptual currency of the modern world has no power to persuade them that they are not living as they should or becoming all that they might be. (p 230)

However, if young people are encouraged to develop certain virtues or general dispositions, such as honesty, fairness or compassion, on the grounds of self-interest, are we in danger of a subtle form of indoctrination or manipulation? Are we perhaps smuggling in some contentious principles as though they were indisputable? The answer, surely, lies in the open kind of justification which is offered for the place of these virtues in human well-being, and the invitation to each subject to determine the relevance to his or her own circumstances.

The possession of certain dispositions still leaves open a huge area of personal moral decision making in particular contexts and with particular personal priorities.

Self-interest and the 'Consultation Values'

We now proceed to examine the relationship between the egotistical values we have outlined and the Consultation Values in Education and the Community (SCAA, 1996).

The value we attach to 'truth, human rights, the law, justice and collective endeavour' is not merely justified in terms of what we might stand to gain through social cohesion, but also by reference to *how we might think about ourselves*, since we risk destroying our own sense of identity if we don't respect the values which identify us as independent, yet social, creatures. Further, in that 'we value others for themselves, not for what they have or what they can do for us, and value these relationships as fundamental to our development' we take cognizance of the significant paradox that we can only serve our own ends by taking seriously others as ends in themselves. Some of the Consultation Values are more obviously self-regarding. If 'we value each person as a unique being' and as individuals 'try to understand our own character, strengths and weaknesses, develop a sense of self-worth, strive for knowledge and wisdom throughout life, etc' then we are quite unambiguously serving our own interests. However, we are also looking to others' interests, since self-worth, for example, generally involves us in earning the respect of others through doing things which they regard as in *their* interests.

So the Consultation Values do not occupy the high moral ground from which those lacking a sense of moral duty or a religious faith are necessarily excluded. They can be seen to appeal to any self-interested person who is prepared to think through the personal consequences of various attitudes, dispositions and types of behaviour.

A key concept would be *enlightened* self-interest, ie taking the longer- rather than shorter-term view. From an educational point of view schools might be expected to do a large part of the enlightening, both through straight subject teaching (particularly in the Humanities and Social Science subjects) and through aspects of the informal curriculum, school ethos, etc. Significantly, moralizing in the sense of ethically persuading would have little, if any, place in such an enlightening process.

Bullying from the point of view of self-interest

We will focus on the phenomenon of bullying because it can be dealt with quite well as a matter of self-interest, and because it is a widespread feature of dysfunctional relationships in all walks of life and amongst all age groups. It is thus a good concrete example of how the self-interest argument might work.

Bullying is a form of aggression where a person or group uses power to gain a favour that would otherwise be denied them and to which they are not entitled. Sometimes bullying takes place for no other reason than for the sadistic pleasure it brings to the perpetrator. In short, it is an aggressive abuse of power.

Bullying tends also to be self-perpetuating. The more bullying a child indulges in, the more likely he or she is to continue (Randall, 1996: 37). Childhood aggression, if unchecked, develops into poorly controlled aggressive behaviour in later life.

So, would bullying be desirable for the perpetuator? Perhaps, but you need a bizarre view of human life if you are to convince yourself. You need to like the idea that you will have poor peer relationships, that you are likely to respond less favourably to training or unemployment, that marital/partner relationships are likely to be less successful, that your own children are likely to model your own aggressive behaviour – to mention a few of the research findings on outcomes for bullies recounted by Randall (1996: 40–41). What is your view of your own selfhood if you effectively distort the selfhood of others? What freedom do you have where anyone's freedom can be destroyed at whim? You need to be satisfied with 'friends' who attach themselves to you because of the spectacle of power you provide, or because of fear that you might turn on them next, but hardly because you are a likeable person. And you need to settle for the realization that bullying is self-perpetuating and that the longer you persist in it the more you restrict your scope for future choices.

Now all this can be resisted by the determined bully. Idi Amin, after all, led a charmed life for a few years in Uganda in the early 1970s. But, as in Amin's case, resistance is easier if you don't understand much about consequences, and who knowingly chooses to acquire the reputation of a dummy?

Conclusion: self-interest and the ethic of duty

Self-interest is far from precluding an ethic of duty, as we have seen.

I have argued the case against bullying in terms of what the would-be bully might *like*, or *not like*, to be or to become, premised on some provisional notion of human well-being. We have also shown how self-interest, as for example in seeking friendship or offering reasons for choices, opens the individual to a wider set of concerns. The choices a bully makes will reflect to an extent the moral values he or she might hold. Thus, a bully might choose to restrain his or her own aggression in order to safeguard his or her marital/partner relationship because he or she believes it is *right* to maintain long-term relationships. Thus, the way in to such traditionally ethical questions may well come through a consideration of what one *wants*.

Further, if Aristotle was right in supposing that men (sic) become just by acting justly, who can say that self-interest would not develop into something more like genuine altruism? In this we might see some parallels with stage-structural theories of moral development, as previously noted. Moreover, unless one fulfils one's duty to oneself one cannot fulfil one's duty to others. We all need a secure base from which to launch ourselves. Self-regarding behaviour thus blurs the distinction between duty and prudence. (SCAA's 'Consultation Values' speak explicitly of 'The Self' as one of four key values, as noted previously.)

So moralists who fear the collapse of the duty ethic may take comfort after all. But their comfort can only be bought at the price of their recognizing that they don't hold a monopoly on moral reasoning, still less on how it develops, and that a liberal education invites informed choice from a range of perspectives and traditions.

The position outlined above helps to reconcile two dichotomous approaches to moral philosophy and moral education represented by the question:

Do we want the individual to attach himself to other people, to care for them, love them as far as he can… or to attach himself to some impersonal ideal, represented by 'duty' or 'justice' or 'being reasonable'? (Wilson, 1990: 111)

Common sense, not to speak of philosophical logic, points to the falsity of that dichotomy.

References

Baier, K (1958) *The Moral Point of View*, Cornell University Press, Ithaca
Carr, D (1991) *Educating the Virtues*, Routledge, London
Griffiths, M (1984) Emotions and education, *Journal of Philosophies of Education*, **18** (2)
Mackie, J L (1977) *Ethics: Inventing right and wrong*, Pelican, Harmondsworth
Peck, R F and Havinghurst, R J (1960) *The Psychology of Character Development*, John Wiley, New York
Piaget, J (1932) *The Moral Judgement of the Child*, Routledge, London
Poole, R (1991) *Morality and Modernity*, Routledge, London
Randall, P (1996) *A Community Approach to Bullying*, Trentham, Stoke-on-Trent
SCAA (1996) *Consultation on Values in Education and the Community*, SCAA, London
Smith, R (1985) *Freedom and Discipline*, Allen and Unwin, London
Straughan, R (1989) *Beliefs, Behaviour & Education*, Cassell, London
White, J P (1984) The education of the emotions, *Journal of Philosophy of Education*, **18** (2)
White, J P (1990) *Education & the Good Life*, Kogan Page, London
Wilson, J (1990) *A New Introduction to Moral Education*, Cassell, London

PART TWO

ISSUES IN EDUCATION IN VALUES

Chapter 6

Legitimating the Moral Curriculum

Paul Yates

Introduction

This chapter attempts an anthropological commentary on the currency of a moral curriculum. What seems to be proposed is a new bolt-on element to the National Curriculum as a response to a perceived moral crisis (SCAA, 1996a, b). Much of the discussion pays scant attention to the fact that schools inevitably are moral agents of the state and that pupils are themselves moral beings. Any changes that may be proposed will not fill a moral vacuum but will have to fight for space in a fully formed existing social world.

I shall argue that a prior issue to that of curriculum content is an understanding of the bases of the legitimacy of schooling. That is to say those ideas, sentiments and actions through which school is regarded as a legitimate institution in our society. This is particularly critical to teachers and pupils who embody the institution. Morality is the systematic organization of social precepts that guide action. It has only phenomenological existence. The point of the book of Leviticus or the Haditha is that they provide a map of possibilities within which individuals locate themselves, and inevitably as is palpably clear in the Psalms, some will locate themselves off the map. Durkheim's (1973) writing on moral education at the beginning of the 20th century tied the morality of education closely to the expressed needs of the state, the creation of a viable French culture. This was not achieved through laboured prescription but via the spirit of discipline. By this, Durkheim meant the capacity to act autonomously and to act as an individual for the social good. Education should be a liberation where freedom was the perfect coincidence between the desire of the individual and the needs of the social.

The most pressing need of the state at the end of the 20th century is not cultural conformity because the shifts have been both towards a globalizing of economic activity and a new emphasis on more local, regional and ethnic sources of individual and political identity. The current priority is to link school to the preparation of children to act in a way that will maximize the state's ability to sustain itself through successful economic competition. I shall argue that the recent reform of schooling, especially the imposition of bureaucratic organization, is not a plausible response to the need to prepare pupils to think and act in terms of the existent and developing global economy.

School is preparatory; it is not an end in itself. The equation of good schooling with measurable cognitive output hermetically seals the system and renders it socially useless. Current notions of success have returned to the human capital model of education, which assumed an automatic link between educational output and economic activity. We have known for some time that this oversimplifies the dynamics of production (Dore, 1976). My argument is that school needs to reflect codes of morality that stress our social nature, an idea that is fundamental to all the Abrahamic religions, and one that is clearly required for our economic and social survival.

The formulation of my analysis as an investigation of moral legitimacy refers to Berger and Luckman's (1967) use of the term. For Berger and Luckman institutions are linguistic constructions that live through the creation and iteration of social knowledge. This knowledge is not primarily theoretical but refers to everyday understanding, 'it is the sum total of "what everybody knows" about a social world' (Berger and Luckman, 1967: 83). It is simply through participation in the life of an institution that it acquires solidity and legitimacy in our eyes as we are incorporated in it and live a part of our social lives through it. The 'knowledge' of an institution can have a wide range of referents but 'On the pre-theoretical level, however, every institution has a body of transmitted recipe knowledge, that is, knowledge that supplies the institutionally appropriate rules of conduct' (Berger and Luckman, 1967: 83).

Giddens (1985) in his theory of structuration suggests that social institutions are recursively structured. Applied to school, that would suggest that school is a dynamic place where members draw on their own practical knowledge and knowledge of the institution and by acting within this framework both sustain and change the institution and themselves.

While institutions strive to sustain themselves they are nonetheless fragile. The breakdown of a moral consensus can render an institution ineffective. What is now referred to (interestingly in the present continuous tense) as a failing school is one where its public purposes are no longer seen as legitimate by its members.

In discussing the question of the legitimacy of schooling I shall examine several areas that contribute to the nature of schools' moral agency. First, I shall examine liberal education as a major legitimating mythology of schooling for both teachers and pupils. I then turn to the impact of the bureaucratization of school and then to the imposition of a quasi-market as fundamental alterations to the basic moral message of school. I shall focus on the curriculum as a moral arena, a set of activities that bear the moral codes of the state and through which moral statements are made and moral definitions sustained. Through the recent work of Pring (1995), I shall look at the place of vocationalism in school as symptomatic of the state's failure to recognize the preparatory nature of school for the whole community. I shall argue that this is compounded by seeing cognitive performance as the legitimate end of schooling. Finally I shall briefly examine the implications of my analysis.

Developments in the legitimating mythologies of schooling

The most powerful of the legitimating mythologies of mass schooling, instituted in response to Britain's relative economic decline against Germany in the middle of the 19th century, was that romantic representation of Plato and Aristotle by Arnold and others known as liberal education. This has underpinned the validity of the academic curriculum and the superior status of education aimed at producing a rational discursive morality, which has been opposed to training aimed at the inculcation of competence.

Hierarchy and unequal access were and continue to be strong features of the social organization of knowledge in school. While school has always been understood as a preparation for securing a living, liberal education and vocational preparation offer radically different alternatives, which Pring (1995) ably attempts to reconcile. This is not an easy task. It is not simply the case that liberal education has no training element in it, it is positively anti-training. Oakshott's (1972) widely quoted apologetic for liberal education sees training as anti-educational. The point of education is the cultivation of '*homo discens* a creature capable of learning to think to understand and to enact himself in a world of human enactments and thus to acquire a human character' (Oakshott, 1972: 22). Oakshott saw school as a place of education in serious decline being substituted by 'socialization', the production of 'fonctionnaires'. To have a broadly moral aim rather than a narrowly functional one is not confined to historical notions of education. The traditional aim of liberal education can also be understood as to produce what Bourdieu (1993: 86) refers to as a habitus, that is an acquisition, 'which has become durably incorporated... as a set of permanent dispositions... [it] is the principle of real autonomy.' The inculcation of a habitus around a broadly based discursive intelligence that emphasized the historical moment is a possibility.

The pure academic curriculum of which Oakshott so thoroughly approved has been at the heart of schooling until relatively recently with widespread cultural approval. However, this has not always been officially endorsed. The Spens report (1938) criticized the grammar school curriculum for being overly theoretical (Pring, 1995: 46). Nonetheless the Butler Act (1944) formalized the role of the grammar school as the benchmark of secondary schooling and it has subsequently been employed as a comparator against which all subsequent forms of secondary schooling have been measured. The then proposed tripartite system of grammar, technical and modern schools with parity of esteem was defeated on the ground by continued public attachment to liberal values in education. What was effectively a dual system came into being with a minority of more cognitively able pupils being competitively selected for a liberal education and the majority for a more elementary and, at least originally, uncertificated experience of a similar curriculum but with some emphasis on practical skills.

In the past 40 years the certification of school experience has expanded and changed dramatically and has been comprehensively extended to accredit vocationally oriented courses. The A level examination has remained in place throughout this post-war period as the apex of liberal achievement in school. It is popularly referred to as the gold standard: the gold being access to the increasingly common good of a university degree. The aim of liberal education is to enable a person to be capable of rational moral discourse. In itself it reflects and values the enlightenment project of the exercise of reason in the pursuit of moral perfection demonstrated through intellectual excellence, and while this is a long way from sitting an A level it is what underpins it as legitimate activity and lends social value to the outcome.

There is another aspect to liberal education as practised in England, and clearly articulated by Oakshott (1972). This is the tendency to devalue anything that is practical and economically relevant and to define it outside the legitimate practice of education. According to Pring (1995: 120), 'This disdain is rooted in our culture and reflected in our educational system at every level.' Pring (1995) quotes Finegold and Soskice (1988) on the consequences of this aristocratic version of liberal education, 'the education and training system has delivered badly educated and minimally trained 16-year-old school leavers to an economy which has been geared to operate with a relatively unskilled labour force'.

Prime Minister Callaghan's Ruskin speech of 1976 calling for schools to bend their energies to preparing pupils for a working life marked the beginning of the state's official disenchantment with the prevalent forms of liberal education in the maintained sector. However, the demands of the state are not necessarily congruent with the aspirations of all sections of the people and the socially regressive professional class continues to see the maintenance of liberal education as in its interests. The Conservative Government's Manpower Services Commission (MSC) began the process of wresting control of the school curriculum from liberally minded teachers and injecting some pre-vocational and training elements into the school curriculum. In the early 1980s the MSC launched the Technical and Vocational Education Initiative (TVEI), which was a fund of over a billion pounds (Pring, 1995: 62) aimed at encouraging schools to develop vocationally oriented courses. However, as Edwards and Whitty (1997: 36) argue, 'TVEI failed to establish a modern curriculum able to compete on equal terms with the attractions of the traditional academic mode.' Further, 'TVEI faced the traditionally low esteem accorded to vocational education' (Edwards and Whitty, 1997: p190). This points to the fact that the continued dominance of academic values in the school curriculum strongly militates against preparation for economic activity being a legitimate activity, except for those who fail to meet the requirements of the academic curriculum. Edwards and Whitty report that TVEI 'predictably failed to attract a due share of the ablest pupils'.

From college to company

The centralization of education through control of the curriculum and of teacher education and, at the institutional level, the Local Management of Schools (LMS) were reforms that brought with them the change in the nature of school as an organization away from the model of the college, characterized by co-operation with a head teacher, notionally *primus inter pares*, towards the current model of school as a commercial bureaucracy with a vertical hierarchy, a line management structure and with powers attached to impersonal roles. This shift in the affective bases of schooling changes its nature as a moral agency and with it the knowledge base from which the dimensions of pupil identity can be drawn. In particular, if pupils understand their relationship to school as contractual (and some schools are now making this explicit with actual contracts) then the pupil role ceases to be a self-defining status. Rather school is seen as merely a service provider that invites no more affective attachment than a modern language college or a crammer.

The bureaucratization of school was massively accelerated by the 1988 Education Reform Act (ERA), which introduced a centrally defined and controlled curriculum. This has been important in undermining the essentially affective nature of pedagogic relationships promoted by liberal education. The imposition of pseudo-markets has also reduced the image of a school as a community because of its emphasis on the contractual nature of relationships. Also marketization has led to the new elevation of school management as the most valued activity and as prior to the business of teaching children. School may no longer be able to inspire affective loyalties because bureaucratic aims, in this case the maximization of accreditation via testing, have replaced the moral aim, the education of children.

The three themes of centralization, bureaucratization and marketization are analytically but not actually separable. However, it is perhaps bureaucratization that is the most deleterious to the achievement of effective moral agency in school. At the turn of the 20th century Weber identified the 'specialist type of man' and the 'older type of cultivated man' as the alternative models upon which public education could be organized. Weber also saw the 20th century as being typified by the increasing bureaucratization of human relations via the continually enlarging state. Until recently the continued growth of state-provided social welfare in Europe, including education, was a major component of the social democratic consensus (Giddens, 1985) that developed after the Second World War. The characteristics of bureaucracy are an emphasis on 'precision, speed, clarity, regularity, reliability, and efficiency achieved through the fixed division of tasks, hierarchical supervision, and detailed rules and regulations' (in Brown and Lauder, 1992: 11). Bureaucratization as a form of organization aims at the rational pursuit of identified objectives. Its major economic success has been in Fordism, that is, the rational analysis of the techniques of manufacturing that led to production line assembly, which can be exemplified by the Ford Company and motor car production.

Attempts to link the processes of education to economic performance more generally may not be best served by bureaucratic organization in what may be a post-Fordist global economy. While the extent and direction of the global economy is a matter for debate the fact of its increasing impact on the European economy is not (Kumar, 1992, 1995; Robertson, 1992). Success in the modern economy may be linked to something more than young people having an expectation of serial employment. Bureaucracies are typically inflexible and self-protective and apparent change may be superficial. The growth and composition of government bureaucracies have changed continually, not least in education. As I shall argue shortly, bureaucratization has an ossifying effect on the epistemological structures of school knowledge at a time when knowledge in the form of information and the ability to use it is central to economic performance and to future development. Lash and Urry (1994: 108) compare production in Britain and America with Japan and Germany and identify the place of knowledge as the critical distinguishing feature. 'The thick interweaving of information structures and production systems in Japan and Germany... means that production itself is more reflexive than in the Anglo-American cases.'

In what is known as the 'Third Italy', Kumar (1992: 60) describes the conditions of post-Fordist production in small-scale enterprises using high levels of technology and with a 'flexible division of labour and flattened hierarchies'. Working relations were characterized by 'little sense of distinction' between the highly skilled workers and their supervisors, allowing for a high degree of mutual support and co-operation. This mirrors precisely those aspects of schooling in a collegial structure that have been made redundant in recent decades in favour of bureaucratized authority. If successful production is no longer predicated on the hierarchically organized transmission of closed knowledge systems, but on an information-based flexible economy, then to reconstitute schooling as a commercial bureaucracy may be literally counterproductive.

Bureaucratic education has distinctive moral features. Brown and Lauder (1992: 23) argue it is characterized by 'low trust' and 'low ability' whereas the emergent economic forms require 'high trust' and 'high ability'. Bureaucratic education also 'generates a large population of "failures"… at the same time those who are successful rarely have the opportunity to gain the transferable social and conceptual skills which are increasingly required by employers'. This is an important point in that the large number of working class pupils who have failed in school have been tolerable because until relatively recently, 'the majority of jobs required little more than the execution of a set of easily learned routines' (Brown and Lauder, 1992: 7).

This stratification aspect of the moral agency of schooling is linked to its culturally regressive nature and also has an impact on pupils' moral being. Broadly speaking, despite the best efforts of the new right reformers of the 1980s, the school system is still geared to the accreditation of the progeny of the professional class and thus to their reproduction. While this management stratum is socially necessary it is questionable whether its needs should continue to drive the structure and moral content of schooling. The manner of its success is in the demonstration of its intellectual excellence in the academic curriculum, which fits it, in its turn, to manage the public and private bureaucracies of government and industry. This process is articulated by a conceptualization of intelligence that is arguably far too tightly bound to a limited range of cognitive performances that have intrinsic worth and symbolic value but most importantly no demonstrable link with the skills required in a rapidly changing global economy. They are more clearly connected with the preservation of a local hierarchy. Educational systems inevitably reflect the social conditions that create them, but which aspects of those conditions they should emphasize is open to debate. Arguably school should prepare pupils for the moral conditions of the emergent future and the inevitability of change rather than inculcate the values and moral habits of a declining social order of settled hierarchies.

The epistemologies of school knowledge

School presents knowledge as naturalistic and largely uncontested, but it is neither. Knowledge is a discursive product, it is made and remade by men and women through the medium of language. Those transactions that produce our knowledge have an inevitable element of power. This is what Foucault (1977) refers to as power/knowledge, with the implication that the two are co-terminous.

School is an ideological apparatus of the state and is constantly subject to politically motivated change. Within the English Conservative Party during the 1970s and 1980s there was a contest between the radical reformers of the new right in the mould and wake of Keith Joseph and what Ball (1994) refers to as the cultural restorationists, those looking to the past to inspire the present. This has caused education to be subject to contradictory pressures. On the one hand the new right reformers emphasize freedom, choice and the market and a curriculum directly relevant to the aspirations of the consumers of education, that is, parents and pupils.

On the other hand the restorationists look to the re-creation of a past condition of education and largely ignore the links between the content of schooling and the economy. In the last Tory administration, the Prime Minister declared an interest in the re-establishment of grammar schools, which put him firmly in the restorationist camp. This idealization of the past in education may have considerable popular support. The preference the English have for dressing school children in outfits based on the school fashions of an earlier age is testament to the triumph of nostalgia over reason.

Grammar schools were originally medieval institutions devoted to the study of the structures and the literature of classical languages. More recently Williams (1958: 172) suggests that 'our present curriculum… was essentially created by the nineteenth century, following some eighteenth-century models, and retaining elements of the medieval curriculum near its centre'. Blackman (1992: 203) argues that 'From the Renaissance until the present century, English education has been dominated by the literary tradition' and that 'Scientific and technological advance have historically been held back by class prejudice, as this "new knowledge" became intimately linked to the training of the lower social classes. And it is from this premise that we derive the modern conception that learning can be undertaken without reference to practicality.'

Originally the grammar school curriculum would have been a practical preparation for the likely vocations of pupils. However, we are left with a set of values that perpetuate a body of knowledge and an implicit model of excellence that ensures the continuance of a form of education that is more akin to the acquisition of an accomplishment, like water colour drawing, than to a preparation for economic or civic life. This was strongly reinforced by the National Curriculum.

The necessity of a National Curriculum is widely recognized throughout Europe where a variety of approaches are taken (Skilbeck, 1994). The core curriculum is critical to its success as an effective preparation for social participation and this requires 'the identification of the values disciplines, areas of knowledge, skills and themes deemed to be essential' (Skillbeck, 1994: 230). Also a divisive National Curriculum is a contradiction and to devise a core that provides 'individually successful and satisfying learning for all students remains one of the great unfinished tasks in education' (Skillbeck, 1994). As Skilbeck (1994) suggests, those who are 'mindful of the wide range of student aptitudes, abilities, interests and socio-cultural backgrounds, are sceptical about a push towards a tough minded academicism'.

The National Curriculum and its legitimation through the associated rituals of assessment is overwhelmingly restorationist in flavour and bureaucratic in form. As Pring (1995: 84) notes, 'the list of school subjects remains relatively stable, and those in the National Curriculum are much the same as those in the 1904 Regulations for secondary schools'. Formative assessment aimed at improving pupil learning is absent while summative measurement of single performances dominates the assessment of the Standard Achievement Tasks (SATS). This is based on the behaviourist model of Measurement-Driven Instruction where the task of the teacher is to train the pupil, understood as passive recipient, towards a prescribed performance. As Torrance (1992: 171) notes, with the National Curriculum 'the focus is on the "delivery" of the National Curriculum via assessment procedures, rather than improving the quality of teaching and learning per se'. Thus, the National Curriculum may be thought to constitute a contradictory set of messages. The content and emphases reflect an historical state of knowledge, what Ball (1994) refers to as 'the curriculum of the dead'. But while the content derives its legitimacy from the liberal model of education, the conditions of its enactment in schools are drawn, not from the idea of education as the development of the rational faculty, but through 'the specification and measurement of basic skills' (Torrance, 1992: 170).

What we refer to by the term intelligence and what is to count as quality are constituents of the moral process of schooling; they are central to its legitimacy and to the moral formation of pupils because they are judged by their performances and these become part of their history and identity and strongly determine their life chances.

The problem of the practical

The construction of knowledge in school, as I have suggested, is not static nor a natural given. It can and does change. There are in England, however, underlying epistemological structures that continue to affect how we value modes of learning and in so doing construct the moral agency of school. Initially we must recognize that the distinction between pure and applied knowledge, which continues to dominate the school curriculum, is not necessarily false, as Pring (1995: 189) would have it but an epistemological distinction that we are free to abandon as detrimental to an effective education. Consequent upon this division is the issue of the status of practical activity in the curriculum, which derives from its inferior conception. Practical knowledge, which is currently being developed in the curriculum, implicitly recognizes the theory and practice divide where it is behaviouristically defined as competence, and where the focus is on the practical not the cognitive performance. The weakness of this form of validation is that once more the performance is the point of legitimation and is itself tightly boundaried. There is still no place in school for the recognition of the discursive practical intelligence that fuels modernity.

In England, vocational training has normally been seen as the concern of institutions other than school, for example colleges of further education and technical colleges, and has taken place post-school. The success of schooling has not been judged by the levels of vocational preparedness amongst leavers, though this is often adverted to, but by their capacity to maintain academic standards particularly through A level examination. In the 1980s the notion that some sort of vocational preparation should begin earlier in a learner's career gained some currency and there were a flurry of government agency-backed initiatives. Pring (1995) and Shilling (1989) both give critical accounts of the attempts in recent years at enriching the vocational content of schooling. The most ambitious of these agencies is the National Council for Vocational Qualifications (NCVQ) with targets aiming to encompass half the workforce by the end of the 20th century and significantly to span both schooling and working life. National Vocational Qualifications (NVQs) were to be the instrument that would provide a vocational element to schooling. Pring (1995: 51) quotes the Chief Executive of NCVQ speaking in 1990: 'If the Government is serious about these ideas it must make a significant amount of room in the timetable. We need a first-class alternative to academic education, like the Germans... It makes a great deal of sense to be looking at provision from the age of fourteen.' However, this is inevitably seen in the light of English attachment to academic values. As Pring (1995: 55) suggests, 'Vocational training has had a relatively low status in Britain... Britain was, until recently, unique amongst the major industrial nations in having the majority of its students leave full-time education or training at the age of 16.'

The focus on the promotion of decontextualized and behaviourally defined competence may result in a limited conception of personal ability. When Pring (1995: 189) suggests that 'Competence as a goal might be limiting', he may be understating the problem. If the pupils' worth is defined by performance alone, whether cognitive or practical, and this is understood as the desirable end of schooling, then it is precisely those performances that become validated in the eyes of the pupils. Thus, the point of learning anything ends with its accredited testing, which confers status but has no directly preparational purpose. Learning in school fails to include a moral future when it is confined to the, albeit absolutely necessary, cognitive core. The abstracted performances that validate school activity are not seen as socially useful by pupils. School knowledge relates to institutional demands. What is absent is the more broadly discursive capacity to extend and develop alongside the acquisition of competence and a place where autonomous and co-operative learning are presented as the vital tools of economic development. Competence needs context.

It is worth noting that school teaching has recently been redefined as a craft rather than a professional activity and given over to an agency of bureaucratic zealotry. In the construction of the National Curriculum, teachers' professional expertise was seen as less significant than the ill-informed whim of politicians (Ball, 1990). The result has been the reconceptualization of teaching as the delivery of a curriculum unalloyed by any personal qualities of the teacher. It has been narrowly redefined, again in behavioural terms, as a set of competences aimed at performance in the classroom. Competence in the classroom has always been necessary to school teaching but has now become sufficient. However, to see teaching confined to its performative aspects is, as Pring (1995: 191) suggests, to turn 'educators into technicians'. The Teacher Training Agency works with a simple Fordist model of teacher production. In promoting teaching as a research-based activity it seeks to sponsor work on classroom performance and the enhancement of cognitive output. This is analogous to the redefining of the practice of law as courtroom performance. Through the extension of financial control over in-service provision and the mandatory induction of head teachers, the Teacher Training Agency has also reinforced a political culture of instrumental pragmatism in schools.

Morality and marketization

What are termed market solutions has been a strong theme in recent political strategy for reform and development. Barber (1996: 163) quotes a treasury official in the 1980s saying, albeit informally, 'It doesn't really matter what the issue is, we know that the question we have to ask is, how do you create a market?' As I have suggested, the conservative interest in education is both to restore an imagined superior past and more reasonably to improve on an imperfect present. Part of the strategy for reform has been the development of a quasi-market in education.

However, education is not entirely regulated by the market. The consumer has no control over the product and no option but to consume. As I have illustrated, England has a school curriculum geared to the requirements of the professional sector and dominated by impractical symbolic knowledge. Therefore one might ask, where the market is unconditionally preferred as an agent of change, is it producing change in a desirable direction? It may be the case that the market is organizing the distribution of an inadequate education.

The impact of market thinking has had some consequences for the nature of school as a moral agency. Enforced market behaviour and market thinking have changed the moral nature of the institution and its relationships with the outside world. For example, competition between schools for pupils is likely to have an effect on local co-operation and make serving the educational needs of the higher ability pupils more attractive than serving others. The picture on the benefits of competition is complicated and it is likely that there are gains and losses. Evidence from the Keele survey quoted by Barber (1996: 110) suggests that only 43 per cent of parents considered examination performance a critical factor in choosing schools. In another study proximity to home was the prime factor in choosing a school for over half the sample. Parents were to have a key role in policing the market reforms (Ball, 1990) but this is a long way from having any control over what is marketed. Hughes (1997), reporting on a large-scale descriptive study, suggests that parents are largely satisfied with school. Seventy per cent were reported as being 'happy with school' and another 18 per cent as 'happy with reservations' (Hughes, 1997: 74). Parents were found to have very limited knowledge of school and its workings and the schools themselves little interest in developing communication: 'They're invited to come in any time if they're not happy, but they don't – so we assume they are happy' is offered as a typical quote (Hughes, 1997: 75).

It may be argued that parents are not in the best position to determine the nature and content of schooling. They will inevitably represent sectional interests with some more able to work the market in their favour than others. This in itself would be unexceptionable if the distribution were as classless as the market language. However, Edwards and Whitty (1997: 40) report that in England 'parental choice is reinforcing traditional hierarchies'. This includes institutional hierarchies: 'A recent OECD (1994) study of choice in several countries concluded that demand side measures were rarely sufficient to create diversity in forms of schooling in highly stratified societies.' Choice and differentiation were meant to be benefits of the market; however, their study also suggests that City Technology Colleges (CTCs), far from being an alternative form of education, were seen by parents in traditional terms and 'as being nearer the top of the local hierarchy of schools than competing comprehensives' (Edwards and Whitty, 1997: 37). Hirsch (1997: 160) in a comparative study of policies for choice in education concludes, 'it is evident that many of Britain's problems with the practice of school choice emanate from the readiness of its citizens to see schooling as a mechanism of sorting people by class, rather than offering potentially equal but possibly different kinds of education to everybody'.

The market is not, as it is presented, a matter of common sense, but of political, that is to say moral, choice. Aspects of the new right agenda for schools – uniforms; a settled understanding of what knowledge is and what its boundaries are; the recognition of learning through testing and an inert culture of deference – are instantly nostalgic and give the illusion of control at the cost of economic relevance. Such a response is simply irrational given the real conditions under which we shall have to make a living. It also reinforces school as primarily for the reproduction of the professional class, the group with most invested in education as a symbolic good and with least interest in the development of a truly entrepreneurial or enterprise culture that would challenge the dominance of bureaucratically organized production.

The introduction of the market as an ideology that governs the conceptualization of education by its participants has strengthened the culture of bureaucracy. In particular, teachers in schools are now clearly divided within a line management system and understand themselves as such. Organizational culture has changed in matters of dress, self-presentation and language and in ways of legitimating activity in school. There has been a dramatic shift in the culture of schooling towards a Fordist bureaucracy concerned with maximal and efficient production. The role of management in school has grown along with the bureaucratization of education. Ball (1994: 71) lists the contents of its brief: 'It is a mechanism for ensuring the delivery of a National Curriculum, and it ties classroom practice, student performance, teacher appraisal, school recruitment and resource allocation into a single tight bundle of planning and surveillance.' However one might understand the need for change, it is open to question whether a bureaucratic management model for school governance is appropriate. It may be the case that within the model compliance is more significant than assent, that behavioural conformity does not betoken a congruence between the values of the institution and all its members. Ball (1994) stresses, 'It (bureaucratic management) drives a wedge between the curriculum- and classroom-oriented teacher and the market- and budget-oriented manager, thus creating a strong potential for differences in interest, values and purpose between the two groups.' Significantly, he concludes, 'This gap is vividly present across our research on educational reform.'

One of the fundamental moral shifts consequent upon the marketization of education is the devaluing of communal life previously upheld by the collegial culture of school. For the New Right, looking to 18th-century ideas of freedom, this may be thought an advance. As Ball (1994: 45) reports, 'The ontology of restorationism is opposed to any conception of human nature as social (except in the narrow sense of family and nation) and conceives instead of private, self sufficient competing individuals.' There is perhaps a moral fit here between an individuated schooling where schools compete amongst themselves for pupils and pupils against one another for certification. League tables are aggregations of individual performances and the league is a production table with quality narrowly associated with single instances of individuated cognitive performances in tests. Value added is an addition to a predictive assessment of individual capacity. School effectiveness (Stoll and Fink, 1996) is finally about the maximization of the production of individuated cognitive performance. These are the real priorities of school management driven by central policy and funding formulae, although interestingly Hardman and Levacic (1997) found no link between high levels of parental preference and school income. Underlying this now dominant form of legitimation is a narrow model of the person and of educational success as determined at the point of production. There is no model of the relationship between what school produces and the relevance of its product for the social and economic forms we might wish to encourage. The judgements that schools pronounce on pupils are based on an instrumental and effectively amoral rationality.

The aim of the collegially organized liberal education was to cultivate traits and capacities. While we retain an outdated curriculum that bears a strong resemblance to those of the past we have jettisoned the cultural forms that gave it meaning. Thus, the content satisfies nostalgic restorationism and also the professional class who are the beneficiaries of bureaucratic organization and are themselves contingent to the new areas of information-based wealth production. The pupils' experience of the curriculum is rendered non-liberal, even anti-intellectual (Ball, 1994: 44) through its legitimation via testing. It is still the case that in our schooling the top band of pupils can secure real social advantage on the basis of a single performance related to an externally given body of knowledge that itself has no practical use. This is delivered and represented as though in some mysterious way these isolated cognitive performances would, without apparent causal connection, improve our relative economic performance. The concern with standards (of individuated performance as a measure of the quality of education) depends upon seeing them as a good in themselves rather than activity that enhances a person's abilities more generally. What is produced is a standard set of impersonally ranked products rather than people with a personal knowledge of their capacities and an engagement in their development within a social and moral context. Many areas of modern economic work require high levels of social skill and above all the ability to act co-operatively, and to understand common ownership of the productive process as an interdependent member of a group. In the analysis of the success of the Third Italy economy the development, maintenance and exploitation of local networks was seen as a critical component in the success of the small-scale enterprises that made up the regional economy. The present arrangements whereby our schools are centrally directed and institutionally autonomous have disembedded them from an economy where region is increasingly significant and likely to become more so with the growth of information-led production.

The moral reconstitution of school

The educational reforms of the recent Labour administration, and those of the preceding Conservative administrations, are partly aimed at tightening the links between education and our social and economic life. However, the initial radicalism has been reversed and the means to a part of education, the management of maximal cognitive output, has become its sole end.

The central focus on the raising of standards of cognitive ability within the maintained sector is primary to an effective education and necessary. But in the achievement of this, the moral agency of school has been bureaucratized and thus rendered incapable of recognizing and promoting a moral framework for national cohesion and continuing prosperity. The combination of bureaucracy, individuation and legitimation through cognitive testing provides, at best, the foundations of a self-orientation and manifestly encourages dependency through engineering deference in both the teachers and the pupils.

In examining the moral agency of school I have argued that its current condition is inimical to the creation of a moral order, a habitus, that will provide pupils with an impetus, and the range of social and conceptual capacities, to enable them to work within the global economic frame that increasingly controls local conditions. Success in the world beyond is now the only truly reasonable end of schooling for the individual. This can be realized in the recognition and exploitation of the interdependency of persons and the social nature of being. Pupils will not flourish in the dependency engendered by the equation of success with conformity.

What is now required is a future-oriented and economically aware analysis of how school can be remodelled to fulfil a truly national role that serves the whole people. There are still critical voices that seek to empower the moral agency of school. Barber's (1996) informed polemic is both reasoned and radical. Claxton *et al* (1996) offer a model of professional development in teaching suited to a career that embraces planned and intelligent change. Clark

(1996) seeks to make schools open to their communities and to become learning communities in themselves. School has the potential to be the engine house of social cohesion and economic development through nationally defined and agreed goals. The dominance of an emptied-out academic curriculum needs to be replaced with a curriculum that is genuinely rooted in the preparation of pupils for a life of learning. This may require rethinking the polarity between centre and institution, giving scope for the inclusion of regional needs, which will embed collaborating schools in local society and economy. Without returning total control of education to teachers, they must be enabled to develop an authentic educational role in relation to pupils who are encouraged to become skilled and ardent learners over a range of forms of knowledge and competence. Critical to the achievement of these ends is the abolition of education as a function of bureaucratic management.

Finally, there is the question of what sort of schooling will prepare the nation best for the increasing dominance of global cultural and economic factors in the next generation. It is unlikely to spawn the answer, a bureaucratically organized medieval curriculum in a quasi-market.

References

Ball, S J (1990) *Politics and Policy Making in Education: Explorations in policy sociology*, Routledge, London

Ball, S J (1994) *Education Reform: A critical and post-structural approach*, Open University Press, Milton Keynes

Barber, M (1996) *The Learning Game: Arguments for an education revolution*, Gollancz, London

Berger, P L and Luckmann, T (1967) *The Social Construction of Reality*, Penguin, Harmondsworth

Blackman S (1992) Beyond vocationalism, in *Education for Economic Survival: From Fordism to post-Fordism*, ed P Brown and H Lauder, Routledge, London

Bourdieu, P (1993) *Sociology in Question*, tr R Nice, Sage, London

Brown, P and Lauder H (1992) Education, economy, and society: an introduction to a new agenda, in *Education for Economic Survival: From Fordism to post-Fordism*, ed P Brown and H Lauder, pp 1–44, Routledge, London

Clark, D (1996) *Schools as Learning Communities: Transforming education*, Cassell, London

Claxton, G et al (eds) (1996) *Liberating the Learner: Lessons for professional development in education*, Routledge, London

Dore, R P (1976) *The Diploma Disease: Education, qualification and development*, Allen & Unwin, London

Durkheim, E (1973) *Moral Education: A study in the theory and application of the sociology of education*, tr E K Wilson and R H Schnurer, The Free Press, New York

Edwards, T and Whitty, G (1997) Marketing quality: traditional and modern versions of educational excellence, in *Choice and Diversity in Schooling, Perspectives and Prospects*, ed R Glatter *et al*, pp 29–43, Routledge, London

Finegold, D and Soskice, D (1988) The failure of training in Britain, *Oxford Review of Educational Policy*, **4** (3)

Foucault, M (1977) *Discipline and Punish: The birth of the prison*, Allen Lane, London

Gewirtz, S, Ball, S and Bowe, R (1995) *Markets, Choice and Equity in Education*, Open University Press, Buckingham

Giddens, A (1985) *The Constitution of Society: Outline of a theory of structuration*, Polity Press, Cambridge

Hardman, J and Levacic, R (1997) The impact of competition on secondary schools, in *Choice and Diversity in Schooling, Perspectives and Prospects*, ed R Glatter *et al*, pp 116–35, Routledge, London

Hirsch, D (1997) Policies for school choice: what can Britain learn from abroad?, in *Choice and Diversity in Schooling, Perspectives and Prospects*, ed R Glatter *et al*, pp 152–65, Routledge, London

Hughes, M (1997) Schools' responsiveness to parents: views at Key Stage One, in *Choice and Diversity in Schooling, Perspectives and Prospects*, ed R Glatter *et al*, Routledge, London

Kumar, K (1992) New theories of industrial society, in *Education for Economic Survival: From Fordism to post-Fordism*, ed P Brown and H Lauder, pp 45–75, Routledge, London

Kumar, K (1995) *From Post-Industrial to Post-Modern Society: New theories of the contemporary world*, Blackwell, Oxford

Lash, S and Urry, J (1994) *Economies of Signs and Space*, Sage, London

Macbeth, A *et al* (eds) (1995) *Collaborate or Compete? Educational partnerships in a market economy*, Falmer Press, London

Oakshott, M (1972) Education: the engagement and its frustration, in *Education and the Development of Reason*, ed R F Dearden *et al*, pp 19–49, Routledge and Kegan Paul, London

Pring, R (1995) *Closing the Gap: Liberal education and vocational preparation*, Hodder & Stoughton, London

Robertson, R (1992) *Globalization*, Sage, London

School Curriculum and Assessment Authority (1996a) *Education for Adult Life: The spiritual and moral development of young people*, SCAA, London

School Curriculum and Assessment Authority (1996b) *Consultation on Values in Education and the Community*, Com/96/608, SCAA, London

Shilling, C (1989) *Schooling for Work in Capitalist Britain*, Falmer Press, London

Skilbeck, M (1994) The core curriculum: an international perspective, in *Teaching and Learning in the Secondary School*, ed B Moon and A S Mayes, pp 223–60, Routledge, London

Spens Report (1938) *Secondary Education with Special Reference to Grammar Schools and Technical High Schools*, HMSO, London

Stoll, L and Fink, D (1996) *Changing Our Schools*, Open University Press, Buckingham

Taylor, T (1995) Movers and shakers: high politics and the origins of the National Curriculum, *The Curriculum Journal*, **6** (2), Summer, **99**, pp 161–84

Torrance, H (1992) Educational assessment and educational standards: towards an alternative view of quality, in *Education for Economic Survival: From Fordism to post-Fordism*, ed P Brown and H Lauder, pp 161–79, Routledge, London

Williams, R (1958) *Culture and Society (1850–1950)*, Chatto and Windus, London

Chapter 7

The Contribution of Special Education to Our Understanding of Values, Schooling and the Curriculum

Brahm Norwich and Jenny Corbett

Introduction

This chapter discusses the connections between special education and education in general and will illustrate ways in which special education contributes to our understanding of schooling and the curriculum. It will focus on two key changes in the education service over the last decade from a special educational needs perspective: the introduction of the National Curriculum (NC) and the policy move towards greater school specialization. The NC involved an entitlement for all children and included at least in principle all children, even those with significant Special Educational Needs (SENs). This expressed the values of equal opportunities and inclusion. But, with the implementation of the NC, the need for flexibility and differentiation came to the fore. This recognized individual needs and the realizing of potential as values. The term differentiation has now come to refer to within-class curriculum planning and support arrangements. However, it can also refer to organizational arrangements within schools in the class grouping of children by abilities and in the allocation of pupils between schools. This point leads to the second focus of the chapter: the specialization of schools into grant maintained schools, LEA schools, schools with some degree of ability selection, special schools and technology schools. Such a diversity of schools has been justified in terms of the values of meeting different individual needs, but has also been criticized in relation to equality and social cohesion for re-establishing a stratified system of high and low status schooling. Within special educational provision these values of inclusion and individuality have also influenced parental interests in favouring either more mainstreaming on one hand or highly specialist residential or day schools on the other.

The two educational changes show the range of values found in decisions about schooling and the curriculum. These values encompass individual and social aims. Aims for individuals can include realizing each and every individual's potential; intrinsic appreciation of knowledge, understanding, moral and aesthetic experience; developing a sense of self-worth for all and becoming an active and responsible citizen. Aims for society can include community participation; social cohesiveness; equalizing opportunities; maintaining and raising standards; reconstructing society and preserving the best of past traditions. This multiplicity of values can be seen as an expression of the diversity of voices in society. We will argue in this chapter that these voices need to be recognized and integrated in a balanced way. It will also be argued that the issues that arise in educating those with disabilities and difficulties underline the multiple nature of values and highlight the tensions this generates in policy making about schooling and the curriculum generally.

Recent developments in schooling

Changes in the global and national economy, developments in information technologies and changes in the workplace have led many governments to see the critical role of the education system in preparing for and adapting to these changes. This renewed interest in education has been welcomed, even if driven by strong and perhaps hostile economic imperatives. The NC with its national prescription of subjects, programmes of study and assessment arrangements generated much controversy at first and then led eventually to some softening of its demands and inflexibilities. From an SEN perspective, many educationalists see the NC as providing a much needed common curriculum framework and entitlement for all. The significance and value of enacting this principle cannot be ignored even when there has been widespread dissatisfaction with the specific formulations and implementations of the programmes and assessment arrangements. Of course, there are continuing practical issues about how a common entitlement can be meaningfully applied to the diversity of children and young people. One way would be to reduce the content coverage required by the common curriculum so that more teaching time is available for different needs. This would allow some children more time to consolidate key areas of their learning, for others with sensory and motor impairments to gain alternative access to the programmes and for yet others to learn through different methods and settings. Whether the flexibilities introduced after the Dearing revisions to the NC are sufficient for this diversity is not yet known.

Since the introduction of the NC the term *differentiation* has become a way of trying to conceptualize the process of gearing teaching to the diversity of needs. The process of implementing the NC comes to be seen to be one of differentiation. The application of a common framework of subjects, programmes of study and assessment arrangement to the full diversity of children, including those with severe learning difficulties, requires differentiation. However, like many other general abstract concepts in education, differentiation is confusing because of its different uses and associations.

The full range of educational needs has often been separated out neatly into the majority with 'normal' needs and the minority with 'special needs'. There is evidence of the new Labour Government engaging in this oversimplified distinction in its policy documents (DfEE, 1997a; Barber, 1997; DfEE, 1998). One of the key points in our chapter is that this simple separatist position is untenable. Special education is not simply and only a separate part of education, it is inherently connected to all aspects of education. An example of the simple separatist kind of thinking is shown in the renewed interest in within-school ability grouping. From the separatist perspective, decisions about pupil grouping and class teaching strategies have involved the issue of *mixed ability grouping and teaching versus ability grouping and teaching*. These decisions come to be seen as associated with the range of 'normal' abilities and attainments. They have not included within these ability grouping considerations decisions about the grouping and teaching of those with abilities, disabilities and attainments outside the 'normal' range. These decisions come to be seen as part of the separate area of special needs.

The flaw in the separatist perspective is that it fixes *only* on the assumption that learners with special educational needs have special or significantly different needs. It ignores that they also have many 'normal' needs, which are common to the majority, on one hand, and that they are also individuals with unique individual needs, on the other hand. To reject the separatist perspective is therefore to connect needs that arise from impairments to wider needs that are common to all learners, including pupils with SEN. It also reminds us that those with difficulties and disabilities are also unique individuals. The separatist perspective should be replaced by one that sees all pupils, including those with SEN, in terms of several dimensions of need:

1. as having educational needs which they share with all pupils;
2. as having needs which arise from their exceptional characteristics, such as impairments or particular abilities; and

3. as having needs which are unique to them as individuals and which distin-
    guish them from all others, including those with the same impairments or
    abilities.

Therefore, in addressing these different dimensions of need, appropriate
teaching and organizational strategies for pupils with SEN will also have to be
multidimensional. Provision should not be considered only in terms of difference, but also in terms of what is common to all and what is individual to
each pupil. The implication is that differentiation should not be seen only as
an SEN concept.

Differentiation does not just concern itself with effective teaching for individual needs within any particular class. What goes on within a class depends
also on the composition of the class in terms of the pupils' age, gender, attainments and abilities. These in turn depend on how they are grouped within
any school, usually by age, which often goes unquestioned, and sometimes by
attainments and abilities, which is a more controversial matter. But, the composition of classes within a school itself depends on the intake designation of a
school. Schools differ in their acceptance of the kinds of pupils they can accommodate, even comprehensive schools insofar as they coexist with special
schools. To follow this line of analysis is to show that differentiation has to be
treated as a multi-level concept, which encompasses the specialization of
schools, the class grouping of learners within schools and the organization of
teaching within classes. These are central issues in education generally. The
special educational perspective on them is to highlight the full range of diversity to be provided for in the organization of schools, the grouping of pupils
and the organization of class teaching.

Another contribution of the special educational perspective is to highlight
the extent of the national challenge to design a common curriculum for all. As
in decisions about grouping and teaching, designing a common curriculum
for all is also an issue of differentiation. These decisions involve a general curriculum design dilemma: the tension between providing an equal entitlement for all to a common programme, while having the flexibility to gear
programmes to different needs and interests. This is not just a dilemma from
an SEN perspective. They are evident in wider curriculum design debates
about the core requirement for young people in their last stage of compulsory
schooling (key stage 4). These debates concern how much of a common
programme of core and foundation subjects in the NC all learners should be
required to study in view of their different attainments, abilities and interests.
This general dilemma is also found for different kinds and degrees of difficulties and disabilities. For example, with children with sensory impairments,
whether children with severe hearing impairments should be learning foreign languages or learning oral communication methods in English in the

available time; with children with severe intellectual impairments, whether to spend more time on acquiring cognitive learning strategies in maths and science or having experiences of various other subject areas. The point is that designing a common curriculum for all has to take account of difference, and not just the degree and kinds of difference found amongst those with difficulties and disabilities.

Though the NC is consistent with the inclusive principle of a common entitlement, its design bears the hallmarks of the quasi-market schemes introduced into the public services by the previous Conservative Government. This is apparent in the leading role that assessment arrangements played in its design. The principle was that NC assessments reported openly and nationally would provide parents, the users, with information needed for them to choose between the schools, the providers. It was presumed that by bringing schools into competition with each other schools would improve pupil attainment levels. So, introducing an assessment-driven NC was connected with policies to offer greater parental preferences – greater school specialization – and to give schools more management controls of funds – Local Management of Schools, LMS. These policies have been evident in allowing schools to increase their pupil roll and in reducing the central role of local government in the management of schools. This was reinforced by allowing individual schools to opt out of LEAs to become grant maintained schools, funded through a separate central Funding Agency.

As predicted, such a radical restructuring of the school system was bound to have significant effects on provision for SEN. There has been a rising demand on LEAs to provide additional resources for individuals with SEN in the form of Statements. DfEE figures showed a 42 per cent increase in actual Statements over the five-year period from 1991 to 1995 (Parliamentary Question 10965, 20.10.95). The recent Green Paper on SEN identified this increase as a cause for concern (DfEE, 1997a). The current national figure is that 2.93 per cent of the total school population has Statements, of which 58 per cent are in mainstream schools. This pressure on LEAs for additional resources through Statements can be attributed to changes within schools. The restructuring has left schools uncertain about their capability to meet the special needs of those who were supported previously without the formality of a Statement. The squeeze on education funding transmitted through the LMS scheme to schools can also be seen as a factor. The overall effect can be interpreted as pressures that have decreased schools' capability to provide for the diversity of pupils. It was in this context that the Education Act 1993 introduced the SEN Code of Practice. Its introduction can be understood as the outcome of several interests. First, there was the Government's response to the increase in Statementing and the demands on resources. Secondly, there was the related need to specify the relative responsibilities of mainstream schools and LEAs for special provision and so reduce the pressure for additional resources. And thirdly, there was a need to clarify the expectations on schools to adopt SEN as a whole school policy and development matter.

The Conservative Government pushed ahead during the 1990s with its policy of choice and diversity in promoting greater specialization of schools – encouraging more schools to become grant maintained, setting up City Technology Colleges with private funding sponsorships, introducing additional funding for particular LEA schools to specialize in technology and enabling schools to introduce greater selection based on pupils' abilities. The current Labour Government has shown that its priorities are with raising standards and less with the structure of general provision. There will be no more partial selection by schools by academic ability, but it is still uncertain to what extent the diversity of schools will be basically altered. From an SEN perspective, diversity of provision means that parents can pursue their preferences for a range of different kinds of provision, from special schools, including independent ones, to mainstream with support. But, they cannot be assured, for instance, that their preferences for supported mainstream provision will be available in their locality. Popular mainstream schools may also find ways of passing difficult-to-teach children on to other schools. Real choice is not assured and may require lengthy appeals to SEN tribunals, two in five of which are unsuccessful (SEN Tribunal, 1998). Diversity of SEN provision is also costly in resource terms and incompatible with fully inclusive mainstream schools.

Three key contributions from special education

Our position in this chapter is that special education contributes to our understanding of the wider general issues about values, schooling and the curriculum. We will identify three key points about this contribution covering the nature of values in education; the impact of market choice; curriculum priorities with the stress on achievement as a leading value and special educational needs as an aspect of education.

Values in education

The 1990s have seen educational values as the focus of government concern, for both Conservative and Labour governments. This is particularly in relation to conceptions of failing pupils, falling standards and ill-equipped teachers. The dominant imagery perpetuated in Parliament and in the media was of low standards, disintegrating discipline, unruly children and a profession that has lost its way. The new Labour Government has continued this tough-minded approach to schools and teachers but with some positive ways forward to improve the status of teaching (DfEE, 1997a). This contemporary picture of state education in a sorry condition has some similarities with conditions at the turn of the 19th century. It would have come as no surprise to those early critics of the drive towards compulsory schooling towards the end of the 19th century. They condemned Board School committees for educating the labouring poor beyond their social station and attempting to implement an ideology that went beyond practical training in basic skills, which was seen by them as more appropriate (eg DCL, 1878). The previous Conservative Government aimed to create a climate in which teaching literacy and numeracy were seen to compete with anti-discrimination and equal opportunities policies. The two were presented as being incompatible, with the implication that it was the equal opportunities ideologies in schooling that led to falling standards in literacy, numeracy and general behaviour.

Hill (1997) describes the various political factions that have influenced values in education over the past decade:

1. the *neo-liberals* who believed that market forces, competition, diversity of provision and freedom of choice by consumers would raise standards in the public services of health and education;
2. the *neo-conservatives* who wished to restore a culture of 'back to basics' and stress traditional values such as respect for authority, the nation and Britishness, prioritizing the values of a social elite and the importance of a common culture; and
3. the then *official Ofsted discourse* which attacked progressive and egalitarian schooling.

Hill argued that the egalitarian function of schooling was systematically weakened by the reduction in the power of LEAs and the delegation of budgets to schools. Prior to the Education Reform Act 1988, LEAs could provide funding for cross-curricular and extra-curricular developments and were able to fund schools according to levels of need, with schools in socially and economically deprived areas receiving extra funding. LEAs also were more able to implement strategic plans for special educational needs. With LMS, funding became based primarily on pupil numbers, even though some small part of funding was based on indications of social disadvantage (such as free school meals). Popular schools with high attaining pupils, often in socially advantaged areas, were better funded than their lower attaining, less popular counterparts.

Whether the new Labour Government will regulate the operation of the quasi-market in education is still to be seen as its policy proposals move towards legislation and implementation. However, there is to be a renewed role for LEAs in developing plans for raising standards with schools and in supporting school management and leadership. But Labour priorities continue the Conservative focus on raising standards, on one hand, while showing commitment to inclusion, on the other. This has raised questions about how compatible these SEN inclusion policies are with policies to raise standards through literacy and numeracy strategies and target setting (Norwich, 1998). The point we wish to make is that where values are multiple and in tension with each other, it is important that this is recognized and acted on in policy making. It can be said that the very core of education is about the interplay of different values and principles. This is especially well illustrated in the value tensions about mainstreaming: the inclusion of those with difficulties and disabilities in mainstream schools. Much of special education can be understood in terms of this interplay between the general values of individuality (meeting each and everyone's individual needs) and equality (equal respect and inclusion). Special education shows the importance of recognizing the interplay of different values in educational policy.

Market choice

Our second key point about the contribution of special education concerns market choice. We will discuss two significant moves within mainstream and special schooling which reflect the impact of market choice. The first is that parents are increasingly preferring schools that attain high academic results and where the discipline is well regarded (Ball, 1997). Riddell (1996) suggested that the increased exclusion of pupils with social, emotional and behavioural difficulties reflects the dominant values of assessing teacher and school performance rather than a caring approach to all learners. Mainstream schools were becoming more competitive and selective in their intake under the Conservative Government, hoping to attract parents whose children would be effective learners and high achievers. The comprehensive ideology had become seriously threatened in this process. The new Labour Government has committed itself to a modernized version of comprehensive secondary schools, which will use ability grouping as the norm. But, parental preference will continue and we will wait to see how the development of behaviour plans by LEAs, under the Education Act 1997, will affect pupil exclusion.

The other significant development is in regard to parental choice within the SEN Code of Practice (1994) and the use of tribunals, mentioned before. A dominant assumption in the 1980s was that most parents who protested about their child's special provision would be asking for their continued mainstreaming or wanting them out of a special school and into mainstream. This can no longer be assumed. Tribunals have proved to be a classic reflec-

tion of what can happen when market choice is fostered in the public imagination. Specific learning difficulties, such as dyslexia, have been a
dramatically expanding area of special needs, as has attention deficit hyperac-
tivity disorder (ADHD). Both are presented as medically and neurologically
based, related to a degree of minimal brain damage that has influenced patterns of learning and behaviour. This may be seen to reflect a 'back to basics'
move in special education diagnosis and assessment, whereby reliance on
medical diagnosis is given paramount importance.

The use of tribunal procedures, especially in relation to dyslexia, has characterized a market economy in which a narrow and sometimes greedy individualism is legitimated. Parents have, for example, proved to be far more litigious
in the Home Counties than in many other areas, like the rural north (Bryans,
1997). Parents pursuing their 'individual entitlement' as a right to claim resources for individual children, regardless of the limited funding available in
the LEA, has come to replace equality as an entitlement for all. The rhetoric of
consumer rights has encouraged a fierce use of single-issue lobbying, in which
the parents may maximize their child's difficulties to gain their desired provision. In relation to dyslexia, parents are usually very happy to have their child labelled 'dyslexic' and may not be concerned with the resource-worthiness of
their child in relation to other children. This epitomises the market values of
individualism and self-interest, regardless of community needs. The London
Borough of Brent, where there are over 100 languages spoken, reflects these
market values in a pluralist society. Parents often request a special kind of special needs provision, eg a Catholic language unit, Jewish special school or
all-White provision. In this market, parental preference does not just mean exclusion or inclusion but it has to be of a special kind. Thus, the tribunal process
can be seen to characterize market choice in action, offering individual entitlement with a disregard for the wider needs of others.

Market choice for some, usually those with more social and economic
power, may lessen resources available for others and therefore their choice.
Individuals pursuing their own, sometimes narrow, interests may be limiting
the wider public interest. Recent experience in special educational needs il-
lustrates the extent of the operation of these processes. But, as we have argued, we find multiple and sometimes contrary values in education and these
have to be prioritized and balanced. Individual choice has to be balanced
against and therefore limited to some extent by the values of meeting the
needs of others.

Curriculum priorities

Our third key point about the contribution of special education to our understanding of education generally is that high achievement defined in NC

terms can become an over-dominating educational priority. The pressure to raise educational standards, as discussed before, can be understood in the context of economic factors and the growing international focus on education and training as a pre-condition for future economic and social well-being. These national concerns become translated into national educational attainment targets in GCSE, NVQ, GNVQ and SAT terms. The effect of switching into this mode of goal setting on such a scale then refocuses attention on schooling techniques, both organizational and pedagogic, to achieve such targets (Ofsted, 1996 – Report on target setting in schools).

Increasing achievement levels for all is an important value, but it is not the only value in education. Standard setting is the crux of the matter here, as there is a tendency for standards to be set at levels that ignore what is attainable for some individuals, even when they are a significant minority. This is illustrated in the Labour Government's approach to setting targets whereby 80 per cent and 75 per cent at age 11 are expected by the end of the first term of a Labour government to achieve at least level 4 in literacy and numeracy respectively. Target setting in these areas is important, but done in this way it has serious difficulties. Children with SEN are not included in this target, though there is no clear sense of how many pupils this excludes. It is also not clear whether children with SEN are amongst those 20–25 per cent for whom this is not a realistic goal, given adverse social and other factors. It has also been asked whether the effort needed by parents, teachers and children to attain such levels by the age of 11 might undermine these children's learning in other areas and their needs to have a broad and balanced curriculum. There is also no assurance that these levels could even be attained given such a focused investment of effort; current pedagogic techniques might not yet be effective enough. Nor do we know whether the investment of effort will draw attention away from those judged unable to reach level 4 by age 11.

What an SEN perspective contributes to the current interest in general target setting is a reminder of the interdependence and connections between educational values and the risks of over-emphasizing single curricular areas, however important. It also draws our attention to the effectiveness of pedagogic approaches and the context of learning relevant to realistic target setting. Balancing a commitment to high achievement with individual needs and pedagogic realism is better approached through target setting that is individually rather than generally referenced. This would start from individual baselines and then set personally relevant high standards informed by general high standards, rather than start from uniform high standards that are not geared to individuality and difference.

The contribution of special education: concluding comments

Our contention is that the main contribution of special education to our understanding of education is in offering a particular view of the relationship between parts of education to education as a whole. We have argued in this chapter for special education as an aspect of all parts of education and not simply as a separate part of education. Though there has been a move over the past 20 years towards greater integration and the connection between special education and its mainstream counterparts, special education's position is still one of relative isolation and low importance.

Our point can be illustrated by the training of teachers both in initial and in-service courses (SENTC, 1996). Here we find that preparing teachers to understand and relate their practice to a wider range of needs is hived off in separate options, modules and day presentations. A recent example can be found in the initial framework for a national qualification for subject leaders, under development by the Teacher Training Agency (TTA). The SEN aspects of a subject leader's responsibility were not initially thought through in the consultation plans for this national qualification. Our point is also evident in the SEN Code of Practice, which introduced a staged system of identifying and providing for individual children from within the ordinary school's own resources and the formulation and use of individual records and reviews. However, there have been no significant moves to connect the system of individual educational planning (IEPs) with the mainstream planning of the school curriculum and subject programmes of study. This raises critical questions about the relationship between individual planning, general class teaching and the use of in-class support and withdrawal teaching. These had not yet been fully addressed in collaborative work between the DfEE and the Schools Curriculum and Assessment Agency (SCAA), now the Qualifications and Curriculum Agency (QCA), the two agencies with statutory responsibilities. There are also other examples of this apartness, for example in the management of schools and the organization of Higher Education departments of education.

Our point is the more generally applicable one that a rounded concept of education requires that special educational needs not be treated only as a separate part or sub-system of education. This position derives from the nature of education as having multiple ends or aims. In other words, education is guided by multiple values – such as realizing individual potential and meeting individual needs (individuality), doing this for each and every person (equality), promoting social cohesion and participation (inclusion) and raising and maintaining high standards (high achievement), amongst other aims. This means that these aims inevitably have to be pursued jointly and need to be connected to each other, so when they come into tension they have to be balanced against each other.

One practical implication of this position is that special provision, understood as additional or different provision, has a precarious basis as it might be incompatible with some key educational values. For instance, special school provision that does not raise standards for its pupils compared to additionally resourced mainstream provision would be doubly unjustified, in terms of both inclusive values and high achievement values. On the other hand, separate special classes or schools could be justified in curriculum and achievement terms. This would depend on maintaining connections with the mainstream in curriculum, organization, social interaction and teaching terms, in support of inclusive values. Justifications would ultimately depend on what actually happens: on the actual organization, the quality of provision, the learning outcomes and the links with mainstream.

The main point in this chapter is that special education makes a significant contribution to our understanding of education in general. It is a point that depends on a particular conception of special education. It is a conception of an educational endeavour that connects to other parts of education, while being a distinctive aspect concerned with the needs and interests of those with difficulties and disabilities (Norwich, 1996). As a *connective specialization* of education, special education is neither to be dissolved fully into other parts of education nor to be separate and isolated. It is through this connective feature that it can make a wider contribution to education.

References

Ball, S (1997) On the cusp: parents choosing between state and private schools in the UK: action within an economy of symbolic goods, *International Journal of Inclusive Education*, **1** (11), pp 1–19

Barber, M (1997) *A Reading Revolution: How we can teach every child to read well*, Preliminary Report of Literacy Task Force

Bryans, T (1997) Tribunals and dyslexia, Talk at the Institute of Education, University of London, 7 March

Corbett, J (1997) Include/exclude: redefining the boundaries, *International Journal of Inclusive Education*, **1** (1), pp 55–65

DCL (1878) *The Education Craze and its Results: School Boards, their Extravagance and Inefficiency*, Harrison and Sons, London

Department for Education and Employment (DfEE) (1997a) *Excellence in Schools*, White Paper, DfEE, London

DfEE (1997b) *Excellence for All: Meeting SEN*, Green Paper, DfEE, London

DfEE (1998) *National Literacy Strategy*, DfEE, London

Hill, D (1997) Equality in primary schooling: the policy context, intentions and effects of the Conservative reforms, in *Promoting Equality in Primary Schools*, ed M Cole, D Hill and S Shan, Cassell, London

Norwich, B (1996) *Special needs education, inclusive education or just education for all*, Inaugural Talk, Institute of Education

Norwich, B (1998) Aims and principles, in *Future Policy for SEN: Responding to the Green Paper*, ed SEN Policy Option Steering Group, NASEN

Ofsted (1996) *Setting Targets to Raise Standards: A survey of good practice*, DfEE, London

Riddell, S (1996) Theorising special educational needs in a changing political climate, in *Disability and Society: Emerging issues and insights*, ed L Barton, Longman, London

SENTC (1996) *Professional development to meet special educational needs*, Report for the DfEE

SEN Tribunal (1998) *Annual Report*

Chapter 8

Citizenship Studies, Community Service Learning and Higher Education

John Annette

Introduction

In the recent Crick Committee report on *Education for Citizenship and the Teaching of Democracy in Schools*, citizenship and service learning has made a welcome reappearance on the educational agenda, and the consultation document on Millennium Volunteering, for young people between 16 and 25, has placed an important emphasis on civic values. Religious leaders, including the Archbishop of Canterbury, Dr George Carey and the Chief Rabbi, Dr Jonathan Sacks, have called for a renewed sense of moral responsibility. At present all the three main political parties appeal to the electorate's sense of civic responsibility and the New Labour Government sees this as a key feature of the supposedly new third way in British politics.

It would appear that the issue of citizenship, with all its complexity, has become central to contemporary political debate and a strategic subject area within the academy. Why is this the case? The growing public perception of the limitations of liberal social democracy and its alternative New Right minimal state has created in the United States, and now in Britain, a scepticism about the future of social democratic politics and the resulting search for an alternative politics of meaning (cf Dionne, 1991; Greider, 1992; Gray, 1997; Crewe *et al*, 1997). In addition, there is an increasing awareness that the problem of encouraging participation in governance is not just one of electoral politics or office-holding but one of participation and leadership in the associations and organizations of civil society (cf Dionne, 1998; Barber, 1998a, 1998b; Wuthnow, 1998; Putnam, 1995, 1996). In the UK this has resulted in an increased recognition of the importance of the voluntary sector and the civic and educational importance of volunteering (cf Prior *et al*, 1995; Giddens, 1998). In such a context the key issue is not merely one of constitutional reform (à la Charter 88), but the very definition and meaning of social democratic politics itself. It is not surprising then that the theorization of citizenship has become central to political debate. We cannot shrug it off as merely a political fashion, or effective form of political rhetoric, handy for political soundbites.

We are all citizens now – but do we know what it means to be one?

Since the late 1980s, there have been a number of developments which have put the issue of citizenship on the political, academic and educational agenda (*vide* Oliver and Heater, 1994). In 1988, the Home Secretary, Douglas Hurd, gave his Tamworth Address in which he stressed the importance of civic obligation. In the same year, the Charter 88 movement was established, highlighting the growing public interest in the theme of constitutional reform, and calling for a written constitution and a Bill of Rights. It was not long before the broader political attention moved to education and by 1990 the Speaker's Commission on Citizenships was expressing concern about the ways in which students were learning about citizenship. In 1991 the Government's Citizen's Charter and the citizens platforms of both the Labour and Liberal Democrats parties were established. For the Government there began a significant shift from an emphasis on active citizenship, in the speeches of Hurd and Patten, to that of the consumer rights of the Citizen's Charter while for New Labour the language of citizenship replaced that of class and class conflict.

In the 1990s the growing influence of Professor Amitai Etzioni, *The man with the big idea?* (*Sunday Times*, 9 October 1994), helped put the ideas of communitarianism on the political agenda (cf Etzioni, 1993, 1994; Tam, 1998). Seen as a third way between the welfare state and the libertarian individualism of the free market, communitarianism, in its political form, represented by the writings of Amitai Etzioni, has criticized the overemphasis on individual rights and called for greater responsibility in family life and child-rearing, workfare, punishment as a public ritual, community service and moral education in schools. Communitarianism in its political form, as compared to philosophical critique of liberal political philosophy, is an increasingly heterogeneous body of thought, which includes both conservative and liberal variants. In the United States, communitarian ideas have been hugely influential in the Clinton presidency (especially with the appointment of William Galston as Deputy Assistant to the President for domestic policy, who is now the chair of the National Commission on Civic Renewal) and in Britain, communitarianism is represented both by the civic conservatism of David Willetts and the interesting combination of Demos new think and Christian ethical socialist thinking, which appears to be influencing Tony Blair, David Blunkett and Jack Straw. The extent to which this civic moralism is actually shaping New Labour politics, and therefore government policy in Britain, is an important and interesting question.

In the academy the study of citizenship and its relationship to political identity had become, by the 1990s, a major growth area in the social sciences with an increasing number of conferences, newly established research centres and numerous publications, including the recent international academic journal, *Citizenship Studies*, edited by Professor Bryan C Turner (cf Kymlicka and Norman, 1995; Shafir, 1998). At the same time, within the study of political theory, the communitarian critique of liberal individualism became a major subject area with its own extensive theoretical literature (*vide* Mulhall and Swift, 1996)[1] and both historians of political thought and political theorists have examined the elisions between the discourses of liberal individualism, popular constitutionalism and civic republicanism (cf Oldfield, 1990; Terchek, 1997; Daggar, 1997; Petit, 1997). Within democratic theory, the theorization of the politics of difference and the rise of multiculturalism and the politics of recognition have raised the very real issue of whether or not a shared political identity is either realisable or desirable (Elshtain, 1995; Taylor, 1994; Wolin, 1993; Kymlicka, 1995). The revival of the concept of citizenship in contemporary political discourse and the study of it in the academy have led to some fundamental questions being asked about the nature and purpose of education, including higher education itself.

In the early 1990s the public concern with the decline of civic participation became an important issue on the agenda for educational reform. Following on from the establishment of the national curriculum in 1988, in 1990 the National Curriculum Council produced its Curriculum Guidance Booklet 8 on Citizenship Education, which provided a set of objectives but not a definitive syllabus for citizenship education as a cross-curriculum theme in England. (For Wales, for example, the concept of community was used.) The objectives of this education for citizenship, stated in terms of knowledge, skills and attitudes, were to be pursued by developing personal and shared moral values. These were not clearly defined and to a large extent the proposals shared the objectives of the schools programmes for Personal and Social Education (PSE), which had already been created in many schools in the mid- 1980s (cf Sedgwick, 1994). What the curriculum booklet did not make clear was how the philosophical, moral and political issues concerning citizenship would be addressed in the new national curriculum. Nevertheless, the work of the Centre for Citizenship Studies in Education at Leicester University, the Institute for Citizenship Studies, set up with corporate backing, and the Citizenship Foundation, created by the Law Society, attempted to promote and develop programmes of citizenship education (cf Jones and Jones, 1992; Edwards and Fogelman, 1993; Speaker's Commission, 1990). By 1994, however, the Dearing Report, in reducing the scope of the national curriculum, contained no reference to citizenship education and this reinforced the lack of any obligation for schools to undertake it as a cross-curricular theme.

The apparent neglect of citizenship education as a cross-curricular theme in schools since 1990 has also highlighted the issue of the lack of time and training for teachers in this subject area. There is a great deal of innovation and variety in Personal and Social Education but the effective teaching of citizenship would require teachers being able to develop skills in critical thinking (cf Costello, 1995)[2] as well as the knowledge required for political literacy. The very real difficulty of defining citizenship and therefore its context also contributes to the limited development of citizenship education. A study of trainee teachers on the concept of citizenship by Madeleine Arnot and Gabrielle Ivinson showed that less that 10 per cent of a sample of 375 secondary school teachers in England and Wales said that they felt uncomfortable teaching education for citizenship. This was because many felt that citizenship was a value-laden and inappropriate concept to impose on multicultural classrooms (THES 31 January 1997; Tomlinson, 1992; Callan, 1997).[3] Yet at the same time, Dr Nick Tate, the QCA chief executive, while developing an open-minded approach to defining what should be civic education, has also argued that British values should be a central part of citizenship education. The issue of multiculturalism and the politics of difference raises crucial questions about how citizenship is defined and how an education for citizenship can recognize difference while providing the framework for a shared political identity based on historical traditions and contemporary social and political reality. Perhaps the most fundamental criticisms of the NCC Curriculum Guidance 8 booklet on Citizenship Education centres on the general lack of clarity of what the values of citizenship might be and that such a definition of values raises the question of whether conflicting beliefs and values should be part of the schools curriculum (Porter, 1993). The teaching of 'political literacy' advocated by Bernard Crick and the Programme for Political Education (1974–77) called not only for the toleration of different political values but also the knowledge and skills necessary to argue critically about political attitudes and values, and it is still an important document for considering the development of a curriculum for education in citizenship (Crick and Porter, 1978).

The recent Crick Committee report (QCA, 1998) on *Education for Citizenship and the Teaching of Democracy in Schools* has reintroduced citizenship and service learning as a key feature in the debate over the structure and delivery of the national curriculum. According to the excellent research being undertaken by David Kerr of the National Foundation for Educational Research (NFER), there are a wide variety of opinions as to what should constitute an education for citizenship in the UK (Crick Report, 1998; Kerr, 1997; Kennedy, 1997; Hahn, 1998). The development of active citizenship is seen as including education in critical thinking, political literacy, moral values, spiritual values, emotional literacy etc, and increasingly there is also recognition of the importance of the principles of experiential learning. CSV and other voluntary sector organizations have highlighted the importance of encouraging awareness of the importance of civil society and social responsibility alongside political awareness and political participation. Many schools in the UK and the United States provide school students with the opportunity to engage in experiential learning based upon community service and this has been termed service-learning (Potter, 1990; Erickson and Anderson, 1997). In schools, the problem for teachers will be to integrate education for citizenship, including the opportunity to engage in service learning, into a national curriculum that is already overcrowded. The Crick Committee report has recognized that: 'However, if citizenship education is to be accepted as important, not only for schools but for the life of the nation, it must continue beyond the age of 16' (Crick Report, Sect. 5.5). This consideration about the teaching of democratic values and the place of service learning in the community in schools is one that also raises some important questions about the organization of the undergraduate curriculum in higher education in Britain.

One of the main aims of higher education, according to the Dearing Report on *Higher Education in the Learning Society*, is to contribute to a democratic, civilized and inclusive society. Indeed the Robbins Report on higher education (1963) had argued that one of the main aims of higher education was to transmit a common culture and standards of citizenship. The emphasis on citizenship highlights the need for the curriculum in higher education to prepare graduates to become active citizens and to participate not only in formal politics but also play a leadership role in civil society. This emphasis on citizenship should not only be on social responsibility or duty but also on rights and democratic participation. The challenge for higher education in the UK will be to consider how such a development will take place in the curriculum, which is organized largely on the centrality of academic disciplines and in which there will be unease about providing education for citizenship. The increasing emphasis in the Dearing Report on *Higher Education in the Learning Society* on the organization and outcomes of the learning experiences of students and the achievement of key skills and capabilities, and not just subject-based knowledge, as the aim of a higher education is part of the post-Dearing debate about what will be the future of higher education in Britain. It is in this context that I would like now to examine some ways in which citizenship education has been introduced into higher education in Britain and the United States since the late 1980s.

Higher education in Britain is rapidly becoming a mass system, perhaps on the model of the United States. With a participation rate approaching 35 per cent and the ending of the binary divide, the higher education system in Britain now faces the challenge of its own Dearing Commission Report and the implications of the upgrading of the status and role of further education. According to Peter Scott, the result is a disjunction, even a paradox. British higher education has become a mass system in its public structures, but remains an elite one in its private instincts (cf Scott, 1995; Oakley, 1992; Halsey, 1995). The development of the mass system of higher education in the United States began in the 1960s during a period of sustained economic growth and an optimistic political age. In Britain, its development in the 1990s has been against a background of scepticism and uncertainty. The rise of the multiversity began in the 1960s and is made up of many academic departments and institutes, where the totality of the whole is organized on the pragmatic principles of administrative convenience. The multiversity was seen as crucially producing and reproducing knowledge through the semi-autonomous activities of its professors, departments, institutes, colleges and faculties. For A H Halsey (1995), this whole process of change in Britain has resulted in what he terms the decline of donnish dominion. Yet the process should not be seen as a simple linear one, nor determined by the US model. Much of the literature of the subject has either focused on the history of changing institutional forms and systems or emphasized the university as a mainly research-oriented institution. The academic study of the higher education curriculum, however, raises some important questions about how we can understand the changing nature of the higher education system. These changes, rather than being viewed as a threat to academic standards or even academic freedom, can also be seen as a process of integrating the university into democratic society.

A central feature of higher education since the late 19th century has been the power and influence of the academic disciplines and their professional identities and organizations. I raise the topic of disciplines for two reasons: one – because citizenship study as a subject area is essentially interdisciplinary and it therefore faces the challenge of crossing disciplinary boundaries, and two – the subject area is a meta-discipline, as it attempts to contribute to the development of a curriculum framework for the whole academic community.

In many recent studies of higher education the specialization of academic disciplines has been seen as one of the main factors in the disappearance of a common academic community. According to the Carnegie Commission Report on the Undergraduate Experience in America, 'Too many campuses, we found, are divided by narrow departmental interest that become obstacles to learning in a richer sense. Students and faculty, like passengers on an airplane, are members of a community of convenience' (Boyer, 1987: 83; cf Barnett, 1994). Professor Ron Barnett, in his study of the idea of higher education (1990), has written, 'So, a key curriculum question in higher education is this: Can a discipline based curriculum fulfil the wider objectives, objectives which call for individual disciplines to be transcended? Can a programme of studies which is organized around a particular discipline engender an understanding of its limitations, and indeed a place in the total map of knowledge?' (Barnett, 1990: 177; Becher, 1989; Bender and Schorske, 1997). The question of what will be the future of academic disciplines is a complicated one. According to the anthropologist Clifford Geertz, there has been a 'blurring of genres' as academic disciplines as interpretive communities seek to establish new configurations for the organization of the production and reproduction of academic knowledge and in doing so, begin to move across disciplinary boundaries. While academic disciplines may provide obstacles to rethinking the curriculum they could also provide the possibility of producing new interdisciplinary and multidisciplinary perspectives from within their disciplinary configurations. The development of a core curriculum in higher education might possibly lead to a reconfiguration of the map of academic knowledge and a change to the dominance of the academic disciplines. The challenge facing the academic disciplines is how they will respond to these changes by not only rethinking the teaching and assessment practices within the disciplines but also by contributing to the discussion about what a core curriculum might be for undergraduate education.

In the United States, the conflict between the idea of multiversity and the search for academic community and the demand for public accountability has led some conservative critics, like Allan Bloom, Dinesh DSouza, Roger Kimball, *et al*, to criticize the university for morally failing or even corrupting its students. This debate about the curriculum has centred on the role of classic or canonical texts in the liberal arts curriculum, which are being challenged by the rise of post-modernism, feminism, multiculturalism and the politics of difference on the campus (Annette, 1994).

In a very important book, which also brings us straight to the nub of the problem, *The Aristocracy of Everyone* (1992), Benjamin Barber writes:

'Where Tocqueville saw in the gradual development of the principle of equality... as a Providential Act, Bloom, Bennett and company are moved by anxiety, sometimes, it seems almost by terror, and rush forward to reclaim a vanished past... We live today in Tocqueville's vast new world of contractual associations – both political and economic – in which people interact as private persons linked only by contract and mutual self interest; a world of diverse groups struggling for separate identities through which they might count for something politically in the national community'. (p 128)

For Barber, the fundamental problem facing higher education is not moral corruption or post-modern nihilism, but the challenge of providing students with the 'literacy required to live in a civil society, the competence to participate in democratic communities, the ability to think critically and act deliberately in a pluralistic world, the empathy that permits us to hear and thus accommodate others, all involve skills that must be acquired' (Barber, 1992: 4). The debate about political correctness is therefore much more fundamentally about how a university education can provide students with the knowledge and skills to participate fully in a democratic society. While recognizing the politics of difference it should also provide students with an historical and critical understanding of a shared moral and political vocabulary to enable them to participate in what Michael Oakshott described as the 'poetry of the conversation of mankind' (Oakshott, 1951). I would argue that service learning in the community provides one of the most effective learning experiences, which establishes a way of realizing an education for citizenship in higher education. I would also argue that it enables students to develop key skills and capabilities and that it is one of the best examples of active learning, which prepares graduates for lifelong learning.

The Dearing Report (NICHE, 1997) follows on from an increasing range of work done since the 1970s, which has emphasized the importance in higher education of the development of what has been termed transferable, personal, core or key skills (cf Drew, 1998). In the report the four key skills that graduates should develop are communication skills, the ability to use number, the use of information technology, and learning how to learn. The final skills of learning to learn are seen as essential for preparing students for lifelong learning in an age in which specific knowledge can quickly become obsolete. The challenge for higher education is to provide an academic framework that is based on the acquisition of critical knowledge, which is mostly structured upon the present framework established by the academic disciplines, and which provides students with the opportunity to develop essential key skills and capabilities. The Dearing report also emphasizes the need for higher education institutions to foster an active approach to learning and it argues:

> For this to be possible, students must have access to more than just the articulation of knowledge in the form of books and lectures. They also need practical experiences that rehearses them in the professional or scholarly skills of their field, and the opportunity to develop their own understanding and point of view in an environment that gives constructive feedback... Such a vision puts

students at the centre of the learning and teaching process and places new challenges and demands upon teachers... We believe that achievement of our vision will establish the United Kingdom(UK) as a leader in the world of learning and teaching at higher levels. (NICHE, sect 8.3)

It is important to recognize that the organization and delivery of such learning involves essential partnerships between academic teaching staff and academic administrative staff, including staff in careers advice services, placement offices and, increasingly, community service learning offices. It is interesting to note that it was often these academic non-teaching staff, alongside pioneering academic teaching staff, who made a major contribution to the development of and research into key skills and capabilities learning since the 1970s, eg the work funded by the Enterprise in Higher Education and the research work on work experience funded by the Department of Employment. More recently, the DfEE has been supporting development work into key skills and work experience in higher education and its significance is reflected in the CVCP/DfEE report on *Skills Development in Higher Education* (CVCP/DfEE, 1999).

An important way in which students can develop key skills through work experience and experientially realize education for citizenship is through service learning. At the core of community service learning is the pedagogy of experiential learning, which is based on the thought of John Dewey and more recently David Kolb *et al* and which has paralleled the growth of cognitive and development psychological analysis of moral development linked to the writings of Carol Gilligan, Lawrence Kohlberg, etc (Kolb, 1984; Weil and McGill, 1989). In the United States the National Society for Experiential Education (NSEE) has since 1971 been engaged in the development of and research into experiential education. More recently, the American Association of Higher Education (AAHE), in partnership with the Corporation for National Service, has commissioned volumes by leading academic figures to examine the importance of service learning in higher education. What is impressive about the work of the NSEE and the AAHE is that there is research done on not only pedagogic practices but also, going beyond anecdotal evidence, there is research into the evaluation of the learning outcomes of service learning.[4] The Dearing Report 'endorses the value of some exposure of the student to the wider world as part of a programme of study'. And it states that 'This may be achieved through work experience, involvement in student union activities, or in work in community or voluntary settings' (NICHE, Sect. 9.26). In the UK the DfEE has supported research into work experience but only recently has it begun to support research into community service learning, eg FDTL projects such as CoBaLT (Brennan and Little, 1996; Harvey, 1998; Little, 1998).[5] What is important about community service learning is that it is multidisciplinary and can be integrated into a wide variety of academic disciplines and learning experiences, which could also include environmental and global study and the opportunity for students to undertake community service learning while studying abroad, especially through the EU-funded Socrates network. Community service learning can be established generically across a university but a major challenge facing universities will be to encourage disciplinary and multidisciplinary community service learning in the subject-based curriculum.

The provision of the opportunity for students to participate in community service learning also requires partnerships with the university's local communities. It is interesting to note that the CVCP report on *Universities and Communities* (1994) highlights the role of universities in local and regional development but, except for the appendix by John Mohan, it does not consider how university and community partnerships will impact upon the curriculum of higher education (CVCP, 1994; cf Elliott, 1996). The increasing recognition of the need to provide students with the opportunities to develop key skills and capabilities in higher education, in order to prepare them for lifelong learning, should hopefully encourage academics to consider how learning in the community will best provide such learning experiences. It should also encourage them to examine how the delivery of the curriculum will best meet the needs of local communities (cf Watson and Taylor, 1998).

In the United States there has since the 1960s been a tradition of community service learning based upon the principles of experiential education. A very large number of higher education institutions now provide support for community service learning and increasing numbers of university presidents have committed their institutions to this type of learning through membership of the organization Campus Compact (Jacoby, 1996). Professor Benjamin Barber, in a number of influential articles and books, has advocated the education for active citizenship in higher education through engaging in critical thinking and through community service learning. At Rutgers University, Professor Benjamin Barber has established the Citizenship and Service Education (CASE) programme, which has become an important national model of such an education for citizenship.[6]

While there has been a tradition of community-based internship and experiential education since the 1960s, the new emphasis in the United States since the 1990s has been on citizenship education (cf Rimmerman, 1997; Reeher and Cammarano, 1997; Guarasci and Cornwall, 1997; Battistoni and Hudson, 1997). This is reflected in the growing influence of communitarian politics, especially in the administration of President Bill Clinton. In May 1993, President Clinton outlined proposals for a new type of national service in which one or two years of post-school national service would be paid in the form of a grant towards the cost of education or training. Later in that year, the

National and Community Service Trust Act (NCSTA) was passed into legislation. At present the Corporation for National Service administers a number of programmes that support service in the community and it also provides backing for research into community service learning in schools (K-12) and higher education (cf Mohan, 1994; Waldman, 1995). In Britain, James McCormick in a pamphlet on Citizens Service for the Institute For Public Policy Research (1994) has argued for a national voluntary Citizens Service initiative and David Blunkett has discussed the possibility of a national programme of community service (cf McCormick, 1994; Gorham, 1992).

What was disappointing about the Dearing Report was that it did not more directly address the issue of what would be the role of universities in relationship to their local communities. In particular, it did not consider how the re-thinking of the university curriculum should take into account the needs for citizenship education and the benefits of service learning in the community. (This criticism is perhaps unfair given the vision of the report and the range of topics covered.) The Community Service Volunteers (CSV) have, for example, been promoting and facilitating service learning in higher education by working in partnerships with a number of institutions of higher education in Britain and its SCENE network is now renaming itself the Council for Citizenship and Service Learning (CCSL). The aims of this national multidisciplinary and community-linked network is to promote community service learning through higher learning that is accredited or certified for key skills and which meets community needs (Buckingham-Hatfield, 1996, 1999). Some of the partner universities are the Interchange project in Liverpool (linking Liverpool, Liverpool John Moores and Liverpool Hope Universities), the Community Exchange project in Manchester (linking UMIST, Manchester, Salford and Manchester Metropolitan Universities), Napier University and the Edinburgh University Settlement Programme, The Northern Ireland Science Shop (linking the Queens University Belfast and the University of Ulster), the Roehampton Institute, etc. At Middlesex University, in addition to a large number of accredited modules in a variety of academic subjects which provide for experiential community service learning, there has recently been validated a joint-honours programme in Citizenship and Community Studies, which is the only degree programme in citizenship and community studies education offered in the UK. In this programme students achieve academic credit not only for taught modules but also for experiential service learning both within the university community and in the local communities around the university. An increasing number of universities are now offering students the opportunity to engage in student mentoring and are examining ways in which this could be either given academic credit or certified for key skills attainment. The problem with many of these programmes is that they only involve a comparatively small number of students. The debate about the need for universities to provide the opportunity for developing key skills and also for providing an education for active citizenship raises the possibility that citizenship education and community service learning could be an important feature of the core educational experience in higher education in Britain.

The challenge of introducing the study of citizenship and experiential service learning raises some central questions about the future of higher education in the post-Dearing era. With increasing access and public debate about purpose and accountability, how will the curriculum in a mass system of higher education address the needs of the academic community and its wider communities? How will generic education like citizenship and community service learning fit into the continuing dominant disciplinary framework? To what extent does student-centred learning and the use of experiential learning, as a basis of enabling students to develop key skills and capabilities, and not just to acquire knowledge, reflect how the curriculum will be organized in the future? If we are to move beyond soundbites or empty phrases about citizenship and community, it is now central for education both in schools and in higher education to debate openly the issues of education for citizenship and service learning in the community and its place in the curriculum.

Notes

1. For the philosophical statements of communitarianism the best introduction is now Mulhall, S and Swift, A (1996).
2. I would like to thank Sally Mitchell for this reference.
3. For the philosophical discussion of pluralism versus civic idealism see Callan, E (1997).
4. Cf The National Society for Experiential Education (NSEE): www.nsee.org; The American Association for Higher Education (AAHE): www.aahe.org; The Michigan Journal of Community Service Learning: www.umich.edu/ocsl/MJCSL
5. And the Community Based Learning Teamwork (CoBaLT) project: www.bham.ac.uk/cobalt
6. Cf http://www.scils.rutgers.edu/case/case.html for the CASE home page. The Web site of the Citizen's Practices network is www.cpn.org

References

Annette, J (1994) The culture war and the politics of higher education in America, in *The War of the Words*, ed S Dunant, Virago, London

Barber, B (1992) *The Aristocracy of Everyone: The politics of education and the future of America*, Oxford University Press, New York

Barber, B (1998a) *A Passion for Democracy*, Princeton University Press, Princeton

Barber, B (1998b) *A Place for Us: How to make society civil and democracy strong?*, Hill and Wang, New York

Barnett, R (1990) *The Idea of a University* (SRHE), Open University Press, Milton Keynes

Barnett, R (ed) (1994) *Academic Community: Discourse or discord?*, Jessica Kingsley, London

Battistoni, R and Hudson, W (eds) (1997) *Experiencing Citizenship: Concepts and models for service learning in political science*, AAHE, Washington, DC

Becher, T (1989) *Academic Tribes and Territories* (SRHE), Open University Press, Milton Keynes

Bell, G (ed) (1995) *Educating European Citizens*, David Fulton, London

Bender, T and Schorske, C (eds) (1997) *American Academic Culture in Transformation*, Princeton University Press, Princeton

Boyer, E (1987) *Carnegie Commission Report on the Undergraduate Experience in America*

Brennan, J and Little, B (1996) *A Review of Work Based Learning in Higher Education*, DfEE, London

Buckingham-Hatfield, S (1996) *Community Enterprise in Higher Education*, CSV, London

Buckingham-Hatfield, S (1999) *Student Community Partnerships in Higher Education*, CSV, London

Callan, E (1997) *Creating Citizens: Political education and liberal democracy*, Oxford University Press, Oxford

Costello, P (1995) Education, citizenship and critical thinking, *Early Child Development and Care*, **17** (107)

Crewe, I, Searing, D and Conover, P (1997) *Citizenship and Civic Education*, Citizenship Foundation, London

Crick, B and Porter, A (eds) (1978) *Political Education and Political Literacy*, Longman, London

CVCP (1994) *Universities and Communities*, CVCP, London

CVCP/DfEE (1999) *Skills Development in Higher Education*, CVCP/DfEE, London

Daggar, R (1997) *Civic Virtues*, Oxford University Press, Oxford

Dionne, E J (1991) *Why Americans Hate Politics*, Simon and Schuster, New York

Dionne, E J Jr (1998) *Community Works: The revival of civil society in America*, Brookings Institution Press, Washington, DC

Drew, S (1998) *Key Skills in Higher Education: Background and rationale*, SEDA Special No 6, March

Edwards, J and Fogelman, K (eds) (1993) *Developing Citizenship in the Curriculum*, David Fulton, London

Elliott, J *et al* (1996) *Communities and Their Universities: The challenge of lifelong learning*, Lawrence and Wishart, London

Elshtain, J B (1995) *Democracy on Trial*, HarperCollins, New York

Erickson, J and Anderson, J (eds) (1997) *Learning with the Community: Concepts and models for service-learning in teacher education*, American Association for Higher Education (AAHE), Washington, DC

Etzioni, A (1993) *The Spirit of Community*, Simon & Schuster, New York

Etzioni, A (1994) The man with the big idea, *The Sunday Times*, 9 October

Etzioni, A (1995) *New Communitarian Thinking*, University Press of Virginia, Charlottesville.

Fogelman, K (1991) *Citizenship in Schools*, David Fulton, London

Giddens, A (1998) *The Third Way: The renewal of social democracy*, Polity, Cambridge

Gorham, E (1992) *National Service, Citizenship and Political Education*, SUNY Press, New York

Gray, J (1997) *Endgames: Questions in late modern political thought*, Polity, Cambridge

Greider, W (1992) *Who Will Tell the People?*, Simon & Schuster, New York

Guarasci, R and Cornwall, G (eds) (1997) *Democratic Education in an Age of Difference*, Jossey-Bass, San Francisco

Hahn, C (1998) *Becoming Political: Comparative perspectives on citizenship education*, SUNY Press, New York

Halsey, A H (1995) *The Decline of Donnish Dominion*, Clarendon Press, Oxford

Harvey, L *et al* (1998) *Work Experience: Expanding opportunities for undergraduates*, Centre for Research into Quality, University of Central England, Birmingham

Jacoby, B (1996) *Service Learning in Higher Education*, Jossey-Bass, San Francisco and Campus Compact: www.compact.org

Jones, E B and Jones, N (eds) (1992) *Education for Citizenship*, Kogan Page, London

Kennedy, K (ed) (1997) *Citizenship Education and the Modern State*, Falmer, London

Kerr, D (1997) *Citizenship Education Revisited – National Case Study: England*, National Foundation for Educational Research, Slough

Kolb, D (1984) *Experiential Learning: Experience as the source of learning and development*, Prentice Hall, Englewood Cliffs, NJ

Kymlicka, W (1995) *Multicultural Citizenship*, Oxford University Press, Oxford

Kymlicka, W and Norman, W (1995) Return of the citizen: a survey of recent work on citizenship theory, in *Theorizing Citizenship*, ed R Beiner, State University of New York Press, Albany

Little, B (1998) *Developing Key Skills through Work Placement*, CIHE, London

Lynch, J (1992) *Education for Citizenship in a Multicultural Society*, Cassell, London

McCormick, J (1994) *Citizens Service*, IPPR, London

Mohan, J (1994) What can you do for your country? arguments for and against Clinton's national service legislation, *Policy and Politics*, **22** (4) and the Corporation for National Service: www.cns.gov

Mulhall, S and Swift, A (1996) *Liberals and Communitarians*, 2nd edn, Blackwells, Oxford

National Committee of Inquiry into Higher Education (NICHE) (1997) *Higher Education in the Learning Society (The Dearing Report)*, NICHE, London

Oakley, F (1992) *Community of Learning: The American college and the liberal arts tradition*, Oxford University Press, New York

Oakshott, Michael (1951) *Political Education*, Bowes and Bowes, Cambridge

Oldfield, A (1990) *Citizenship and Community: Civic republicanism and the modern world*, Routledge, London

Oliver, D and Heater, D (1994) *The Foundations of Citizenship*, Harvester Wheatsheaf, London

Petit, P (1997) *Republicanism*, Oxford University Press, Oxford

Porter, A (1993) Impoverished concepts of citizenship in the debate on the National Curriculum, in *Diversity, Citizenship and the National Curriculum Debate*, ed J Gundara and A Porter, Institute of Education, London

Potter, J (1990) *A Guide to Community Service Learning*, CSV, London

Pring, R (1995) *Closing the Gap: Liberal education and vocational preparation*, Hodder and Stoughton, London

Prior, D *et al* (1995) *Citizenship: Rights, community and participation*, Pitman Publishing, London

Putnam, R (1995) Bowling alone: America's declining social capital, *Journal of Democracy*, **6**

Putnam, R (1996) The strange disappearance of civic America, *America Prospect*, Winter (www.epn.org/prospect/24/24putn.html)

QCA (1998) *Education for Citizenship and the Teaching of Democracy in Schools: Advisory group on citizenship (Crick Committee)*, QCA, London

Reeher, G and Cammarano, J (eds) (1997) *Education for Citizenship*, Rowman and Littlefield, Lanham, MD

Rimmerman, C (1997) *The New Citizenship*, Westview Press, New York

Scott, P (1995) *The Meanings of Mass Higher Education*, SRHE, Open University Press, Milton Keynes

Sedgwick, F (1994) *Personal, Social and Moral Education*, David Fulton, London

Shafir, G (ed) (1998) *The Citizenship Debates*, University of Minnesota Press, Minneapolis

Speaker's Commission on Citizenship (1990) *Encouraging Citizenship*, HMSO, London

Tam, H (1998) *Communitarianism*, Macmillan, Oxford

Taylor, C (ed) (1994) *Multiculturalism and the Politics of Recognition*, 2nd edn, Princeton University Press, Princeton, NJ

Terchek, R (1997) *Republican Paradoxes and Liberal Anxieties*, Rowman and Littlefield, Lanham, MD

Tomlinson, S (1992) Citizenship and minorities, in *Education for Citizenship*, ed E B Jones and N Jones, Kogan Page, London

Waldman, S (1995) *The Bill: How legislation really becomes law – the case study of the National Service Bill*, Penguin Books, New York

Watson, D and Taylor, R (1998) *Lifelong Learning and the University*, Falmer, London

Weil, S W and McGill, I (eds) (1989) *Making Sense of Experiential Learning*, SRHE and Open University Press, Milton Keynes

Wolin, S (1993) Democracy, difference and re-cognition, *Political Theory*, **21** (3)

Wuthnow, R (1998) *Loose Connections*, Harvard University Press, Harvard

PART THREE

TEACHER EDUCATION AND VALUES

Chapter 9

The Moralization of Teaching: A Relational Approach as an Ethical Framework in the Professional Preparation and Formation of Teachers

Michael Totterdell

Introduction

In recent years educators have been trying to open up a neglected theme in the curriculum of teacher education for critical scrutiny and reconsideration; to identify issues in a relevant educational context that might be the focus for others to analyse and debate. The theme in question is how the moral gesture of teaching – which implies that not only what is taught, but how it is taught has to carry values assurances – might be transposed into an ethical orientation worthy of a democratic profession.[1] Because teachers will stand as gate-keepers to increasingly powerful forms of knowledge and to the powers of discrimination required to use them wisely and for the good of others, many foresee an increasing emphasis on ethics in the teacher's role. In what follows, I have written to provoke questions and thought about the 'state we're in' and to make a tentative proposal rather than to attempt a definitive analysis. However, by seeking to set forth a case for a teaching orientation process involving an ethical focus, I hope to press for a realistic but visionary strategy.

The new National Curriculum for Initial Teacher Training (DfEE, 1998) has been widely perceived by educationists as a 'deficit model' (Wilkins,

1999). What now seems clear is that as a consequence of disappointing learning outcomes among pupils and related poor inspection performance amongst teachers, a curative educational policy has been implemented with the express purpose of raising the standards of teacher preparation. While the standards specified for newly qualified teachers are largely unobjectionable in and of themselves, they do tend to reduce 'teaching' to programmatic competences or operational skills amenable to 'success criteria' and judgements about quality based on inspection evidence (see eg Ofsted/TTA, 1997/98). By emphasizing a narrowly conceived professionalization and underestimating the relational dynamics of teaching and learning, there is a real danger that the preparation of teachers may serve not so much to 'demystify' teaching and return it to its supposed simplicity as to demoralize [sic] it. Thus intercultural issues which stress the interactive element in the learning process are largely avoided and attention is diverted from any consideration of the vices and virtues in the practice of teaching – that is, what makes the practice of teaching bad and what makes it good.

But it is not only the structure of teacher preparation programmes that poses a problem for identifying a clear educational–professional ethic. There are also intrinsic difficulties. 'Don't try to teach a pig to sing,' said a teacher once. 'It's a waste of your time, and it irritates the pig!' Such sentiments nicely capture the feelings many teachers harbour about teaching morality; teacher educators hold similar reservations. Even operating under the more subtle auspices of 'professional ethics', they genuinely fear the prospect of creating stridently moralizing environments. Yet most will readily affirm that education is a moral endeavour, not a neutral one; if moral concerns about values, relationships and purposes are not at education's heart and are not cultivated as such, the whole enterprise disintegrates. Moreover, teaching likes to think of itself as a profession and professionalism is about the ability to articulate and defend that which one does on behalf of others – not just in instrumental or prudential terms, but also in moral and ethical ones.

Is it then the case that teacher educators are faced with a stark choice: either go with their intuition and abjure from any appearance of transmitting a prescriptive ethic, or attend more assiduously to the logic of their own moral sentiments and be in the business of moral tutelage. I would hazard a guess that the vast majority of educationists would feel unhappy with such 'either/or' approaches. On the one hand, I suspect they regard moral issues as far too slippery for a concern with the moral dimension to lead one willy-nilly into moral instruction. But on the other, they may not be able so readily to identify where it does lead. In part, this may well stem from the prevailing intellectual viewpoint that there is now no recognized moral knowledge upon which projects of fostering moral development could be based. However, as Mary Midgley (1995) has recently reminded us, this reticence may also derive from the discernment that there is something paradoxical about the interplay of the intellectual and moral aspects of life that education somehow highlights. Morality occupies a place between instinct and reason and cannot be reduced to either. Attempts to promote moral wisdom which seeks to extrude the moral via the intellectual in a crude manner, or 'content-free' strategies for moral development grounded entirely in some 'process' which tends to obfuscate any responsibility for acquiring an ethical orientation, are likely to be equally unacceptable (cf Pring, 1995: 134ff).

Nevertheless, if teaching is to sustain its claim to professional status, it not only needs a professional structure, supported by a framework of national standards, but also a professional ethic based on a sense of collective responsibility which reflects its obligations and aspirations. In turn, this will need to rest on educational values and principles attuned to democratic community and to the civic competencies and axioms of social justice that underpin it. Thus, it seems highly desirable that the preparation and formation of future teachers should carry with it accountability to established colleagues, to other stakeholders and to society in general, not only for high, consistent and common standards of didactic and pedagogical competence, but also for comparable standards of ethical conduct and integrity. In so doing, it would be deepening the moral culture of teaching.

The moral dimension, after all, is a pervasive and inescapable fact of our human existence and moral autism in teachers is clearly intolerable. For morality is not just one human enterprise among others, it is the base that makes other enterprises such as teaching and learning possible, and the vantage point from which they are judged. Moralities as ethical systems parallel languages as linguistic ones: we do not invent them by our individual choices, but they must be learnt. Hence part of the task of educational leaders is to equip their protégés with a usable moral vocabulary and exercise them in the grammar of its use. It is quite misguided to claim we can produce effective teachers with 'high standards', attested by classroom performance, without giving comparable attention to their values base and character. Indeed, because they are crucial to finding effective solutions to the challenges of social regeneration and to ensuring the flourishing of human beings in society-at-large in the global context of the 21st century, we cannot renege on our duty both to strengthen the moral disposition of beginning teachers and to cultivate their attachment to a coherent ethic as part of their professional formation.

Moral muddle, cultural attenuation and the déshabillé of professionals

There is also an urgency about the need to bolster the ethical self-consciousness and moral engagement of the teaching profession. It derives from three closely related factors that reflect the seriousness of the current situation both in schools and society. The first is the perception of moral breakdown and the associated belief that our young people are growing up without any adequate values. As Christopher Lasch (1995), one of the more perceptive and independently minded observers of our time, has put it:

> Many young people are morally at sea. They resent the ethical demands of 'society' as infringements of their personal freedom. They believe that their rights as individuals include the right to 'create their own values,' but they cannot explain what that means, aside from the right to do as they please. They cannot seem to grasp the idea that 'values' imply some principle of moral obligation. They insist that they owe nothing to 'society' – an abstraction that dominates their attempts to think about social and moral issues. (p 180)

The widespread phenomenon of disaffected youth has given rise to growing public disquiet and to a certain wariness in the profession itself.[2] Many worry that moral education has been played down in schools and too many children receive what Etzioni (1993) has labelled a 'morally careless education'. After years of neglect, there has been a renewal of public debate about how the moral values necessary to a free and orderly society can best be imbued in the next generation.

The second factor is the common perception of the decay of our culture and its social fabric in the face of remorseless change, with a consequent crisis of cultural authority and what Jonathan Sacks (1997) has described as the 'fraying of the civil bond'. Regardless of how one describes the times in which we live – the post-industrial age, the post-modern or late-modern era, or the new global era – the change-rich factor seems to increase exponentially and our demographics become ever more liquid. The result is the culture of the transitory and the momentary: a lust for immediate gratification, a universal concern with the self and what Vattimo (1988: 40) profiles as 'a new ideal of emancipation based on oscillation, plurality and, ultimately, on the erosion of the very "principle of reality"'. Our post-religious, secular society is no longer able to live off the moral capital of the creeds it has rejected nor defend the fading remnants of a dying culture by saving the appearances. In the context of what is now generally recognized as a spiritual and moral deficit in the West, how can educators resist what Philip Rieff (1985), addressing fellow teachers, describes as the 'downward identification' that threatens any form of culture at all? On what basis can they undertake an inventory of values so as to reclaim depth, meaning and a sense of connections in life? Some such revaluation of what education is for and what it should be attempting to provide for young people seems essential. Otherwise, how are their teachers to help them grow up in a complex and rapidly changing world and encourage them to build their identities on something other than their appearance – with the consequence that in this shrunken existence, we find virtually no substance behind the appearance and "meaning" gets hollowed out of their world and replaced with "image"' (Sherman, 1996: 31).

The third factor is the corrosion of professionalism that comes with the transformation of the ethos of public service into a contract culture. In the public sector, institutions with a long history of civic service have been 're-formed', 'modernized' and redefined into 'commercial delivery systems'. The emphasis on recontextualizing schools, colleges and universities within an educational marketplace where performance is judged by outcomes against set targets has led to difficulties in planning for the long term as people feel they have little control over their employment futures. These developments dilute any sense of connection to the workplace and to the community and have led among both aspiring and practising teachers to a waning of the *frisson* that characteristically accompanied a sense of vocation to pioneering work in urban schools and a blurring of the concomitant moral impulse for attempted socio-cultural transformation (cf Grace, 1997).

Neo-capitalist management strategies that focus exclusively on cost effectiveness and efficiency leave limited opportunities for people to construct a coherent narrative of their lives and make it difficult for them to build a sense of self-respect and self-worth out of their working lives (cf Sennett, 1998). Consequently, in the world of education, whereas formerly what has aptly been described as a 'community of educated people' (Pring, 1995) lived in the service of demanding ideals and exacting standards, it is now difficult to find a sense of 'the learning community' that is anything other than contemporary. Obsessed by cultivating the ability to stay on top of the latest trends, educators, in Lasch's (1995: 40) words, 'find it difficult to imagine a community of learning that reaches into both the past and the future and is constituted by an awareness of intergenerational obligation'. For professionals working in education, as elsewhere, ambition no longer seeks a 'competence' to raise the quality of work, in the sense of its integrity, so much as a licence to move up to places of higher consideration.

Whatever the combination of causes that have led to the destabilization of modernity – the cultural revolution of the 1960s, the erosion of truth and the loosening of the semantic base of meaning consequent upon the waning of the authority of tradition, the voices of growing national pluralism and the partisan nature of special interest groups, the rise of consumerism and the ethos of choice, etc – public life no longer has a single guiding vision. There is a growing consensus in the face of what amounts to a democratic malaise that we should demonstrate a greater openness to the need to reshape the concept of democratic public life by investing it with greater ethical specificity (Raz, 1994). The vital connection between obligation, choice and relationship needs, I suggest, to be reforged into a robust public ethic that can support the civic spirit necessary for communities of character and compassion to thrive. Otherwise, starved of civil affection and without a sense of mutual obligation, a 'remissive' culture like ours cannot long survive.[3] Leslie Lipson (1993: 3) has observed that the starting point for such a project is 'a clearer intellectual comprehension of what is at stake, resulting in a sufficient goal to impel us into collective and individual action'. Educators surely need to be a party to this. For the issue at stake is as big as whether a pluralistic society, distrustful of authority, can endure; whether, that is, it can reconstitute and sustain its sense of commonwealth and communal purpose or must inevitably abandon itself to disorientation and discord.

Reinstating the primacy of the moral gesture of teaching

If I am right in thinking that there is a certain importunity that now attaches to refocusing on the moral fabric of teaching and being explicit about the ethic underpinning it as a social practice, then what are the prospects for doing so? An emerging emphasis on the concept of reciprocal obligation as being the necessary counterpoint to the extension of choice in our society has prompted efforts to crystallize and envalue a core set of professional values and ethical principles (see eg Sockett, 1993). Furthermore, the pivotal changes in the state's programmatic purposes for education – from the 'building-a-nation' agenda, through creating autonomous active citizens for social democracy, to equipping the workforce of the future so as to compete in the global marketplace and eradicate social exclusion – together with the ideological undercurrents that have shaped its response, provide a spur to fashion an ethical framework that is sufficiently robust to reclaim some effective integrity of purpose for education as a practice in its own right. That is, the profession as such has, I suggest, a strong self-interest in wresting education from the custodianship and interventionism of the state and curbing its predilection for easy captivity to the ideologies of competing socio-political forces. An educational-professional ethic, which could be operated by teachers driven by moral purpose and which provided the means to establish a clear and accountable professional realm, might help recover and defend a conviction of education's own inviolable, albeit limited and accountable, sovereignty.

Of late, the philosophical literature on the discourse of ethics has become more diffuse (see eg MacIntyre, 1990 and Stout, 1988). This notwithstanding, I think that there is scope to strike out in a new direction by harnessing the primacy of the moral gesture of teaching through framing our professional expectations within a relational ethic. By ethic, of course, I mean not only considerations of conduct, but also concern for the pursuit of life's essential *telos*, that is the 'good life' of human flourishing in community. The renovation of a practical ethical framework – by which I understand both the nurture of an archaeology of day-to-day virtue[4] and the identification of guiding principles which will promote 'good' teachers' – is one way in which educationists can directly shape the structures that affect society. The advent of the long-awaited General Teaching Council, a burgeoning interest in professional ethics, and the scope for recasting teacher preparation and continuing professional development in terms of new models of accountability, all combine to make such an initiative timely. And besides, there is a more basic factor: rejuvenating education and the wider society with a sense of positivity is contingent upon a recovery of the kind of 'feel-good factor' recently postulated in an interview with Melvyn Bragg (Storkey, 1996: 19): 'Fundamentally, people have to feel good about being good in order for any good to happen.'

A relational ethic and a role-centred conception of moral life

A relational ethic is one that recognizes that relationship is one of the base dimensions of existence and central to human life. The significance of our relational infrastructure is apparent once we acknowledge that, in the words of Schluter and Lee (1993: 3), 'we do not, first and foremost, exist as individuals with rights against society, or as members, with responsibilities to society. We are persons in mutual relationship.' We need to retrieve in our professional discourse about teaching a sense of the person situated within, and partially constituted by, relationship with others. As John Macmurray (1961: 12) once put it, 'the personal relation of persons is constitutive of personal existence'. Acknowledging the primacy of relationships as fundamental to human flourishing leads us to advocate an ethic based on a clear-eyed estimate of the consequences of behaviour on human well-being and yet responsive to a vision of goodwill as being integral to any project of 'making good'. Furthermore, the prospect that such an ethic may exhibit a particular 'fitness for purpose' in the world of education becomes clear once it is recognized that teaching is primarily a relational occupation because a teacher teaches something to *someone*, is in a dialogue with *someone* and is responsible for *someone*. Good teaching therefore implies that there is a level of mutual trust and obligation between teacher and taught which leads most surely to learning. A relational ethic builds naturally on the close logical relationship that obtains between intimacy and good teaching (cf Merttens, 1995), as well as on a more general perspective which claims that each of us is involved in a web of

communicative relationships with others because he or she is 'a lan-
guage-using member of a community, in which interpersonal relationships
are the norm' (Scruton, 1994: 493f).

Developments in the broader cultural milieu are encouraging for retriev-
ing what Sacks (1997) calls the 'ecology of freedom' from both collectivism
and individualism. There seems to lie a growing recognition of
connectedness and mutuality in the socio-political thinking of liberalism –
for example, Ralf Dahrendorf's (1979) concern with building ligatures, encouraging the creation of norms, and reconstituting the social contract – as
well as in Communitarianism – for example, Jonathan Boswell's (1990) ad-
vocacy of 'associativeness-in-liberty'. As Alan Wolfe (1989) suggests, we need
a third way of thinking about moral obligation, one that locates moral obligation neither in the state (collectivism) nor in the market (individualism) but
in common sense, ordinary emotions, and the customary affirmations of everyday life.

Arguably, the idea that relationships matter is implicit in any com-
mon-sense view of human life. Expanded into its full conceptual and interdisciplinary framework (see Schluter and Lee, 1993), with an emphasis on
social and personal values in the ordering of public life, it distils out an ethic
based upon the principle of reciprocity and its associated requirement to engage in a reversal of perspectives (Benhabib, 1992) – one on which professionals representing diverse world-views and traditions can agree. In so far as
it implies a definition of human flourishing that recognizes human beings'
need to be understood in their inherent relatedness and deals in attributes all
members of society share, it holds out the promise of furnishing a moral consensus from which a substructure of professional relationships strong
enough to carry mutual commitment, trust and good faith can be built. Fundamental to such consensus is the recognition of a moral conception that
gives a central place to the Golden Rule ('Do unto others what you would
have them do to you') and inculcates a professional ethos in which all need to
take responsibility for the right use of power seriously. Thus responsibility is
deployed in our dealings in the world and with others such that a good relationship is to be understood primarily as a morally good relationship. Inter-
face becomes interdependence; one is responsible for and to others.

Freedom is often regarded as the key word in our definition of ourselves in
the 'modern' West; it is widely regarded as the foremost moral value of liberalism. However, this freedom can be neither absolute nor abstract but is mediated and qualified by materiality and history. Therefore, a relational ethic
holds out the possibility of a morality grounded not in negative freedom as
separation from, but rather in the question of the correct relationship between self (as it indwells the order of things) and others. The self is understood as being constituted within the discursive space of moral meaning

embodied in various social practices and traditions. Ordinary language usage of terms like 'right' and 'good' and the fact that we still seem to mean something by them is taken as giving us reasonable grounds for trusting them as indicative of the fact that it is possible to identify a broad consensus about some necessary conditions for being human and to communicate meaningfully about moral issues across boundaries. Moreover, the subtle dictum of 'doing as you would be done by', while not a description of moral behaviour *totidum verbis*, nevertheless provides a relational rule of thumb which is a powerful rallying point for professionals whose particular concerns will differ, but whose aims will in practice coincide across large swathes of policy and practice. Furthermore, while it does not demand a metaphysic, it is compatible with the core ethic of a number of world religions and can be integrated with a faith perspective.

Only the briefest sketch of the philosophical contours of a relational ethic can be attempted here (but see, *inter alia*, Thayer-Bacon, 1997). It is derived from the axiological approach of Brentano (1952) and the 'relationship-responsibility' model of Curran (1985) and offers several advantages to moral theory compared with traditional deontological, teleological or utilitarian approaches. In keeping with the insight that there is an intimate connection between morality and benevolence, it claims that any adequate conception of moral life must be derivative from, and thus centred on, goodwill. Therefore one of the central and basic questions must be, 'Is this action, trait, desire, etc, conducive to goodwill in the appropriate and relevant way?' On a relational construal, a person's moral life comprises certain salient relationships or roles he or she stands in – parent, friend, guardian, teacher, citizen, neighbour, etc. Because morality is concerned with one's roles or relationships with others, one's moral life is largely a matter of being the sort of person who fills such roles in a satisfactory way. It is, for example, a matter of having the virtues and lacking the vices of a good teacher (to somebody). In whatever role, then, virtue is recognized as a reinforced practice and vice as exceptionable within the self, the community and the wider society.

A conception of morality that is role-centred has a pleasing richness, for not only does the vocabulary of virtues seem most sensible in the context of roles, the same is true of duties and rights, obligations and choice, goodness and badness, and of 'ought' evaluations in general. In order to defend and clarify any claim that someone has a duty or obligation to someone else, we commonly specify that we meant he or she ought or has a duty as a 'something' to whomever. Thus rights, duties and virtues are relative to the roles one has, and this will be true of any putative profession to the extent that there is a shared conception of what the quality of the distinct human practice of its central good consists in.

Within the conception of morality I have been outlining, one's moral life is a matter of discharging well the various morally significant roles one fills in the lives of various persons. In each such role, being good in it depends crucially on being benevolent in some relevant way. For some roles, such as that of teacher, this consists in willing some relatively particular type of human good, for example, education – understood as initiation and induction into forms of knowledge and understanding and the cultivation of wider sensibilities. For others, the relevant notion of benevolence is a less specific one. But the basic idea of benevolence, what constitutes virtue and the common standard of duty for all these roles, is that of willing for someone the basic components of a flourishing human life. This is what virtue and the duty of goodwill are all about and suggests that moral attributes are essentially linked to the will. Malevolent desires and intentions tend to make us bad in our roles, while benevolent ones make us good in our roles.

Goodwill, then, is the ultimate duty, and any failure to exhibit it needs to be justified. An ethic that takes seriously the fact that one's moral duties are owed to this or that person on account of the role(s) one fills in the person's life will entail the fact that to act wrongly is *to wrong someone* by violating one's relationship with him or her. However, we are neither able to will to secure every good for each person, nor willing to will anybody all the good we could will him or her. In view of this limit on our goodwill, it seems reasonable to establish a floor beneath which we will not go in our departures from goodwill. In morality we need a line drawn between the kinds of deviations from goodwill which are sometimes justifiable on the grounds simply of our own projects and interests and those which are not. With an adequate account of the goods, devotion to which is constitutive of the virtues and duties of a teacher – viz., a code of ethical guidelines, we should be able to apply a similar line of argument to derive the impermissibility of breaching certain exceptionless norms of professional obligation – viz., a code of practice (cf Thompson, 1995 and Tomlinson, 1997).

Towards a pedagogy to address professional ethics

A relational ethic construed as role-centred will look first to the nature and moral purpose of the service provided by professionals, then turn its attention to the dispositions necessary for and responsibilities inherent in the proper *practice* of their good offices. This in turn provides a basis for identifying the common virtues standing on common principles, which should characterize them as moral agents. Part of the challenge remains to articulate afresh the moral purpose of teacher education. For only by contributing to building a moral community can we also be serious about creating the social capital needed for an agreeable society.[6]

How can we help beginning teachers to internalize a sense of moral conviction about a worthy 'mode of being' – one that requires them to 'be' (self identity) as they should want to be (professional image) in any particular and concrete situation, or in response to the immediacy of any contingent and specific moment? Given that values change with age and experience, on what basis can teacher education foster in these intending professionals the sort of integrity required to negotiate increasingly demanding situations?[7] Clearly there is a place for the structural embedding of ethical principles in course design and programming. More important, however, is the need to find pedagogical strategies that will facilitate the curricular integration of ethics and so encourage commitment to pertinent expressions of the profession's ideals. We should, from the start, rule out any attempt to assert ethical proprietary rights over teachers-in-the-making or their mentors. Otherwise we inevitably close rather than open doors for others in an attempt to obscure the ever-vulnerable nature of the search for moral truth and secure what Martha Nussbaum (1986) has described as 'a life of goodness without fragility'.

Also unsatisfactory are approaches that provide little or no moral sustenance but instead rely solely on 'values clarification' – with the unfortunate implication that good values are 'what one values' based on personal preference or social convenience. Nor should we substitute 'dilemma' ethics for 'basic' ethics, so that students lose sight of the fact that some things are clearly right and others clearly wrong and come to believe the very idea of a stable moral tradition to be an archaic illusion. Such approaches, while they may have legitimacy as part of a broader strategy designed to help aspiring teachers develop shared values, if used exclusively implicitly deny a structured way to develop values and abjure the teacher's traditional concern with edification.

Hopefully, too, we can learn from the failed experiment of liberal education to advance moral education in schools solely via the canon of reason. Moral reflection does not just provide a guide to action. It, and the actions that result from it, both reflect our self-understanding and crucially contribute to it. Teachers not only need a cognitive awareness of the moral realm but also a predisposition to act ethically. Indeed, rather than granting priority to reason as arbitrator of moral experience and human relating as the liberal tradition has been prone to do, we should recognize that good moral habits actually enhance one's capacity for rational judgements.

As Pádraig Hogan (1995: 15f) has argued in his powerful critique of Western education, teaching is best characterized as 'a special kind of cultural and communicative art, which seeks in essence a 'courtship of the sensibilities' – a sensitizing awareness of the fate of civilization, an openness to experience and a fostering of discrimination. Building on this insight, I offer a brief description of approaches that might contribute to the refocusing of pre-service and induction programmes and facilitate the emergence of a professional persona among beginning teachers which conspicuously exhibits an ethical orientation. I consider it desirable to counterbalance an over-reliance on generalized standards of proficiency by urging a reinstatement of values and dispositions as essential elements in teacher formation. Notions of competence, while they may have a currency in the dominant 'official' discourse of teacher training, need to be re-appropriated within a framework which gives more space for the exploration of educational values underlying 'good' practice and encourages a morally serious conversation about the insights and aspirations of education.[8]

Discussion-based learning

This first, and arguably most fundamental approach, regards 'conversation' as being a useful metaphor for a pedagogy appropriate to moral education; it seeks to build, therefore, on the 'ideal speech situations' of structured conversation, open discussion and disciplined dialogue. It can focus on a document, for example the proposed code of ethics for the teaching profession (see Tomlinson, 1997), or it can seek to dissect a problem, for example school exclusions. Alternatively it can consider a range of relevant issues – conceptions of purpose, human nature, actual and ideal communities, perceptions of value, epistemological assumptions and attitudinal contexts (see Beck and Murphy, 1994). In addition, it can seek to clarify and sort out the different ways in which we choose personal values and identify our own primary mode(s) of moral reasoning – authority, logic, experience, emotion, intuition, or 'science' (see Lewis, 1990). The resulting 'ethical criticism' may take the form of a staff supervised but peer-led communal enquiry – with students working together synergistically, following some kind of intersubjective and 'checking' methodology which hinges around four questions: what is this about?; what do we need to know and understand?; how far can we answer these questions or tackle these issues?; what questions are we left with? Alternatively, dialogic reflection may take the form of 'critical friend' dyads – engaging with another person through simulated recorded interviews which encourage talking with, questioning, even confronting, the trusted other in order to examine presuppositions and putative actions. This technique can be structured in such a way as to provide a safe environment within which self-revelation can take place. Beginning teachers are able to distance themselves from their actions, ideas and beliefs, holding them up for scrutiny in the company of peers with whom they are willing to take such risks. The interview process, and subsequent analysis of its content, creates an opportunity for giving voice to one's own thinking while at the same time being heard in a sympathetic but constructively critical way.

Narrative learning

It has long been recognized that the 'best way to convey a world adequately stocked with good and evil is a story'. 'People cast and recast themselves as they follow narratives', in the process making themselves like those who have 'good in them' because 'this is where the moral sympathies permanently reside and retain their primitive power and influence' (Martin, 1992: 238f). Furthermore, as MacIntyre (1985) notes, every agent engaged in a practice must (even if only implicitly) appeal to some narrative in which self-understanding is possible. This narrative will inevitably suggest to the practitioner some idea of his or her *telos*, ie the point or purpose of what he or she is doing. A professional must integrate some such ideal into his or her practice – there is a sense in which we are all involved in scripting our professional lives. Given that recent research and literature on teachers' lives has emphasized notions of personal identity, integrity, educational experience and philosophy (Goodson, 1992), the professional formation of teachers should provide opportunities for the beginnings of sustaining narrative for their conscious and conscientious practice. This will enrich not only preparation for the teaching process but the experience of teaching itself – equipping teachers to become moral companions to young people, who with cultural mores so enervated, find it difficult to muster an internal dialogue and appreciate the examined life is worth(y) living.

Once the beginning teacher becomes engaged with the issue of what kind of person to be, and how to become that kind of person, the problems of ethics become concrete and practical, and for many, moral development is looked upon thereafter as a natural, even inescapable undertaking. The value of the narrative method is that it can facilitate the sort of inquiry that searches for the meaning of pivotal moral words and metaphors and of the implications of moral-type actions of characters in narrative contexts. Because characters must choose, they are inherently valuing beings. Every choice implies an underlying value – a because, an ought. In the context of our professional lives, such an awareness encourages understandings and shared commitments that are central to a collective sense of moral purpose and accountability. However, we must learn to overcome our distrust of pedagogically unmediated experience and allow considerable space for reflection on a wide range of authentic literary and other perspectives, otherwise the exercise can degenerate into solicitude and didacticism.[9]

Case studies and modelling

By looking at case studies we are forced to enquire about more general principles, which can then be transferred. Case method teaching has long been the staple diet at Harvard Business School; its potential has recently begun to receive serious attention in teacher education (see Wasserman, 1993 and McAninch, 1993). With its key features of cases, study questions, small group work, debriefing the case and follow-up, it is a methodology that lends itself admirably to the context of developing professional ethics. It forces beginning teachers to eschew dependency patterns of learning, reminds them that all teaching involves the ethical in consideration of the relationship between teacher and taught and helps them to accept that in their professional roles as teachers, they have to make some difficult ethical choices about how and what to teach and why.

Complementary to the case study approach are methods based on modelling, that is, models that would mimic real-life situations through 'coded' descriptions. Ormell (1995: 3, 33) identifies modelling as the natural form of modern cognition: as he puts it, 'To cast human knowledge in an explicitly modelling form is to give maximum scope to the imagination in using and entertaining that knowledge'. It engages beginning teachers in a form of 'projection-through-imagination' which energizes the learning process and fosters 'a form of mental effort and mental discipline to be able to "go beyond the information given" and vividly entertain its implications'. Ormell incisively recognizes that it is precisely these kinds of 'fluent envisaging... imagining... and empathizing skills', the absence of which 'gives rise generally to moral aberrations', which can be harnessed by 'modelling' – whether this be through the kind of role play espoused by conflict resolution studies, via intuitive fictional models of potential human reality, or effected through computer-mediated virtual reality.

Conclusion

It is important that we should resist the sort of revisionism that, in the words of John Gray (1996), would claim that 'by returning to the hidden or neglected verities of liberal thought we can find a prescription for living together'. Wherever life's meaning is spelt out in terms of a single uni-dimensional plane of existence, its richness is attenuated and responsible living is undermined. Liberal moral perfection, in whatever principle it is idealized, is a chimera. Yet, accepting the contingency of liberal culture (as we must) can, as Lasch (1995: 87) warns us, lead to the erosion of common standards:

> The suspension of ethical judgement, in the conception or misconception of pluralism now prevalent, makes it inappropriate to speak of 'ethical commitments at all'... To refer everything to a 'plurality of ethical commitment' means

that we make no demands on anyone and acknowledge no one's right to make demands on ourselves.

Clearly we require a more invigorating ethic than the tolerance of indifference. We need to clarify how a subject involved in historical currents can acquire authentic character and apply principles to situations so as to act responsibly. Given that no one can transcend a formative milieu very far and that this matrix of thought determines one's personal calling, it is now timely to deliberate on the question of how trainee teachers might be helped to develop the insights and language to engage in meaningful discourse about ethical issues as these impinge on their professional lives. Educators will need to take on board the essential intellectual resources provided by a reconsideration of ethical traditions. Our task is to take the many parts of a complicated social and conceptual inheritance and stitch them together into a pattern that meets the need of the moment. This creative intellectual task involves moral *bricolage* – in the good sense of selective retrieval and eclectic reconfiguration of traditional linguistic elements in the hope of solving the problem at hand – but need have nothing to do with what critics in the bad sense think of as decadent postmodernist jouissance (cf Stout, 1988).

Of course, issuing a call to the teaching profession to have the courage of its convictions and refurbish its moral credentials rests on an implicit assumption. It is that the profession is ready to take seriously the possibility that education contains within itself the potential for creating an ethos among its members, to which beginning teachers will submit themselves for training and for which, because it is both politically and professionally acceptable, it can elicit support from the wider society. I have suggested that this ethos should be derived from the relational basis of teaching, and inculcated through a pedagogy appropriate for professionals who are confronted by problems which have both an immediate practical aspect and a deeper, philosophical dimension. However, if it is to constitute more than an intellectual drawbridge, which goes up once teachers withdraw from the environs of higher education and retreat behind the classroom door, it will have to become habituated in an appropriate way within every teacher's own pedagogical stance.

If we are to have some prospect of achieving such an outcome, educationists will need to take the conscious step of moving beyond the sterile debates between left and right: traditionalists and progressives do not represent mutually exclusive or exhaustive options. We can induct novice teachers into a more comprehensive and rich pattern of ethical duty towards society than that allowed by entrenched schemes either of cultural transmission or radical liberation. As an initial step, socialization: not into professional culture as a seamless web or total world-view, rather what Wittgenstein

(1969) regarded as a sort of '*vor-wissen*', a context of living and a paradigm for further inquiry. Then criticism: not as a major current which problematizes all but the critical moment, rather an awareness through Socratic-like activity that this substantive vehicle of continuing enquiry is contingent, and therefore subject at least to some extent to critique, leading in turn to a more profound apprehension of truth. Finally, contemplative imagining of comprehensive visions, which seek a view of how things are or should be in the most inclusive sense possible. Thus schooling as a liberal institution can be conceived of as oriented towards a provisional *telos* – a widely shared but self-limiting consensus on the highest good achievable under circumstances like ours. But it is a *telos* with community latent in its concepts and inherently relational in its social practices, one that justifies a kind of tolerance and openness foreign to classical teleological tradition. It rightly combines the vocabulary of virtue – which fosters the uninhibited activity of the well disposed resulting in the peaceable commerce of human beings one with another – with rights-talk – which makes it possible for everyone to take part – and thus directs our moral attention to something our forebears often neglected, namely the injustice of excluding people from social practices because of their race, gender, religion, or place of birth.

Such a curricular model will be witnessed where there is a diachronic rather than merely synchronic scholarly sensibility – open to the insights and conscious of the limitations of pre-modern, modern and post-modern perspectives (cf Lyon, 1994) so as to encompass past actualities, present alternatives and future possibilities in a way that makes possible authentic choice. This will involve what Hogan (1995) calls the 'interplay of ventured standpoints'; a conversation between horizons of interpretation concerning human being and well-being. It will invite participation in debate over the role of education in shaping the nature and direction of present-day society. It will seek to cultivate a shared sense of collective purpose, communal solidarity and participatory ethos by which any public morality can alone be sustained. It will also contribute to teachers becoming what Wilson (1992) describes as morally educated persons in the sense of having the ability to make both worthwhile attachments and judgements of merit. Of course, this is something of an educational high road; sadly, to this point, it has been a road less travelled.

Notes

1. Renewed interest in professional ethics in teaching is evidenced by the work of the Universities Council for the Education of Teachers (Tomlinson, 1997), the contribution of the Association of Teachers and Lecturers' professional development

officer Meryl Thompson (1995), and, most recently, the SCETT seminar given by the Chief Executive of QCA, Nicholas Tate, on 'The spiritual, moral, social and cultural development of pupils: implications for training and developing teachers' at the NATFHE Conference Centre, London, 1998. A related but rather different agenda is addressed in Selmes and Robb (1996). Similar developments in American Teacher Education can be traced in Strike and Soltis (1998) and are explicitly addressed in a special edition of the *Journal of Teacher Education* (Ducharme and Ducharme, 1998) on the theme of 'Ethics and Teacher Education'.

2. Widespread public disquiet reached its zenith, perhaps, at the time of the Bulger case. As Robert Whelan (1994: 1) observed, 'Can we, the adult population, really feel that we are fulfilling our obligation as citizens to civilize and socialize the next generation, when we peer into the moral void which the stories of Jamie Bulger's killers seemed to reveal?' The wider context is equally worrying according to David Cracknell (1997: 9) who, in his presidential speech to the Society of Education Officers, DEMOS, in collaboration with MORI, studied the attitudes of young people towards democracy and politics. A 'disconnection index' was devised which showed that 54 per cent of people under 25 years of age registered as profoundly disconnected from society's core institutions, their neighbourhoods and the nation itself. The American experience suggests that this dissonance is not just embedded in the message of the media (Condry, 1993). It is also apparent in the daily communication that occurs between young people and adults in both home and school (Good and Brophy, 1994).

3. Many social commentators have examined our contemporary inability to hold people responsible (see eg Wolfe, 1989). Christopher Lasch (1995: 107) captures the heart of the problem we face when, having noted with approval the Communitarian call for compassion on those needing help, he then adds, 'But it is our reluctance to make demands on each other, much more than our reluctance to help those in need, that is sapping the strength of democracy today.' A trenchant critique of contemporary moral evasion is provided by David Selbourne (1999).

4. I borrow the phrase 'archaeology of virtue' from Jon Davies (1994: 7f) to indicate that level of moral life in which certain values such as honesty, reliability, trust and integrity are simply taken for granted, like the flatness of footpaths or the oblongness of bricks; the day-to-day unquestioned, ubiquitous attitudes and characteristics of 'deep culture' which form the fabric underpinning normal social habits of living.

5. Primarily, it recognizes that our intellectual work in education can no longer be carried on within the context of the 'modern' world-view typified by traditional approaches. It also accommodates much of the recent revolution in moral philosophy, which abandons the pursuit of an abstract ideal in an ethics of principle in favour of concrete ethics of virtue (with its implications for the development of moral character), while retaining a notion of commensurable ethics which incorporates what Seyla Benhabib (1992) calls 'interactive universalism'. Finally, it leads directly from value judgements to claims about how people should respond by analysing the former in terms of the latter. This is relevant as in ethics our interest is in value response more than the value itself.

6. In recent years sociologists have realized that the social relations that exist in the community constitute a form of capital which can be measured. This 'social capi-

tal' is broadly understood as involving the processes between people that establish networks, norms and social trust, and facilitate co-ordination and co-operation for mutual benefit. Schools, according to James Coleman (1988), can only be effective to the extent that they are embedded in communities that have social capital. Moreover, the amount of social capital is vital to the transmission of values.

7. Given that professionalism is in large part about how one justifies the way one's work is done (Davis, 1991), professional integrity is being willing to say, 'I am governed in my conduct by something other than my own desires' (Carter, 1996: 6). Fundamental too is the capacity to identify a baseline standard below which you will not go; a threshold of principle and practice from which you will not depart.

8. Competence should then involve a sense of vocation (implying a belief in the intrinsic value of a given line of work and its link to the public good), combined with the attributes, capacities and skills required to undertake it effectively. As such, it would be participatory and have rich moral overtones. For, to have a vocation is to be prepared to subordinate one's own personal beliefs, will and interests to the requirement of professional relationships that are unique in involving complex dimensions of power and trust (cf Weber, 1946).

9. Thought provoking examples of how this can be done are provided by Mary Midgley (1991); see also the collected papers edited respectively by Witherell and Noddings (1992).

References

Beck, L and Murphy, J (1994) *Ethics in Educational Leadership Programs*, Corwin Press, New York

Benhabib, S (1992) *Situating the Self*, Routledge, London

Boswell, J (1990) *Community and the Economy: The theory of public co-operation*, Routledge, London

Brentano, F (1952) *The Foundation and Construction of Ethics*, Humanities Press, New York

Carter, S L (1996) *Integrity*, Basic Books, New York

Coleman, J S (1988) Social capital in the creation of human capital, *American Journal of Sociology*, **94**, pp S95–S120

Condry, J (1993) Thief of time, unfaithful servant: television and the American child, *Daedalus*, **122**, pp 259–78

Cracknell, D (1997) Interdependence Through Learning And Leading, *Presidential Speech for Annual Meeting of Society of Education Officers* (17 January), pp 1–13

Curran, C (1985) *Directions in Fundamental Moral Theology*, University of Notre Dame Press, Notre Dame, IN

Dahrendorf, R (1979) *Life Chances*, Weidenfeld and Nicolson, London

Davis, J (1991) Professions, trades and the obligation to inform, *Journal of Applied Philosophy*, **8** (2)

Davies, J (1994) Re-sacralising education and re-criminalising childhood: an agenda for the year 2132, in *Teaching Right and Wrong: Have the churches failed?*, ed R Whelan, IEA Health and Welfare Unit, London

Department for Education and Employment (1998) *Teaching: High status, high standards*, Circular Number 4/98, HMSO, London

Ducharme, E R and Ducharme, M K (eds) (1998) Ethics and teacher education, special September/October theme issue of *Journal of Teacher Education*, **48** (4), pp 243–313

Etzioni, A (1993) *The Spirit of Community: Rights, responsibilities and the communitarian agenda*, Crown Publishers, New York

Good, T I and Brophy, J E (1994) *Looking in Classrooms*, HarperCollins, New York

Goodson, I F (ed) (1992) *Studying Teachers' Lives*, Routledge, London

Grace, G (1997) Politics, markets, and democratic schools: on the transformation of school leadership, in *Culture, Economy, Society*, ed A H Halsey *et al*, Oxford University Press, Oxford

Gray, J (1996) What liberalism cannot do, *New Statesman*, 20 September, pp 18–20

Hogan, P (1995) *The Custody and Courtship of Experience: Western education in philosophical perspective*, The Columba Press, Dublin

Lasch, C (1995) *The Revolt of the Elites*, Norton, New York

Lewis, H (1990) *A Question Of Values*, HarperCollins, San Francisco

Lipson, L (1993) *The Ethical Crisis of Civilisation: Moral meltdown or advance*, Sage, London

Lyon, D (1994) *Postmodernity*, Open University Press, Buckingham

MacIntyre, A (1985) *After Virtue: A study in moral theory*, 2nd edn, Duckworth, London

MacIntyre, A (1990) *Three Rival Versions of Moral Enquiry*, University of Notre Dame Press, Notre Dame, IN

Macmurray, J (1961) *Persons In Relation*, Faber and Faber, London

Martin, D (1992) Making people good – again: the role of authority, fear and example, in *The Loss of Virtue: Moral confusion and social disorder in Britain and America*, ed D Anderson, The Social Affairs Unit, London

McAninch, A R (1993) *Teacher Thinking and the Case Method*, Teachers College Press, London

Merttens, R (1995) *Pedagogy and Intimacy*, University of North London, London

Midgley, M (1991) *Can't We Make Moral Judgements?*, The Bristol Press, Bristol

Midgley, M (1995) Can education be moral?, *Prospero*, **1** (1/2), pp 10–11

Nussbaum, M (1986) *The Fragility of Goodness*, Cambridge University Press, Cambridge

Ofsted/TTA (1997/98) *Framework for the Assessment of Quality and Standards in Initial Teacher Training*, HMSO, London

Ormell, C (1995) Canonical modelling, the natural form of modern knowledge, *Prospero*, **1** (1/2), pp 30–33

Pring, R (1995) The community of educated people, *British Journal of Educational Studies*, **43** (2), pp 125–45

Raz, J (1994) *Ethics in the Public Domain*, Revised Edition, Oxford University Press, Oxford

Rieff, P (1985) *Fellow Teachers*, Chicago University Press, Chicago, IL

Sacks, J (1997) *The Politics of Hope*, Cape, London

Schluter, M and Lee, D (1993) *The R Factor*, Hodder and Stoughton, London.

Scruton, R (1994) *Modern Philosophy: An introduction and survey*, Sinclair-Stevenson, London

Selbourne, D (1999) *The Spirit of the Age*, Chatto, London

Selmes, C S G and Robb, W M (1996) *Values In Teacher Education, Volumes One and Two*, NAVET/CAVE, Aberdeen

Sennett, R (1998) *The Corrosion of Character*, Norton, New York

Sherman, A (1996) Hope dreams: looking for good news in the inner city, *Books and Culture*, **2** (3), pp 3 and 31–33

Sockett, H (1993) *The Moral Base For Teacher Professionalism*, Teachers College Press, New York

Storkey, E (1996) A tentative certainty – interview with Melvyn Bragg, *Third Way*, **19** (5), pp 16–20

Stout, J (1988) *Ethics After Babel: The languages of morals and their discontents*, James Clarke and Co, Cambridge

Strike, K A and Soltis, J F (1998) *The Ethics of Teaching*, 3rd edn, Teachers College Press, New York

Tate, N (1998) The spiritual, moral, social and cultural development of pupils: implications for training and developing teachers. Address at the NATFHE Conference Centre for the SCETT seminar

Thayer-Bacon, B J (1997) The nurturing of a relational epistemology, *Educational Theory*, **47** (2), pp 239–60

Thompson, M (1995) *Professional Ethics and the Teacher: An educated talent in the service of society*, ATL, London

Tomlinson, J (ed) (1997) *Code of Ethical Principles for the Teaching Profession*, Universities Council for the Education of Teachers Occasional Paper No. 7, UCET, London

Vattimo, G (1988) *The End of Modernity*, Polity Press, Cambridge

Wasserman, S (1993) *Getting Down to Cases: Learning about teaching from studying cases*, Teachers College Press, New York

Weber, M (1946) Science as a vocation, in *From Max Weber: Essays in sociology*, ed H H Gerth and C Wright Mills, Oxford University Press, New York

Whelan, R (ed) (1994) *Teaching Right and Wrong: Have the churches failed?*, IEA Health and Welfare Unit, London

Wilkins, M (1999) *The Role of Higher Education in Initial Teacher Education*, Universities Council for the Education of Teachers Occasional Paper No 12, UCET, London

Wilson, J (1990) *A New Introduction to Moral Education*, Cassell, London

Wilson, J (1992) Moral education, values education and prejudice reduction, in *Cultural Diversity and the Schools; Vol. 2: Prejudice, polemic or progress*, ed J Lynch, C Modgil and S Modgil, Falmer Press, London

Witherell, C and Noddings, N (eds) (1992) *Narrative and Dialogue in Education*, Teachers College Press, New York

Wittgenstein, L (1969) *On Certainty*, Blackwell, Oxford

Wolfe, A (1989) *Whose Keeper? Social science and moral obligation*, University of California Press, Berkeley

Chapter 10

A Code of the Ethical Principles Underlying Teaching as a Professional Activity

John Tomlinson and Vivienne Little

Introduction

In any circumstances where an individual or group of individuals takes responsibility for aspects of the lives of others on the grounds of special knowledge or expertise, whether in a context of public funding or not, ethical issues arise and some form of guidance for action is required. This is most emphatically the case when the recipients are below the age of consent. The UCET Conference of November 1995 set up a Working Group to propose some Ethical Principles of Teaching that might be commended to teacher educators, recognizing that, irrespective of whether there is a formal curriculum of moral education, teachers inevitably and properly convey moral ideas and principles. This chapter examines whether ethical principles are fundamental to the process of teaching itself, and if so what they are.

Advice about a curriculum of 'moral values' has been devised by national authorities for transmission through the education system. The background is a moral fear among some influential groups that 'basic values' have broken down and that the social structure will not survive unless codes of belief and behaviour are introduced. Within the surrounding public and professional debate, a difference of view is evident between those who think that attention to the development of the whole child/student is a necessary basis for teaching and those who want to limit the teacher's role to intellectual development. A further disagreement is evident between those who wish any moral teaching to assume a society in which the nuclear family is the basis, and those who accept the existence of many patterns of partnership and child-rearing. Such differences of view illustrate the perils of attempting any statement grounded in general principles, namely that it is difficult to know where the borderline of an activity so fundamentally human as learning and helping people learn can properly be set.

The values that teachers display in teaching and in managing pupils, other staff and resources are part of the values curriculum of schools. Many pupils come to recognize the usefulness and delight of scholarship and learning and the life-enhancing qualities of engaging interests through contact with teachers willing to express personal enthusiasm and excitement. Some of the most important lessons pupils learn about social relationships are derived from the ways teachers behave towards them and towards others. Are children spoken to with the same politeness accorded colleagues? Do they receive apologies if inconvenienced, misled or wrongly accused; gratitude if helpful? If so, they learn that persons are to be respected whatever their age or status. If not, they learn that rank and power are salient in relationships. Teachers who emphasize care of property and show concern for aesthetic quality, comfort and order in the classroom may convey expectations and standards that relate to wider environmental questions. Insistently and inevitably the values of teachers pervade the school curriculum.

Moreover, now societies have moved 'beyond the stable state' and change has become a constant, curricula, including values curricula, will continue to develop, just as the explosion of knowledge and the growth of a multicultural and pluralist society have been a cause of so much change since the 1950s.

Given the provisionality of knowledge and the multiplicity of values in the modern world, however, it seems that any definition of professionalism should imply loyalty to goals that may embrace but must transcend self-interest. The notion of professionalism has suffered from the intellectual assertions of the 20th century. It has become fashionable to believe that humans are not capable of altruistic acts. Altruism is just another form of self-interest, serving the purpose of the individual rather than the recipient. Thus true professionalism, rooted in serving the needs of the client rather than the donor, is a mirage. At worst, it can become a screen for self-serving acts or, as Bernard Shaw put it, a conspiracy against the laity. Such a view has been one of the causes of the demeaning of the teaching profession.

Yet any analysis of the problems of a pluralist society, where there can be no single 'common good' beyond cohesion and effectiveness, suggests that the sense of the personal and social responsibility of each individual is the key to survival. A moral sense, acknowledging both independence and interdependence, is essential. In that situation the rearing of the young in these values – lived not merely preached – becomes paramount, and the schools as the single, formal common process must play their part. This is not to indoctrinate but to liberate.

In schools of that purpose teachers see the moral growth of their pupils as pre-eminently important and thus regard for them must be their prime concern. The basis of professionalism, self-denying interest in the well-being of another, is triumphantly reconstituted. A sense of his or her personal responsibility is essential to the teacher. It needs to be maintained by continual acts of will, whatever the external pressures towards conformity to an instrumental curriculum.

A degree of autonomy for the teacher is needed, alongside the requirement for public accountability. If the intellectual and moral nurture of each new generation were in the hands of technical-rationalists it would ensure the very cultural and economic disaster that successive attempts at educational reform were designed to avert.

A balance needs to be struck between professional responsibility and public accountability. And professional responsibility, like public accountability, needs to be both individual and collective. It involves working at the enduring curriculum of humanity, that slow growth of meaning and values, which is above and beyond the official curriculum. Personal and collective professionalism has at least two aspects: conscience and a sense of vocation. Together, they give the knowledge that teaching meets your nature. Such an imperative is the opposite of the personally indulgent. The teacher's professionalism, based in education, training and experience and driven by conscience and a sense of vocation, is the best safeguard the public can have against unprincipled and inchoate value references.

To quote Mike Bottery (1997) from his paper for the UCET group:

> It seems clear then that any comprehensive reflective practice – and any comprehensive professional ethics – must embrace the wider 'ecological' dimensions of professional endeavour, as well as the principle of political independence of mind and action. (p 15)

Thus the ethical principles which inform teaching assume fundamental importance.

Analysing various approaches

Moral philosophers have usually based their work on one of two arguments, authority or purpose. That is to say that an ethical principle or basis for action may derive either from the authority accorded a precept or argument; or from the nature of the purpose intended to be achieved by the action. Broadly these are the arguments from ontology and teleology. (Ontology is to do with the nature of existence, substance and appearance, for example; teleology is to do with purposiveness in existence.)

Typically any popular morality seems to be a mixture of these two kinds of thinking. Authority is often evoked or implied – God, or the bible, or law and order, or parental duty or the duties of state and citizens within a social contract. But so is purpose; certain actions are required of citizens in order that there should be social order, family life, etc.

The same mixture seems to apply to statements about teaching. Some things done or believed by teachers derive from what is understood about the nature of children's minds and bodies and therefore about learning processes that are appropriate. Particular action by teachers appears to be based on the authority to be derived from these understandings. The understandings, of course, may change with time or, even more confusingly, rival interpretations of the nature of childhood or learning may exist at the same time. Can this kind of authority, which is based in the knowledge accepted by society and/or its teachers at any time, be said to be the kind of authority on which an ethical principle can rest or from which it can be derived? If any such derivation is to be deemed an ethical principle, because it is a description of right human action towards other humans, then the potentially transient nature of its basis entails the need to keep it under review. A philosopher might say that the authority is now epistemological, not ontological, and that teaching would entail the duty to act ethically in the sense of what is held to be most conducive to good at a particular time and in a particular situation.

Let us now look at the other possible basis for ethical principles in teaching, namely purpose.

Expressions of purpose for educators are plentiful. For the sake of argument, two may be chosen from early and recent stages of the Great Curriculum Debate 1976–96:

> 3.11 Education is not concerned only with equipping students with the knowledge and skills they need to earn a living. It must help our young people to: use leisure time creatively; have respect for other people, other cultures and other beliefs; become good citizens; think things out for themselves; pursue a healthy life-style; and, not least, value themselves and their achievements. It should develop an appreciation of the richness of our cultural heritage and of the spiritual and moral dimensions to life. It must, moreover, be concerned to serve all our children well, whatever their background, sex, creed, ethnicity or talent.

> 3.12 It is the primary school teacher who must begin to fulfil these objectives. I am very conscious of the challenge many primary school teachers face, receiving as they do children from very different backgrounds – social, economic, ethnic, religious – and varying greatly in their readiness to learn. But if children do not leave primary school with a firm grasp of the basic skills of literacy and

numeracy, with an appetite for learning and with a belief in themselves and their talents, their future progress will inevitably be stunted. Dearing Review (1993)

or, the eight 'aims of the schools' set out in the 1977 Consultative document *Education in Schools*:

1.19 Schools must have aims against which to judge the effectiveness of their work and hence the kinds of improvements that they may need to make from time to time. The majority of people would probably agree with the following attempt to set out these aims, though they might differ in the emphasis to be placed on one or the other.

(i)   to help children develop lively, enquiring minds; giving them the ability to question and to argue rationally, and to apply themselves to tasks;

(ii)   to instil respect for moral values, for other people and for oneself, and tolerance of other races, religions, and ways of life;

(iii)   to help children understand the world in which we live, and the interdependence of nations;

(iv)   to help children to use language effectively and imaginatively in reading, writing and speaking;

(v)   to help children to appreciate how the nation earns and maintains its standard of living and properly to esteem the essential role of industry and commerce in this process;

(vi)   to provide a basis of mathematical, scientific and technical knowledge, enabling boys and girls to learn the essential skills needed in a fast-changing world of work;

(vii)   to teach children about human achievement and aspirations in the arts and sciences, in religion, and in the search for a more just social order;

(viii) to encourage and foster the development of the children whose social or environmental disadvantages cripple their capacity to learn, if necessary by making additional resources available to them.

Both these formulations attend to both the cognitive and the affective sides of educating children. That is, knowledge, understanding and skills on the one hand and personal and social attitudes, emotional development and beliefs and behaviours on the other. They are set implicitly in the well-documented analysis of curriculum as containing three elements: the transmission of knowledge, the development of the individual's powers of mind and body, and cultivation of the morals required by the society in which the teacher and student are set. It is the confusion surrounding the third element together with the post-modernist assertion of the relativity of all values that has contributed to the current public concern about the need to 'teach morals'.

This line of thinking leads us to suggest some ethical principles of teaching which derive from a mixture of both authority and purpose. We can cite authority when we speak of knowledge, its various forms and tests for truth etc. It is the authority of epistemology – the best that has been said and written and the best systems for examining the world and ourselves that have been devised.

In the affective domain, the basis may be to do more with purpose since there must be an explicit or implicit model of the good person and the good life.

A code of ethical principles for the teaching profession

If, as has been argued, ethical principles deriving from epistemological authority and from professional purpose can be said to be fundamental to teaching, what are these principles? This chapter suggests that they inhere in three dispositions essential to teaching: the disposition to rationality; the disposition to promote the interests of those taught; and the disposition to humility in relation to the provisionality of knowledge, the fallibility of those who claim to know and the partnership of learners in the process of education. There is a sense in which the disposition to rationality includes the other two, because it entails impartiality, fairness and a willingness to consider a range of points of view, but it is helpful to delineate its applications in distinct areas.

Ethical principles

I In those areas of the exercise of reason that concern the quest for truth, however elusive and provisional in a post-modern context, teachers must:

1. **respect the nature of knowledge; and the canon of knowledge;**
   This involves 'subject' methodology – how the knowledge is derived, the processes of investigation, evidence, tests for truth, etc which are different in important respects for each domain of knowledge, and 'subject' record – the accumulated attainments of the exercise of the methodology and a lively scepticism with regard to both.
   Shorthand: *have Intellectual Integrity*.

2. **respect professional knowledge, skills and experience;**
   This involves the requirement to remain current, to extend one's insight and repertoire of skills and to mix and match in order to be pedagogically effective with a range of pupils in varied contexts and settings.
   Shorthand: *have Vocational Integrity*.

3. **show independence of mind and action.**
   This involves willingness to teach subject matter or use methods that are unpopular or officially frowned upon, if intellectual and/or vocational integrity so demand.

   Shorthand: *show Moral Courage.*

II In those areas that concern the interests of those taught, teachers must:

4. **discern and respect the interests of persons taught;**
   This involves setting those interests ultimately above their own, cultivating appropriate self-esteem in those persons, and recognizing that education is an interactive process, dependant on the contributions of learners as well as those of teachers.

   Shorthand: *exercise Altruism.*

5. **acknowledge social interdependence;**
   This involves avoiding and preventing exploitation of one individual or group.

   Shorthand: *exercise Impartiality.*

6. **respect the families and social situation of those being taught;**
   This involves sensitivity to diversity, to multiplicities of influence and the avoidance of stereotyping; and seeking to ensure equality of educational opportunity.

   Shorthand: *exercise Human Insight.*

7. **exercise and accept responsibility for influence which may be long term.**
   This means realizing that experiences in classrooms are truly formative and taking care to leave a positive imprint on the lives of those taught.

   Shorthand: *assume the responsibility of Influence.*

III In those areas concerning humility, teachers must ultimately embrace a self-denying ordinance, for their most significant measure of success is a pupil who can learn without their aid! In pursuing this teachers must:

8. **recognize their own fallibility;**
   This involves being willing to acknowledge that one may be mistaken in respect of knowledge and of behaviour.

Shorthand: *exercise Humility.*

9. **respect and work co-operatively with professional colleagues;**
   This entails listening to and learning from others, recognizing that disciplines have common as well as separate concerns and accepting a duty to work together for the benefit of those taught.

   Shorthand: *exercise Collegiality.*

10. **recognize and put to work the contribution of those taught and their associates in education;**
    This involves taking account of and making use of, as far as possible, the talents and expertise of those being taught, their families and social situation.

    Shorthand: *exercise Partnership.*

11. **be willing to promote professional values, expertise and interest, by commenting publicly on education policy.**
    This means speaking and writing openly about the implications of public policies for the practice of education.

    Shorthand: *exercise vigilance with regard to Professional Responsibilities and Aspirations.*

Conclusion

The short titles seem to be or imply statements of values and we are pleased by this since we cannot conceive of a set of ethical principles that is not based on values which are declared as a prior condition. *Principles are values in action.*

If such a set of principles is to be both appropriate and useful, it must be helpful to the resolution of ethical dilemmas, which arise in the course of professional practice. In action, principles are often in conflict.

Some examples may illustrate the point:

1. One expression of the disposition of professionals to act morally is the duty of placing the interests of clients, patients, pupils, ahead of one's own. Teachers in modern universities face a double dilemma in this regard. Students need individual academic counselling, study skills, revision classes and, above all in the case of trainees for the social professions, a great deal of personal support, as they are initiated into practice. These demands go well beyond what can be fitted into timetabled contact hours. Universities require staff to undertake research and publication and indeed reward success in such activities over success in teaching, as essential

to the business of Higher Education. What constitutes an ethical response in these circumstances and can the principles help? Altruism may entail the giving of time and energy to the pedagogical imperatives at the expense of personal advancement, but what of collegiality? Is the essential characteristic of universities to impart what is known or to discover the new? If one settles for altruism and pedagogical integrity, foregoing personal advantage, is one showing moral courage in challenging prevailing value systems or compromising intellectual integrity and traducing collegiality?

2. Granted the disposition to place the interests of pupils ahead of one's own, what does one do when there is conflict or opposition between the interests of one (or a few) and those of the many? To take a routine example: Assessment systems involve deadlines for the completion of assignments. Individuals, for a variety of reasons – the least complicated of which are health problems – fail to meet them or recognize in advance that they will do so. Humaneness dictates a system of extensions for individuals sympathetically administered. Students, via representative councils, however, complain of injustice, suggesting that the system can be/is being subverted by dishonest students, who thus secure advantage over their peers. Is such a system altruistic or does it fly in the face of human interdependence? Would it be ethically more justifiable to have no exceptions or would that show lack of insight?

3. Assuming the disposition to act in the interests of those taught, what does one do when the interests of the individual pupil are at odds with those of the enterprise? The university is dedicated to the imparting of academic values and standards and, in teacher education, also to the 'delivery' of effective professionals. What is the ethical response to:

- the student who is diligent and 'good with children' but academically limited?
- the student whose self-esteem is inhibitingly low, possibly because of previous experience of failure, whose work has improved but has still not reached the required standard?
- the student who has listened to and taken one's advice but complains because work has still been graded below the level at which it is aimed?
- the student who is able and conscientious but dogged with health problems which are unlikely to improve by the time QTS is attained?
- the student who meets all demands, but whom intuition suggests should not be a teacher?

Here adherence to principles 1 and 7 are to some extent in conflict with principles 2 and 3. Moreover, what are academic standards in the context of the current debate?

It may be concluded either that the principles must therefore be placed in a hierarchy, or that since they do not in practice provide clear guidance for action they are neither use nor ornament. To take either view, however, is to deny the essence of professionalism, which lies in the ability of teachers to perceive the dynamic relation between the principles and willingness to accept the responsibility of selecting for guidance those most relevant to particular situations. Those teachers who seek to educate teachers must make explicit the values and encourage adherence to the principles both in precept and by example.

Who is a teacher?

Having got this far, we must ask 'Who is a teacher?' To whom are these precepts addressed? In one sense, in a participative democracy, everyone is a teacher: 'It takes a whole village to educate a child.' And Aristotle argued that to be virtuous one must live in a virtuous state. You can see what he meant, but the argument seems circular. For practical purposes we suggest that a teacher is anyone who is in a contractual relationship with the state (or a proprietor in the private sector) and/or client where the main object of the contract is to instruct. That rules out parents who are not paid, but brings in all phases of the state and private education service. It leaves out other professionals who have an element of teaching in their work, health visitors for example, because they have professional codes that refer to their work generally, including the element of teaching.

Not all teachers who might wish or be encouraged to adopt the principles proposed above would be registered teachers. We assume that registration – at least compulsory registration – will continue to apply to those working in the compulsory education phases, where parents have a legal obligation to send their children (unless they teach them 'otherwise') and teachers are expected to be *in loco parentis*. That is, where the State makes teaching compulsory, it registers its teachers and the public can reasonably expect a code of good practice to be followed. There are voices now pressing for government to impose a Code; the arguments here are advanced in the hope that teachers in all phases of education will accept the principles of the above code as a voluntary act.

Points for reflection and discussion

- Are the ethical principles here proposed universal, applying to all kinds of settings in which teaching may occur?

- Are the 'demands' on teachers implicit in the Code realistic and reasonable, given the pressures of modern public education systems?
- Is the dimension of 'care', given prominence in this chapter and in the Code, integral to the process of teaching itself, and thus appropriate for all settings and purposes; or only for some; or for none?
- Is it considered that the introduction of wider discussion of the ethical principles underlying teaching, whether in the form of a Code or otherwise, would be helpful in the present context, or might only serve to provide another instrument with which to oppress teachers?
- Is it the case that the ethical principles proposed are not in conflict with, but would positively support, the Values in Education and the Community being proposed by the National Forum set up by SCAA? If that were so, it is of interest – not least because the work on ethical principles, done by those involved in teacher education and training, was done separately and completed before the Forum's first proposals were published.

References

Bottery, Mike (1997) Some Thoughts on the Completion of Professionalism, and the Implications of this for a Code of Ethical Principles for the Teaching Profession, *UCET Occasional Paper*, **7**, UCET, London

DES (1997) *Education in Schools Green Paper*, DES, London

DfE (1993) *Review of the National Curriculum, Dearing Final Report*, DfE, London

Chapter 11

The TTA Consultation Documents on ITT: What, No Values?

Stuart Ainsworth and Andrew Johnson

Introduction

On 15 January 1996, Nick Tate, chief executive of the School Curriculum Assessment Authority (SCAA), hit the headlines proclaiming that schooling was failing to promote an adequate sense of moral values (*The Times*, 15 January 1996). A key institution singled out for criticism by Mr Tate was teacher education. The then Minister for Education and Employment, Gillian Shephard, was reported to have approved of his remarks (*The Times*, 16 January 1996).

In February 1997 the Teacher Training Agency (TTA), at the behest of Gillian Shephard, sent out for consultation proposals for 'Standards and Requirements' for teacher training in England and Wales (TTA, 1997). Based on a technicist 'competency' model, nowhere did these proposals seriously tackle the issues of moral education raised by Tate. Further, there was no indication in them of their general underlying educational values.

This chapter stemmed from the 1997 Antiracist Teacher Education Network (ARTEN) annual seminar (April 1997), which centred around producing a response to the TTA proposals. It drew on the ARTEN analysis, which concluded that the consultative proposals were dangerously inadequate and in some ways racially biased.[1] Additionally, omission of any serious reference to the teacher as a reflective, self-monitoring professional was held to render them inadequate at a very fundamental level.

As well as the lack of consistent direction between the TTA and SCAA, attention was drawn to the fact that aspects of Department for Education and Employment (DfEE) policy were also not reflected in the TTA proposals. By way of contrast salient features of Scottish teacher education were outlined. Not only was the position there already radically different, more recent proposals and decisions from relevant bodies showed Scotland in some ways to be moving in the opposite direction to the 1997 TTA proposals.

This updated version of the chapter argues that a change of government, to one which committed itself during the May 1997 election to social justice, has made little real difference to key aspects of the TTA's final set of 'standards' (TTA, 1998). This, it will be argued, is particularly significant at a time when a public inquiry into the murder of Stephen Lawrence has raised public awareness of issues connected with racism, especially what is called 'institutional racism'.

'Competency'/'Standards' models of education and the work of Frankena[2]

The TTA consultation documents nowhere discussed the validity of the competency-based approach adopted. This is in marked contrast to educational approaches that take as fundamental the need to base proposals on argument, evidence and reasoning. As will become clear, this almost cavalier attitude to justification is not entirely at odds with the managerialist competency model itself.

The theory of 'competences' itself has undergone a process of evolution. Boyatzis (1982), for example, adopted a person-centred notion of competence, stating that:

> a job competency is an underlying characteristic of a person in that it may be a motive, trait, skill, aspect of one's self-image, or social role or a body of knowledge which he or she uses. (p 21)

O'Hagan (1992) argued that by merging person-centred and work-related aspects, competence is a wide concept which embodies the ability to transfer skills and knowledge to new situations within the occupational area. It encompasses the organization and planning of work, innovation and coping with non-routine activities, as well as those personal qualities that are required in the workplace to deal effectively with colleagues, managers and colleagues.

Such all-encompassing definitions have, however, been criticized for being too vague. In an attempt to increase the degree of specificity, the suggestion has been that 'competences' should be operationalized. As a result of such developments in the theorizing of competency strategies, competence-based education and training can now be located broadly within the twin theoretical orientations of behaviourism and functionalism. Both of these are associated with shared goals of prescriptively laying down tight guidelines about what individuals ultimately should do, so that this may be readily assessed.

Driven by the appeal that this has a heavily managerialist mentality, the competency model has by degrees pervaded all aspects of education in the past decade, until it has now assumed a pre-eminent position which is not seen to require explanation or justification. So deeply embedded are the 'taken for granted' presumptions involved in the adoption of this model that there is often little realization of how heavily ideological and questionable the process has become. Indeed there are a number of important ways in which the competency-based approach may be seen both to restrict the development of imaginative teachers and to coincide with questionable political ends.

Firstly it has been argued that the approach is grossly reductionist in that it assumes that the sum of prescribed competences can encapsulate the overall competence of the professional (Hyland, 1995). A narrow assessment process, focusing primarily on observable behaviours relating to specific criteria, excludes certain kinds of knowledge (such as what counts as an appropriate value or moral base and from whence it derives) and raises critical questions about what is excluded and the nature of the knowledge perceived to be integral to a profession such as teaching. As but one example of the ideological implications of competence-based training, this chapter demonstrates that the TTA managed to excise from its consultation documents any meaningful concern about, or consideration of, the knowledge which would allow teachers seriously to address the manner in which discrimination and other iniquitous practice occurs.

Frankena, values and teacher education

In this context it is worth considering a philosophical analysis derived from Frankena. Summarizing the work of other philosophers, he suggests that a normative philosophy of education has two parts: a comparatively philosophical and theoretical line of reasoning involving A, B and C in Figure 11.1 to show what excellences are to be cultivated by education, and a practical line of reasoning involving C, D and E.

Noticeably the 1997 TTA consultation documents, in outlining what Frankena would call 'the list of excellences' against which trainee teachers should themselves be judged, concentrate on 'standards' and 'requirements' which relate almost exclusively to D and E, with E being defined largely in terms of teaching subject content. The TTA documents, therefore, omitted any serious reference: a) to teachers developing an understanding of any values which they are supposed to foster; and b) to teachers developing as reflective professionals who should be critically concerned with the ethical justification of their practice.

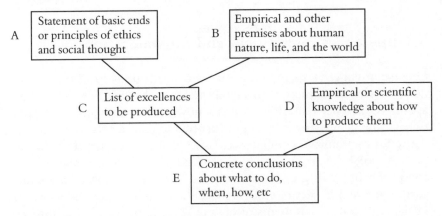

Figure 11.1   *Model derived from W K Frankena (1965)*

By contrast with the TTA proposals, any serious consideration by teachers of values and morals in education – for example along the lines urged by Nick Tate – would surely at least have to contemplate the philosophy of education and any assumptions being made about the nature of our society. Begging the question of which values should underpin education, the TTA's competency model, however, neatly excludes reference to the relationships between A, B and C and focuses almost exclusively on D and E, on what has to be taught and how.

In another context, Hodgkinson (1995: 61) has described such an approach as 'rampant managerialism' and it is not difficult to identify the approach in a wide range of government educational documents. As Collins (1991) notes, knowledge has become defined by a narrow and technocratic approach to education, which is increasingly influenced by bureaucratic corporate demands. More broadly, as Apple (1993) suggests:

> The Right in the United States and Britain has thoroughly renovated and re-formed itself. It has developed strategies based on what might best be called authoritarian populism. As Hall (1985) has defined this, such a policy is based on an increasingly close relationship between government and capitalist economy, a radical decline in the institutions and power of political democracy, and attempts at curtailing 'liberties' that have been gained in the past. This is coupled with attempts to build a consensus, one that is widespread in support of its actions. (p 21)

This 'close relationship' is perhaps nowhere more profoundly expressed than in a business-derived 'competency' ethic, which excises from the agenda that which cannot easily be prescribed and measured, and hence much that requires both sustained analysis and critical evaluation.

'Competences', assessment and fragmentation

One major concern, therefore, is that assessment processes are narrowed down to what has sometimes been referred to as the 'painting by numbers' approach. Teacher education students now often focus quite disproportionately on identifying work simply in order to produce the necessary evidence for each unit of competence. Issit (1995) argues that the reflective professional, by contrast, must be concerned with the holistic and dynamic complexity of teaching contexts which are more than simply a sum of their parts. For example, teachers may well have a full and proper understanding of the technical requirements of how to teach topic X or Y. If, however, there is no requirement for them to acknowledge the principles involved in, for example, eliminating the self-fulfilling prophecy or understanding the social and cultural dynamics of labelling in the school and classroom, then there is much evidence to indicate that outcomes for certain pupils will be iniquitous.

Secondly, Ramsay (1993) argues that the fragmented and prescribed nature of competences may undermine the creativity and innovation of workers' practice. There is no need for the student to go beyond that which is prescribed (indeed there is some anecdotal evidence that to do so can be met with some hostility) and therefore the development of a necessary autonomy for the teacher is denied.

Thirdly, the focus of competences on outcomes as opposed to the process of student learning promotes a form of narrow instrumentalism. According to De Maria (1992), there then prevails a tendency for students themselves to become more self-centred, conservative, competitive and authoritarian. As a result, superficial and narrow learning becomes the basis of good practice.

In our experience, this often means that good students become bored with merely 'reporting' around alleged key 'competences'. Intrinsic interest and excitement in the process of working with new concepts and creating new ideas is lost as learners become mere labourers and technicians. In the classroom, initiative, collaboration and risk taking – a necessary excursion for the practising and developing teacher as she or he explores the thrill of teaching – are increasingly removed from an agenda that seeks only technical requirements. In these senses, competency education easily becomes oppressive, stultifying and some would say even banal.

Fourthly, as Issit (1995) has noted when discussing 'equal opportunities' in further education, the inherent individualistic and technocratic rationale can be seen to perpetuate oppressive structural inequalities because it merely focuses on learning at the individual level whilst often projecting merely the illusion of tackling injustice. It can be seen as a process whereby the complex, structural power relations within society are implicitly ignored and a simplistic, grossly distorted and quite inadequate solution to oppression manufactured in its place.

As if to highlight the inadequacy of a simplistic competency model of teacher education, the Scottish Office Education Department document, *Guidelines for Teacher Training Courses (1992)* – in marked contrast to the TTA consultation 'standards' – state unequivocally under 'Competences Related to Professionalism' that:

> professionalism implies more than a mere set of competences. It also implies a set of attitudes which have particular power in that they are communicated to those being taught.

Though still labelled 'competences' this set of requirements for teachers, which will be analysed more fully later, is couched in terms of what the TTA documents exclude – commitments.

ARTEN and the TTA documents on ITT

The ARTEN analysis of the TTA consultation documents mirrored the general criticisms of a technicist model. Noting that the 1997 TTA proposals were not based on any rigorous intellectual framework, nor referred to recent research, the ARTEN document directly took issue with the TTA designation of initial teacher preparation as 'training' as opposed to 'education'.

Lack of a value base

The ARTEN document also noted with concern the lack of any explicit value base for the proposals. This, it was argued, should be remedied by an explicit statement of values in the documents' introduction. More specifically, the ARTEN paper argued that four major elements should be included:

- enabling students to become reflective, creative and critical thinkers;
- the facilitation of an analysis of what constitutes social justice;
- enabling students to understand and identify how discrimination operates and how to develop strategies to counter it;

● enabling students to recognize, accept and work with differences in a positive way.

The list was not seen as exhaustive. Reference to concerns about the environment should, it was argued, be added; as should reference to intellectual virtues such as honesty, and commitments to the search for truth and the impartial weighing of reasons, evidence and argument.

A 'colour blind' approach?

ARTEN also took issue with the lack of any sustained reference to the importance of diversity in our society. In this the TTA proposals appeared to adopt a basically 'colour blind' approach, in line with a speech given by the then Prime Minister, John Major, at the January 1997 celebration of 50 years of independence for India and Pakistan. Apparently unaware of the law (or perhaps more mindful of other priorities), John Major talked about 'positive discrimination' as though it were legally permissible. He added, 'Policy must be colour blind – it must just tackle disadvantage' (Commonwealth Institute, 1997: 7). This is certainly at odds not only with the research of Gillborn and Gipps (1996) but also with the policy conclusions reached by the Office For Standards in Education (Ofsted):

> Failure to address ethnic diversity has proved counter-productive at the school level. Where schools have adopted 'colour-blind' policies, for example, inequalities of opportunity have been seen to continue. In contrast, research has begun to examine the benefits of addressing diversity as an important and changing part of school life.[3]

The ARTEN (1997) document also refers to the 10-point action plan for educational attainment and 'ethnic minority' students drawn up by the DfEE as a consequence of the Ofsted recommendations. Point eight of the plan specifically refers to a commitment by the DfEE to:

> work with the TTA on the skills needed with a view to enhancing initial teacher training and professional development.

Nowhere in the TTA proposals was there any reference that would indicate that this was being made a reality. And, if there is no reference to such collaboration there by the TTA, where would it be found and how would it be made a reality?

There was also little evidence in the TTA proposals of a recognition of linguistic diversity, apart that is from a negative description of pupils who 'are not fluent in English' (TTA Paper 2 & 3: 13). Nor was there, ARTEN argued, any evidence in the TTA documents of a significant understanding of the power of pupils' cultures in relation to schooling. The pressing need for the claimed collaboration between the DfEE and TTA could hardly be made clearer than by these shortcomings.

'Neutrality', monoculturalism and the TTA proposals

Additionally ARTEN took issue with a lack of awareness in the TTA documents that subjects and their concomitant knowledge are not neutral. If the TTA was at all aware of the dangers of ethnocentrism, or the 'structured omission' of references to worldwide contributions to knowledge, this was not apparent from the documents.

This general criticism was sustained by ARTEN when analysing the specific proposals in the documents. The TTA documents make reference to the need for students to be aware of 'common misconceptions' (TTA, Paper 2). An ARTEN illustration of how this could have an antiracist perspective (currently lacking) made reference to misconceptions about British imperial history, misconceptions about particular religious beliefs and misconceptions about practices and values concerning literature from different parts of the world. With respect to Mathematics the ARTEN document pointed out a failure to recognize 'that young children's everyday experience of number and shape will be diverse and culturally mediated' (ARTEN: 6). In addition the ARTEN document made clear that Paper 3 on Primary English 'relates entirely to monolingual pupils learning English as a first language. It is presenting a linear model of language learning unsupported by recent academically sound research' (ARTEN: 5).

Any illusion that Britain is, or ever was, monocultural has been exposed by theorists such as Mike Cole (1989). There was, however, little to be found in the TTA documents that was not consistent with a determinedly monocultural stance on education.

There is a reference in the section D, 'Other Professional Requirements', to 'teachers' legal liabilities and responsibilities relating to... anti-discrimination legislation' (TTA, February 1997: 11). But this hardly constitutes the most ringing endorsement of a multicultural, multiracial society. Indeed it may seem more in line with the policy of some institutions, where 'equal opportunities' policies, for fear of punitive legal judgements, appear to be introduced so as not to fall foul of the law. If this appears excessively pessimistic, or even ungenerous, reference should be made to the almost complete lack of other more positive statements within the TTA documentation.

Certainly the reference to 'setting high expectations for all pupils notwithstanding individual differences, including gender, and cultural and linguistic backgrounds' (TTA, 1997: 8) lies open to the charge of rehearsing some very unfortunate stereotypes. The important point, again, is that one searches in vain for countervailing references that could put this into any different, more positive, perspective. As the ARTEN document made clear, there was no shortage of places where those genuinely concerned with equality work in education could (indeed, in many cases almost certainly would) have inserted quite naturally a word or a phrase making such concerns clear. For example, the requirement that intending teachers must demonstrate that they 'understand how young children learn and how this is affected by their physical, intellectual, emotional and social development' (TTA, 1997: 5) could easily have referred also to children's cultural development.

Teachers as reflective, self-evaluating professionals and the TTA proposals

It has been commonplace in relatively recent educational theorizing to see teachers as reflective professionals who evaluate the appropriateness of their teaching for those in their charge. Such a model requires teachers to have a responsibility for exercising their judgement against a set of values, with professional self-evaluation being a critical element in this.

One might expect some of this to inform the TTA consultation documents' statements of 'requirements', especially in the section 'Other Professional Requirements' (TTA, 1997: 11). Very little at all could be found. Whilst they contained a reference to evaluation it was at best vestigial. It is the last point in its section, is tied to 'effectiveness' rather than 'appropriateness', and doesn't feature (as ARTEN recommended) in the title of the section (TTA, 1997: 8). One can't help reflecting that if this one reference to evaluation could have been excised it would. In implying some form of teacher autonomy it appears at odds with almost all of the rest of the documents.[4]

In fact, these documents look for all the world like a prescription based on the application of industrial management principles, not those of education. There are isolated references to 'pupils' needs' (TTA, 1997: 9) and to the 'requirement' to 'plan opportunities to contribute to pupils' spiritual, moral, personal, social and cultural development' (TTA, 1997: 7). They would have carried greater conviction if they were supported by 'requirements' that indicate where and how intending teachers are supposed to develop the understanding required, and against what set of general value commitments these 'requirements' are to be judged.

It was this lack of a clear set of value commitments in the TTA documents that was crucial in the opinion of ARTEN. 'Matching the approaches used to… the pupils being taught' (TTA, 1997: 7) could, of course, be interpreted as helping to meet the needs of widely disparate pupils, and could take due cognizance of, for example, different cultural backgrounds. There is, however, nothing in the documents to ensure that teacher education establishments would raise such issues. Quite the reverse, as evidenced by the lack of serious reference to the needs of bilingual pupils.

What, no values? 'Common sense' the default position?

It is apparent from Frankena's analysis – to say nothing of insights to be drawn from David Hume[5] – that, despite the surface appearance of an education which is practically value free in the TTA's documents, values of some description will inevitably lie behind any proposals for education. More specifically, and especially relevant in the present context, R F Dearden (1968) has argued cogently that 'in no system of education can the teacher escape responsibility for the direction which things take' (p 13).

And there is a sense in which it could be argued, with some justice, that much of the foregoing about technicist models exaggerates any actual position in education. All but the most blinkered, measurable, behavioural objectives disciples would surely have to agree that judgements involving values are intrinsic to teaching in schools. Whether it be simply the selection of materials, examples or modes of questioning, there are judgements to be made which implicitly rest on value positions. And this is to say nothing about the myriad different interactions between staff and pupils, staff and other staff, staff and parents, or about matters like discipline.

Powerful arguments can, then, be mounted that the model of the school as some sort of glorified baked bean factory to which time and motion studies may be applied (though a salutary metaphor for some current, grossly simplistic theories) couldn't actually ever reflect the real complexity of education. Try as some politicians and others might to prescribe standards that will allow teachers minimum room for professional judgement, values cannot be excised from the teaching process. Judgements will have to be made, evaluation will take place and teachers will be responsible for some very important choices.

Quite so. The question, however, is on what basis these choices will be made. In the absence of any overt guidance, discussion or agreement whatsoever on the values that are to permeate and inform education, what is the default position to which teachers will revert? Here relatively recent heavy political reliance on invoking 'common sense' springs to mind.

Without rehearsing the wealth of evidence and argument available to substantiate the position, and mindful of the need not to oversimplify to the point of caricature, it can fairly safely be asserted that, in the absence of a reflective consideration of values during initial teacher education, the default position for many new teachers would be a predominantly middle class, predominantly white, and predominantly monocultural set of assumptions, which would not of itself challenge, for example, heterosexist and able-bodied assumptions about 'normality'. In today's social, political and economic climate it may well also have an overwhelmingly 'instrumentalist' orientation to learning and a pretty limited and conventional view of what is 'basic' to education.

Finally, reliance on 'common sense' (which under the TTA consultation proposals newly qualified teachers could well have to fall back on) is precisely that which anti-racist education – and other anti-discrimination education – often has to confront, analyse and expose as being not just inadequate to the task of helping build a more equitable society but, in fact, one of the greatest barriers to its realization.

The Scottish context

The context within which teacher education takes place in Scotland is in many significant respects quite different from that south of the border. Scotland has for a very long time had its own distinctive educational system. Not only this; during the period of the 18 years of Tory government, Scotland exhibited a marked resistance to the importation, by politicians such as Michael Forsyth, of 'English' educational ideas and values, eg in the form of league tables, opting out and selection. Such policy had only very limited success. Partly this was due to the different history and structuring of educational management in Scotland. But in no small measure it was also due to the marked resistance from parents, unions and local authorities, to say nothing of many active teachers.

SOED (Scottish Office Education Department) 'competences'

Whilst reserving the right to be critical of the Scottish Office Education Department (formerly SOED, now the SOEID) 'competences' model and of some of its contents, it is striking that by contrast with the TTA documents much of the 1993 SOED document can be seen as answering to the model of teachers as educated, reflective, self-evaluating professionals. The very first 'competence' states that the new teacher should be able to:

> demonstrate a knowledge of the subject or subjects forming the content of his or her teaching which meets and goes beyond the immediate demands of the school curriculum.

The document adds that the new teacher should be able to:

> justify what is taught from knowledge of the learning process, curriculum issues, child development in general and the needs of his or her pupils in particular.

Not perhaps the most startling of 'requirements' but, in referring to 'curriculum issues', a far cry from the general tone of the TTA consultation documents. There is also a marked difference when it comes to 'evaluation'. Several places in the document refer specifically to the need for teachers to 'evaluate' their methodology, their management and their teaching.

The point is not that such guidelines necessitate a 'liberal' teacher education: it is that teacher education institutions have plenty of pegs on which to hang an education that is not narrowly instrumental and technicist. As already noted, however, the biggest difference lies in the section 'Competences Related to Professionalism' which states that 'professionalism implies more than a mere series of competences'.

Cashed out in a series of 'commitments' these additional requirements include 'a commitment to views of fairness and equality of opportunity as expressed in multi-cultural and other non-discriminatory policies'. What is especially interesting is that the national profile, drawn up by the Scottish Office Education Department, requires teacher education institutions, as part of their final report, to evaluate each new teacher specifically on these commitments.

The GTC, anti-sexism and anti-racism

Perhaps the biggest current difference between Scotland and England is the General Teaching Council, a body independent of the government and the Scottish Office.[7] Its role is to oversee the teaching profession in Scotland and no one can teach in a Scottish school without being registered with the GTC. But most significantly, for present concerns, its approval is necessary before any teacher education course can be validated in Scotland.

From the specific perspective of ARTEN (and its Scottish equivalent SARTEN) it is highly significant that the GTC has published strong anti-discrimination policies, *Gender in Education* (GTC, 1992) and *Multi-Cultural/Anti-Racist Education* (GTC, 1994). The following selected quotes give something of their flavour:

> The Council believes that effective gender equality policies must embrace the concept of anti-sexism.

> Anti-racist education takes as its starting point the unequivocal assertion that ours is a multi-cultural and democratic society in which all citizens have a right

to equity and justice. It means acknowledging that the existence of racism and racist attitudes creates for black pupils an experience of education that is often negative, with the result that their life-chances are often diminished.

The council therefore believes that the main thrust of MCARE must be a direct assault on racist behaviour, language and practices, both institutional and individual.

The commitments are unequivocal. In addition the GTC makes crystal clear that it sees its recommendations as relevant to all schools, whether or not they include black pupils.[8] Unlike many other documents, there is also a very strong section on bilingualism, especially in the full GTC MCARE document (GTC, 1994). Of even more direct relevance to the ARTEN analysis, and its recommendations for the revision of TTA proposals, the GTC MCARE document is quite specific on teacher education:

> The Council believes that MCARE should be included in all courses of teacher education and that all institutions should have in place monitoring systems to ensure that coverage is effective... A special unit or module in addition to the permeative approach should be considered and students should be encouraged to incorporate MCARE principles in their teaching.

Concerning the status of teachers as reflective professionals the full GTC MCARE document could hardly be more explicit, or mindful of the pitfalls of reliance on 'common sense':

> The General Teaching Council is committed to the concept of the teacher as a reflective, self monitoring professional. If teachers are to contribute effectively to the development in their pupils of a critical awareness of how racism and prejudice can be perpetuated and a more positive attitude towards cultural diversity, it is important that they be given the opportunity not only to question their own perceptions but to examine their professional activities from a MCARE perspective.

The foregoing does not, of course, ensure that there will be no shortcomings in anti-discrimination work in Scottish schooling. What it does mean is that those who are serious about such work have very significant policy statements to which they can refer. The latest document from the GTC, *Report of the Working Group on Partnership in Initial Teacher Education* (GTC, 1997), in its section 'Rationale', provides an effective summary of how the GTC views teacher education in general:

> Teaching is recognized to be a complex activity requiring more than a set of routine procedures. It involves the ability to understand and use a wide range of professional insights and it is for this reason that teacher education courses have

developed in a way which recognizes the essential interaction between reflection and action.

It later continues:

> It is increasingly acknowledged that teaching requires a well-considered and reflective commitment to certain values such as justice, respect for others, truth and rationality.

These are precisely some of the key value commitments that are lacking in the TTA proposals. They are, however, embedded in other documents relevant to English schooling.

SCAA and the NFVEC on values

ARTEN made it clear that the TTA documents lacked a frame of reference supplied by a statement of values. In theory such a statement could merely make explicit the narrowly technicist, and largely monocultural, position evident in the 1997 TTA proposals. Given the nature of morality and moral discourse, though, it is hard to imagine any rationally defensible statement of values that did not take seriously concerns of equity and justice.

It is, therefore, not an accident that the draft values statement of the National Forum for Values in Education and the Community (drawn up for the School Curriculum Assessment Authority) included important references to equity; nor is it surprising that these found a ready and widespread acceptance. In *Principles for Action* it is stated that we should:

> accept diversity and respect people's right to religious and cultural differences, provide opportunities for all, contribute to, as well as benefit fairly from, economic and cultural resources.

These – especially the latter – go far beyond Nick Tate's own original formulation of 'fair play'. If acted upon seriously, they would take education much further down the road to genuine equity than many existing 'equal opportunities' policies. Also, a genuine commitment to 'make truth and integrity priorities in public life' would be seen by most as a much needed reassertion of fundamental principles. Additionally, this latter principle could readily be translated, in an educational context, into something approaching the intellectual virtues outlined earlier.

The following values statement in the NFVEC draft embraced many of these principles above: 'We value truth, human rights, justice and collective endeavour for the common good of society.' It certainly marks a refreshing change from the flawed philosophy which spawned the idea that 'There is no such thing as society' (Thatcher, 1987).

No simple statement of values will satisfy all. And there are some causes for serious concern in the document. One is the principle enunciated that we should 'try to live up to a shared moral code'. Powerful arguments can be mounted that any society needs some shared moral notions, and even that some particular values such as integrity and generalized truth-telling are basic requirements for any sustainable society (Ainsworth, 1976). Nevertheless, it needs to be asserted that there is, over and above a shared basic social morality, no sufficient reason to think that on all other moral matters (eg sexuality or the place of religion) there has to be one shared value position. That would, for one thing, cut across the cultural diversity espoused earlier in the NFVEC document. And those who, from a determinedly moral stance, seek to preserve such diversity do not deserve to be vilified as they were, for example, by Nick Tate in his January 1996 statements.

That said, there is certainly much in the SCAA-sponsored values position which could have informed the TTA documents. Allied judiciously to the points raised by ARTEN and the steps outlined in the DfEE 10-point plan on education and 'ethnic minorities', they would have transformed the TTA documents. Not only would the notion of the teacher as educated reflective professional have been reinstated, the 1997 TTA documents could have helped move us closer to the Scottish GTC aspiration of 'a multicultural and democratic society in which all citizens have a right to equity and justice'.

More recent developments: An introduction

Since this chapter was originally prepared, a number of major developments have taken place in addition to the continuation of the TTA consultation on ITT. What should be one of the most significant of these was the election in May 1997 of a Labour Government with a huge majority. Three features, at least, of the election campaign by the Labour Party are highly relevant to the issues addressed here. They are a pledge to make 'education, education, education' a top priority; a commitment to social justice and combating social exclusion; and a promise of 'joined up' government.

As one result of the change of government, Scotland elected its own parliament, with responsibility *inter alia* for education, in May 1999. And, on a UK-wide basis, the Home Secretary, Jack Straw, has introduced further legislation to combat 'racially aggravated offences' (Crime & Disorder Act, 1998). But, perhaps of greatest significance, an inquiry was set up by Jack Straw, headed by Sir William Macpherson, into the Metropolitan Police Force's handling of the murder of black teenager Stephen Lawrence. The report (Macpherson, 1999) found there to be widespread 'institutionalized racism'. Amongst other sweeping proposals it recommended that, in addition to changes in the 1976 Race Relations Act, education should, through the National Curriculum, tackle issues of racism. Subsequently there has been an Ofsted report – also identifying institutional aspects of racism – which is critical of the way 'race' has been dealt with (or rather not dealt with) by many schools (Ofsted, 1999).

The TTA consultation processes

The original TTA (DfEE, 1997) consultation process for the ITT national curriculum was eventually issued in Circular 10/97. A subsequent consultation process, aimed at extending the ITT national curriculum from simply covering Primary English and Maths to also covering Primary Science, Secondary Science, Secondary English and Secondary Maths (as well as prescriptions about Information and Communications Technology for all teachers), was issued in Circular 4/98 (DfEE, 1998), which incorporated and replaced the previous circular on ITT.

In essence, both Circular 10/97 and Circular 4/98 retain the emphases and serious omissions of the original ITT documents. The approach is still technicist. Moreover, there is not even the briefest outline of the values that should be aimed at in the education of teachers. In addition, the subjects prioritized in the latest document – the so-called core subjects – reflect this ostensibly value-free approach since, apart from English, they are not those that by their very nature treat of human motivations, social interactions or ethical values. Sadly, in the case of English, where one surely could expect an exploration of language and human values, there is little in the latest document to necessitate a serious approach by intending teachers to developing an understanding of the power of language, through meaning, to condition social relationships.[10] Indeed, so very far from the TTA understanding this, its own documents were subject, during the latest consultation exercise, to serious criticism for their overly prescriptive 'tone' in repeatedly insisting 'trainees must be taught' (TTA, 1998).

Also criticized during this consultation process was what many saw as the 'tick list' approach of the TTA's documents. Rather ungenerously referring to this as a 'widespread misconception' the TTA seems to have fallen short of some of the criteria it eventually laid down for effective communication in the teaching of English (DfEE, 1998: 40, 91). The TTA was, therefore, obliged to add two paragraphs to Circular 4/98 to try to correct this.

Reminiscent of Issit's (1995) earlier criticism of 'competency' approaches, part of the clarification given is to the effect that:

It is necessary to consider the standards as a whole to appreciate the creativity, commitment, energy and enthusiasm which teaching demands, and the intellectual and managerial skills required of the effective professional.

Whether this will suffice to rescue the process from fragmentation remains to be seen. It may well not since this clarification itself studiously omits any reference to the values that would give the process point and coherence.

Certainly, there is one reference to teachers setting a 'good example... through their presentation and their personal and professional conduct'. But this rather conjures up images of teachers in twin sets or suits, and calls to mind the earlier criticism that, under the TTA's proposals, the operative values could very well be narrowly conventional. What Circular 4/98 certainly doesn't do, in an era supposed to be one of 'joined up' government with a top priority of education, is address the far more substantial issues of social justice, including poverty, marginalization and social exclusion; issues that are said to be high on the Government's agenda elsewhere.

Equity and the revised TTA documents

It is clear from the most recent consultation document that issues concerned with equity were raised in serious criticism of the TTA proposals by many of those who attended the 1998 conferences on the ITT national curriculum or who responded in other ways (TTA, 1998). From the TTA's response, these appear largely to have consisted of concerns not about providing opportunities for learning about equity issues in society but rather about access for individuals to the curriculum under the heading of 'equal opportunities', and requests for pointers about this in the final documents. There was one exception to this noted in the TTA summary report; namely that English is a good vehicle for promoting 'cultural diversity... as an asset'.

Passages related to the concerns about 'equal opportunities', in terms of access to the curriculum, can now be found in the final Circular, 4/98. But, rather unfortunately, references to the contributions of various civilizations to the development of Mathematics and of Science are couched in terms of 'different' civilizations. Further, though welcome, such references may simply represent what is at best a 'soft' multicultural approach. If this is not accompanied by genuine anti-racist education, or worse is seen as a substitute for it, major issues concerning equity in our society may simply not be addressed. Sadly, a similar criticism can be made of the reference, under Secondary English, concerning what are called 'attitudes to language use': the example given is simply the neutral and rather vague expression 'attitudes to gender in language'.[12]
The contrast, here, with the Scottish GTC policy on gender, could hardly be

more marked when it says, 'Erasing sexism from our vocabulary is the first step towards removing it from our thinking' and later asks of all schools, 'is the eradication of sexist language a key aim of the policy?'

Comparison with the Scottish context

The lack of reference in the TTA document to its fundamental values is reflected in a lack of serious reference to equity concerns in the requirements for all teachers. There is the previously mentioned, and by ARTEN heavily criticized, requirement that teachers simply know the law that applies to them in equity areas. This is in sharp contrast to the Scottish situation. Now referred to as guidelines for 'teacher education', the new Scottish guidelines – to be operative from session 1999/2000 – build on the previous 'commitments' by listing a series of 'values, attributes and abilities'. These specifically require of the teacher that:

> [He or she must] value and promote equality of opportunity and fairness and adopt non-discriminatory practices, in respect of age, disability, gender, race or religion. (SOEID, 1998)

Not all recent developments in Scottish education make explicit such a commitment, however. The white paper *Targeting Excellence* (Scottish Office, 1999), whilst talking about social inclusion, fails to explore its relation to the various forms of discrimination. Further, the document *The Short Term Working Party on Initial Teacher Education* makes specific reference only to the need to 'ensure the recruitment of an adequate supply of teachers for the denominational and Gaelic medium sectors'. Silences can speak volumes. If this passage excludes other religious groups and other languages it may well effectively marginalize many black Scots. Such marginalization raises fundamental questions about how citizenship is to be conceptualized in a country that is about to embark on a new political experience with its own elected parliament.

Further, draft curriculum guidelines for secondary schools have been sent out for consultation by the Scottish Consultative Council on the Curriculum (1998) to replace the previous document drawn up in 1987. The previous document, under 'permeating elements' clearly identified what it called 'equal opportunities' and suggested several different strategies for ensuring 'permeating elements' were covered. The new draft document, by contrast, makes only one passing reference to equality issues and does nothing about the continued privileging of Christianity under Religious Education and Religious Observance. Indeed, given the fact that it explicitly restates that privileging, it is not clear how teachers can also live up to the requirement quoted

above: that they should 'adopt non-discriminatory practices, in respect of...
religion'. It remains to be seen whether this potential contradiction is removed when the final document is published.

Other educational developments

In the case of England and Wales, in addition to recent developments concerning teacher education, other important government papers have been
issued concerning education. More specifically, the document *Teachers: Meeting the challenge of change* (DfEE, 1999) and its attendant technical paper set out
consultative proposals for a form of 'payment by results' for teachers and
schools. Containing at present a strange admixture of different forms of criterion referencing and norm referencing – the criteria for teachers vary at different points and schools have to 'compete' for a limited amount of additional
funds – nowhere do these criteria seriously attend to issues of equity and values in general.[13] Worryingly – given what is already known from investigations done by the Commission for Racial Equality into the experiences of
ethnic minority teachers – the danger is that, if not amended, the new proposals will increase the number of points at which such teachers could face the
sort of discrimination they have already suffered in promotion (CRE,
1988a).[14]

At a conference specifically called to discuss the English documents, issues
of values and equity were forcefully raised, not least in the very warmly received contribution by Professor Gus John (1999). In answer to a question
about values, equality, the TTA 'Standards' and the 10-point DfEE plan on
the education of ethnic minority students, Anthea Millet – chief executive of
the TTA – said that there was now a working party looking at these matters
but that any change in the 'Standards' would probably have to wait for another three years.

What does seem evident in this whole process from 1997 onwards is that,
for whatever reason – and there is some suspicion that it may have to do with
votes and government perceptions of the prejudices of 'middle England'[15] –
there has been a marked reluctance to spell out the values which should inform teacher preparation, especially in the area of equity issues. It seems fairly
clear that this was probably policy from the very top during the years of Tory
government and became embedded institutionally in bodies like the TTA.

Along with others ARTEN has, since 1996, lobbied the TTA and government ministers – including David Blunkett – for clear anti-discriminatory
practice to be an integral part of education, especially teacher education. To
judge by the TTA documents since Labour came to power it may be that, at
least until very recently, the Labour Government was intent at the structural,

political level on following very much the same path as the previous government. Evidence for this comes not just from the TTA documents produced since the 1997 election but also from a lack of sustained analysis of equity issues in the final Crick report on citizenship and democracy in schools (QCA, 1998).[16]

The Stephen Lawrence Inquiry and 'Institutional Racism'

What may throw a very different perspective on all of this now, and will probably be a litmus test for 'joined up' government and genuine commitment to social justice, is the report into the Metropolitan Police Force's handling of the murder of the black teenager Stephen Lawrence. Macpherson found evidence of 'institutional racism' not only in the practices of that force but said that 'education and housing also suffer from the disease' (Macpherson, 1999).

One clear recommendation from Macpherson, which it could well be very difficult for the Government now to resist, is that education via the National Curriculum has a crucial role to play in eradicating the racism that is endemic in so many institutions. Education is seen as having a 'particularly' important role in this 'from pre-primary school upwards and onwards'.

'Institutional racism'

If this is to be so, any institutional resistance within the TTA itself to genuine anti-racist education will have to be overcome. And, if teachers are genuinely to be prepared for such a process, a lot of work will need to be done on what the Commission for Racial Equality and the Swann Report identified 14 years before: developing a proper appreciation of what 'institutional racism' actually means.[17] This is not something that can simply be left to 'common sense', which is often itself deeply implicated in 'institutional racism'. Indeed, the Stephen Lawrence report comments favourably on evidence given by Dr Benjamin Bowling who, *inter alia*, said, 'some discrimination practices are the product of uncritical rather than unconscious racism'. In this respect it is well worth referring again to the Scottish GTC emphasis in its full MCARE policy that:

> it is important that [teachers] be given the opportunity not only to question their own perceptions but to examine their professional activities from a MCARE perspective.

The early signs, however, are not necessarily hopeful. Responses, both by some police officers to the Stephen Lawrence Report and by some union leaders to the Ofsted report, have shown a marked hostility to accepting that either institution could have sets of practices whose effects are racist. David Hart, the general secretary of the National Association of Head Teachers, said, for example, on Radio Four's *Today* programme, 'I categorically reject the idea that there is institutional racism in schools' (BBC, 10 March 1999). And Doug McAvoy of the National Union of Teachers, whilst welcoming that 'At long last Ofsted [had] recognized the importance and contribution of schools in tackling racism', is quoted as saying that teachers would interpret the term institutional racism as implying that they were racist. This is despite Sir William Macpherson's definition of 'institutional racism' stressing that racism could be unwitting.[18]

Here it is important to quote Herman Ouseley's comment on Sir Paul Condon:

> We should be deeply disappointed by the unwillingness of Sir Paul Condon to acknowledge that institutional racism exists within the Metropolitan Police service because of the impact of such an acknowledgement within the service and within the larger community. He may still misunderstand what institutional racism really means and what is involved in eradicating it. The failure by those in leadership roles within the Metropolitan Police service to recognize the need to change the culture of racism reflects the influence of this culture.

Though far from being new – as Sir Paul had tried to insist – the idea of unwitting institutional racism has, it seems, simply not been understood by many who have almost instantaneously reacted to it as implying a slur on police officers or teachers. And many of these have been in critical leadership roles. This predisposition to define racism in terms largely of individual and intentional behaviour seems so deeply rooted as to be almost immune to reasoned discussion.

More importantly, if it is true that teachers and police officers generally do interpret racism simply in personal and intentional terms, it demonstrates that the normal practices of these institutions – and their own schooling – have failed sufficiently to inform members of these professions of the complex nature of racism. There could be no clearer sign of the 'structured omission' of sustained and serious work in these areas. It is an omission which is itself a critical aspect of 'institutional racism' and which parallels the 'structured' institutional silence in much schooling which by default helps reproduce other forms of discrimination, such as heterosexism, as well. Even to those familiar with such an analysis, it is still startling to read that the evidence to the Lawrence Inquiry:

> demonstrated that not a single officer questioned before us in 1998 had received any training of significance in racism awareness and race relations throughout the course of his or her career.

The Macpherson definition also states that institutional racism can be 'detected in processes, attitudes and behaviour which amount to discrimination through unwitting prejudice, ignorance, thoughtlessness and racist stereotyping which disadvantages minority ethnic people'. There is much in this which is helpful, indeed necessary, but it doesn't perhaps stress enough, what the previous Swann/CRE definition concentrated upon 14 years ago, namely the critical role played by 'the normal workings of the system'. With regard to misunderstanding of what institutional racism in its fullest sense means, it is also somewhat unfortunate that it is defined by Sir William Macpherson in terms of a failure to provide:

> an appropriate and professional service to people because of their colour, culture or ethnic origin.

'Structured silence', institutional practices and schooling

Such a 'consumerist' definition, whilst catching some important aspects of where shortcomings lie, unfortunately omits other critical aspects, particularly in relation to schooling. The determination in the DfEE 10-point plan for ethnic minority students to improve their educational attainment is to be applauded as a vast improvement on simply celebrating festivals, as happened in some forms of multicultural education. And tackling harassment and the quite disproportionate exclusions of some groups of students, which has also been highlighted by the latest Ofsted report, are self-evidently important issues. Nevertheless, concentrating simply on these matters omits – as did David Blunkett's pronouncements in the *Daily Express* – the critical role played by structured silence about racism (and many other serious issues of social justice) in the curricula of many schools.

If the problem of schooling's role in the reproduction of racism was simply about 'service delivery' and qualifications this might not matter. However, report after report testifies to the fact that, even with identical qualifications, black people are far less likely to be employed or to be given a particular job than white youngsters with the same qualifications. A critical issue that needs to be addressed is the question of what the schooling of all citizens (and their subsequent education or training) has done to make them aware of the ways in which the 'normal' processes of institutions often discriminate; so that, to take one key example, employers can understand how their advertising, interviewing and selecting for jobs can all be racially biased. Classic instances of this are the CRE reports into the St George's Medical School (CRE, 1988b), into the shortcomings found in the middle management selection process of London Underground Limited (CRE, 1990) and into the difficulties experienced by Asian rail guards who wanted to become train drivers. More specifically, in the context of education, questions also need to be asked as to whether their own experience of racism within schooling – which still for many includes an education drawn up to an almost exclusively white agenda – prevents many black people from seriously contemplating teaching as a career.[19]

Additionally black people are still subjected, both within and without employment, to discrimination, harassment and assault because they are black. And this says nothing of murders infused with racism, such as those of Ahmed Iqbal Ullah and Stephen Lawrence. What has schooling done, for example, to disabuse those carrying out all of these acts from categorizing people into 'them' and 'us', assuming that black people really 'belong' elsewhere and assuming, for example, that black people are favoured by 'positive discrimination'? The reporting of the Stephen Lawrence Inquiry recommendations in the press and on television has been replete with notions of 'quotas' and 'positive discrimination', notions which can themselves be used divisively. The reporters involved were apparently quite unaware that the Race Relations Act itself makes these illegal. What chance, then, that disaffected youths, often with serious social problems of their own, are going to know any better, especially if schools themselves have been institutionally silent about the nature of racism and the law of the land?

This is the sort of 'structured' ignorance that is most dramatically displayed in Sir Paul Condon's apparent complete lack of awareness, 14 years after major aspects of it had been clarified by Swann and the CRE, that racism operates often in normal practices, sometimes from well-meaning motives and often out of ignorance, as well as in failing to take seriously complaints about harassment within a service and in failing to provide proper training for staff.

Schooling is the one institution that one might imagine should be dedicated to combating ignorance. But the evidence is that, as a matter of public policy, its priorities in England and Wales have been structured in a way that makes sustained consideration of equity issues (of all kinds) very difficult and certainly not essential. It is small wonder that misconceptions, stereotypes, distorted assumptions, loaded language, myths and downright falsehoods can flourish if serious anti-discrimination work is effectively structured out of school experience. Against such an impoverished educational background, it is hardly surprising that prominent and influential news reporters perpetuate falsehoods about race and the law, and that the most senior police officer in England has been operating for six years with a definition of racism so deficient that he couldn't possibly have used it effectively to tackle racism – in all its forms – within his force.

Paradoxically, in early years' development and child care plans the DfEE requires local authorities to ensure that an equal opportunity strategy be put in place. Further, the Early Year's Trainers Anti Racist Network (EYTARN) has recently published a report containing a framework for equality. This has been sent by the DfEE to every local authority in England and Wales, has been highlighted in its latest guidance and is to be used in its approval of early years excellence centres (EYTARN, 1998).

Conclusion

Hopefully, in an era of 'joined up' government, such a lead could be followed by the TTA in consultation with the teachers' committee which, at the time of writing, is advising it in relation to the DfEE 10-point plan on the educational achievement of ethnic minority students. ARTEN has made strong representations to, and indeed is represented on, that committee. But unless it succeeds in making clear to the TTA that tackling racial inequality is as much about educating all students about racism (and other forms of discrimination) as it is about better meeting the specific needs of ethnic minority students – and, crucially, unless the TTA takes such advice seriously and puts it into practice – the job that needs to be done will remain at best part done.

Such an outcome would, however, sit ill with Jack Straw's statement made in relation to his acceptance of almost all of the 70 recommendations in the Stephen Lawrence report, on the BBC's *Nine O'clock News* (23 March 1999):

> What the Lawrence process, the inquiry process, did was to open the eyes of the white community to what it can be like to suffer the unfairness in our society simply from being black or Asian. We've got to change that.

If there is now genuine understanding and sufficient political will, it may be that, with reference to issues of race, the TTA Standards will have to be revised or added to well before three years have elapsed. To be effective they will have to reflect the major elements enunciated by ARTEN in response to the original TTA ITT documents. But these should apply to all equity concerns, not just racism. To single out this one area could easily create a dangerous and divisive hierarchy of oppressions.

Any revision should, therefore, be the occasion for an explicit acknowledgement of the general values that should underpin teacher education, with work to counter all forms of discrimination at its heart. Only then will provision for teacher education in England and Wales start systematically to address the issues about teacher education raised by Nick Tate in January 1996. We would argue that this will entail dropping any pretence of an ideologically neutral position and departing from the present, seriously flawed, technicist/standards/efficiency model in the preparation of teachers. It is a model that is quite inadequate to the task of teacher education.

Notes

1. This chapter is indebted at many points to Jane Lane of ARTEN, who also co-presented the earlier version at the conference in the Institute of Education.
2. We are indebted, in this section, to Gavin Heron – research student at the University of Strathclyde – for providing insights and references into his exploration of related issues in the context of social work.
3. The TTA's apparent lack of appreciation of this recent evidence sat badly with its own requirement that teachers should be aware of recent classroom research. See *Standards for the Award of Qualified Teacher Status*, February 1997, TTA, p 3, point A 1 viii.
4. In Circular 10/97 and Circular 4/98 this reference to evaluation has indeed been deleted.
5. See Ainsworth, C S (1976) Rationality and a secular humanist view of Values I, in *Values Education*, University of Waikato, Hamilton, NZ. Following on from insights to be drawn from Hume, it is argued there that a fully developed notion of rationality that is objective and value free is logically incoherent.
6. *Guidelines for Teacher Training Courses*, op cit. There is, for instance, little in the document that could be construed as attending specifically to what have been called here the 'intellectual virtues'.
7. A similar body is now planned for England and Wales. See *Teachers: Meeting the challenge of change*, DfEE, London, December 1998.
8. The GTC makes clear that by the term 'black' it means all those who experience discrimination because of their colour.
9. See, for example, Rationality and a secular humanist view of Values: II, Ainsworth, C S (1976) in *Values Education*, University of Waikato, Hamilton, NZ.
10. See, for example, ibid, p 36, where any reference to value judgements is omitted in para 3e iii: 'how language can be described in terms of various functions'.
11. This is not to deny that such issues are important. It is rather that, as we later argue, they don't go to the heart of many of the ways in which schools, often by default, help to reproduce inequality – racial or otherwise.
12. There is not space here to address all the relevant issues in detail but, significantly, the same 'neutrality' about values is not adopted in the passages that stress (partly at the behest of teachers of these subjects) the value and importance of Physical Science and Mathematics.
13. *Developing the Teaching Profession – Meeting the Challenge of Change,* London, QMW Public Policy Seminar, 11 February 1999. At the conference specifically concerning these documents (which included an address by the minister Estelle Morris) the senior civil servant present, whilst trying to convince the audience that teachers' pay at least would be criterion referenced, used the expression 'the most able teachers' to describe the beneficiaries, without appearing to understand that this appeared to signify that in principle not all teachers would be able to meet the cri-

teria. And as to how schools which are 'competing' for limited funds can also be expected generously to share their best practice with other schools was left as something of a mystery.

14. On the experiences of black teachers see also Osler, A (1997) *The Education and Careers of Black Teachers: Changing identities, changing lives*, Open University Press, Buckingham.

15. Similar suspicions about the Government and its perceptions of prejudices have been voiced concerning the issue of homosexuality and Labour's promise to repeal Section 28 of the Local Government Act 1988, in Paul Burston, *Tony's Fairy Tales*, Channel 4, 13 March 1999.

16. For a critical analysis of such issues, see Ainsworth, C S (1998) Citizenship, inclusiveness and countering discrimination, in *Values Education for Democracy and Citizenship*, ed D Christie *et al*, University of Strathclyde, Glasgow, Gordon Cook Foundation.

17. 'Institutional racism is described... as a "range of long established systems, practices and procedures" which have the effect, if not the intention, of depriving ethnic minority groups of equality of opportunity and access to society's resources. "Institutional racism" operates through the normal workings of the system rather than the conscious intent of the prejudiced individual.' Commission for Racial Equality (1985) Swann: A response from the Commission for Racial Equality, CRE Publications, London, p 2. Though agreeing with the definition used in the Swann report, the Commission expressed concern that, apart from one section, the notion of institutional racism had 'not [informed] the remainder of the report', ibid, p 3.

18. The full definition of 'institutional racism' given in the report is 'The collective failure of an organization to provide an appropriate and professional service to people because of their colour, culture, or ethnic origin. It can be detected in processes, attitudes and behaviour which amount to discrimination through unwitting prejudice, ignorance, thoughtlessness and racist stereotyping which disadvantage minority ethnic people.' Op cit, p 28, par. 6.34.

19. See, for example, Johnson, A, Arshad, R and Kelly, E (1998) *University Ethos and Ethnic Minorities: Overcoming barriers to access and developing institutional support systems*, in Flexibility in Teaching and Learning Scheme (2): Dissemination Report, Scottish Higher Education Funding Council, Edinburgh. See also Johnson, A, Identifying and addressing the causes of discrimination in higher and further education: a discussion paper, *Proceedings of the Racial Equality Conference in Further and Higher Education*, Scottish Higher Education Funding Council in collaboration with the Commission for Racial Equality, Edinburgh.

References

Ainsworth, C S (1976) Rationality and a secular humanist view of Values: II, in *Values in Education*, University of Waikato, Hamilton, New Zealand

Apple, M (1993) *Official Knowledge: Democratic education in a conservative village*, Routledge, New York and London

ARTEN (1997) Report of the Annual Seminar, ARTEN, Glasgow

BBC (10 March 1999) *Today Programme*, Radio Four

Boyatzis, R (1982) *The Competent Manager: A model for effective performance*, John Wiley and Sons, Toronto

Cole, M (1989) Monocultural, multicultural and anti-racist education, in *The Social Context of Schooling*, The Falmer Press, London

Collins, M (1991) *Adult Education as Vocation*, Routledge, London

Commission for Racial Equality (February 1988a) *Medical School Admissions: Report of a formal investigation into St George's Hospital Medical School*, CRE, London

Commission for Racial Equality (CRE) (March 1988b) *Ethnic Minority School Teachers*, CRE, London

CRE (1990) *Lines of Progress: An inquiry into selection and equal opportunities in London Underground*, CRE, London

Commonwealth Institute, Saturday 18 January 1997, p 7

The Crime and Disorder Act: 1998

Dearden, R F (1968) *The Philosophy of Primary Education*, Routledge and Kegan Paul, London

De Maria, W (1992) On the trail of radical pedagogy, *British Journal of Social Work*, **22** (3), pp 231–52

DfEE (July 1997) *Teaching: High status, high standards, requirements for courses of initial teacher training*, DfEE, London

DfEE (May 1998) *Teaching: High status, high standards, requirements for courses of initial teacher training*, DfEE, London

DfEE (February 1999) *Teachers: Meeting the challenge of change, op cit, and Teachers: Meeting the challenge of change: Technical consultation document on pay and performance management*, DfEE, London

EYTARN (1998) *Planning for Excellence: Implementing the DfEE Guidance Requirements for the EOP Strategy in Early Years Development Plans*, EYTARN, London

Frankena, W K (1965) *Philosophy of Education*, Macmillan, New York

General Teaching Council (1992) *Gender in Education: GTC Leaflet 8*, GTC, Edinburgh

General Teaching Council (1994) *Multi-Cultural/Anti-Racist Education: GTC Leaflet 9*, GTC, Edinburgh

General Teaching Council (February 1997) *Report of the Working Group on Partnership in Initial Teacher Education*, GTC, Edinburgh

Gillborn, D and Gipps, C (1996) *Recent Research on the Achievements of Ethnic Minority Pupils*, Ofsted (HMSO), London

Hall, S (May/June 1985) Authoritarian populism: a reply, *New Left Review*, **151**, pp 115–24

Hodgkinson, P and Issit, M (eds) (1995) *The Challenge of Competence*, Cassell, London

Hyland, T (1995) Behaviourism and the meaning of competence, in *The Challenge of Competence*, ed P Hodgkinson, and M Issit, Cassell, London

Issit, M (1995) Competence, professionalism and equal opportunities, in *The Challenge of Competence*, ed P Hodgkinson, and M Issit, Cassell, London

John, G (1999) Potential change in the quality and inclusiveness of education: 'drifters and visionaries', *Developing the Teaching Profession – Meeting the Challenge of Change*, QMW Public Policy Seminar, London, 11 February

Macpherson, Sir William (1999) *The Stephen Lawrence Inquiry: Report of an Inquiry by Sir William Macpherson of Cluny*, The Stationery Office, London, February

Ofsted (1999) *Raising the Attainment of Minority Ethnic Pupils: School and LEA responses*, London

O'Hagan, K (1992) *Competence in Social Work Practice*, Jessica Kingsley, London

Osler, A (1997) *The Education and Careers of Black Teachers: Changing identities, changing lives*, Open University Press, Buckingham

Qualifications and Curriculum Authority (1998) *Education for Citizenship and the Teaching of Democracy in Schools*, London, September

Ramsay, J (1993) The hybrid course: competences and behaviourism in higher education, *Journal of Further and Higher Education*, **17** (3), pp 70–89

Scottish Consultative Council on the Curriculum (1998) *Curriculum Design for the Secondary Stages: Guidelines for schools, consultative draft*, Dundee

Scottish Consultative Committee on the Curriculum (1987) *Curriculum Design for the Secondary Stages: Guidelines for headteachers*

Scottish Office Education Department (1992) *Guidelines for Teacher Training Courses*, SOED, Edinburgh

Scottish Office (1999) *Targeting Excellence – Modernising Scotland's Schools*, SOED, Edinburgh

SOEID (October 1998) *Guidelines for Initial Teacher Education Courses in Scotland*, SOEID, Edinburgh. Sexuality and aspects of sectarianism are still excluded

TTA (February 1997) *Standards for the Award of Qualified Teacher Status*, London, TTA, p 11

TTA *Paper 2*, London, TTA, p 6

TTA *Paper 3, Primary English*, London, TTA

TTA (April 1998) *Initial Teacher Training National Curriculum: Consultation Summary*, TTA, London, p 7

Thatcher, M (1987) quoted in *Woman's Own*

Chapter 12

Communities in Search of Values: Articulating Shared Principles in Initial Teacher Education

Val Fraser and Mick Saunders

Introduction

There are numerous reasons why 'values' should be high on the agenda for those concerned with teacher education. One is that the worth of the enterprise is frequently called into question, not, significantly, by students or teachers, but by those with a more remote perspective. Another is that there is a reductive discourse abroad, which borrows from commerce a vocabulary of competition, and the claimed value of the disciplines of the marketplace. Teachers are to be trained rather than educated. What they need is an apprenticeship in which skills are demonstrated, practised and acquired. The standard of training can be straightforwardly described and measured, and from such measures league tables drawn up and published. Beginning teachers and schools are conceived of as customers needing information about a product or service. The response to alternative and more appropriate ways of describing the purposes and processes of teacher education is frequently one of aggressive dismissal.

It is not surprising that in the face of such reductive notions and combative stances there is disquiet in teaching and in teacher education. It is not, however, to be explained by the failed and dated theories of what is frequently labelled the 'educational establishment' – whatever that might be. Rather it is to do with the difficulty of promoting and sustaining a sense of the worthwhileness of teaching when so many current initiatives seem bent on deprofessionalizing those who undertake the work.

It is important therefore to be clear about the values that underpin teacher education. These can never be in the nature of settled and unchanging precepts. They will relate to the individuals involved in particular courses, to the social circumstances in which they operate, and to what emerges from processes of enquiry, reflection and evaluation. What follows is an account of on-going discussion and debate amongst the team of people responsible for the PGCE course at the University of Nottingham. Our hope is that the account will:

- accurately describe what has motivated and directed our discussions;
- indicate how our work serves an educative as well as a training function;
- encourage and contribute to a wider debate concerning value and principle in teacher education;
- offer a clear description of the theories of learning in which our practices are grounded.

The background

By way of introduction we should put what we are seeking to establish at Nottingham in a general perspective. Like colleagues everywhere we work to agendas not of our own making or choosing. In preparing student teachers to work to a National Curriculum claimed to be agreed, it is necessary actually to acknowledge the degree to which it has been a contested imposition. This is a challenge shared by teacher educators across the system. (Neither is this purely a concern in the UK. Similar developments are in train in the USA and Australia.) In the space of 36 weeks we have to make students familiar with what is statutorily required of them, offer a course which fulfils the specifications of Circular 9/92, and work to the competence model which that Circular makes compulsory. Yet also, if the process is to be properly educative, we must invite people to examine how the curricula for schools and teacher training have come about, and the nature of the relationship implied between teacher and taught through the statutory frameworks currently in place. We have to draw attention to a looking glass world:

> 'When I use a word,' Humpty Dumpty said in a rather scornful tone, 'it means just what I choose it to mean – neither more nor less.'
> 'The question is,' said Alice, 'whether you *can* make words mean different things.'
> 'The question is,' said Humpty Dumpty, 'which is to be master, that's all.'
> (Lewis Carroll, *Through the Looking Glass*, 1871)

Edgar Stones (1994) opens his book *Quality Teaching* with this quotation in order to call attention to a notable characteristic of governmental discourse. The 1973 DES document, *Education, a Framework for Expansion,* led, he says, to 'a sphincteral contraction in education provision in Britain'. The 1983 DES document, *Teaching Quality*, offered an account of the teacher's role that was limited, limiting, and thoroughly misconceived. Such examples could very easily be amplified *(Choice and Diversity,* for instance,) to indicate more extensively how political power has allowed words to mean what the masters want them to. It becomes the responsibility of teachers and teacher educators to examine such Orwellian doublespeak. It is a challenging position to be in.

Numbers of commentators have pointed to the significant shift in the political control over the curriculum taken forward by successive Conservative administrations since 1979. Protherough and King (1995, pp 9–10), for example, remind us of how Keith Joseph's *Curriculum Matters* consultation papers strategically curtailed discussion with professional groups and justified the formulation of policy directly through legislation. The strategy allowed Kenneth Baker later to make 'agreed national objectives' mandatory in the Education Act of 1988, and to impose not only a crude and content-dominated version of the curriculum, but also a strait-jacket of external assessments at all Key Stages which privileged a particular and highly contestable view of teaching and learning.

> Education is being reduced to a mechanistic process for turning out well-programmed, but unquestioning, operatives for the Thatcherite New Jerusalem. (A British teacher quoted in Hextall, 1988: 74)

It seems therefore that teachers face the dilemma of having to fulfil statutory obligations whilst taking a legitimately critical stance towards them. In turn teacher educators, if their courses are to be accredited, have to prepare beginning teachers for those inescapable but possibly unwelcome responsibilities, whilst offering a more sustaining and value-led version of what it is to be a teacher.

The need for an agreed language

A common feature of analyses of the National Curriculum and the Circulars that govern teacher education is the identification of a reductive and inappropriate terminology. Richard Pring (1996) points to:

> the adoption of metaphors from the world of business in place of those which have normally described that transaction between teacher and learner as together they try to make sense of, to find value in or to examine critically. Hence

the effort by the National Council for Vocational Qualifications to reduce the complex life of learning to lists of competences. Hence, too, the attempt to separate *the product from the process of learning, assessment from the curriculum*. (p 111)

The determination of the Teacher Training Agency to bring Initial Teacher Education similarly within an NVQ framework is therefore a depressing prospect, and makes an alternative account of the professional responsibilities of the teacher a pressing necessity.

A problem to be faced is the debasement of terminology, which should signal proper attention to matters of quality, value and professionalism. 'Quality assurance', for example, is an expression associated with bureaucratic and mechanistic interventions and devices. All institutions seem to boast mission or vision statements more often than not viewed with scepticism by those whose principles and activities they are meant to describe. Ofsted has developed a reputation for misrepresenting its findings in thoroughly shoddy ways. So terms like quality, standards and vision become suspect. This makes the reclaiming of such vocabulary an urgent matter, involving not simply a definition of terms, but an engagement with the variety of meanings a particular idea might carry. Neither should we suppose that we will finish up with easy, neat or settled agreements. T S Eliot memorably expresses how meanings are struggled towards, are particular to time and circumstance, and have to be reconsidered and remade in a continual and sometimes circular process:

And so each venture
Is a new beginning, a raid on the inarticulate
With shabby equipment always deteriorating
In the general mess of imprecision...
There is only the fight to recover what has been lost
And found and lost again and again: and now, under conditions
That seem unpropitious.
(*Four Quartets: East Coker*)

These are lines which resonate in the circumstances in which we find ourselves – concerned to make meaningful the work we do and the professional lives we lead at a time when conditions seem unpropitious.

The raid on the inarticulate has always been an essential and value-laden activity for teachers as much as poets. How do we get beyond the crudeness of the terms we are currently obliged to use – attainment targets, key stages, levels of attainment, levels of competence and so on? How do we nurture and make apparent the value of complexity and ambiguity in preference to unjustified certainty? How do we nevertheless conduct ourselves so as to make possible a more precise language for exploring and clarifying worthwhileness and principle?

Traditions of enquiry

There are discourses which go some way to address such questions and which have been good to be reminded of in our Nottingham circumstances: not to provide ready-made answers but to provide focus and structure to the discussions in train. Richard Pring's contribution to *Values in Education and Education in Values* has already been mentioned. In his chapter he usefully revisits and restates the arguments for, and the problems with, the traditional version of a liberal education. He reminds us too of the significance of the work of R S Peters which merits continued attention and refinement by those who are concerned with what is educationally worthwhile. What to teach cannot be a matter settled once and for all by QCA or the TTA. How forms of knowledge are defined, developed and made available to learners are questions that require to be periodically addressed, both for themselves and in relation to the constantly changing cultural and social conditions in which such learning takes place. Philosophical analysis remains an appropriate and essential activity, therefore, for those concerned with the curriculum.

The same may be said about the important tradition that has taken the moral responsibilities of teachers as its field of enquiry. Jasper Ungoed-Thomas's (1996) chapter in *Values in Education and Education in Values* has as its title 'Vision, values and virtue'. Not surprisingly, questions of vocabulary and definition are to the fore in this area too. The single word 'school' might mean (or have meant) significantly different things to different people in particular contexts. Victorian schools, for example, with an aim to inculcate Christian values, were built in ways that echoed ecclesiastical architecture and had a curriculum and teaching methods reminiscent of the catechism. The characteristic contemporary paradigm of the school for Ungoed-Thomas, as much as for Richard Pring, is a factory:

> At its apex is the senior management team, deploying such techniques as line management and total quality control, and concerned to compete effectively in the marketplace. To this end, budgets are kept and scrutinized by accountants, press officers try to ensure a positive image, and performance indicators are put in place to monitor output variables. Above all, there is concern that the product, that is the student, should be delivered effectively and efficiently, in accordance with the requirements of the various customers, for example, employers, government, further and higher education and parents. (pp 144–45)

Again, we can point depressingly to the measures currently being applied to initial teacher education in order to come to a judgement as to its quality: the cellular inspection framework, the NQT and employer questionnaires, the necessity for information to be capable of tabular presentation, and the ultimate production of a league table whose connection with what it seeks to represent is at best tenuous.

In setting out what we wish schools to do and be, we have to seek to understand what the current sets of possible meanings might be and in which directions the ideological winds are presently blowing. The language we have to do this with is inescapably analogous and metaphorical. This is by no means an impediment if what we are interested in are values. But it does make necessary a close attention to the particular senses or associations we wish to attach to particular words and the ideas they embody. Ungoed-Thomas is therefore keen to restore some credibility and precision to the word 'vision':

> Authentic vision is of crucial significance for schools. In the first place, it should help inform and guide the moral development of students. There is a necessary connection between real vision, as contrasted with fantasy, and moral behaviour.
>
> If we are to develop fully as persons we can hardly manage in the absence of a moral vision. As Iris Murdoch has put it, 'we can only move properly in a world that we can see, and what must be sought for is vision'. (p 146)

Vision resides in people, not institutions. People articulate, develop and sustain vision. Of course, if we don't like the term, we can choose another, but the bringing together of the sense of an imagined ideal and of clear-sightedness is actually useful in thinking through educational values and their necessary rootedness in the actions of particular people in particular situations. Whatever term we choose, it needs to allow a focus on the process of defining practices and principles which in turn permit and encourage the allegiance and commitment of those engaged in educational activity. For it is impossible that an imposed or unexplored vision could meet with or encourage properly educative outcomes.

Ungoed-Thomas's argument is for the fullest possible understanding of what vision implies and what associated implications follow. In pursuing the matter he refers to the work of MacIntyre (1985):

> MacIntyre has proposed a particular approach to interpreting the meaning of virtue... It places due emphasis on the cultural contexts and social traditions within which notions of virtue arise and develop. It does not, however, adopt a stance which is either necessarily relativistic in moral terms, or which denies the significance and integrity of the idea of a person. It is, in fact, a perception of virtue which is consistent with the idea of a school as I have discussed it. (p 150)

Virtues should be regarded as human qualities necessary to take forward what MacIntyre calls worthwhile practices or activities, in which education would be included. That is his first stage of defining virtue. The second stage is connected with 'those qualities necessary to sustain us in our personal search for the good'. The third stage incorporates the notion that virtue must be socially as well as individually expressed. Worthwhile human goals 'can only be elaborated and possessed within an ongoing social tradition' (MacIntyre, 1985: 273). In these respects the concept of virtue, like that of vision, is an apt one to pursue, both in relation to schools and the education appropriate to those preparing to teach.

In summary, Ungoed-Thomas (1996) offers the following assertions. Schools are essentially concerned with developing individual people. They should therefore teach and embody the virtue of respect for persons. In relation to the curriculum and the forms of knowledge that legitimately make it up, the governing virtue should be regard for truth. Perhaps we should say that virtue resides in the proper understanding of the means by which truth in particular areas of the curriculum is established and tested. Obviously schools are communities. In relation to community the abiding virtue should be fairness, and in relation to citizenship, another fundamental value that schools are charged to promote, the virtue should be responsibility. These are attractive hooks on which to hang an examination of what educative communities should espouse and practice. Within such a framework there is the possibility and necessity to give these principles a local habitation and a name, both in terms of cultural traditions which give them particular context and expression and in looking to support individuals in the search for their personal vision of the good life and right behaviour. These statements are useful starting points for a consideration of what values might inform a programme of initial teacher education. The philosophical concerns and traditions of moral education encourage us to think beyond classroom competences to engage with personal and social questions of more compelling significance.

Other perspectives lead to similar ends and similarly call into question the adequacy of the apprenticeship model of teacher training. Much to be preferred is what is implied in the term teacher education. In a School of Education it is clear that, just as within a school, there is a need to achieve a sense of what are agreed and shared values and commitments, and how individuals can make and develop their particular contributions to that collaborative enterprise. We need to be able to indicate clearly to student teachers what principles underpin the courses and experiences we offer, and how they are intended to allow for both personal and professional development. This is true to what actually happens on successful courses. Students will say that they have learnt as much about themselves as about teaching through the experiences undergone and through reflection upon them. By the same token, amongst the purposes of teacher education must be the movement beyond introspection and personal concerns to an acknowledgement of the professional imperative to look to the development of others. Of course the personal and the professional perspectives are not and cannot be mutually exclusive. A similar point can be made about the necessary connection, for teachers and for teacher educators, between practice and theory, teaching and research. The work of Edgar Stones (1994), from a psychological starting point, exemplifies the essential interdependence of these fields of enquiry and practice.

Like Pring and Ungoed-Thomas, Stones finds it necessary to examine particular metaphors customarily applied to teaching. For instance, teaching is frequently referred to as a craft, and beginning teachers as frequently characterized as apprentices. These are impoverished and unsustaining descriptions in his view, largely because they are put forward usually by those who deride theory as irrelevant to the real work of delivering the curriculum and winching up standards. However:

> Advances in education and teaching, in distinction from administrative and bureaucratic changes, are totally dependent upon a highly skilled teaching force with real understanding of theory – especially of learning but also of the impact of wider social pressures. (Stones, 1994: 13)

It is interesting to note how the individual and social come together as clearly in an approach underpinned by educational psychology as it does from the perspectives of philosophical analysis and moral education. The question of value remains central. Theory in Stones' terms involves the establishment and the examination of principles. Craft knowledge, if that is a helpful term to employ, is by no means ruled out – but it is not sufficient. No teaching can be atheoretical. It is therefore essential to be explicit about theory so that the practice supported by it is open to scrutiny.

Constructing a theory of teaching precisely describes the educative function of a programme of initial teacher 'training' and by extension the continuing professional development that should properly be the entitlement of serving teachers. For teaching ought to be an enquiry-led activity. Teachers look to solve pedagogical problems and meet pedagogical challenges. Native intelligence may take some people some of the way, but knowledge of illuminating theory is also a requirement for informed and creative action. It is worth quoting Stones at length on the matter because he puts the case so well:

> Inquiring teachers will see teaching as an activity of great complexity which we hardly yet begin to understand. They will see it as open-ended exploration in which they express their pedagogical knowledge in action that will not only improve the conditions of learning for their pupils, but also enlarge their theoretical understanding. This follows from the view of teaching as inquiry informed by a self-consciously held body of principles in which the principles are put to the acid test of practice. In fact, the theory and the practice are best conceived as

two aspects of the same process, so that it might be said that practice is also tested in the light of theory. The two are mutually refining. (Stones, 1994: 15)

The Nottingham Values Group

We now offer a description of how the process of articulating values has been pursued at Nottingham. We expect the perspectives outlined thus far to continue to inform what we do. In our particular circumstances we have also begun to explore what the school improvement movement can offer us, for reasons that should become clear.

As a team of PGCE tutors representing many subject disciplines, we have embarked upon a programme of professional development to explore further the central issues that underpin our collective work. Recognizing that the purpose and nature of particular areas of the curriculum (or forms of knowledge) may vary, we believe that the methodological issues that emerge from pursuing lines of enquiry into basic questions of teaching and learning are essentially shared. They centre on the fact that all educational activity is socially constructed and capable of having aims and outcomes defined and evaluated. If this is true of learning in schools it is similarly so for student teachers. We are looking therefore to establish and make public the principles that give coherence to the PGCE programme: the common ground occupied by all participants in the process irrespective of their subject specialisms.

We have an agreed professional development programme that brings us together as a staff for a minimum of one day each term. We have used those occasions to present and discuss our current practices, and to establish what is shared and what is legitimately distinct in the method courses we offer. As a result we have become better informed about each other's work, have learnt from each other's good practice, and have sought to give real substance to the principle of collegiality. This programme was already well established when a new professor and Head of Department arrived. We particularly welcomed David Hopkins' potential contribution to the process of staff and institutional development as his research interests and activities focused on school improvement. Much of the work of supporting beginning teachers necessarily involves thinking through what makes for successful schools, both in relation to pupils' beaming and to the models of teaching and reflection offered. It was particularly appropriate therefore to invite David to brief us about his work on the Improving the Quality of Education for All project (IQEA) as part of the staff development programme.

We subsequently agreed to see whether the principles and findings that related to school improvement could find an application in the School of Education, and in particular how the developing frameworks for staff and pupil development in schools might (or might not) apply to higher education in an environment of change and required accountability.

Like schools, we seek stability against a background of imposed reform. Initiatives that demand we formalize our relationships with partner schools and prescribe curriculum content for initial teacher education have arrived and continue to dominate our planning. However, as the IQEA project directors acknowledge, 'change and improvement are not necessarily synonymous... and such changes are (not) always desirable' (Hopkins *et al*, 1996).

Given that much educational change arises from external pressure and is imposed upon institutions, how can a school, or a School of Education, manage change and continue to raise student achievement? Our discussions focused on the need to be clearer about what changes should be resisted, adapted, accommodated or welcomed. Alongside our concerns about our own working conditions and practices, we were keen to clarify our role in helping beginning teachers identify appropriate responses to imposed change. These concerns did not present themselves to us as separate from one another.

What emerged as fundamental was the need for a statement of values. In the case of an individual, including an individual student teacher, this would be an informed personal theory of teaching and beaming; in the case of a collection of individuals or an institution, this would in some cases take the form of a set of shared understandings/beliefs that characterized and disciplined the work collectively undertaken. The connection with the traditions of enquiry described earlier has become quite clear to us. Additionally the IQEA Project has provided some telling parallels. 'Schools are most likely to strengthen their ability to provide enhanced outcomes for all [students] when they adopt ways of working that are consistent with their own aspirations as well as the current reform agenda' (Hopkins *et al*, 1996). If we were to use the impetus of external reform for internal purposes then we needed a collaborative approach to setting our goals and establishing our priorities which reflected a core set of values. In this way we would be better guided to respond appropriately to change whatever its provenance.

Change has certainly become endemic. For example:

- Circular 9/92 has required an incremental formalizing of the working relationships with schools.
- The development of the Framework for Inspection marries notions of quality and funding and demands an immediate audit of current policy and practice.
- The National Curriculum for Initial Teacher Training intends to result in 'the biggest shake-up in teacher training for a generation'.
- The Research Assessment Exercise commits universities to programmes

of research and publication with consequent implications for the priority accorded to teaching.

- In response to diminished funding the University has instituted what is euphemistically termed a restructuring exercise.

The effects of such initiatives are felt by and are visited upon individuals and departments. How could we, with integrity and wisdom and in ways that were helpful to our students, respond to such agendas? Defining our aims and values and developing a shared and understood language was, we felt, essential. However much we debate the quality of teaching, 'This will not lead to enhanced levels of student achievement unless we, as an educational community, expand and define more precisely our vocabulary of teaching' (Hopkins, 1996).

In making our values explicit we:

- make available implicit knowledge/understanding;
- sharpen up this implicit knowledge, develop it, adapt it or discard it;
- are able to give a greater sense of what we are about to our students in a way that is helpful to them, especially in assisting them to clarify their own informed theories and values;
- can synthesize this work with the many other projects that PGCE colleagues are involved in and seek to reach wider and more public audiences;
- are working together in ways that are helpful to our collective and individual self-esteem rather than feeling belittled and powerless in the face of relentless requests for change.

The PGCE Values Group was set up following the in-service events described above. Membership of the group is open to any PGCE staff member – this applies to attendance at meetings and to contributions to the written work that we have already undertaken, and intend in the future to produce. The group has a core representation of all the subject areas taught in the PGCE course. In this respect we were putting into practice at least three of the five principles outlined in the IQEA Project:

- The vision of the school should be one that embraces **all** members of the school community as both learners and contributors.
- The school will see in external pressures for change important opportunities to secure its **internal priorities**.
- The school will seek to develop structures and create conditions which encourage collaboration and lead to the **empowerment** of individuals and groups (Hopkins *et al*, 1996).

In our first meeting there was the sense that we were conducting illuminating and new work. The group had attracted newly appointed and more established members of staff, but not one of the large number present could remember debating at whole course level the philosophy which underpinned our practice, though of course this had happened at team and subject level. So we began by defining terms (What do we mean by values?) and clarifying our aims (What do we want to achieve in the short, medium and long term?). We then cross-referenced subject documentation written for students, which contained aims and objectives, in order to examine common themes. We also took advantage of the presence of a visiting scholar who had been involved in the Values Review of the National Professional Development Program in Western Australia to assist us in developing our work.

A further in-service event was planned to focus on the issue of establishing values. The collation of the subject documentation was fed into that day as was the intention to define and articulate more precisely our underpinning theories of teaching and learning. Colleagues were asked to work in groups and make explicit what they understood by the term 'an educated person' and then to set out their views on what constituted good teaching and good teacher education.

A first draft from one group read as follows:

> We believe that an educated person will of course be literate, numerate, able to communicate effectively and argue rationally. He or she will have the capacity to be autonomous in their learning but have also the understanding that knowledge is framed and achieved socially and so be able to critique knowledge and information and the value systems underpinning them. He or she will see themselves with a degree of self-awareness and placed within a set of communities from local to global. Evidence for this would include empathy, an ability to collaborate, and a sense of responsibility for mutual development within their communities. So they would possess the necessary intellectual and social skills for the furtherance of their own and others' learning. He or she would also possess a set of personal beliefs or theories which would enable them to act with integrity and wisdom.

The collective views on good teaching were collated and discussed in the light of emerging themes. From that discussion has come a draft document addressed to PGCE students:

> In choosing to train as a teacher, you are committing yourself to contributing to other people's learning as well as developing your own. We see teaching and learning not as separate activities but interconnected parts of a whole.
>
> There is a set of national competences against which you and your tutors will measure your performance over the year. However, above and beyond that

framework, we seek to create a learning environment at Nottingham which allows you to develop your own informed personal theory of teaching and learning. You will also be given opportunities to consider the principles upon which an education system is based and this will involve you in exploring other disciplines related to the study of education as well as the expertise you bring to your main method. You will be encouraged to examine the links between these two complementary aspects of the course. With this in mind, we would like to make explicit the values which underpin our definition of good teaching.

Good teachers operate on five levels:

1. They are secure in their knowledge, and convey confidence and enthusiasm for their subject and its place within the broader canvas of education.
2. They have a clear sense of what they are doing and why, and model their educational theories in their daily practice.
3. They have a sensitive understanding of how students make most progress in the classroom and because they understand the social aspects of learning they see school as a place where people can learn from one another.
4. They present themselves to students as learners as well as teachers and are committed to developing pupils' independence and curiosity.
5. They take seriously the need to help students develop their social and moral awareness and responsibility, both within school and outside it.

A decision was made to not only encourage our beginner teachers to aspire to become teachers who operate on these five levels but to hold ourselves accountable as teachers to this model. To this end we have embedded the above statements into the tutor evaluation system which is undertaken by all PGCE students at the end of the course. This meets with the requirements of the fifth principle of the IQEA Project. 'The school will seek to promote the view that **monitoring and evaluation of quality** is the responsibility which all members of staff share' (Hopkins *et al*, 1996).

Our current tasks involve the collation of the values underpinning the statements which colleagues submitted concerning the principles and purposes of teacher education. Here is our first attempt.

Good teacher education:

- is made possible by teacher educators who operate on the five levels identified in the earlier statement;
- articulates what we mean by student entitlements and takes account of the individual needs and values of student teachers;
- is committed to meeting children's needs;
- is underpinned by a set of shared understandings and principles which is made explicit to the learners and which includes the links between their subject and broader educational development;

- introduces ways of recognizing orthodoxies and helps to develop a professional response and a professional identity;
- encourages the recognition of education as an intellectually rigorous discipline requiring wide reading and discussion to develop an informed personal theory of teaching and learning;
- demonstrates the inextricable links between theory and practice as well as between the application of theory and reflection, and provides a balance of practical, supported guidance and theoretical perspectives;
- empowers teachers to explore different teaching and learning strategies which offer a variety of learning;
- experiences and encourages teachers to continually develop their own style through collaborative endeavours and critical autonomy;
- requires students to reflect on their and others' practice with a view to improving the learning experiences of pupils, continuing their professional development, and contributing to that of others;
- encourages a global understanding of the role of the teacher in making explicit the interconnectedness of communities to which an individual belongs and in helping to prepare pupils to become global citizens of the future;
- offers qualified optimism and provides the impetus and motivation for a commitment to life-long teacher education, including an introduction to the support and stimulus provided by wider educational communities.

In setting out our stall in advance of the arrival of the National Curriculum for teacher trainers, we accepted that our version would have to exist alongside that document. However, these external pressures for change will provide important opportunities to secure our internal priorities and adapt such imposed calls for change to the School of Education's own purposes. It is in this way that we hope to respond in a principled way, whether it is to resist, adapt, accommodate or welcome such reforms.

We hope that a major outcome of our work will be improved learning for student teachers. If the first principle of school improvement is that it is 'a process that focuses on enhancing the quality of students' learning' (Hopkins et al, 1996), we would look to outcomes for student teachers that would show capacities for creativity and critical thinking, improved self-esteem and enhanced prospects for employment in schools informed by intelligently established theories of teaching and learning. For tutors we would hope to see 'increased collegiality, opportunities for professional learning, increased responsibility' (Hopkins et al, 1996) as well as a sense not only of surviving changes intact but of emerging with a feeling of personal and professional self-worth.

Conclusion

In describing this programme of discussion, and in setting out the first drafts of statements of value and principle, we are aware of the ordinariness of what we are doing. If the response of a reader were to be 'What's so special about that?' we would have to reply with all due modesty 'Not very much'. Nevertheless, it has been brought home to us that in the general rush and hurry of our daily business, made incrementally more busy by the insistent agendas of outside agencies, it has required an effort of will to keep first principles vital and under review. However unsurprising the end results, the process is proving important and affirming in a number of ways. To frame our discussions by referring to those discourses touched on in the first sections of this chapter has contextualized the work within respected and valuable traditions. To look for connections with school improvement has similar potential, perhaps, for offering perspectives that go beyond the immediate and parochial. Our guess is that most colleagues in teacher education are engaged in very similar efforts to retain and develop clear values to inform what they do in unpropitious times. We would be very pleased to hear from them, to be informed of work elsewhere, and to contribute to a wider and more extended exchange.

References

Hextall, I (1988) Educational changes in England and Wales: the impact of the New Right, in *Making the Future: Politics and Educational Reform*, ed E B Gumbert, Georgia State University, Georgia

Hopkins, D (1996) On the need for a language of teaching, in *The Primary School Manager*, Pitman Publishing, London

Hopkins, D, Ainscow, M and West, M (1996) 'Unravelling the complexities of school improvement', a case study of the 'Improving the Quality of Education for All' (IQEA) Project in the Open University Course E838 Reader *Organizational Effectiveness and Improvement in Education*, Open University Press, Milton Keynes

MacIntyre, A (1985) *After Virtue: A study in moral theory*, Duckworth, London

Pring, R (1996) Values and education policy, in *Values in Education and Education in Values*, ed J Halstead and M Taylor, Falmer Press, London

Protherough, R and King, P (1995) *The Challenge of English in the National Curriculum*, Routledge, London

Stones, E (1994) *Quality Teaching*, Routledge, London

Ungoed-Thomas, J (1996) Vision, values and virtue, in *Values in Education and Education in Values*, ed J Halstead and M Taylor, Falmer Press, London

PART FOUR

RESEARCH FOR EDUCATION IN VALUES

Chapter 13

Valued Educational Research: Reconceptualizations of the Curriculum

David Scott

Introduction

This chapter explores the role of values in researched accounts of educational systems, institutions and curricula. It contrasts methodologies that can be broadly located within positivist/empiricist frameworks with those that incorporate a hermeneutic dimension, and identifies the way values are concealed in the former, but made explicit in the latter. This element of reflexivity, it is argued, is central to the construction of research encounters and determines the way we come to conclusions about educational processes. This builds in a critical dimension to educational research and this chapter will therefore examine those values that underpin texts and curricula.

Positivism

Positivism, for so long the dominant tradition in educational research, has been understood in a number of ways. However, Kolakowski (1972) argues that a positivist conception of the world includes four elements: phenomenalism, nominalism, the separation of facts and values, and the unity of the scientific method. Briefly, phenomenalism refers to the belief that as observers of the world we are only entitled to deal with phenomena as they appear to us and not to hidden or concealed essences. Natural and social scientists therefore deal with the relationships between these observed phenomena as they manifest themselves in regular patterns. The second element is nominalism. This is where the world is said to consist of objects which cannot be reduced in any way – in short, that we can discover facts about the world, which can then be used as building blocks in the development of theory. These facts exist by virtue of what the world is and do not depend in any way on their perception or cognition by social actors. This would seem to suggest that the relation between the world and our descriptions of it is unproblematic. Indeed, that a simple correspondence theory can be adduced to explain the relation, so that words and numbers are simply the means by which such phenomena are made intelligible.

The third element is the separation of facts and values and logically follows from the nominalist doctrine discussed above. As Kolakowski (1972: 13) argues: 'the phenomenalist, nominalist conception of science has another important consequence, namely, the rule that refuses to call value judgements and normative statements knowledge'. Logical positivists (cf Ayer, 1954, among others) would go further and suggest that those branches of philosophy such as ethics and aesthetics which deal primarily with issues of judgement and value cannot legitimately be described as knowledge at all. Thus ethical judgements are understood as emotive outbursts which cannot be evaluated as true or false. We may express value judgements about the world but we cannot expect them to be anything other than arbitrary choices and certainly they cannot qualify as scientific statements. The fourth element is the fundamental belief in the unity of the scientific method; which is that there is only one correct way of understanding natural and social phenomena and that scientific detachment and objectivity constitute the right method.

These four principles lead to a view of knowledge which is concerned with the establishment of general laws or nomothetic statements about the world (both in its physical and social forms). These laws allow replicability of research, in that their discovery can be verified by other researchers who adopt similar procedures – these procedures or rules consist of public or verifiable criteria by which descriptions of the social world can be judged. These general laws consist of 'the constant conjunction of atomistic events or states of affairs, interpreted as the objects of actual or possible experience' (Bhaskar, 1979: 158).

A number of objections have been made to this way of understanding. The first is that data about the world are always underpinned by theoretical frameworks: the world is pre-understood. The second objection follows from this and suggests that this implies a close relationship between knower and known which cannot be accommodated within a model of the disinterested observer of events. Thus, at the very least this implies a reconceptualization of the notion of objectivity. It is important to understand that accepting this reconceptualization and certainly weakening of the naive objectivist position does not imply that it is not possible to adopt a realist position. What it does imply is that any realist position has to take into consideration the inescapable limitations imposed on us by our locatedness in discourses, power-plays, environments and time.

The third objection stems from the inability of social scientists to develop general laws and suggests that because social life, and more particularly the relationship between constructs developed by observers and those used by social actors, is so arranged, then nomothetic descriptions of educational activities are rarely possible. The double hermeneutic referred to here, with its two-way relationship between social actors' and social observers' interpretations, at best allows structures or persistent relations to be only relatively enduring. Furthermore, the interpretive element involved in this means that we cannot take for granted that the categories we use to determine social facts are accurate unless we build a self-referential element into our research methodology. As soon as we do this we create open systems whereby we cannot be sure that the cases we have used to determine patterns of social life are in fact the same across time and place.

The fourth objection again follows from this. If it is difficult to imagine social laws being developed, then the predictive power of social descriptions is considerably weakened. Furthermore, unlike the natural sciences, any predictions we do make may influence the activities of those affected by them thus changing their nature and at the same time decreasing our certainty about those predictions. The fifth objection is alluded to above and suggests that if we are only concerned with events and their constant conjunction, we are concerned merely with appearances and ignore fundamental or underlying essences. Finally, an objection is made that the universalizing of method by which we can come to understand the world ignores the fact that method is both constitutive of the data we collect and immersed in specific and time-bound epistemological frameworks, or, as MacIntyre (1988) calls them, 'traditions of knowledge'. Furthermore, understanding these 'traditions of knowledge' can only be attained from within; that is, in order to critique such frameworks, we can only do so from within the traditions of thought that sustain them.

Paradigmatic debates

Research/evaluation, therefore, cannot be thought of as a pragmatic activity. Researchers/evaluators need to offer answers to philosophical, in particular epistemological, questions such as: what is the proper relationship between the researcher and participants in their research? How can we know reality? What is it? As a consequence, researchers, knowingly or not, are always located within methodological frameworks that implicitly answer some of the questions posed above. Denzin and Lincoln (1995) suggest that there are four different ways of conceptualizing this debate. The first is where those criteria used to judge natural scientific work are thought equally appropriate for the study of the social world (this is a paradigmatic perspective). The second position is opposed to this since the argument is that the social and natural worlds are qualitatively different and thus different criteria are appropriate for making judgements about each (this is a di-paradigmatic perspective). The third position is that there are no appropriate criteria for the study of the social world (this is a multi-paradigmatic perspective). Finally, there is a fourth position which is that new criteria need to be developed which are appropriate for all forms of research but which explicitly involve a rejection of the epistemological and ontological assumptions that underpin positivism (this is a uni-paradigmatic perspective).

These debates are not purely esoteric, but have real and material effects on the business of evaluation and research. Contra Bryman (1988) researchers/evaluators are confronted by a number of dilemmas in the field that cannot be solved pragmatically, but only by reference to epistemological and ontological perspectives. Bryman (1988: 125) argues that fieldwork is a social activity and thus appropriate fieldwork behaviour cannot be ethically or normatively orientated, but is fundamentally a practical activity. In a sense, this viewpoint acknowledges its own flaw, which is that it conflates normative and descriptive accounts of research. That researchers in the past have paid scant attention to epistemological and ontological concerns is no guide as to how they should have behaved or should behave in the future.

The qualitative/quantitative divide

The most profound divide is between qualitative and quantitative researchers. The two main forms of quantitative research are experimental (or quasi-experimental where it is not possible to choose randomly groups or individuals for comparative purposes) and correlational. Each of these is problematic. Experimental researchers have been criticized on a number of grounds. In essence these criticisms are fourfold. First, many things are not easy to test for. Effects may be more subtle or difficult to conceptualize than experiment allows for. This point is particularly relevant to the time dimension of experiments, since effects of interventions are deemed to show up either partially or completely at certain definite moments of time which the experimenter is able to identify and thus appropriate as testing moments. Second, the experimental researcher studies human interaction in artificial settings and as a result it may be difficult to draw valid conclusions which relate to real-life situations; in other words, experiments may be ecologically invalid. Third, experimenters may not be able to capture the culture of the setting being investigated, operating as they do by reducing aspects of social life to sets of variables, which, for the purposes of producing mathematical models, they then operationalize by reducing complex human activities to numbers. Indeed critics (Giddens 1984 and others) would go further and suggest that social phenomena cannot be properly understood without referring to the explanations given by social actors for their behaviours and activities. This last point refers to both experimental and correlational research.

In addition, correlational researchers need to address a number of issues. The first concerns the implicit uni-linear mode of causation they subscribe to. Educational practice may be conceived as deliberative action designed to achieve certain ends. What this implies is that there may be a number of ways that are equally appropriate to achieve those ends. Indeed, participants in research projects may respond in different ways to different initiatives. However, the use of mathematical models to describe educational settings and the production of prescribed lists of specified behaviours would suggest a uni-linear approach to, for example, schooling. Quantitative modelling necessarily leads to certain ways of understanding these settings and precludes others.

The second issue concerns the relationship between correlations and causal mechanisms. Even if a correlation can be established between two variables, it is still not possible to assert that the one caused the other to happen in an unproblematic way. There is always the possibility of a third variable causing variance in both. Furthermore we cannot be sure as to which variable is prior to the other. Correlations are no more than the recording of relationships of variables or the constant conjunction of events. Realists such as Bhaskar reject the notion that these constant conjunctions of events necessarily represent reality. He argues that there are two different realms – the epistemological and the ontological. Causal mechanisms reside in the ontological realm; constant conjunctions of events reside in the epistemological realm. The problem for educational researchers is to bridge the gap between the epistemological and ontological, if it is understood that there is inevitably a gap between appearance and reality. Reality, as Bhaskar understands it, can be characterized in four ways: there are certain truths about the world whether we can know them or not; our knowledge of the world is always fallible because any claims we make about it can be disputed; there are transphenomenalist truths of which we can only have knowledge of their appearances and not necessarily of underlying structures or causal mechanisms; and even more importantly, there are counter-phenomenalist truths in which those deep structures actually have misleading appearances, that is those appearances may be in conflict with the mechanisms that sustain them.

There are two consequences of this division between appearance and reality. First, the designation of correlations does not necessarily lead to the uncovering of causes. If we conflate the two, we are guilty of what Bhaskar calls the ontic fallacy, that is the mixing up of epistemological and ontological phenomena. This is most obvious in some well-known examples. A hooter in London signalling the end of the day's work in a factory does not cause workers in Birmingham to pack up and go home, even if a correlation can be established between the two phenomena. A good correlation has been discovered between human and stork birth rates over a period of time in various regions of Sweden, but it is clear that the one does not cause the other to happen. Both these examples show what may be called spurious correlations in that the regularities so described do not relate in a straightforward manner to the causal mechanism that produced them. There may be two reasons for this. First, as suggested above, a third variable may have acted on both to create the pattern we have observed. Second, as Bhaskar suggests, deep structures may have contradictory appearances. Evaluators of educational activities may therefore have to be extremely careful about ascribing causal relations to the observed constant conjunction of events. Furthermore, if this is correct, then there are two methodological solutions. The first is the use of experimental or quasi-experimental methods. The second is a qualitative or ethnographic approach.

Meanwhile, we come to the other problem with mathematical models of educational activities, and this is their ability to predict outcomes. If we uncover causal mechanisms, and the claim is then made that those causal mechanisms apply in other circumstances, whether in place or time, then we are claiming that it is possible to develop laws about human activity, in a similar way to those laws developed by natural scientists. However, for us to be able to do this, we have to understand human beings and human activities in specific ways. First, they are subject to laws of nature which compel them to behave in certain definite ways. Regardless of their complexity, the claim is made that if certain conditions are met, human beings will behave in certain predictable ways. As a result, it is possible for us to produce prescriptive lists of best possible educational practice, confident as we are that if we set in motion the right intervention, it will have the desired effects. Second, that it is possible for us, given our locatedness in specific temporal and geographical localities, to uncover those mechanisms. For Bhaskar, those mechanisms anyway are only 'relatively enduring' and they are subject to decay because of the double hermeneutical nature of social reality and social research.

Interpretive perspectives

Human beings both generate and are in turn influenced by social scientific descriptions of social processes. What this means is that any law-like statements we can make about educational activities are subject to evaluation and re-evaluation of their worth by practitioners acting subsequently. This re-evaluation means that those causal mechanisms inscribed in laws are suddenly no longer simple mechanisms that work on human beings, but ones that now have added to them a further interpretive element. As Giddens (1984: 31) argues, this 'introduces an instability into social research' which renders data and those findings produced by experimental or correlational methods problematic:

> The social sciences operate with a double hermeneutic involving two way ties with the actions and institutions of those they study. Sociological observers depend upon lay concepts to generate accurate descriptions of social processes; and agents regularly appropriate themes and concepts of social science within their behaviour, thus potentially changing its character. This... inevitably takes it some distance from the 'cumulative and uncontested' model that naturalistically inclined sociologists have in mind.

This notion of the double hermeneutic points to a further sense we can give it. This is that human beings are reflexive and intentional actors who are engaged in interpretive activity throughout their lives. However, researchers themselves, in making interventions of whatever sort, are also engaged in interpretive activity. Thus, we have a situation – this is the act of doing research – in which researchers are interpreting interpretations made by social actors. The nature of these interpretations is especially crucial in research settings, constructed as they are in terms of unequal distributions of power and knowledge, vested interests and inadequate exchanges of information. This is so because the act of interpretation involves selection, the filtering out and organizing of a mass of data into a coherent pattern, which conforms to and has an effect on the way the researcher already understands the world.

Reconceptualizing knowledge

If the values of the researcher and equally the values of the researched are essential components of any knowledge gathering activity, then it is important to address questions about the nature of that knowledge and its curriculum implications. I will begin this section by examining the work of the French philosopher, Michel Foucault, and in particular, his central theme of power-knowledge, that is: a particular configuration of the two that would seem to exclude them operating independently. He has argued that:

> Truth is a thing of this world; it is produced only by virtue of multiple forms of constraint. And it induces regular effects of power. Each society has its regimes

of truth, its general politics of truth, that is the types of discourse it accepts and makes function as true, the mechanisms and instances which enable one to distinguish true and false statements, the means by which each one is sanctioned, the techniques and procedures accorded value in the acquisition of truth, the status of those who are charged with saying what comes as truth. (Foucault, 1986, pp 72–73)

Thus power-knowledge as opposed to power and knowledge of power is what is being proposed.

This seems to point to its self-refuting character as an argument. If knowledge of anything only comes about as a result of power arrangements within society, then that knowledge is conditional; or to put it another way, what confidence can we have in the alleged relationship between power and knowledge, when our knowledge of that relationship is presumably subject to power arrangements in society? In addition, the identification of power with knowledge would seem to disallow events, activities, procedures which operate within the rules (the rules of discursive formation) of one episteme being understood within another. This is reinforced in two ways. First, Foucault's notion of genealogy as opposed to archaeology ties closely together discursive formations with power arrangements in society at the time the discursive regime is operating. Second, Foucault is not interested in the human subject as such. The history of ideas has been dominated by the idea of a human subject and a human subject saying something that is taken up in various forms and guises by other people. The traces and connections constitute its history. But Foucault wants to concentrate his critique at the level of concept, idea or text, not person. Thus he would seem to be ruling out the idea that there is such a thing as a human being who can in any way transcend the episteme in which she or he is positioned, and understanding only occurs in terms of the prevailing arrangements (and this of course includes epistemological arrangements) then in existence.

The third problem is even more serious. Unless we want to distinguish between epistemology and ethics, arguing that the latter has some universal quality, whereas the former is firmly located within particular and specific discursive formations (and he shows no inclination to do so or produce arguments to support a universal theory of value), then he would seem not to be able to distinguish between different regimes of truth or different regimes of power (because that is what they are). He deliberately does not develop a theory of ethics, though it is interesting to note that privately (that is, outside of his philosophical work) he was extremely committed (against the death penalty, against inhumane conditions in prison etc). So different regimes are only different in kind and not in value. History is cleansed of any teleological or progressive elements. Benign and brutal prison regimes are equally bad or good. Progressive (and I am using this now in a different way) education is no better or worse than educational regimes based on overt forms of fear.

So we are left with three compelling arguments against this notion of power-knowledge: a) the argument of self-refutation; b) the argument of paradigmatic commensurability; and c) the argument of ethical nihilism. Before I address each of these, let me suggest that the argument is complicated by other factors. First, there is ample evidence from his whole body of work that he changed his mind, or certainly that he emphasized some aspects at the expense of others at an early stage of his writing and de-emphasized them at a later stage (ie he republished *Mental Illness and Psychology* with a substantially rewritten second part; his last years were spent on the first stages of the development of an ethical philosophy, something which he set his mind against during most of his working life). Second, the bulk of his writing would seem to suggest that he had little truck with the relativistic element involved in power-knowledge. He was perfectly happy to accept that some truths may be valid across societies, only that methods and occasions of generating truth will ultimately depend on some aspect of a society's power arrangements.

In order to defend him we need to make reference to a well-known distinction in philosophy; between the conditions for the production of truth and the means of its production, or to put it another way: between judgement and procedure. A truth may be produced because of certain arrangements in society (this would refer to issues of access, availability, dissemination, suppression, obfuscation etc), but its truth value is not determined or dependent on any of these. This is a tempting way out for Foucault. However, if this were so, it would make redundant the close conjunction of the two terms: power and knowledge; indeed, it would make unremarkable the connection he sought to suggest between the two. Second, he may actually be referring to a distinction make by Bhaskar (1979, 1989) (referred to above), which is the distinction between epistemology and ontology, in which he argues that epistemology is always transitive and therefore by definition as much a product of prevailing power arrangements in society, but that ontology, certainly with regard to the human sciences, is relatively enduring and thus has a degree of intransitivity about it.

Now it seems to be that Foucault's defence would go somewhere along the following lines. He is concerned to uncover deeper-lying structures (ie power, and if we think about this notion, it only seems to be manifest in action or actions, and some manifestations of it are hidden or covert), but knowledge of them, and of course of ways of knowing about them, are transitive and therefore subject to existing arrangements in society. Now this doesn't of course get round the problem of self-refutation, because this argument is essentially located within the realm of epistemology or knowing (and someone like Popper would want to argue this), then our knowledge of those mechanisms by which truths are established (and these would include procedural as well as judgemental mechanisms) can necessarily only be limited. These truths are not so much provisional as speculative, partial and incomplete (this is of course Rorty's defence of epistemic relativism), and that is as far as we can go. The point is that if our knowing is always epistemically relative (and we can never know if it is or not), then how we determine truth from falsehood (and this is of course not procedural but judgemental) must be determined by prevailing power relations in society. If criteria for judgement are universal (that is trans-epistemic), then power relations play a lesser role in judgement, but this is not a synthetic truth but an analytical one. The conclusion simply follows from the premise. As a consequence, it doesn't tell us anything about the likelihood of those judgemental criteria being universal.

The position that Foucault takes is not that different from the philosopher Alistair MacIntyre (1988), though the latter refers to traditions, rather than epistemes, even though they still encompass the epistemological. MacIntyre's notion of tradition-bound rationality points to the second problem we identified earlier; which is that if we are located within one episteme or one discursive formation, then we literally cannot understand or make sense of ideas, events, activities located epistemologically elsewhere. Foucault developed two methodological approaches. The first is archaeology in which the archaeologist seeks to uncover the epistemological assumptions underlying the formation of ideas in society. In other words, he or she seeks to uncover the rules concerning relations between statements within the discursive formation which allow expression, understanding and use of some ideas to the exclusion of others and, as importantly, the rules concerning the development of the discursive formation. Discursive formations limit the number and type of alternatives. The speaker is positioned by the discursive formation: 'takes up a position that has already been defined'. Foucault identifies the four stages of the development of a discourse: the threshold of positivity, the threshold of epistemologization, the threshold of scientificity and the threshold of formalization. Archaeology then looks at discursive matters. Foucault's later notion of genealogy looks at relations between discursive and non-discursive matters, or between ideas and power relations in society.

A number of points about this need to be made. First, he argues that archaeology cannot operate outside of discursive relations, which are situated in time and place. It does not and cannot operate 'independently of all discourse or all objects of discourse'. However, this seems to be merely a covering note. We are told that these are the stages through which a discourse goes during an evolutionary path – not just that all discourses in the past have fitted this pattern, but that this pattern will be sustained in the future. Foucault in his *Archaeology of Knowledge* (one of his earlier works) had yet to develop fully his notion of genealogy in which these discursive formations and their evolution would be more firmly located within power arrangements in society or within non-discursive formations. Though these matters concern discourse and ideas within discursive formations, they are not ideological or necessarily located in systems of ideas, but have a material base. They are in effect nomothetic; this is how society works. They are examples of Bhaskar's mechanisms but are they absolutely or briefly enduring and if not, what is their status; merely historical artefacts? And, secondly, since we have knowledge of them and furthermore knowledge of a method by which they can be discovered, is this epistemological knowledge briefly, relatively or absolutely enduring?

The next problem associated with this is more serious. Does Foucault have a method? And what underpins his method? He certainly has a theory of time, or more precisely a theory of causation. Some events can be placed before other events and are responsible for bringing them into being. He has a theory of association that some events have a greater relevance to the development of theory than others; and finally he has a theory of reference – ideas refer to material artefacts, ie power relations. If method was absolutely located within an episteme, then it could be used to identify events, activities of a different epistemic nature. If human beings are located within discursive formations which exclude them from certain ideas and these discursive formations are located historically, then are all those historically located human beings operating under the same epistemic spell at the same time? When one episteme gives way to another, does this mean we see things differently in every way? By introducing an historical method to describe the formation of discourse, Foucault has settled for a transcendental mechanism that seems to have the status of a historical truth.

I referred earlier to the problem of finding a consistent reading of the whole of Foucault's oeuvre, and here, it seems to me, is an example of that inconsistency. On the one hand he suggests that knowledge of everything is related to power arrangements in society, and on the other, he describes certain mechanisms for the production of discourse which seem not to relate to any particular and specific arrangements of power. In order to cite the Bhaskar defence outlined earlier, he would have to argue that knowledge of these rules is transitive, a position he seems reluctant to take. And the reason he has to take this position is because he wants to discuss arrangements in different epistemes and make comparisons between them. He can only do this from one perspective, his own epistemic perspective, but presumably the historical or archaeological method which is located within his own epistemic perspective is going to produce different types of truth about different epistemic arrangements and therefore the comparison certainly becomes invalid. His insistence on tying closely together discursive formations with specific historical periods means that the subsequent account of human societies is, as

Archer (1988) argues, too all encompassing. She refers to this as 'the myth of cultural integration', and she argues that it has created 'an archetype of culture(s) as the perfectly woven system, in which every element was interdependent with every other – the ultimate exemplar of compact and coherent organization' (Archer, 1988: 2).

The main problem is the reduction involved in his account of human beings. As we have noted already, the history of ideas is stripped of people. In their place are concepts, ideas, texts, mechanisms. Again this has contributed to the third of our critiques – that of ethical nihilism. By refusing to take up specific political and ethical positions, he is forced to treat all power formations as equal. Power becomes a monolithic concept:

> because it is produced from one moment to the next, at every point, or rather in relation from one point to another. Power is everywhere… because it comes from everywhere. (Foucault, 1979: 93)

This goes beyond the ethical. It is not just that, within the framework offered by Foucault, one cannot judge between different regimes of power, it is that this notion of power becomes singularly unhelpful in explicating different degrees and types of power exercised on human beings. A word that covers everything refers to nothing and has no explanatory usefulness. So when we compare progressive and non-progressive ideologies, since both are equally power-imbued, we cannot distinguish between them. That is, we cannot distinguish between them at the explanatory level. Clearly they refer to different phenomena, but Foucault's notion of power cannot allow us to make interesting and valid comparisons between the two. If power is present in all human interaction, it becomes impossible to distinguish between the different instances of its application. The essential ingredient that is missing is that some people possess more power than others, or to put it in another way, power is differentially distributed. Furthermore, unless we have some notion of agency, we are in danger of reducing human beings to the role of 'unwitting dupes' of structural forces beyond their comprehension and influence.

Boundaries, knowledge and the curriculum

So far, I have argued in this chapter for a number of axioms:

- Values are central to the activity of research, that is both the values of the researcher and the values of those being researched.
- Research, therefore, is inevitably a 'fusion of horizons' (Gadamer, 1975), in which different sets of values fuse to produce new knowledge.

- These values, or conceptual frameworks, are located within historical contexts or 'traditions of knowledge' (MacIntyre, 1988).
- The production of knowledge, therefore, has a close relationship with the way society organizes itself. However, to understand knowledge and power as inseparable is to erect too rigid a strait-jacket on the relationship between social arrangements and knowledge (both about them and other matters).

I now want to extend this argument to the realm of curricula or to the way knowledge is produced and reproduced in educational institutions by examining one aspect of the process – the way knowledge is organized (its boundary definitions). In addition, as Bernstein (1996) suggests, there is always a pedagogic dimension, though this is beyond the scope of this chapter. The argument, I will suggest, is that the way we divide up knowledge has an effect on the way we can understand the world.

Each discursive field has a history, is composed of individuals with different projects who form and reform in different alliances at different moments. There are, therefore, micro-political struggles within the history of each field. But, more importantly, at the level of the academy, those struggles involve the establishment of various organs of dissemination and of criteria by which the knowledge-producing activity may be judged. In the first place, a new field needs to produce books and articles in academic journals; new journals which reflect the epistemological assumptions of the field; positions of office in universities; access to the popular media; the development of a cadre of taught and research students; research funding for projects; and the establishment of a coterie of referees for journals and research projects. The paraphernalia of field formation is often hard-won, frequently involves excursions down blind alleys, and is a risk-taking business.

But more importantly, the field needs to establish three sets of criteria before it can be considered to be fully formed: first, it has to have created a set of criteria by which its knowledge may be evaluated; second, it needs to have formalized a set of definitional criteria which includes and excludes what is considered proper knowledge; third, it needs to be able to offer a set of methodological criteria with which an initiate may operate – a set of procedures that delineate a practitioner from a non-practitioner. Whilst some of these moves are more successful than others, they are, as MacIntyre (1988) points out, subject to decay, argument, dispute and change. The field itself always has to operate within other discursive fields, for example the wider field of policy. Macro-political influences, therefore, have an influence on the way the field comes into being, and indeed, practitioners (especially in the field of education) may deliberately shape their thinking to chime with policy moves, either actually in existence or projected.

Two examples will suffice. This first is ethnography, not understood as a field in its own right, but as a subset of the wider field of methodology. Forty years ago, this would not have been considered appropriate as a knowledge-producing activity. It is now acceptable in the academy, as its organs of dissemination are now well enough established to sustain it as a serious activity. However, it is not acceptable within wider contexts such as policy-making forums, and is therefore to some extent weakened by its inability to participate in macro-political processes.

The second example is the school effectiveness/school improvement movement, which has risen to prominence in the field of education in recent years. The creation of such a discourse has come about as a result of a number of moves made by important players in the academy: for example, the marginalization of existing forms of knowledge, such as the sociology of education, the philosophy of education and curriculum studies. This process has been accomplished by the cementing of alliances between policy-making bodies such as the DfEE and the academic community; and more importantly, the setting in place by government of a number of apparatuses (eg Ofsted Inspection, National League Tables, etc) which better facilitate the successful operation of the discourse, and which at the same time act to circumscribe and set boundaries to the field. In addition, the movement has sought to market itself and thus establish a bridgehead to the world of practitioners, ie by the use of marketing devices and by sustaining close relationships with knowledge users.

These two examples, incomplete as they are as histories, suggest that knowledge in the Academy represents a fluid configuration, which is always in a state of flux. Subsequent reconfigurations, which may or may not be influenced by older typifications of knowledge, merely confirm the flexible and changing nature of knowledge typifications. However, as Foucault reminds us, these manoeuvrings have material effects – that is, they open and close discursive possibilities, and limit and delimit what can be said about education.

Note

Some of the material in this chapter is taken from Scott and Usher (1998), Scott (1998a) and Scott (1998b), for which permission has been received.

References

Archer, M (1988) *Culture and Agency*, Cambridge University Press, Cambridge
Ayer, A J (1954) *Knowledge, Truth and Logic*, Gollancz, London

Bernstein, B (1996) *Pedagogy, Symbolic Control and Identity*, Taylor and Francis, London
Bhaskar, R (1979) *The Possibility of Naturalism*, Harvester Press, Brighton
Bhaskar, R (1989) *Reclaiming Reality*, Verso, London
Bryman, C (1988) *Quality and Quantity in Social Research*, Allen & Unwin, London
Denzin, N and Lincoln, Y (eds) (1995) *Handbook of Qualitative Research*, Sage, London
Foucault, M (1972) *Archaeology of Knowledge*, Tavistock Publications, London
Foucault, M (1979) *Discipline and Punish*, Penguin Books, London
Foucault, M (1986) *The Foucault Reader*, ed P Rabinow, Peregrine Books, London
Gadamer, H G (1975) *Truth and Method,* Continuum, New York
Giddens, A (1984) *The Constitution of Society*, Polity Press, Cambridge
Kolakowski, L (1972) *Husserl and the Search for Certitude*, Yale University Press, New Haven
MacIntyre, A (1988) *Whose Justice? Which Rationality?*, Duckworth, London
Scott, D (1998a) Approaches to evaluating health promotion, in *Evaluating Health Promotion*, ed D Scott and R Weston, London
Scott, D (1998b) Afterword, in *Values and Educational Research*, ed D Scott, Bedford Way Paper, London Institute of Education
Scott, D and Usher, R (1998) *Researching Education: Data, methods and theory in educational enquiry*, Cassell, London

Chapter 14

Education for Integrity: Values, Educational Research and the Use of the Life History Method

Paul Armstrong

Introduction

In a chapter on values and the life history method, it is appropriate to introduce some elements of autobiography in order to make sense of the issues to be raised and discussed. My own interest in the use of the life history method for social research goes back to my postgraduate days of 1973–76. It is significant that I had received training in sociology, and sociological research methods, firstly at the University of York, and subsequently at Essex. The theoretical paradigm in which I had undertaken my research apprenticeship was interactionism. My Masters' dissertation was entitled *Sad tales and other stories: motivational accounts of shoplifters*. The dissertation was heavily influenced by the writings of Erving Goffman, C Wright Mills and Peter Berger, with a focus on the meaning individuals attribute to their social actions. In particular, as the subtitle of the dissertation suggests, the interest was in the accounts that shoplifters gave, and the social meanings they constructed through their accounts. Awareness of the audience was a significant factor, since it was clear that the stories shoplifters told varied depending on who was listening to the stories.

In my subsequent PhD research, I took up and extended the notion of accounts, which were episodic and fragments of people's lives, which had pragmatic value in excusing or justifying a specific piece of (deviant) behaviour, which functioned to enable them to resist the power of labelling ('criminal') so that it did not become incorporated into their self-identity. Whether they were moral holidays, momentary lapses of reason or unavoidable consequences of poor socialization, the stories served to deflect any need to accept a deviant identity. However, in carrying out qualitative research for my PhD, I realized that I needed to contextualize episodes in terms of the *whole* – the person's life history. I therefore developed an interest in the life history method of research.

Whilst it was not a new method – indeed, it could be traced back to the Chicago School of the 1930s – it was relatively unusual at the time I was writing, though coincidentally during the time I was doing my PhD, the number of articles on the subject of autobiographies and doing life histories books began to proliferate (Bogdan, 1974; Carr-Hill and MacDonald, 1973; Denzin, 1978; Faraday and Plummer, 1979; Klockars, 1977; Thomas, 1978; Watson, 1976).

The sociological perspective in which I served my apprenticeship had also sensitized me to the ethics of doing social research. The focus on the study of deviant actions through participant observation in the late 1960s and early 1970s had thrown up questions about the issue of 'objectivity' and 'taking sides'. One proponent of taking sides was Howard Becker, who – characterizing liberal ideology – argued that value freedom and objectivity is a myth, since all researchers cannot but have views that shape their definition of the research problem, influence their methodology, constrain their analysis and determine their reporting (Becker, 1966). For Becker the answer was simply to expose their values to view, and then permit them to be taken into account when reading and interpreting the results of the research. Sociologists at that time were accused of over-identifying with the 'underdog', the 'criminal', the 'deviant' – those who were supposedly powerless in their struggles against the dominance of the ruling classes to draw the boundaries between acceptable and not acceptable behaviour, between normal and deviant activities, between law-abiding and law-breaking actions (Gouldner, 1968).

I have to confess that my own postgraduate research reflected this liberal avoidance of the problem of values, which although worthy of discussion, was not seen as the primary methodological problem, since its consideration was given a lower priority than the issues of reliability and validity. I failed to recognize the complexity of values and ethics in research over and beyond stating that values are not facts, but socially defined.

My postgraduate research was primarily in the area of the sociology of deviance. It was a few years later, whilst teaching research methods to postgraduate students on adult education programmes, that I came to consider the application of the life history method to educational research (Armstrong, 1982; 1987). Initially, I undertook to describe the life history method, in theory and practice, and to give practical advice to postgraduate students in how to approach life history research. In the revised edition, I extended the discussion of the theoretical underpinnings of the methodology, and having undertaken a thorough literature review, selected some illustrative case studies, taken largely from social rather than educational research. Having said that, there were signs even then of the beginnings of the growth of the use of the methodology in education, including in adult education research.

In the decade since this publication, there has been a significant expansion in the number of studies published that have utilized the life history method; moreover, there is a European network specialist (Hoar, 1994), a number of books and articles, and at least one Masters programme (University of Sussex) that specializes in the life history method. Although my publication could do with a serious update, this is not the purpose of this chapter. Here, I only need to give an indication of this growth, to account for it, and to relate it to the contemporary debate about values.

I was made aware of the developments in the use of the life history method research through participation in a national adult education research conference, which I have attended continuously since 1979. The Standing Conference on University Teaching and Research in the Education of Adults (SCUTREA) began in 1970. A review of the annual conference papers over a period of 26 years shows that the earliest reference to 'biography' was made in 1985, in a paper on social work and adult education (Hale and Coull, 1985). At the 1988 conference, the first two papers to focus specifically on the life history method as an 'alternative' research strategy appeared (Finger, 1988; Jarvis, 1988). In subsequent years, the respectability of the biographical or life history method has been established. Within five years, this so-called 'alternative' perspective, or 'new paradigm research', had established itself sufficiently to become a major focus of the 1993 conference. A whole strand of the conference was devoted to biographies and autobiographies. There was a series of eight papers (out of a conference total of 45), some dealing with the autobiographical experiences of the researcher, whilst others narrated the stories of adult learners. In 1994, five papers (out of 35) focused specifically on biographies; others were developing the notion of identity, self and values. In 1995 this increased to eight (out of 38), and in 1996, the position consolidated with seven out of 54 papers (Figure 14.1).

This is taking evidence from only one annual conference, albeit the one in Britain that provides the primary opportunity for research papers in university adult education to be presented. I now want to account for why this 'alternative strategy' has established itself in the mainstream.

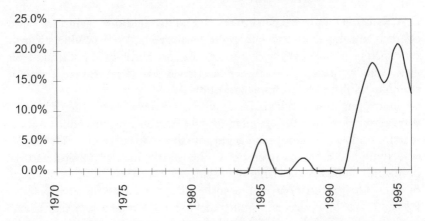

Figure 14.1   *Percentage of life history papers at SCUTREA conferences*

Life histories and educational research

I have noted that the first systematic contribution to the raising awareness of the use of life histories as an 'alternative' research strategy came in 1988. Borrowing from contemporary concerns in sociological theory with hermeneutics, phenomenology and critical theory (Habermas), Finger (1988) announced the life history method as the emergence of a 'new hermeneutical paradigm in adult education research', which respects the subjectivity of the adult, as well as the totality of the person and their formative process. This 'new paradigm not only allows, but even requires learning during the research process as a necessary condition for understanding [one's formative processes].' At the same conference, Peter Jarvis (1988) reported his research on adult learning which focused on reflections on alternative realities, and on the disjunction between adults' biographies and experience. Again, the origins of this research interest stem from reading Habermas, though mediated through the work of Mezirow (1981).

These two papers were among the earliest to recognize that the study of adult learning would gain much if it moved away from mainstream psychological concerns for theories of learning, and pointed in the direction of looking at rather more socio-cultural phenomena that underpinned the adult learning processes. As I have noted, within five years, this so-called 'alternative' perspective, or 'new paradigm research', had established itself sufficiently to become the major focus of the 1993 conference. In between times, the context of university – indeed, all – adult education had been changing. The very purposes and values of adult education had been challenged. Those who had previously been critical of the liberal tradition in university adult education found themselves wishing to defend that tradition against the radical overhaul coming from the 'new right' (Armstrong, 1989a). Within Europe, there had been the crossing of borders, and the blurring of political ideologies. These were indeed 'new times', and it was appropriate to take stock of research in adult and continuing education.

Educational research had already witnessed a paradigm shift. There had been a struggle within the liberal tradition of establishing that educational research could have as an acceptable purpose that of social change. The myth of objectivity had been sustained but in the meanwhile the political and economic milieu had been changing, leaving traditional views of research outmoded. This is reflected in the surge of activity in evaluative research. Research *was* for a purpose – policy making, accountability, cost efficiency, performance measurement. The notion of the neutral academic researcher had been successfully challenged, not by those on the left who had failed to transcend the hegemony of liberal ideology, but by those on the political right.

Funding for higher education had become linked to success in attracting research grants and amount of research undertaken, and published outcomes. Funding-driven research had turned the academic world upon its head. In the introduction to the 1993 Conference Proceedings, Miller and Jones (1993) wrote:

> The critical importance of research in adult and continuing education was underlined in 1992, with many person-hours being devoted to the completion of returns for the Research Assessment Exercise, and threats to the continued funding of research by the HEFC. The emphasis on research output in the assessment of research has brought about a shift in the climate of adult and continuing education departments, with what was at one time a relatively relaxed attitude to the production of research papers giving way to a desperation to publish (p 5).

This was reflected in the marked expansion of papers offered to the SCUTREA conferences during this period, and there was a need for the conference planning teams to begin to limit both the number and size of papers it could accept. Cynics may want to question the motivation for this sudden increase in interest in presenting conference papers, and having articles published. There was a genuine risk that to satisfy the demand for quantity would lead to a reduction in quality. For that reason, paper selection needed to be based on a set of professionally defined and publicly agreed quality criteria. The sophistication of research and methodological discussion became very important. One of the criteria for the acceptance of papers was that the papers would go beyond mere description of research, but provide critically reflective accounts – 'telling the story' – of the research project. Political as well as philosophical and epistemological issues became more urgent methodological considerations. The increasing blurring between theory and practice became a focal concern, particularly in repositioning research in terms of the issue of objectivity and value freedom.

Values and ethics in research

Of course, for those trained in sociological research methodology, none of this was new. The politics of social and educational research had its legacy in the 19th-century writings of Durkheim and Weber, and had been continuously revisited throughout the 20th century. The social sciences are littered with case studies of ethical dilemmas that provoke debate about the very purpose of research and its practice (Adelman, 1984; Bulmer, 1982; Kimmel, 1996; Penslar, 1995; Sjoberg, 1967). For many years, it was felt that the natural science model of research, with its emphasis on quantitative data gathering and analysis, was less susceptible to the challenge of subjectivity, although there has always been a certain unease about the politics of the consensus about what constituted worthwhile scientific problems that should be encouraged and supported. There was at the same time a distancing between the research problem, the research process, and the implications or operationalization of the results of the research within science. In social science, dealing with human beings, such distancing was always more problematic.

A more thorough analysis of the status of research as a scientific activity would need to take account of developments within the sociology of science, which is beyond the scope of this chapter. Nevertheless, we will need to retain an interest in what counts as knowledge, the Durkheimian problem of objectifying social facts, and the issue of truth. One approach to 'solving' ('avoiding' is probably more appropriate) these issues is to deal with them as though they were merely a collection of technical matters, which could be dealt with by improving training in research techniques and skills; or they were professional matters that could be resolved by an appeal to a published code of ethics. Certainly many of the ethical issues that social researchers face fall into either one of these categories. For example, *confidentiality* – the professional code will require members to protect the interests of those being researched, and the technical training will suggest ways in which this can be done. However, quite often the illustrations and examples that are used in codes do not neatly fit the real-life examples that confront researchers, and whilst the code might provide some guidance, and a basis for decisions, it can never provide *the* answer.

It is worth reflecting on the notion of an ethical *dilemma*. What makes it a *di*-lemma in the first place is that there is no right or wrong answer. There are at least two answers, each of which have both favourable and unfavourable outcomes. If it did not, then there would not be a dilemma. A characteristic of a dilemma is that it requires an awkward decision. One of the reasons that a decision is hard to reach is that we logically think that *there ought to be a right answer*. No amount of training or codes of ethics will provide *the right answer*. Those who subscribe to objectivity *avoid* making the decision.

The value position I take here is one which argues that social and education researchers must take responsibility for making choices in a condition of continuous uncertainty, and be prepared to be responsible for any 'wrong' choices. Ethical codes absolve us from the responsibility of being responsible for making the wrong choices – indeed, absolve us from the possibility that we could even make the wrong choice. As Arendt (1958) said, the 'agony of choice' has gone as we are freed not only from the responsibility for 'wrong', but also from the possibility of doing 'wrong'; our guilt can be eliminated.

This moral position on doing and being responsible for research is clearly some distance away from the liberal view of research. Far from being objective, such a view recognizes the inevitability of subjectivity in all research activities, and taking responsibility for that subjectivity. The recognition of the values behind this moral position is integral to the notion of a paradigm shift in research referred to earlier. Elsewhere (Armstrong, 1989b) I have expressed some sympathy for the notion of 'new paradigm research' as represented in Reason and Rowan's *Human Inquiry* (1981). In this book they put forward an alternative approach to traditional research as a strategy to do justice to the 'humanness' of all those involved in the research process. They suggest that their book is different from traditional textbooks, in that they *do* tell the reader what to do. They criticize traditional texts for being too flat, too insipid, too diplomatic and lacking in energy and commitment. However, they believe they can only define their approach in antithesis to those traditional methods they wish to transcend. Their approach to research begins with what they call 'naïve inquiry', which is most certainly subjective, involved, committed, intuitive and alive, but at the same time committed to the pursuit of rigorous and systematic enquiry. Like Becker, they feel a need to confess their own political standpoint, not just to be taken into account when interpreting the research results, but as a vital part of the story.

It is interesting to consider their manifesto for research:

Research
- is never neutral;
- is praxis;
- inevitably connects to issues of social change;
- involves a reciprocal relationship between researchers and researched;
- shares language;

- produces active knowing and generates self-determination;
- is learning through risk-taking in living and knowing;
- is a tight and rigorous synthesis of subjectivity and objectivity;
- shows respect for individual particularity and diversity;
- retains its interest in generalization;
- accepts person-in-context;
- uses interdisciplinary or multidisciplinary frameworks for understanding;
- respects people as people;
- seeks to reveal the hidden consequences of the research process on people;
- has knowledge as an outcome for knowledge is power.

To this I would add:

Research is
- purposeful;
- more of a process than an end in itself;
- a moral activity requiring commitment and responsibility;
- a critically educative activity.

Life history, values and integrity

Reason and Rowan do not recommend a particular research method within this overall strategy of humanistic inquiry. Indeed, in their book there is no recognition of the biographical or life history approach to research. Nevertheless, I wish to conclude by bringing together the points made in this chapter, in order to stress the value of the life history approach in meeting the points in the revised research manifesto. In particular, I want to focus on the life history as a method for restoring integrity.

That the life history method will raise issues of values and ethics should not be in doubt. I would, however, like to go beyond my original discussion of ethics and life history research in which ethics are seen as 'a further traditional methodological consideration', which needs to address confidentiality and anonymity. I go on to say:

> There is an alternative view to be considered here. Whenever the issue of ethics and confidentiality is raised, this reminds us of the traditional bias of much research and reflects the power of the researcher over the subject, and in a sense this concern is at the same time patronizing in the effort to restore the balance. The alternative view of life history research as consciousness-raising technique in a praxical sense should obviate the need to be unduly concerned with this tra-

ditional issue, since the researcher should no longer be the powerholder and the subjects powerless. The two are working in collaboration, and in theory the outcome should not do damage to the individual but to the benefit of all. In practice, a realistic assumption is that engaging in 'subversive' political research against the dominant and commonsense perspective might mean that the interests of some individuals have to be sacrificed in the interests of the common good, and if this happens, the researcher is forced to confront the contradiction between individuals and their society. (Armstrong, 1987: 28)

I do come very close to denying responsibility here, through the vocabulary of sharing power, with the intention of benefiting all. To some extent, the second part of the paragraph rescues this by containing a clear value position, though its conceptualization of theory and practice remains inadequate.

In using life history research, it is important to recognize how the stories being told are reconstructions; they have little to do with 'truth' or 'reality' (which, after all, are socially constructed), yet they have meaning, however transitory. My initial perspective on this, gleaned from reading Berger (1966), was that the past is not fixed, immutable or invariable, but is continuously constructed and reconstructed; that reconstruction is always in terms of where we are now, not where we were at that time. This may not be an entirely random process, and behind the life history is a meta-narrative, or the story of the story.

As researchers, how can we make sense of the possibility that those engaged in life history are trying to make sense of themselves, and that their story is both a process as well as a (temporary) end in itself? How do we sift through the multiple realities in order to make sense, to reintegrate our fragmented selves and lives? And why do we want to achieve integrity? I would suggest that the answer to this lies in the nature of these 'new times'. This is not an argument for psychological theories of cognitive dissonance, nor for Parsonian structural functionalism, which has integration as one of its four pattern variables. In the first, there is an assumption that the individual needs to restore a sense of equilibrium if, for example, actions are dissonant with beliefs; in the second, there is an assumption that the social system has a natural tendency to equilibrium which will be naturally restored from a state of disequilibrium. I would challenge these on the grounds of first that there is a separation of the individual from society (psychology versus sociology), and secondly that equilibrium or integration is a natural phenomenon. Rather, I would hold that the individual has a dialectical relationship with society, which is both critical and creative in the process of social construction of meanings, and that there is a tendency continuously to check and recheck the validity of our values. One feature of these 'post-modern' times is superficiality and appearance. But nothing may be what it seems at face value, which provides a task for the researcher to get beyond surface appearances. Bauman

(1995) suggests that if postmodernism succeeds in tearing off the mask of illusion, this does not necessarily mean that beneath it we will find unpatterned, chaotic, fragmentary, incoherent and disintegrated sets of values and ethical principles. After the failure of the modernist project to establish universal moral certainty, we are left with moral dilemmas and unresolved conflicts, but at the same time, we have our moral selves, a moral conscience, which may have been 'anaesthetized, not amputated'. Bauman argues that rather than a twilight for values and ethics, these have been emancipated from the false consciousness entailed by modernity, and enable us to deconstruct our biographies, and reconstruct the fragmented episodes of our life histories into a moral integrity.

Integration, then, has a moral as well as a social meaning. To end this chapter, it is interesting to note that the first-ever reference made to biography in a SCUTREA conference paper was in the context of extending Basil Bernstein's notion of codes into a discussion of an integrated curriculum:

> 'Integration', however, goes beyond Bernstein's limited concern with knowledge to incorporate the 'subjective' components of learning and to integrate this with the 'objective'. Thus is included the impact on learning of subjective experience via individual biography and social career, and also via ongoing social interaction as the group pursues its work. Finally, the concept of 'integration' captures the everyday life of the educational institution – its roles, relationships, structures and practices – to forge a process of learning ordered to accommodate objective and subjective dimensions. Integration, therefore, is of the totality of educational context in which the curriculum is but a central pivot. (Hale and Coull, 1985)

Summary

The purpose of this chapter is to examine the current popularity of the life history method in educational research, especially in the study of adults learning, and to review its worth in exploring values as a dimension of the educational process. The chapter argues that in these 'new times', the life history method has particular strengths, as a strategy for exploring values.

It is argued that, as a research method, life histories are particularly appropriate in that they enable both the researcher and the 'subject' to 'make sense' of their lives in the context of social and cultural contexts and change. The life history method facilitates the process by which individuals – who may feel that their lives are in fragments – can begin *to reintegrate* their selves, their social and cultural identities, to restore a sense of wholeness. The life history method is part of the *dialectic*, and develops the understanding of values and integrity as a mutual, democratic and educative process.

References

Adelman, C (ed) (1984) *The Politics and Ethics of Evaluation*, Croom Helm, Beckenham

Arendt, H (1958) *The Human Condition*, University of Chicago Press, Chicago

Armstrong, P F (1982) *The Use of the Life History Method in Social and Educational Research*, Newland Paper No 7, Hull

Armstrong, P F (1987) *Qualitative Strategies in Social and Education Research: The life history method in theory and practice*, Newland Paper No 14, Hull

Armstrong, P F (1989a) Right for the wrong reasons: a critique of sociology for professional adult education, in *Theory and Practice in the Study of Adult Education*, ed B P Bright, Routledge, London

Armstrong, P F (1989b) Is evaluation as a critically reflexive educative activity new paradigm research? reflections on Reason and Rowan, in *Proceedings of 30th Annual Adult Education Research Conference*, ed C Campbell Coggins, University of Wisconsin, Madison

Bauman, Z (1995) *Post Mortem Ethics*, Blackwell, Oxford

Becker, H S (1966) Whose side are we on?, *Social Problems*, **14**, pp 239–48

Berger, P (1966) *Invitation to Sociology*, Penguin, Harmondsworth

Bogdan, R (ed) (1974) *Being Different: The autobiography of Jane Fry*, John Wiley, New York

Bulmer, M (ed) (1982) *Social Research Ethics: An examination of the merits of covert participant observation*, London

Carr-Hill, R A and MacDonald, K I (1973) Problems in the analysis of life histories, in *Stochastic Processes in Sociology*, ed P Halmos, Sociological Review Monograph, Keele

Denzin, N K (1978) *The Research Act in Sociology: A theoretical introduction to sociological methods*, McGraw-Hill, New York

Faraday, A and Plummer, K (1979) Doing life histories, *Sociological Review*, **27** (4), pp 773–98

Finger, M (1988) Hermeneutics, critical theory and the biographical method as an alternative in adult education research, in *Transatlantic Dialogue: A research exchange*, ed M Zukas, SCUTREA, Leeds

Gouldner, A V (1968) The sociologist as partisan: sociology and the welfare state, *American Sociologist*, **3**, pp 103–16

Hale, T and Coull, B (1985) Social work and adult education, in *Papers from the Fifteenth Annual SCUTREA Conference*, ed M Zukas, SCUTREA, Leeds

Hoar, M et al (1994) *Life Histories and Learning: Language, the self and education – Papers from an interdisciplinary conference*, Centre for Continuing Education, Sussex

Jarvis, P (1988) Needs, interests and adult learning, in *Transatlantic Dialogue: A research exchange*, ed M Zukas, SCUTREA, Leeds

Kimmel, A J (1996) *Ethical Issues in Behavioural Research: A survey*, Blackwell, Oxford

Klockars, C B (1977) Field ethics for the life history, in *Street Ethnography: Selected studies of crime and drug use in natural settings*, ed R S Weppner, Sage, London

Mezirow, J (1981) A critical theory of adult learning and education, *Adult Education* (USA), **32** (1), pp 3–24

Miller, N and Jones, D J (eds) (1993) *Research: Reflecting practice – Papers from 23rd SCUTREA Conference*, SCUTREA, Manchester

Penslar, R L (1995) *Research Ethics: Cases and materials*, Indiana University Press, Bloomington

Reason, P and Rowan, J (eds) (1981) *Human Inquiry: A sourcebook of new paradigm research*, John Wiley, Chichester

Sjoberg, G (ed) (1967) *Ethics, Politics and Social Research*, Schenkman, Cambridge

Thomas, E A (1978) Herbert Blumer's critique of *The Polish Peasant*: a post-mortem on the life history approach in sociology, *Journal of the History of the Behavioural Sciences*, **14**, pp 124–31

Watson, L C (1976) Understanding life history as a subjective document: hermeneutical and phenomenological perspectives, *Ethos*, **4** (1), pp 95–131

Chapter 15

Representation in Research: Whose Values Are We Representing?

Jane Erricker

Introduction

Doing qualitative research (for definition see Bogdan and Biklen, 1982) is an endeavour that is permeated with ethical issues. The issues revolve around such questions as:

Whose values frame the research? The researcher or the researched?
Whose values are presented in the research?
In whom does the power to decide these things reside?

In this chapter I will try to analyse, but not resolve, some of these ethical issues by looking at the work of the Children and Worldviews Project and illustrating the issues using data that we have collected.

The Children and Worldviews Project uses a qualitative methodology to investigate how children view the world they inhabit, and how they make sense of their experiences. This is tantamount to gaining access to the framework through which other experiences, including learning experiences, are perceived, and into which they are incorporated.

I chose a qualitative methodology over and above a quantitative one when I began the work of the Project because it felt like the most constructive and ethically sound way to conduct work in this area. I use the word 'felt' deliberately because as well as acknowledging the moral dimension in our research I also place great store in the affective aspect. Using this methodology 'feeling' is allowed. Indeed 'feeling', on behalf of the researcher and the researched, is positively encouraged (see Ely *et al*, 1991). In the areas of spiritual and moral education it is 'feeling' that is the learning objective: the development of the skills of experiencing, reflecting on that experience and using that experience as a key to empathizing with the experiences of others.

The research methodology I use reflects that affective sequence in that I, as the researcher, must be aware of the experiences that have shaped the framework through which I perceive the information given to me by the subjects of the research. In other words, I must be aware of my bias and this is the first of the ethical issues that I wish to address.

One of the main problems may well be that researchers in this area have a strong personal commitment to their work, and may wish to make a case for a particular change in society, education, or the power structures that exist. We must guard carefully against seeing only what will promote our cause in the data that we collect and against only seeing what will evidence our claims in the presentation and analysis of that data. To an extent this cannot be guarded against. We all begin to do research with an idea of a research question, however general. Even if the work is approached with an attempt to ground the theory in the data (Glaser and Strauss, 1967) one must have some idea of where one is going to start anything at all. The ideas that we have collected and the experiences we have had frame our expectations and provide a filter, whether we like it or not, through which we see our data.

In the work of the Project, I use unstructured, semi-structured and focused interviews as the primary methods for collecting data. I am aware of the problem of leading questions and try to guard against using them. I recorded the conversations on tape after asking permission to do so and I transcribed everything that was said. I share transcripts between members of the team and check on our methods. We also share the data with the head teachers and teachers in the schools we use. We keep research logs in which we record any extra information about the research process and the research situation. Any chance conversations, any thoughts or feelings about the research and any analytical ideas are recorded and shared with the rest of the team. Of course the team is made up of like-minded people, and even the head teachers of the schools we use also tend to share our overall philosophy so there is a limit to the identification of bias that will be achieved. Presenting our data to a wider audience in conferences and journals is the last stage in this process.

Representation

It is always possible for the opinions and attitudes of the researcher to appear to impinge on the data in such a way that it opens him or her to criticism. One such criticism that we have experienced revolved around the issue of the representation of a minority group in our data.

I gave a talk with Cathy Ota during which we discussed the way in which 'Asian' boys and girls constructed their identities. They were in a situation where they attended a school which was 99 per cent 'Asian', in a similar area of a city in the south of England. The children talked about the geographical roots of their families, their religious nurture, their position in a white, western society and their identity as either male or female in these contexts.

W, a boy in year 5, showed how many of the children expressed their ethnicity:

W: Like this school cos there's a lot of Asians and a lot of my cousins in this school... I've got a lot of cousins round this area and a lot of friends... there's a lot of Asians round this area as well.

Q: Are you all the same religion?

W: No.

Q: Can you tell me something about that?

S: Yes, me and G are Sikhs and them both are Muslims, I don't know what, are you Bengali? (To N) She's Bengali.

W: Yes, Muslims are quite the same thing here... both religions believe in the same God, Allah.

Q: Right, and you're Bengali (to N) and W?

W: Muslim.

Q: And are you Bengali?

W: Pakistani... like there be some Muslims and different Muslims as well... we're different Muslims that do believe in our own prophet.

Q: Right, so you have your own mosque too?

W: Yes, she goes to this Bengali mosque but they teach the same thing... they appreciate it there more, more comfortable there cos there's a lot of Bengal there.

We noted that the children described themselves as 'Asian', and that their categorization used 'ethnic' (geographical roots) and religious criteria – Bengali, Muslim, Pakistani. However, the differences between the Muslim and Sikh children also caused tension and our research uncovered undercurrents of conflict between children of different cultural and ethnic backgrounds:

> N: There's lots of different people here, there's Pakistani people, there's Hindi people, Indian people, Bengali people.
> Q: What makes them so different?
> N: Because if they're Indian they always listen to the bad angel, not the good one.
> Q: Why's that?
> N: Because they don't like Muslim people, some of them.
> Q: And are people in this school like that?
> N: Yeh.
> Y: Some are different, sometimes the Indian people do listen to the good angels, sometimes, but not all the time.

D (Sikh) and S (Muslim), whom we have already met, spoke about their ambitions for the future:

> S: My Dad wants me to work, get a good job… I think about work-ing… being a house drawer, design houses. I hope I do that and have a big company and all that, I want to be a businessman.
> D: If I become a footballer I'm going to buy a massive, a 32-storey company in New York and when the [football] season's over, I'm going go down and fly out to New York, and control my business there and if I'm not there, I'm going to let my, my secretary take over, or my wife.

D's comment about his wife is indicative of how the girls perceived their role in the future. Many spoke about leaving home and looking after their hus-band's family. N and Y, seven-year-old girls, had a very traditional image of what would happen when they grew up.

Older girls had different ambitions, even though they still acknowledged that their role was to look after a husband and family, as R and H, two nine-year-olds show:

> H: Do you know, when that person is married, they have to go to the boy's house and you know the boy's parents, you have to do some work like for them.

Q: Do you think that might be difficult?

H: Yes, cos we miss our mum and dad.

Q: Is there anything else you'd like to do when you're older?

H: I want to work actually, be a nurse or something.

R: I want to be a airport girl, when you're one of the luggage girls.

Q: Would you be able to be a nurse do you think H?

H: Yes, cos my cousin's a nurse… but when I get married I would stay at home or something.

R: I'd still do a job cos we don't really mind that much.

Staff in the school spoke about how the influence of religious leaders was perhaps not so great as it had been and that parents had aspirations for both their sons and daughters:

The parents I've spoken to, they're saying, 'yes, we want them to have a university education if they're capable of it'.

Ten years ago they would say our daughters can't go onto education, they're with us and staying home. I had one incident when my eldest daughter was year 7 or 8, and one teacher turned around and says to me, 'Oh it's not worth bothering with Asian girls because they end up in the kitchen' and I was really angry about that.

These graphic examples show how the girls' identity in the present is forcibly shaped by their perceived roles in the future. We also found that the way boys and girls relate to each other is affected:

R: You know like in India right, in every Indian religion they don't like girls that much.

Q: What happens in England?

R: Down here they think that they are the same, that boys and the girls are the same… but some men who come from India, they don't like girls, they say like do this, do that, use us as their slave and that… because you know like a girl, it's not really fair on girls cos they have to do all the housework, why not boys and that? So if you treated them the same that would be better.

R's comments that boys should do some housework are unlikely to be heeded; many of the girls spoke of the work they had to do in the home, often while the boys had the freedom to go out as they pleased and play:

A: Girls are the best cos the girls do work for their mothers.
Q: What do the boys do then?
A: Nothing, they just play out.
H: Yeh, boys play computer.

It's probably hard to over-estimate the influence of gender in the development of identity for the girls. For example, many girls recognized that boys were far more preferable in families than girls:

S: We got a baby boy and he be really special.
Q: Why's that?
L: Cos everybody like a baby boy and there should only be one girl in the family cos you need boys.
Q: So what happens if you have more than one girl in the family?
L: It's bad news... but like you still get some money... they get sad because they got girls, the girls are not as good as boys... my mum wishes she had a boy.
S: We're happy now we got a baby boy.

So, within the extracts from transcripts given above we can identify several issues that the children raise. They are very aware of the different groups into which they categorize themselves or are categorized by others; they are aware of Western aspirations in terms of lifestyle and employment; they are aware of the conflict between their 'Western' aspirations and their traditional roles; they are aware of the respective value of each gender in their communities.

In the talk that we gave the transcripts were presented as above. No more analysis was done except for the identification of the issues raised by the children. We felt that we were simply presenting the children's opinions. However, we were accused of misrepresenting the communities the children belonged to, and displaying our own racism in our selection of data. In particular some members of our audience were not happy that the children were using the description 'Asian'.

This was an issue that had to be responded to. We were afraid that in all our efforts to avoid bias we had not been successful and we had to acknowledge that this was the system working – we had presented our data and our bias may well have been identified. This chapter is the result of the consideration of that experience.

On reflection the issue seemed to us to be one of representation. The problem appeared to be that the 'community' was not happy with the opinions and expressions of the children, and feared that these expressions would be taken as those of the community as a whole, and general conclusions would be drawn as a result. In other words, the values and the cohesion of the community would be misrepresented. This caused us to ask the question just who are we representing? Is it us, the researchers? The children? The community? As we have outlined above, we make an effort to ensure that it is not us, but it is bound to be to some degree. The big question is what responsibility do we have to represent the community to which the children belong?

Other research projects have grappled with this problem. The Warwick Project, researching Hindu children in Britain, consulted with all interested parties to make sure that nothing was made public that might result in misrepresentation. Bob Jackson (1996) has indicated how long this chain of consultation may become and I have summarized this in Figure 15.1.

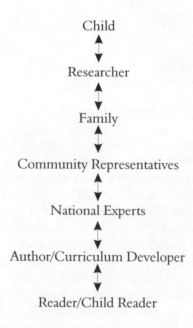

Figure 15.1

While this is a solution of great integrity, at each stage the data is open to censorship; at each stage it passes through the filter of the subjectivity of the reader, who has the power to change what it says, to alter what it communicates to the next person in the chain. We have to ask ourselves what remains of the original voice by the time the final reader lays eyes on it and to what extent it is an accurate representation of that child and what that child, in all honesty and openness, was trying to communicate. The right and the power to represent him/herself have been taken away from that child by this process of consultation and that child's voice is not being heard. The subjects that are chosen for investigation and for publication are those who are in agreement with you, as researcher, and those who are in agreement with the representatives of the community to which your subjects belong. Within the meta-narrative of liberalism, there will be constant correction in the direction of orthodoxy.

The solution we decided upon in our Project was to use the minimum of consultation (Figure 15.2). The children were consulted and asked if they minded their opinions being recorded and being made public. The head teacher of each school was consulted and they read all the transcripts and every potential publication. We always asked the head's opinion about further consultation and acted on that advice, but in the majority of cases no other consultation took place. The researcher, in our case, is also the author of any publication and the curriculum developer if materials for use in the classroom are developed from the data.

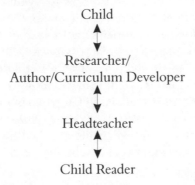

Figure 15.2

The disadvantage of this method is that it opens us up to the criticism that we received at our talk. The advantage is that we confront the issue of power. We would claim that the children who are the subject of the research are disempowered by the long chain of consultation and that our method seeks to empower them. The former does not allow what we would always like to achieve, the real process of communication between the experiencing child and the learning child. We aim to take the narratives of children, revealed through our interviews with children in one school, to the children of another school. We hope that we can facilitate reciprocal relationships, with experiences resonating with each other, and understanding and empathy resulting.

With the subtle and sympathetic intervention of a teacher this process can be facilitated, but it is destroyed by the editing/censoring process. Curriculum materials developed via the long consultation method run the risk of losing their vitality and their immediacy, but also fail to recognize the changing faces of both childhood and communities. The censorship results in conformity and does not reflect the beginnings of change and does not allow issues to be identified. So there is representation of the views of the community but not of the children. Therefore there is a lack of respect for the children's real opinions and reflections on experience because they can be edited out.

We do not pretend that our solution is perfect, but when the issue is who you are representing, a decision has to be made.

Confidentiality and secrecy

A different but closely related ethical issue arose during our work at another school.

Having interviewed children in five schools by this time, we now wished to use their words to invite children in other schools to talk about their experiences. We took a number of storied scripts to a school that was already asking children to discuss issues in regular year meetings and asked if they would be willing for us to come in and introduce their children to other children's stories. By reducing adult intervention in two respects: by providing a stimulus from another child and by allowing children to talk to each other in larger groups, we intended to determine whether what we had already discovered was generally relevant to children's experience and could promote their development. Perhaps this idea could best be answered by the children themselves.

At the outset, following a meeting with the teachers and the head, we collectively decided that the project's involvement would be incorporated into the programme of year assemblies. We would begin by taking a year assembly and interviewing children who wished to be interviewed afterwards.

We deliberately didn't map out its development beyond the initial sessions in order to use the children's responses and involvement to determine how it should evolve. In this way we hoped to empower the children by emphasizing their ability to shape any subsequent planning. Hopefully if it was their agenda they would commit themselves to it, if it didn't resonate with their experience we could revise our approach as a result. Subsequently, we realized the importance of this decision.

The first meeting was with year 6 and included 60 children. We read V's story below as the stimulus.

V: I think that in heaven you can ride a white pony and have marshmallows. Before my Nan died, she told me lots of things because she knew she was going to die and she told me about all the things she was going to do and she said she was going to send me a postcard. Before she went she gave me a piece of paper and stuck a photograph on it. I've still got it.

She said she would be happy and she wanted me to be happy when she died. On that day she got a picture of her and all the family, stuck it on a postcard and wrote on the back, 'I'll see you in your heart'. Now she's always with me. Now I talk to her all the time. I talk to her when I'm lonely. When I've argued with my friends I go and sit on the wall and think about her and talk to her. When I get fed up I sit there and talk to her about my friends. She tells me that she's riding on things. She says she's having a really nice time. She says she's going to ring me up. She says things in my head, she rings up my brain and talks to me. When she went up in heaven she took one of her special secrets. She took it with her and she can just ring me up, it's clever. This special secret makes her able to do that.

I keep on wanting to tell people things but they don't understand. I know everyone's in heaven who has died. Grandma tells me. She works in a cleaner's. She washes all the clouds in heaven. She's got lots and lots of friends in heaven. She hopes we'll stay alive a long time but she wants me to go up there to see her. I'd like to go and see her but if you go up there you've got to stay there. You can't go unless you've died. Heaven is high, high in the sky, it's higher than space.

We were uncertain as to how 10 and 11-year-olds would react to the explanation of a seven-year-old child, but her age was not mentioned. As a strategy for response we gave the following instructions:

Think through what V said and whether you have experienced something similar in your lives.

Talk to each other if you wish and put up your hand if there is something you would like to say.

The tape recorder was passed to those who wished to speak.

They each had a piece of paper and a pen on which to write down a response to V at the end of the session, if they wished.

If they wished to talk further about what they had thought or written, by being interviewed, they were asked to put a tick on their piece of paper.

Initially there was silence after the story. Concerned that we had asked them to do something too difficult or too private in a meeting, we asked them if this was the case. A number of the children said 'No', in an emphatic fashion, but that they needed time to think about it. Conversation started, the atmosphere relaxed and the first hand, a boy's, was raised.

What followed, as the tape recorder was passed continually around the room, was a collection of stories expressing suppressed feelings of loss of different kinds, varying in intensity.

By the end of the assembly 10 children were crying, eight girls and two boys. Other children, both boys and girls, were comforting them. During the break some children wanted to talk further into the tape recorder. We then discussed with the teachers how best to follow up the situation. Since many of the children had explicitly stated, during the assembly, that they wanted to be interviewed and they expected to be interviewed after the break, as was our original intention, we had to decide if this was now the most appropriate thing to do. The written responses gave an indication of the intensity of the children's feelings and the pervasiveness of their felt need.

Of the 60 children present, 47 handed in written responses, some included pictures. Forty-five of those who responded mentioned the death of grandparents (30), uncles (3), animals (3), a sister, or the illness of a relative (4), which worried them.

Three boys wrote about the splitting up of their parents.

'I remember when my mum and dad split up I was very upset because my mum throw a shoe at my dad and take a chunk of skin out of dad's face I still cry when my dad and mum met mum gets very upset so she always takes my out alote to stop he cry and get her mid of this. <u>Please read this</u>.'

'My mum and dad nearly split up. When my mum told me that she was moving into another house I was so upset. They are still married and will be moving back into the same house soon.'

'My mum and dad split up four years ago I feel angry partly with myself but mostly with my dad because he caused of the argument here is a pictur of what he done to my sister (drawn picture of man standing behind girl, man is holding knife and is labelled 'staber' and girl is labelled 'sister' and is saying 'help').'

Thirty-four children asked to be interviewed.

The dilemma for the teachers was created by the nature of the response. What had begun as an extension of the usual year meetings had turned into something the effect of which was significantly different. We had not been able to predict that effect. Though parents had been informed in a newsletter that this research was being carried out, subsequent reports home from upset children might create worry and concern. Also, despite the children's wishes, we had to consider whether they would indeed benefit from further reflection on distressing memories and whether it might be better for them to be given more space to consider their request to talk further. Against this we genuinely wished to respond to the children and affirm their equal involvement. But did that place us, in the children's eyes, in the position of counsellors? This would present us with a responsibility we could not fulfil.

The teachers had the invidious responsibility of making the immediate decision as to whether to interview immediately or not, without recourse to consultation with the head, who was out of school. The decision was taken that we shouldn't interview until we had time to consult over the implications. We returned to the group to break the news.

We explained the difficulties that might result from interviewing them as planned and invited their responses. For the second time that morning we were told we were wrong. They insisted on their wish to be interviewed. We felt the authority did not lie with us. The teachers could not be sure of the outcome.

The concluding decision was made that we would return the following week. Effectively we were buying time and a chance to reassess the situation. As researchers committed to empowering children and promoting their well-being we felt we had hardly been successful so far and it might well be that the school did not feel this venture was worth pursuing any further.

Before the next session a meeting took place with the class teachers and the head. We sensed some uncertainty from the school staff but the head was happy for us to continue.

The following week we agreed to take the assembly and talk further about interviewing. We also raised the question of whether the children felt it was good or not to discuss this sort of issue and what other things they would like to discuss. The teachers were concerned about where this might lead, whether the children had been carried away by their emotions the first time and on reflection would feel differently.

The second assembly sparked a strong debate about what we were doing. Despite the majority of children who spoke wishing to affirm its value, two boys were adamant that it was unhelpful, arguing that it only upset people to go on about it and that it was better to talk about good things. One explained how after the last assembly, he had cried in bed that night as a result of the way it affected him.

The children were asked again to write their comments on a sheet of paper and tick if they wished to be interviewed. As before a few children wanted to speak into the tape recorder after the meeting.

We received 33 written comments, some of them submitted by a pair or group of children. Sixteen wanted to be interviewed, two said they wouldn't mind, three didn't mention wanting to be interviewed but thought it was a good idea to talk about such things, one wanted to talk about good things. Ten children did not want to be interviewed. The following examples express the forcefulness of feeling of some of the children.

'Yes I want to be interviewed. My great-grandad and grandma died in the war and I didn't get to see them. And my dog got put down because he broke his back. He was like my best friend. His name was Sandy.

(Then written at other end of page upside down)

I want to be interviewed but I don't want to be near anyone else. I would like to be alone.'

I think it
would
be a
good idea
to talk
about
good
times

'YES I WOULD DEFINETLY LIKE FOR *SOMEONE*⋆ YOU TO INTERVIEW ME ABOUT THINGS! ON MY OWN. OR <u>WITH FRIENDS BUT</u> I HAVE QUITE ALOT OF ENEMYS AND I WOULD NOT LIKE THEM TO HEAR

(⋆ crossed out)

'I would like to tell Clive about this

It's best to tell people to get it of our chest and have a cry because my dad doesn't like my mum but I still love mum because I realy haven't had lived with mum because I was 3 when mum moved.'

talk about divorse
with children whos
parents are split
like me.

I would like to be interviewed

‘NO! (Written large to fill page)
it was stupided of them to come in because it stated up memories even
thow you let your feelings out
   And don't go on about it enymore
NO’

Reviewing the responses with the head helped us to understand some of these better, particularly in relation to one child, who had argued vehemently that talking about these issues was not helpful in the face of the comments of most of the other children who insisted that such discussion was valuable.

His voice was prophetic in tone as though he was addressing the children rather than just us. He was warning that the result of this enterprise would be failure and disappointment. The reasons for this became clear when his own experiences were recounted to us, during which he had been counselled to the point of family therapy, when the hope of resolution to his own conflicts had foundered. This addressed one of the main concerns that had emerged from the discussions with the children so far, their nervousness as to whether their parents would be consulted over what they had said or might say.

In the interviews that followed the children demonstrated their understanding and compassion for the situations in which their parents found themselves. They, the children, did not want to add to their parents' problems by communicating how they felt. They appreciated that there was nothing anyone could do to put these situations right – parents who had split up and no longer liked each other would not get back together.

‘Like me and my dad, if like, I'm frightened to say if I could go and see my mum and he's saying no, you've got to stay here. Like the other day dad was in the room and I was saying "Why can't I go and stay with mum?" and he just came over and hit me, I can never mention mum when he's in a mood.’

In this situation we, the researchers, were the only people the children felt they could talk to. We were not their parents, whom the children perceived as being the problem or as having too many problems of their own, we were not the teachers, whose role did not include that of confidant and we were not family counsellors, whom some of the children certainly did not trust. The children were very aware that, unlike family counsellors, we could and would not do anything about their situations. All we could do was listen.

But this very trust put us in a difficult ethical position. Should we intervene in any way in the children's situations? We felt very strongly that some provision should be made generally to prepare children for issues that might arise in their lives, and some support should be available when they did arise. But having been made aware of these children's concerns now, should we tell the head? Should we tell the parents? Some of these children were going to go home very upset and all the parents had been told was that researchers were going to be in the school talking to the children. We had come up against an unexpectedly strong response, but if we are not prepared for the unexpected why are we researching?

Our decision was not to inform parents. The children had confided in us, and we felt that that confidentiality had to be respected. Some children told their parents about the session and one parent expressed her approval that issues such as death were being addressed in school. One other parent complained that her child had been upset by the assembly.

Our decision to respect the rights of the children to confidentiality was to some extent vindicated by the actions of the children after the assembly and the interviews. They asked if they could set up a self-help group and that group is operating at the moment. When you respect children's rights, then you free them to take responsibility for their own situations. If we had informed the parents then no doubt actions would have been taken *for* the children and maybe *against* the children, but certainly not *by* the children as did happen.

Reflections

In this chapter I have looked at just two specific research situations which illustrate ethical dilemmas. There are always many more such issues that have to be resolved when carrying out this kind of research. My solution to the problems have been consistent in that what we see as the rights of the researched have been respected. I have tried hard to ensure that the values and the agendas of other interested parties (us, heads, parents, community representatives etc) do not serve to objectify the subject of the research but that their subjectivity has been preserved and been allowed to speak through the publication of the data. This is particularly important for children, whose rights and abilities are so often ignored and undervalued, and for whom decisions are made without consultation. As one of the children we interviewed said:

> Well in a way really L, we are a bit special, the way we have to cope through it all, people are a bit special when they manage to cope with it.'

References

Bogdan, R and Biklen, S (1982) *Qualitative Research for Education*, Allyn and Bacon, Boston
Ely, M *et al* (1991) *Doing Qualitative Research: Circles within circles*, The Falmer Press, London
Glaser, B D and Strauss, A K (1967) *The Discovery of Grounded Theory*, Aldine, Chicago IL
Jackson, R (1996) Paper given at European Association for World Religions in Education Conference, Turku, Finland

PART FIVE

COMPARATIVE STUDIES

Chapter 16

Ethics (Re)placed: Considerations for Educating Citizens in Post-Apartheid South Africa

Robert Balfour

Introduction

I do not, in this chapter, wish merely to retell the history of inequality and systematic impoverishment associated with four centuries of colonial history in South Africa. The consequences of this legacy are now being visited upon educationists, pupils and teachers as they struggle with the effects of inequality, unequal opportunity and differential access to resources, even in the years following the 1994 election. Although these issues are both ethical and historical by nature, it is the ethical nature of a particular historical issue – language teaching and policy for schools – which forms the basis of this discussion. I shall attempt to describe the ethical and religious framework of the Christian National Education (CNE), as an education system devised by successive apartheid governments from 1948–80, with reference to its manifestation in language policy in education.

The consequences and implications of apartheid education are tangible, not abstract; pragmatic, not theoretical. Why, for example, despite the fact that there has always existed a core national curriculum for all schooling, do differences still exist between black and white students' levels of communicative competence? This question begs investigation into the education system itself. With hindsight it seems that Christian National Education, as a means through which the apartheid state, using both its peculiar brand of Calvinism and Darwinism, sought to naturalize the hierarchy of races, appears typically

Sophist in formulation. MacIntyre (1966), in his discussion of Sophist moral-ity, suggests that 'morality is then explicable as a necessary compromise be-tween the desire of natural men to aggress upon others and the fear of natural men that others will aggress upon them with fatal consequences' (p 17). For the purposes of my discussion, I shall retain the distinction made between eth-ics and morality made by MacIntyre, who understood ethics to be the princi-ples upon which we base our thinking about any given issue in order to make a moral choice. Njoroge and Bennaars (1986) define 'normative ethics' as 'the study of conduct in terms of accepted moral codes' (p 174). I shall also refer to Morrow's (1989) analysis of the collusion of the 'grammars' of CNE and Posi-tivism, as a means of illustrating how ideology and philosophy have been used to the detriment of learners in South African language education. In this regard it will become clear why educational reform needs to be ideologically explicit in a way that, during the apartheid years, it never was, in order to be open to con-tinued critique by all stakeholders in South African education.

The Bantu Education Act of 1953 attempted to introduce Afrikaans along-side English as the medium-of-instruction for secondary schooling, whilst also seeking to enforce mother-tongue instruction in primary education. H F Verwoerd, then Minister of Education, favoured mother-tongue instruction because it would keep the 'Bantu' safely out of 'the green pastures of Euro-pean culture' (H F Verwoerd, 1953, quoted in Janks, 1990). Consequently, both mother-tongue instruction and the compulsory use of Afrikaans came to be used alternately as mechanisms for partial access to the 'green pastures' insofar as they enabled Afrikaner nationalist, and mainly English industrial interests, to retain a large unskilled, semi-literate and cheap labour force.

In South Africa, audio-lingual principles of language learning, as defined by Charles Fries (1961) and given pedagogical application based upon the work of behavioural psychologist BF Skinner in *Verbal Behaviour* (1957), found a 'happy home' in Christian National Education, which was enshrined by prominent Afrikaner nationalists as 'philosophy of education'. There is a disturbing similarity between the audio linguist W Rivers' (1964) tabling of the pedagogical foundations of audio lingualism, its methodological practice, and the promoted goals and principles of CNE. Rivers states: 'The meanings that the words of a language have for a native speaker can be learned only in a linguistic and cultural context... Teaching a language thus involves teaching aspects of the cultural system of the people who speak the language' (pp16–22). Piet Meyer, a proponent of Christian National Education, and as-sistant to then Minister of Education, H F Verwoerd, articulated the purpose of CNE in the following manner: 'The Afrikanerizing of the English speaker is an educational task and must start in schools. The Afrikanerizing of the English speaker entails the English speaker accepting the Afrikaner outlook and philosophy of his own...' (Morrow, 1989). Although this task was only implemented to a limited extent, the overarching cultural 'imperialism' that sought to create English-speaking Afrikaners was not extended to the majority of people in South Africa in this form, as it would imply parity with black people. Morrow (1989) argues that to undermine the economic and cultural challenge that English presented to Afrikaner nationalism, CNE, by introducing Afrikaans as the language of instruction in black schools, would simultaneously achieve this aim and stifle black resistance and aspirations to equal education through access to English.

Given that the circumstances of the 1976 Soweto uprising centred on the introduction of Afrikaans as the medium-of-instruction in Bantu Education schools and the enforcement of mother-tongue as the medium-of-instruction in primary schools, the collusion between Positivist theory and CNE educational practice is insidious. Morrow (1989) suggests that: 'CNE in common with Positivism and Pedagogics has as one of its aspects the idea that there can be a universal framework of thinking (or broad educational policy) which… can quite happily accommodate a diversity of educational policies' (p 61). Positivism views knowledge as inherently virtuous and valuable in itself. School knowledge need not be related to the socio-material context of the learner, may not need to locate itself within a defined historical setting or attempt to make explicit the processes by which it is constituted; it is not, in other words, expected to be self-reflexive or to acknowledge and address its own silences. It is therefore not uncommon to find South African school syllabuses for English dominated by a western canon of 'great works' of 'universal' significance (Reddy, 1995).

This kind of system, both political and educational, while purporting to respect 'cultural differences', allowed for the perpetuation of inegalitarian practices. Its consequences are embodied in the debasement of matric qualifications (O level equivalent) and grossly incompetent and disempowered students. For whilst education was centrally controlled by apartheid governments, it was paradoxically administered by 19 racially divided education departments, each using its own variant of a Christian National core curriculum. Historical inequalities between finance allocated to white and black education departments in conjunction with student–teacher ratios of 37:1 in black schools, as opposed to 18:1 in white schools, have material consequences for the pupils and the quality of learning (SAIRRS, 1995). CNE's treatment of ethnic groupings *vis-à-vis* the principle of self-determination is unethical insofar as the inversion of the principle implied the subordination and marginalization of already disempowered populations.

Paulo Freire has noted that 'projecting an absolute ignorance onto others, a characteristic of the ideology of oppression, is that it negates education and knowledge as a process of enquiry' (Freire, 1972: 58). Freire perceives the nature of an oppressive ideology as one that seeks to deny to those whom it positions on its periphery, any knowledge of 'self'. Hilary Janks (1990) has argued that 'language policy (as devised by CNE) and the teaching of literature have to be examined in relation to the racial segregation of education' (p 242). What is noticeable about her account is the way in which it foregrounds, rightly, the fact that language education has meant language impoverishment for the majority of people who did not speak the then official languages of the country: Afrikaans and English. Language education has been exploited in South Africa as a means of dealing with indigenous languages, whilst concurrently enforcing the observance of Euro-centric values and norms on people 'othered' by Apartheid.

The irony of Christian National Education is that while it paraded itself – in typically Calvinistic terms – as a moral system based on the justification of difference between God's chosen and 'others', the fact remains that as a moral system, which articulated itself in terms of quasi-religious notions of right and destiny, CNE lacked any ethical basis that allowed either adherents or subjects a degree of self-reflexivity. It is hardly surprising that CNE was able to assimilate seemingly progressive language learning theories such as Communicative Language Theory (CLT) (Hymes, 1972) and the Natural Approach (Krashen, 1988) as part of its apparatus to reinforce and sustain power relations between dominant and subordinate groups. Both the former Transvaal Education Department (white) (TED, 1988) senior school syllabus for English, and the former Department of Education and Training (black) syllabus, use communicative principles for the selection and teaching of material.

Since 1990, the South African government, in response to growing pressures for change, appeared to make provision for an integrated education system with the introduction of Model C schools. Despite its seeming acknowledgement of the necessity of integration, the government merely devolved segregationist powers onto local school communities, which, given the fact of racially segregated living areas, allowed for limited integration on the following terms: 'Given that one of the stipulations of desegregation under the Model C schools is that the "ethos" of the school should not change, it is unlikely that state authorities under the existing dispensation will introduce formal curriculum changes in response to desegregation' (Christie, 1993: 113). 'Ethos' in this context may be understood to include the language of the school community prior to integration, curriculum content, theoretical-textual approaches for literary analysis, as well as pedagogy. Although policy has changed to desegregate schools, the nature of such institutions belies policy initiatives with the consequence that no meaningful integration of the learners' lived experience with school knowledge is achieved. Although the ideology is critical, more humane, and may seemingly no longer cohere with still inadequate theoretical approaches to pedagogy and syllabus design – such as audio lingualism and the transmission model discussed earlier – these approaches continue to be borne out with devastating effect in classroom practice. As Reddy (1995), a critic and teacher from a Model C school, has noted: 'Under such conditions, traditional subject groupings, the transmission mode of teaching and conservative assessment and examination procedures have frequently held sway.' Assimilationist policies continue to demonstrate the paternalism of schools, which assume that black pupils will be brought into an essentially European value system.

Drawing from Bourdieu's Reproduction theory with its concept of 'cultural capital' and Giroux's Resistance theory, Lisa Delpit (1988) identifies in US education a series of silences in the contested terrain of educational policy and praxis, which are also evident in reform initiatives in South African education. There is, she suggests, a tendency of those within the dominant group, especially 'progressives', to avoid acknowledgement of the cultural and social power they possess over subordinated groups. Whilst 'liberal' educators aim to provide the same education for everyone, their good intentions mask the fact that parents who do not belong to the same cultural and dominant group often want more than 'the same for everybody' (p 3). They see the role of the school as providing children with an awareness of 'discourse patterns, interactional styles and spoken and written language codes' that will allow them access to and protection from the dominant culture. Liberals' attempts to impose forms of schooling that are 'culture-specific' – under the familiar guise of respecting cultural difference and diversity – are viewed as a plot to deny the subordinate groups access to participation in the 'culture of power' (Delpit, 1988).

A second assumption held by progressive educators is that child-centred learning and process approaches, as derived from CLT and the Natural Approach, work best for all children because they make common sense. In the classroom where the process is held to be implicitly more important than the product, learners are being denied knowledge about a set of rules that govern the dominant culture where one is judged according to what one produces. One need only think of how language-register, according to Bernstein (1975), determines status and access to power. Many teachers who belong to the dominant culture are reluctant to make their authority explicit in the classroom because this style of teaching has been labelled as authoritarian and sometimes even fascist by progressive educationalists. The teacher's resistance, suggests Delpit (1988), to exhibiting power in the classroom is 'tentatively attributed to the mistaken notion that to exhibit one's personal power as an expert source is often the equivalent to disempowering students' (p 6). Furthermore, whilst progressive teachers seldom see the necessity to use explicit language, often 'using veiled commands and indirect requests for adherence to an unstated set of rules', it has become increasingly obvious that in working-class contexts or second language classes, this approach frustrates and confuses students, thereby disempowering them (Heath, 1983: 28). Delpit (1988), Wong-Fillmore (1985) and Cope and Kalantzis (1993) argue for teachers not only to accept differences between student groups but to accept responsibility to make evident the ways in which difference affects access to power. Encouraging students to believe that there are no 'gate-keeping mechanisms', in terms of language deficiencies, is criminal because it 'sets them up' for failure in the employment sector where they discover that it matters not only what they produce but how that production is articulated (Balfour, 1995).

A reaction to the absence of transparency and ethical critique in education may be found in the development of what has been termed as 'people's education'. 'People's education appears to display – in its formulation as set out by Newfield (1992) – an awareness of the need for an ideology which is more humane, redressive and inclusionary, but which is also more critical of its aims than Christian National Education. Moreover, 'people's education' seems to be grounded within a Critical approach to the construction of knowledge and language. The following may be regarded as constituent parts of the Critical approach. First, there is an assumption that ideological critique is as necessary as action based upon that critique. Most critical theorists are concerned with the mapping-out of injustice and inequalities within systems of governance and power. McLaren suggests that 'the dialectical nature of Critical theory enables researchers to see the classroom not only as an arena of indoctrination or the site of instruction, but also as a cultural terrain that promotes learner empowerment and self-transformation' (1989: 167).

In schools where there exists language homogeneity, and in Model C integrated schools, which display multicultural and multilingual student populations, the question: whose language, for which purposes, in whose interests? is one that needs to be debated in an ethical fashion. A seemingly simple question such as this masks conflicting interests between the state and communities. The state may be concerned with nation building, based on a sense of national identity and a shared sense of values, whereas the local or regional community's investment in protecting the particularity of its own culture or language in schools within given geographical regions may militate against that sense of collective identity. Add to this the individual's or family's interest in securing the education necessary for social mobility and material upliftment within the national tertiary education framework, and one is able to understand why an apparent desire for separation occurs. Examples of that desire are evidenced in the 'Volkstaat' movement by Afrikaner conservatives in 1996, or the Inkatha Freedom party's KwaZulu-Natal drive for federalism and the devolving of power from the central state to the provinces. Newfield's

(1992) overview of the aims of 'people's education' is appropriate for English teachers, and indeed all teachers concerned with innovative curriculum development, because it displays, explicitly, its ethical principles in such a manner as to suggest their dialogic relation in South Africa's past and the present challenges facing education in the country:

> First, to understand the aims of apartheid and to think and speak in non-racist, non-sexist and non-elitist ways. Second, to play a creative role in the achievement of a non-racial democratic South Africa. Third, to enable people to determine their own destinies and free themselves from oppression. Fourth, to express and consider the issues and questions of their time. Fifth, to transform themselves into full and active members of society. (Newfield (quoted in Evans, 1992), p 42)

Newfield's analysis of the aims of 'people's education' has parallels with the Critical approach which may be employed potentially as an ethical framework to inform issues discussed in this chapter.

By focusing on the injustice and inequality, Critical theory attempts to create an awareness of 'subject-positioning' within the dominant discourses of society thereby creating a basis for radical and reasoned transformation. Critical theory seeks to expose oppressive education through a sensitivity to 'false-consciousness' and espouses the related concepts of 'critical thinking' and 'empowerment'. In this regard, the following premises are put forward. The essential characteristics of empowerment depend on the capacity of the teacher/learner to engage in reasoned questioning and self-reflexivity. Critical thinking is not generic but is contextualized within specific genres, discourses and subject areas. MacIntyre (1966) suggests that 'if we define knowledge in the Socratic sense then we beg the question concerning how that knowledge is transmitted to what ends' (p 21). From Socrates it is possible to deduce that knowledge which is founded on an understanding of one's ignorance is the kind of knowledge which is self-reflexive, critical and continually questioning of itself and the environment in which the learner is situated. In South African history, where an ostensibly 'moral' education system has been paradoxically unethical in its treatment of communities and learners, one might invoke, as the first ethic, the need for radical critique from within a socio-historical web, to help inform the choices citizens make concerning issues, such as language policy and education, in post-Apartheid South Africa. And this in order that moral accountability between the state and citizens be established and that ethics be re-placed in South African education.

References

Balfour, R (1995) *An Enquiry into Classroom Dynamics and Teaching Methods in the Department of English at the University of Natal*, Durban, MA Thesis, University of Natal (Durban), South Africa

Bernstein, B (1975) *Class, Codes and Control*, Routledge and Kegan Paul, London

Christie, P (1993) School desegregation and curriculum in South Africa, in *Inventing Knowledge: Contests in curriculum*, ed N Taylor, Maskew Miller Longman, Cape Town

Cope, W and Kalantzis, M (eds) (1993) *The Powers of Literacy: A genre approach to teaching writing*, Falmer Press, London

Delpit, L (1988) The silenced dialogue: power and pedagogy in educating other people's children, *Harvard Educational Review*, **58** (3)

Evans, E (1992) *Reading Against Racism*, Open University Press, Buckingham

Freire, P (1972) *Pedagogy of the Oppressed*, Penguin Books, London

Fries, C and Fries, A (1961) *Foundations for Teaching English*, Kenyushka, Tokyo

Heath, S B (1983) *Ways with Words*, CUP, Cambridge

Hymes, D (1972) On communicative competence, in *Sociolinguistics*, ed J B Pride and J Holmes, Penguin, Harmondsworth

Janks, H (1990) Contested terrain: English education in South Africa (1948–1987), in *Bringing English to Order*, ed I Goodson and P Medway, Falmer Press, London

Krashen, S (1988) Second Language Acquisition and Second Language Learning, Prentice Hall, Hemel Hempstead

MacIntyre, A (1966) *A Short History of Ethics*, Routledge and Kegan Paul, London

McLaren, P (1989) *Life in Schools: An introduction to critical pedagogy in the foundations of education*, Longman, UK

Morrow, W (1989) Philosophies of education in SA (4), in *Chains of Thought*, ed W E Morrow, Southern Book Publishers, Johannesburg

Newfield, D (1992) in *Reading Against Racism*, ed E Evans, Open University Press, Buckingham

Njoroge, R and Bennaars, G (1986) *Philosophy and Education in Africa: An introductory text*, Transafrica Press, Nairobi

Reddy, S (1995) *Reconstructing the Current Senior Secondary Literature Syllabus in KwaZulu Natal: A critical emancipatory approach to textual studies in the post-apartheid classroom*, MA Thesis, University of Natal (Durban)

Rivers, W M (1964) *Teaching Foreign Language Skills*, University of Chicago Press, Chicago

Skinner, B F (1957) *Verbal Behaviour*, Appleton, Century, Crofts, New York

South African Institute of Race Relations (1995) *Race Relations Survey 1994–1995*, Calvin & Sales, Cape Town

Wong-Fillmore, L (1985) When does teacher-talk work as input?, in *Input in Second Language Acquisition*, ed Gass and Madden, Rowley Press, Newbury House, USA

Chapter 17

Researching Values in Cross-cultural Contexts

Elwyn Thomas

Introduction

The United Kingdom is not the only place where there is a growing concern about what role values education in the context of rapid societal change should have. The subject has also been high on education agendas in many countries in different parts of the world. One region of the world where quite strenuous efforts have been made to make values education more relevant to the school curriculum has been in Asia, and especially in North and South-East Asia (Thomas, 1997c).

This chapter sets out to discuss some of the issues that relate to the recent developments in attempting to make the school curriculum more sensitive to the need for a relevant values education programme, and also examines some of the problems concerned with researching values in the context of curriculum planning and pedagogy. In the course of the chapter, reference will be made to the author's experience in the Asian region and specifically to data collected from a number of North and South-East Asian countries. As many countries that make up the Asian region (especially those in South-East Asia) are pluralistic societies, the issue of cultural diversity, linked to the inclusion of cultural values in the school curriculum, provides us with a particularly interesting and sensitive dimension to the study of values. The problem is even more challenging, especially when it comes to carrying out research as a prerequisite to the planning of a values curriculum that needs to have a broad appeal to the different cultural groups that make up a nation. This chapter will address four key questions:

- What are values, and to what extent are values culture related?
- Why is it necessary to research values within different cultural contexts?
- What are the key areas that need to be considered when developing plans for researching values education within different cultural contexts?
- What research methodologies are best suited to study values and values education in different cultural contexts?

As a working statement, **values** will be defined as centrally held sets of enduring predispositions, which can determine both deep-seated and peripheral attitudes, which have the propensity to motivate a person's behaviour (Thomas, 1997a). Values education refers to teaching political, social, religious, aesthetic and environmental values, while moral education might be thought of as a Kantian universally oriented conception of justice (Habermas, 1982) and a code of behaviour which could be included in a values education programme. **Culture** is viewed as a series of encounters that may be either transient or enduring between members of a group, which are transmitted over time to members of that group (Thomas, 1992a), while **cross-cultural** comparisons are made between cultures for the benefit of exploring the generality or otherwise of human behavioural traits.

It is the contention of this chapter that for any programme that sets out to provide a meaningful and effective values education curriculum, it is necessary that well-thought-out research strategies be developed by educators, in order that such programmes will be relevant, sensitive and adaptable to change for all cross-cultural contexts.

What are values?

There are a variety of views that are expressed by various authors coming from different disciplines in the way they interpret what they mean by values. Therefore as a backdrop to what is being discussed here, let us examine briefly some of these views.

For social psychologists, values are perceived as a central core construct which relate to moral concepts and specific attitudes as peripheral elements. Perhaps one of the most well-known authors in the field is Milton Rokeach (1973), whose seminal work on the nature and understanding of human values has provided us with a classification which distinguishes between **terminal** and **instrumental** values. The work of Kluckholm and Strodtbeck (1961) showed that value orientations serve an important function in guiding one's behaviour and assisting the individual to solve problems. Attitude systems, which include particular dispositions to authoritarianism, Machiavellism, prejudice and so on, reflect the inner core or central values, and are elements of an individual's personality. This interpretation has been used in cross-cultural research on values systems in Taiwan (Yang, 1986). The seminal work by Rotter (1966) on locus of control has provided interesting revelations on how self-perceptions of one's beliefs may determine an individual's behaviour under different conditions. In value transmission, it is often useful to analyse the balance between conditions that favour internality over externality when developing strategies for values learning in schools.

Trying to understand human values from the perspective of **how we develop** our perception and understanding of values, and especially moral values, has been a hallmark of the theories of Dewey (1933), Piaget (1932) and Kohlberg (1976). In essence, these theorists suggest that our understanding of values and the decisions we take that involve judgements about values go through a sequence of phases from childhood to adulthood. The process of development is thought to be partly one of maturation and partly influenced by learning. All three theorists occupy similar ground concerning the nature of human development. Each stage of development is at a qualitatively higher level than the preceding one. Stages are invariant and part of a hierarchical system of cognition.

The work of Peter McPhail (1972, 1982) focuses on moral values in the context of other persons and how they interact. McPhail sees moral education solely in terms of **consideration for others**. To him, the essence of moral behaviour is consideration, care and mutual respect. McPhail works on the assumption that moral behaviour is a direct consequence of what we take from our environment and the people that make up this environment. The message the consideration model delivers is that human values are essentially *caught rather than taught*. On the face of it, the consideration model would have something to offer many developing countries, as it focuses on several priority values that emphasize harmony and group cohesion inside and outside school. Indeed, the Government of Singapore has used some of McPhail's work in their current Civics and Moral education programme for these and other purposes (MoE, 1991).

The philosophical approach by Wilson (1990) provides an interesting framework for introducing moral values into school. Rather than using indoctrination to teach a particular set of values or moral code, Wilson's approach is to explore ways that teachers might use to rationalize problems relating to values. Wilson believes that as there are ways of *doing science* there are also ways of *doing morality*.

Values education and cultural processes

The process of values education, like that of learning, cognition, socialization

onality development, takes place within a complex of human interac-
ome of which provide enduring agendas that may or may not be
socially transmitted to successive generations through the agencies of language and traditional customs. In other words, the mainstream of these trans-
missions constitute what may be called *culture* (Thomas, 1992a). Value
systems are an integral part of any cultural context and where several cultural
contexts meet, as they do in pluralistic and multi-ethnic societies, questions
inevitably arise relating to the existence of universal values and culture-
specific (relativistic) values, and how a balance can be achieved between both
when it comes to developing a values curriculum that must have a common
appeal.

The relationship between cultural universals and cultural specifics has a
major place in the study of cross-cultural behaviour. Cross-cultural psychologists refer to universals as psychological rather than cultural as they
confine their scope to human activity, rather than the products of that activity. Triandis (1978, 1979) and Lonner (1980) have argued that the search for
psychological universals is perhaps one of the highest priority items for
cross-cultural psychologists to tackle, possibly leading to a global understanding of human behaviour. However, research on universality of human
behaviour is embryonic and what there is may be considered to be somewhat tentative. The value of psychological universals seems to lie mainly in
their potential for cross-cultural comparisons. For a cross-cultural psychologist such as Jahoda (1979), universals would help test the generality of psychological explanations and principles giving possibly more prediction to
human actions.

Determining the precise nature of psychological universals is also likely to
lead to a more meaningful debate about globalization and the impact of
'global culture' on education and schooling (Thomas, 1997b). However, for
an increasing number of cross-cultural researchers, psychological and cultural universals are not key issues in understanding human behaviour.
Scribner and Cole (1973), Davidson (1994) and Schweder (1990) stress the
importance of intra-cultural and indigenous approaches to behaviour in different cultural groups, and view the issue of seeking out universals as less important than finding out about how individuals interact with one another in
their own cultures. The recent work of Teasdale and Teasdale (1994) on Australian aborigines, Aikman (1994) with Peruvian indigenous Indians, Nunes
(1994) with Brazilian street children and Tanon (1994) with West African rural children from the Ivory Coast point to the fact that the development of a
school curriculum for these cultures stands to benefit when researchers concentrate on finding out more about the day-to-day patterns of living, and the
relevance they have for making schooling not only more effective but worthwhile as well.

Recent developments in values education in the Asian region show that in countries such as Malaysia (Mukherjee, 1988), Singapore (Gopinathan, 1988; Eng, 1989; Thomas, 1990) and to a lesser extent Burma, Thailand and Vietnam (Thomas, 1997c), there have been conscious efforts to arrive at varying degrees of consensus when it comes to drawing up a school curriculum, which in reality attempts to tackle the problem of universals and cultural specifics. In principle, it is natural that both universal and culture-specific values are given their rightful place in a school curriculum. However, who makes the decision about choice and balance, and who sets out the rationale for the whole process will always be problematical issues, especially in pluralistic societies.

Understanding the nature of human values, as seen from the foregoing discussion, provides us with no shortage of views. However, planning a school curriculum that aims to reflect both universal as well as relativistic cultural values that may assist a pluralistic society to exist in harmony will be a strong challenge whatever the circumstances.

The precise nature of the *challenge* arises in finding out what values are the most relevant and how best they can be presented in the life of the school. It is evident from a perusal of the recent literature on values and moral education in most countries that little attention is being given to developing research strategies that will translate into a sound basis for values teaching and learning, both inside and outside school. The remainder of this chapter will examine the problems relating to researching values in several Asian societies that are currently experiencing profound change.

Researching 'Asian values'

In the past decade or so considerable efforts have been made by the governments of most of the Asian tiger economies such as Korea, Singapore and Malaysia, as well as the less developed economies in the region like the Philippines and Indonesia, to concern themselves with what they call the threat to their system of values. These values are often referred to globally as 'Asian values'. Cummings (1996), in his attempt to couple Asian values with education and its effect on national and economic development, describes Asian values as an expandable and flexible system in which the new values of the market and the individualism of capitalistic ideology have become incorporated. This in effect has provided a culture of *'Asian pick 'n' mix'*.

While on one hand this *'Asian pick 'n' mix'* may have been a factor in the success of these economies, the leaders are worried by the detrimental effects which parts of the Asian mix are having on young people. Among the perceived detrimental effects are the decreasing respect shown by young people for the older members of the family and society, the challenging of authority and the move away from the extended family towards nuclear and satellite structures. Another feature is the rise of individualism and the drive for greater youth independence. There is, however, little by way of research findings to justify the above worries.

Nevertheless, protection against values erosion has become a very political affair in most of the South-East Asian tiger economies, and this is reflected in political and educational decisions affecting cultural and religious values. Educational decisions that resulted in the omission of certain key cultural values from a curriculum could be perceived by a particular cultural group as a threat to its cultural identity. While the *'Asian pick 'n' mix* may be seen as stemming the erosion, it could also be argued that its use could be a convenient umbrella term to subsume diverse cultural values, and deter the demands for too much cultural diversity, proving in the long run to be counter-productive to national cohesion and a national identity.

To examine some of these problems, several key countries in the region met in 1989 in Japan (UNESCO/APEID, 1992) to discuss in some depth the place of a substitute for values education in the school curriculum. The outcomes of this meeting produced a blueprint for a movement termed 'Education for Affective Development'. This blueprint was an attempt to embrace values education as part of a wider scheme for educating young people in becoming responsible citizens for the future. Although the true impact of the development is yet to be realized, the whole issue of values education at a regional level came to the fore. In countries like Indonesia, Singapore and Malaysia, the Curriculum Development Centres had already begun to develop, over the last decade or so, many examples of curriculum materials for the teaching of values in both primary and secondary schools. Colleges of Teacher Education have also included in their curriculum values education programmes to meet the needs in the schools.

A trend that seems to recur most frequently wherever such programmes are initiated is that ideals and expectations are never matched with the realities. In fact, as has been found in Singapore over the years, the gulf between the ideal plans and their implementation is often so large that the Singaporean curriculum planners are constantly initiating brand-new initiatives, aimed at better measures of relevance and practice, all, it seems, to be changed again and again (Eng, 1989).

There is an urgent need to research values in the context of curriculum planning, for what we have at present, at least in South-East Asia (and probably in other regions of the world), is a somewhat muddled approach to the problem. It is clear, when one examines the various values education programmes in most countries in the region, that over-arching questions need to be addressed. Let us consider some of these questions. Why in the first place is it necessary to have values education as part of the school curriculum, in countries where family and community values are relatively still so strong? With the constant reference to so-called 'Asian values' from countries within the region, would it be necessary for us to know what exactly are Asian values? If Asian values are under attack, in what ways are they being threatened, and is it really a case of irreversible erosion? If, as the evidence seems to indicate, Asian values are becoming more eclectic (Paige, 1975; Cummings, 1996), what role does the school and the workplace have in promoting these changes? Another more urgent question lies in the fact that different countries that call themselves Asian, and adhere to some form of Asian value system, will perceive the growing influence of westernization differently. For instance, the Malaysian and Indonesian values programmes for secondary schools have been purposely developed in order to counteract the detrimental effects of what their government leaders have called 'value erosion', mainly due to western influences (Thomas, 1997c), while in Singapore, Taiwan and South Korea the approach appears to be more 'accepting' of the changing nature of Asian values. This may be due to the broad Confucian traditions that underpin the thinking of many of the government decision makers in these countries. Such thinking appears to be able to accept that the older traditional values can exist side by side with the more individualistic and competitive values of capitalism, and the need to be successful in the newer culture of market forces (Thomas, 1997d). These and other leading questions about Asian values may need to be considered, in order that we can attempt to trace the relationship between these values and educational development and so provide a basis for policy making in these countries. Answers to these questions are also likely to be of interest to many western countries, which look with envy at the economic success of the tiger economies.

The need for policies before plans

There will always be a need for governments to provide a framework in which the direction, rationale and raison d'être for a programme of values are spelt out as clearly as possible. In Indonesia, Malaysia and Thailand, policies on school values education programmes are founded to a greater or lesser extent on either a religion or a religious philosophy. In Indonesia and Malaysia, the principal driving force is Islam, while in Thailand, Burma and Cambodia it is Buddhist philosophical ideas and practice. In all cases, a values blueprint is provided by a dominant religious/philosophical underpinning.

In Taiwan and Singapore, because of the large Chinese populations, the influence of Chinese traditionalism, mainly tempered with varying amounts of Confucianism, Menciusism, Taoism and Christianity, affects directly or indirectly not only what values are selected for the school curriculum, but how they may be presented. However, in Singapore, since ethnic Malays make up 14 per cent and Indians 7 per cent of the population, these ethnic groups are given a strong say in any policy on values education which would affect the teaching of their own values. The Malays are almost all Muslim, and most Indians are either Hindus or Muslims; some are Christians. In Japan and South Korea, policy for the teaching of values in schools seems to be influenced in the main by Confucian and Zen Buddhist philosophy. Recently in Korea, there has been an upsurge in the number of Koreans attending various Christian denominations. It is not certain, however, to what extent Christian values are having an impact on policies for values education in Korean schools. This would clearly be an interesting subject for research in itself. It would appear that the policy frameworks for values education in the countries mentioned above are strongly influenced by either a long-standing pervasive philosophy embedded over centuries into the culture of these nations or influences derived from Islam or Christianity.

A policy of teaching values in these countries will have either a decidedly religious complexion, or a secular/philosophical one, or a mix of all of them. In Indonesia, the five principles of Pancasila are an attempt to embrace both secular and religious values as a blueprint (Ribera, 1990), and the same may be said of Malaysia's National Philosophy (ICSS, 1989). However, a careful scrutiny of these blueprints cannot disguise the fact that the shadow of Islam is not far away. Nevertheless, each national philosophy provides a strong statement of policy for the teaching of values in schools. In the other countries discussed above, the situation is less clear due to the more open attitude and approach towards the teaching of values.

Values such as hard work, thrift, achievement and tolerance are catered for mainly out of school as part of family and working life. Therefore, should a policy for researching values re-examine the place of what Rokeach calls terminal values in a proposed values education? Furthermore, should research be carried out to explore the extent to which Asian values may be positively influenced by the importation of newer values, such as greater individuality, personal independence, being more competitive and showing greater self-reliance? If that would be the case, should the new Asian mix be part of a values programme? Do existing values such as being filial, being tolerant, being thrifty, need to be revisited through research to see what these values are like in this day and age, and to what extent they have changed?

Developing values programmes that attempt to address the above questions requires the existence of clear policies which assist decisions to be made as to whether or not consensus would be a desirable goal, or whether there should be separate programmes answering to the needs of each cultural group or religious persuasion.

Key areas for cross-cultural research in values education

There are four key areas that can be identified for any research plan for the development of values education in societies which are culturally diverse, and these are discussed below.

Policy-related research and values education

Programmes like *The Good Citizen* and *Being and Becoming*, developed by the Singapore Ministry of Education during the 1980s, took as their overriding policy one that attempted to cover values that had a general appeal to all ethnic and religious groups that made up the Republic. In Malaysia, the expression of a national policy on values education has been the introduction in 1988 of a National Philosophy (ICSS, 1989), with its emphasis on mainly spiritual values, which is expected to pervade all teaching in both primary and secondary schools. A similar policy exists in the case of Indonesia with its National Policy of Pancasila, also aiming at providing a school curriculum that develops in the pupils (and the teachers) a sense of moral and social well-being for the nation. However, in all three countries and to different degrees, there appear to be varying accounts of success for these programmes. There is little published on programme evaluation and so it is difficult to get a true picture. Also, the position of pupil assessment in values programmes is ambiguous. It is not always the case that the subject of values is assessed, and where it takes place, teachers are far from satisfied with the measures. This has prompted the most recent values programme in Singapore called *Civics and Moral Education* (MoE, 1991), to virtually abandon formal assessment altogether, and to replace it with a loose system of teacher feedback.

In countries like Vietnam, Burma, Laos and Cambodia, the issue surrounding a values education policy is somewhat different. These countries have to address the changing political landscape and reassess the place of former ideologies that filtered into the school curriculum as civics or political education. The key issue, it seems, centres around the extent to which former values can be incorporated into existing curricula in which former Marxist and Leninist values hold sway. This is an especially pertinent problem for Vietnam. The large ethnic minorities in the north also provide tough challenges for curriculum planners as they have to serve the many cross-cultural contexts.

In the light of the above, future research might concentrate on the following areas as far as policy is concerned. Firstly, why has a consensus approach to a values education been only partially successful in South-East Asia? A second area might examine to what extent each cultural or religious group should develop its own values education programme in preference to the eclecticism of a consensus policy. A third area would involve looking at comparative data from countries such as Britain, Australia, Canada, the United States and New Zealand, which have developed policies of multiculturalism that attempted to give a framework for curriculum planning. A fourth area might consider why some values should be included and not others.

Researching the nature of values for the curriculum

There has been a tendency for most values education curricula to provide lists of values that are thought to be both desirable and necessary, during school-ing. The lists mainly reflect the earlier work of social psychologists such Mil-ton Rokeach (1973), Kluckholm and Strodtbeck (1961) and Rotter (1966), but the recent and more relevant cross-cultural research of Schwartz and Bilsky (1987), Bond (1986) and Yang (1986) has yet to be consulted. There is a decidedly psychological flavour to the lists of values selected, while philo-sophical and sociological influences are sparse. However, in countries where there are substantial ethnic Chinese minorities as in Malaysia, there is evi-dence from the teaching materials that Confucian and Buddhist philosophi-cal values have been included, albeit rather sparingly. A Confucian values programme for Chinese ethnic Singaporeans in the early 1980s was also developed (CDIS, 1985; Tu, 1984), based entirely on a modern interpreta-tion of Confucian philosophical values. It unfortunately appears to have had only limited success.

Blueprints for values education programmes published by the Ministries of Education in Singapore, Malaysia, the Philippines, Indonesia and Japan not only provide long lists of values, but invariably categorize them, eg spiri-tual, moral, intellectual.

Lists and categories certainly have a place in the planning of a values educa-tion programme but behind the lists and the categories a key research prob-lem exists relating to what a particular value means to a particular culture. This raises once again the question of cultural universals. For example, does trust or obedience have the same connotations for Malays as for Japanese? Take freedom of the individual as another example. In many parts of Asia, in-dividual freedom is perceived to be profoundly different from western no-tions, and even within the Asian region there would be crucial differences in what freedom means to citizens from Vietnam and China and their counter-parts in Singapore. Kohlberg's (1976) *Stage of Universal Ethical Principles* con-tains tenets that produce considerable unease in countries which feel that *they*, and *they alone*, should have their own national and cultural agenda on univer-sal ethical principles. Issues such as corporal and capital punishment as part of the criminal justice system and restrictions on citizens to openly criticize gov-ernment policy in the press are constantly cited by the governments of Malaysia and Singapore as being their *own* affair and should not be dictated by the international media.

Where there is agreement on including a value for study purposes in a programme, that may not be the end of the matter. In research carried out by the author (Thomas, 1990) on perceptions of filial piety among Singaporean adolescents, it was found that while most subjects ranked filial piety as the most important value for them, their reasons for the high ranking were not accompanied by a blind acceptance of the value in any situation.

Before embarking on a values education curriculum, especially one that may have to address several cultural agendas, research into what specific values mean and how different groups in the population perceive and understand them is not only desirable but essential.

Researching teacher education and pedagogy

Added to the difficulties of developing a successful values curriculum are problems of recruiting staff with suitable qualifications who have relevant experience and a strong commitment to the subject. In company with both pedagogical and professional demands that are made in teaching values, another problem is the question of assessment. There is little doubt that pupils who are aware of the fact that a values education programme is compulsory but not assessed will not take the subject seriously. What is more, in countries with a high reputation for academic achievement as in Singapore, Hong Kong and Taiwan, parents and even teachers will see the whole exercise as having little value and will give it either minimum or no support.

Closely related to the discussion above is the way teachers are trained for values education. In Singapore and Malaysia teacher training institutions have compulsory curricula for training all students in various moral and civics education programmes. In the main, students do not take these programmes as seriously as they should (Thomas, 1992b). There are several reasons given. One relates to the fact that values or moral education is generally not assessed as part of their overall teaching qualifications. Another and more serious reason is that the approaches used in teaching values are not sufficiently innovative.

Turning to the pedagogies that could be used in the teaching of values, there have been some significant developments during the last decade or so. For example, the development and application of *discourse pedagogy* in teaching moral and values education, which puts emphasis on children developing their own point of view while respecting the views of others, is discussed at some length by Oser (1986). The ethical principles of justification, fairness, consequences and universalization which form the basis to *discourse pedagogy* are ways of making the teaching of values more interesting and probably more relevant. However, Oser does not appear to address the situation in which children and teachers come from different cultural traditions and religious persuasions.

For most cultural groups that form the populations of Asia, allowing young children and adolescents to express their own point of view in class is hardly the norm. Such an approach would quickly run counter to traditional forms of discourse between pupils and teachers, and between children and their elders. However, some form of discourse pedagogy is encouraged in the Singapore Civics and Moral Education Syllabus for primary and secondary schools. *Developing character and integrity as well as becoming a useful member of society* are themes that underpin the programme.

A careful analysis of themes such as *Nation before Community* and *The Family as a Unit* shows that social cohesion is understandably at the top of the Singapore agenda. However, a more cynical view might be that this may be a way of ensuring political control by the state through inculcation.

The four approaches of: *Cultural Transmission,* which identifies desirable values from a culture and transmits them to future generations; *Consideration,* focusing on care for others; *Modified Values Clarification Model,* which leads pupils to accept and take responsibility; and *Cognitive Developmental,* which focuses on various stages of moral reasoning, are all fused in an eclectic manner to match the needs of the Singapore school learner.

Singapore is some way ahead of its South-East Asian neighbours as it has been experimenting for many years with different approaches to the teaching of values. In Malaysia, Islamic studies are taught only to Malays using mostly a didactic approach, while children of other ethnic groups receive their values education as part of civics. In countries like Thailand and the Philippines there is some evidence that the cognitive developmental model has some influence on the teaching of values.

Research in this area needs to be carried out on a number of fronts. First, there is an urgent need to find out from both teachers and teacher trainees their perceptions about the value and relevance of the values education that they teach. Second, little is known about pupils' perceptions as far as their attitudes towards content suitability and content presentation are concerned. Third, parents are rarely consulted on what should be taught in the school curriculum. Fourth, while there are small piecemeal evaluations available in some countries like Singapore and Thailand on the effectiveness of some programmes to date, no large-scale evaluation has been published in these countries. There is also no recent report about the impact of Pancasila on the attitudes of Indonesian teachers and pupils towards the values curriculum, and similarly in Malaysia on what effect the National Philosophy is having on secondary school teaching.

Finally, a fifth area might consider the case for research to be carried out on how a values education programme might fit within a *culture-sensitive pedagogy*.

The idea of a *culture-sensitive pedagogy* is presently being developed by the author (Thomas, 1997b), consisting of epistemological, contextual, process and personalistic components. The components are so structured and integrated with one another that they actively reflect and prescribe culture-specific knowledge, behaviours, attitudes and skills. These culture-specific attributes should complement basic learning requirements common to schooling. In order that values be included in this form of pedagogy, research would need to be carried out on the cultural contexts and origins of values. Aspects of *discourse pedagogy*, discussed earlier, could fit comfortably within the contextual and process components of the culture-sensitive model.

Research methodologies

The discussion so far has focused on the *why* and the *what* of researching values. The final area to be discussed here will briefly look at the *how;* in other words, the research methods that are used in collecting data. Like all research studies that aim to collect data, the choice of the means by which observations are collected will depend on the nature of the research problem and the preference of the researcher to follow a particular research approach. The use of survey methods for large-scale research about a problem that addresses the relative importance of values, or a problem about exploring the attitudes of teachers and learners towards the introduction of a new values programme, can produce useful data from which more in-depth probing can be developed. Methods that use questionnaires, inventories, multiple choice and other test measures often help the researcher to get an overall perception about a particular value.

The seminal work of Rokeach (1973) and Kluckholm and Strodtbeck (1961) relied on mainly survey data, which led eventually to the development of measures that were both reliable and valid. The use of survey methodology also set the scene for the work of Feather (1986) and more recently the work of Schwartz and Bilsky (1987), Bond (1986) and Yang (1986), which provided useful knowledge about trends across different national groups concerning certain values. Therefore, not only do these methods provide the opportunity for developing valid measures, but they also provide much needed cross-cultural insights into the perception of values.

Quantitative methods do not in general enable researchers to get an intimate picture of a person's behaviour. For this we need to use the interview and other qualitative research tools such as focus group interaction and interpretative observation. The interview is a widely used research tool in values research. However, as there are several types of interview, eg structured, semi-structured, free running, the choice will depend on the questions the researcher is posing. Researching into moral development has had a long tradition of using interviews as a means of collecting data from respondents. The methods employed by Piaget (1932) and Kohlberg (1976) are testimony to this. This would also be true if discourse approaches such as those used by Oser (1986), McPhail (1982) or Wilson (1990) were to be used, for there are few better ways to really probe a respondent's thinking about a moral choice and its justification. Similarly, the author's work in moral development in Singapore and Malaysia (Thomas, 1990) used both survey and interview data from secondary school pupils. However, it was the interview data that helped to focus on the cues thrown up by the survey data that provided the many fresh insights on how adolescents really felt about moral concepts such as filial piety and trust. Nevertheless, interview methods have been criticized for their subjectivity, and are generally inadequate as reliable and valid measures. However, employing both free-ranging and semi-structured interviews enables the researcher to get to the heart of a person's thinking, and when combined with the additional use of valid and reliable survey instruments, a detailed as well as a more total picture is likely to emerge. The use of ethnography, with its emphasis on natural observation and human interaction, is another approach that has its merits in probing the appreciation of values. Ethnography would be particularly useful if one is trying to develop an indigenous cross-cultural paradigm for values development. Another merit of employing ethnographic methods is that they focus on natural settings, often producing much unplanned, spontaneous and valuable data.

Researching values in cross-cultural contexts benefits from the use of both quantitative as well as qualitative methods. Quantitative methodologies aim to provide us with the wider context to the expression of one's values systems, whereas qualitative approaches enable the researcher to experience the intimate sensitivities that abound at the level of the individual and which are so crucial to a real understanding of what human values are all about, in whatever cultural context we are studying them.

References

Aikman, S (1994) School curriculum as a forum for articulating intercultural relations with particular reference to the Peruvian Amazon, in *International Perspectives on Schooling and Culture: A symposium proceedings*, ed E Thomas, pp 197–218, Institute of Education, University of London

Bond, M H (1986) *The Psychology of the Chinese People*, Oxford University Press, Oxford

CDIS (Curriculum Development Institute Singapore) (1985) *Confucian Ethics Textbook-Secondary Three*, Education Publications Bureau, Singapore

Cummings, W K (1996) Asian values, education and development, *Compare*, **26** (3), pp 287–303

Davidson, G (1994) Cultural, cross-cultural or intercultural? comment on Lonner, Dasen and Segal, *Cross-Cultural Psychology Bulletin*, **28** (1), pp 1–4

Dewey, J (1933) *Experience and Education*, Collier Macmillan, London

Eng SP (1989) *Moral Education in Singapore: Dilemmas and dimensions*, Proceedings of CCU-ICP International Conference, Moral Values and Moral Reasoning in Chinese Schools, Taipei, Taiwan, pp 678–98

Feather, N T (1986) Cross-cultural studies with the Rokeach Value Survey: the Flinders program of research on values, *Australian Journal of Psychology*, **38**, pp 269–83

Gopinathan, S (1988) Being and becoming: education for values education in Singapore, in *The Revival of Values in Education in Asia and the West*, ed W K Cummings, S Gopinathan and Y Tomoda, pp 131–45, Pergamon Press, Oxford

Habermas, J (1982) *A Communicative Approach to Moral Theory*, Paper presented at the International Symposium of Moral Education, Fribourg

ICSS (1989) Curriculum Development Centre, Ministry of Education, Malaysia

Jahoda, G (1979) Theoretical and systematic approaches in cross-cultural psychology, in *Handbook of Cross-Cultural Psychology Volume 3*, ed H C Triandis and W Lonner, Allyn & Bacon, New Jersey

Kluckholm, F R and Strodtbeck, F L (1961) *Variations in Value Orientations*, Row Peterson, Evanston, ILL

Kohlberg, L (1976) The cognitive developmental approach to moral education, in *Moral Education: It comes with the territory*, ed D Purpel and R Kevin, McCutchan, Berkeley

Lonner, W (1980) The search for psychological universals, in *Handbook of Cross-Cultural Psychology*, ed H C Triandis and W Lonner, Allyn & Bacon, New Jersey

McPhail, P (1972) *Social and Moral Education*, Basil Blackwell, Oxford

McPhail, P (1982) *On Other People's Shoes*, Longman, London

MoE (1991) *Civics and Moral Education Syllabus*, MoE Publication, Singapore

Mukherjee, H (1988) Moral education in a developing society: the Malaysian case, in *The Revival of Values Education in Asia and the West*, ed W K Cummings, S Gopinathan and Y Tomoda, pp 147–62, Pergamon Press, Oxford

Nunes, T (1994) Cultural diversity in learning mathematics: a perspective from Brazil, in *International Perspectives on Schooling and Culture: A symposium proceedings*, ed E Thomas, pp 357–70, Institute of Education, University of London

Oser, F K (1986) Moral education and values education: the discourse perspective, in *Handbook of Research on Teaching*, 3rd edn, ed M Wittrock, pp 917–41, Macmillan, New York

Paige, J M (1975) *Agrarian Revolution*, Free Press, New York

Piaget, J (1932) *The Moral Judgement of the Child*, Routledge and Kegan Paul, London

Ribera, J (1990) A national identity in the process: the Indonesian experience, in *Education, Culture and Productive Life*, ed J J Boeren and K P Epskamp, CESO Paperback No 13, The Hague

Rokeach, M (1973) *The Nature of Human Values*, Free Press, New York

Rotter, J B (1966) Generalized expectancies for internal versus external control of reinforcement, *Psychological Monographs*, **80**

Schwartz, S H and Bilsky, W (1987) Toward a universal psychological structure of human values, *Journal of Personality and Social Psychology*, **53**, pp 550–62

Schweder, R A (1990) Cultural psychology: what is it?, in *Cultural Psychology: Essays on comparative human development*, ed J W Stigler, R A Sweder and G Herdt, Cambridge University Press, Cambridge

Scribner, S and Cole, M (1973) Cognitive consequences of formal and informal schooling, *Science*, **182**, pp 552–59

Tanon, F (1994) A cultural view of planning: the case of weaving in the Ivory Coast, *Cross-Cultural Psychological Monographs*, Tilburg University Press, Tilburg

Teasdale, R and Teasdale, J (1994) Culture and schooling in Aboriginal Australia, in *International Perspectives on Culture and Schooling: A symposium proceedings*, ed E Thomas, pp 174–96, Institute of Education, University of London

Thomas, E (1990) Filial piety, social change and Singapore youth, *Journal of Moral Education*, **19** (3), pp 192–205

Thomas, E (1992a) Schooling and the school as a cross-cultural context for study, in *Innovations in Cross-Cultural Psychology*, ed S Iwawaki, K Koshima and K Leung, pp 425–41, Swets & Zeitlinger, Amsterdam

Thomas, E (1992b) Moral development, cultural context and moral education, in *Moral Perspectives and Moral Education*, ed K C Chong, pp 47–68, University of Singapore Press, Singapore

Thomas, E (1997a) Teacher education and values transmission: cultural dilemmas with difficult choices, in *Educational Dilemmas: Debate and diversity*, ed K Watson, Cassell, London

Thomas, E (1997b) Developing a culture sensitive pedagogy: tackling a problem of melding 'global culture' within existing cultural contexts, *International Journal of Educational Development*, **17** (1), pp 13–26

Thomas, E (1997c) Teacher education in South-East Asia: prospects for a north–south dialogue with a difference, in *Global Perspectives on Teacher Education*, ed C Brock, pp 123–51, Triangle Journals, Wallingford

Thomas, E (1997d) Values old and new: curriculum challenges, in *Education and Development: Tradition and innovation 3*, ed J Lynch, C Modgil and S Modgil, pp 154–69, Cassell, London

Triandis, H C (1978) Some universals of social behaviour, *Personality and Social Psychology Bulletin*, **4**, pp 1–16

Triandis, H C (1979) The future of cross-cultural psychology, in *Perspectives on Cross-Cultural Psychology*, ed A J Marsella, R G Tharp and T J Ciborowski, Academic Press, New Jersey

Tu, Wei-Ming (1984) *Confucian Ethics Today: The Singapore challenge*, Singapore Federal Publications, Singapore

UNESCO/APEID (1992) *Education for Affective Development: A guidebook on programmes and practices*, UNESCO, Bangkok

Wilson, J (1990) *A New Introduction to Moral Development*, Cassell, London

Yang, K S (1986) Chinese personality and its change, in *The Psychology of the Chinese People*, ed M H Bond, pp 106–70, Oxford University Press, Oxford

Chapter 18

Can Those Children Become 'Good Cats'? Dilemmas in Curriculum Reform in the Schools of Beijing, China

Xiaopeng Li

Introduction

Since the early 1980s there have been a series of social and economic reforms in China. In the school curriculum, many efforts have been made to promote an 'all-round' education – this means pupils are more comprehensively trained and teaching covers moral, mental and physical education, labour skills, aesthetic education, and many other aspects. While in the policy there is emphasis on being 'all-round', in practice, teaching and learning in many schools merely focus on what is to be examined in public examinations. In this chapter, the main features and background of school education reforms and the new focus in the curriculum policy in China are introduced, with analyses of how and why teaching and learning is against all-round education. Potential solutions are discussed.

Recent important changes in education and new focuses in the school curriculum in China

'Whether white cats or black cats, they are all good cats if they can catch mice.' This is a famous saying of Deng Xiao-ping.[1] Deng's ideas have greatly influenced the social and economic reforms of China since the early 1980s (background information will be introduced in the later discussion on changes in education). The saying reflects Deng's emphasis on being realistic and practical and his idea that more attention should be paid to the development of the country, not to ideological struggles as happened in the 1960s and 1970s.

From the mid-1980s until the early 1990s, two important steps were taken in education in China. One was the 1985 Education Reform. The second was the National Programme for Educational Development 1992–2000.

In the 1985 Reform, a focus was to develop vocational and technical education. Policy makers believed that the socialist modernization drive needed senior technical experts and managers as well as intermediate technicians and skilled workers. The streaming of students into different career paths was to take place between the junior and the senior secondary school and secondary education was to serve the goals of both academic and vocational/technical education. As Figure 18.1 shows, while some children, after leaving the junior division of regular junior secondary schools, would enter the senior division in which teaching was mainly to prepare pupils to go on to higher education, others would go to vocational secondary and technical schools.

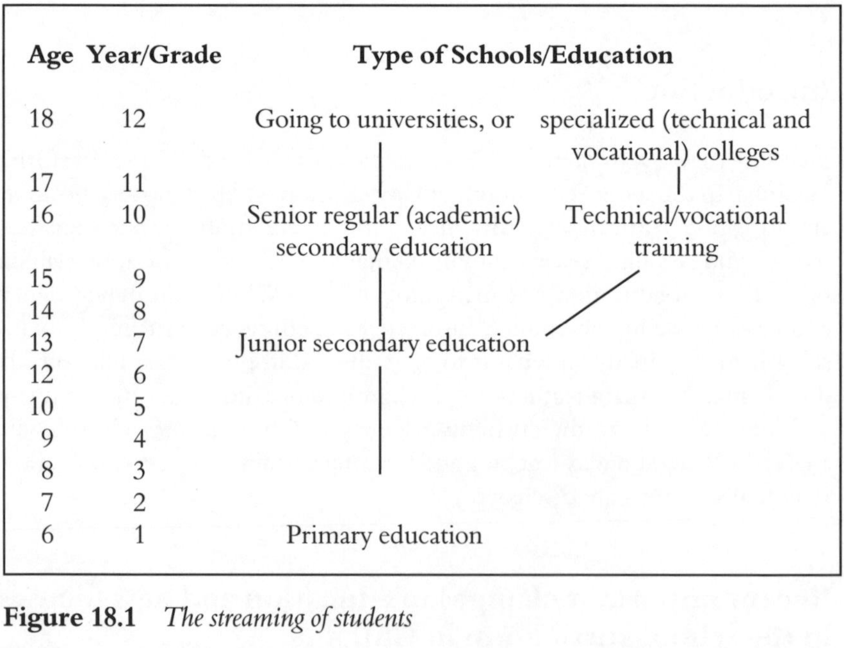

Age	Year/Grade	Type of Schools/Education	
18	12	Going to universities, or	specialized (technical and vocational) colleges
17	11		
16	10	Senior regular (academic) secondary education	Technical/vocational training
15	9		
14	8		
13	7	Junior secondary education	
12	6		
10	5		
9	4		
8	3		
7	2		
6	1	Primary education	

Figure 18.1 *The streaming of students*

A division between keypoint and regular schools was not mentioned fully in the main reform document, but it had been part of official policies since the early 1980s. Locally there have always been schools which have enjoyed a much higher reputation than others. In general, at the secondary level, regular (academic) schools are divided into keypoint (first-class), second-class and third-class schools; within the first category there are national, provincial, city and district keypoint schools. They were designed to identify early the academically outstanding students who were to be groomed for higher secondary and university education. The keypoint schools are controlled directly by the high-level education authorities, have both the best teachers and the most advanced teaching facilities, and are mostly located in urban areas.

Table 18.1 shows that between 1980 and 1985 the number of vocational and technical schools increased sharply. Table 18.2 shows that for the academic year 1991–1992 in the country as a whole, the number of junior secondary graduates entering vocational training was almost equal to those going to regular academic schools. All the same, it also shows that there were 6,144,757 pupils (56.6 per cent) who were left out of senior secondary education.

Table 18.1   *The numbers and entrants of specialized (technical) schools and vocational senior secondary schools*

| | Specialized (technical) secondary school | | Vocational senior secondary school | |
Year	Schools	Entrants	Schools	Entrants
1980	3,069	467,600	3,314	240,600
1985	3,557	668,300	8,070	984,900
1990	3,982	730,100	9,164	1,038,300
1991	3,952	780,000	9,572	1,140,000

Source: People's Education Press, 1992

Table 18.2   *The streaming of junior secondary graduates, 1991/92*

		Persons	%
Total junior secondary school graduates		10,855,053	100%
Students going to	regular senior	2,438,157	22.5%
	vocational senior	1,139,999	10.5%
	specialized technical	1,132,500	10.4%
Residue		6,144,757	56.6%

Note: Summarized from *Education Statistics Yearbook* 1992, People's Education Press

In 1992, the 14th Congress of the Chinese Communist Party put forward the *National Programme for Educational Development 1992–2000*. The Programme states, 'to fulfil the need to set up a socialist market economy and to promote political and scientific reforms, the reform and development of education needs to be quickened so as to train more technical personnel for the socialist modernization' (p 1).

With regard to secondary school education, the Programme states that 'the nine-year compulsory primary and junior secondary education must be well implemented', and that 'the primary and secondary education needs to change from an "education for examinations" to a thorough enhancement of the level of students in morality, cultural and scientific knowledge, labour skills and physical and psychological quality' (p 7). There is emphasis on a wider coverage in the curriculum.

There are by-policies of the 1985 Reform and Programme 1992–2000, for example the policy to cancel the public Year 6 Examination and to allow primary school graduates to enter nearby secondary schools directly in those areas where junior secondary education was popularized (Wang, 1996). According to the statistics of 1996 and 1997, most cities have cancelled the public Year 6 Examination (Wang, 1996). Policy makers believed that with this change pupils would have a lighter examination burden and develop more fully and more happily (Liu, 1993).

The background of the 1985 Reform and Programme 1992–2000 relates to policy oscillations in education, which are largely associated with the struggle between the left- and right-wing leaders within the Party. In the early 1950s, Liu Shao-chi's ideas gained the upper hand within the Party. He favoured more emulation of the Soviet model and stressed the importance of expertise. In education, emphasis was on training more technical personnel. At the primary level, there were programmes to achieve mass literacy. Secondary education was developed on polytechnic lines. Efforts were accelerated to provide teacher training for the required teachers. However, between 1958 and 1960, under the guidance of Mao Tse-tung, the Great Leap Forward set out to break the monopoly of schools and universities, as well as the privileges of degree-holding intellectuals. The famous slogan was, 'Education combined with productive labour'. Although academic expertise was very briefly re-emphasized in the early 1960s when the Great Leap Forward movement ran out of control, ideological conflict continued between Mao and other Party leaders. The polarization within the leadership led to the major upheaval of the Cultural Revolution (1966–76). In this period, ideological and political struggles were intense. In schools, regulations were abolished or suspended; the courses were reduced or simplified. Liu Shao-qi and Deng Xiao-ping were formally criticized as capitalist promoters. Political ideology dominated the curriculum and greater emphasis was given to the importance of being 'red'. It was not until the early 1980s when the right-wing leaders regained power that the policy focus shifted back to academic expertise. In the early 1980s, Deng Xiao-ping regained power. In the wide-ranging social and economic reforms launched since the early 1980s, some ideas of the human capital theory (HCT) seemed to have a strong influence on the policy making. A typical example is the speech of Deng Xiao-ping at the National Conference on Education in 1985:

> The economy of our country may approach the level of the developed countries at its 100th anniversary. One of the reasons we say so is that we possess the power to develop education well, to increase the scientific and technological level and to train hundreds of millions of all kinds of qualified manpower at all levels in the time before the 2040s. Our country, its power and the potential of economic development depend increasingly on the quality of labour and on the quality of the intellectuals. (Deng, 1985)

Deng's underlying idea seems to be: investment in educational training would increase individual productivity and lay the technical base for the types of labour force necessary for rapid economic growth (Dore, 1976).

It is against this background that there is educational reform which aims at continuous, compulsory and 'all-round' six-year primary and three-year junior secondary education, and the rapid development of technical and vocational education at the senior secondary level. The efforts made in abolishing the public Year 6 assessment also partly reflected the idea of this large reform programme.

What problems have been encountered?

An objective of policy makers is to provide pupils with an 'all-round' primary and junior secondary education. However, teaching and learning in many schools is to and for exams (Pan *et al* 1991; author's field study in 1995).[2]

This is mainly because, although much effort has been made to cancel some examinations, the education system is still selective, and schools are still judged by the public and/or the educational authority on the basis of their achievements in examinations, especially the exam success rates. In a teacher's own words:

> How well students have performed in examinations, and if the success rate is high, have almost become the only yardstick of a class and a school. Schools which have a lower rate of success in examinations would even run into the problem of finding applicants... once the rate has gone up, people will look at

you differently; you may be given such honour as 'model teacher', and you may talk to the authorities about improving the conditions of the school. (Author's interview)

The content of teaching and learning has been dominated by inflexible exercises on examination questions. Since the aim is to get high scores, some teachers and pupils have used any means to achieve this. For example, in creative writing, when the author interviewed a schoolboy in a recent field study in Beijing, the boy described how his teacher instructed them to prepare for the composition section in the Year 9 exam:

The boy: In the test, the essay questions are always about narration, exposition or argumentation. So, my teacher asked us to prepare a composition for each type before the test. Classmates have tended to memorize model essays, or good articles in some other books; during the exam they use these with some changes. This year we are told that the composition in the test is likely to be a narration on an event.

Author: You think that's going to be the test?

The boy: Well, our teacher told us. I believe that. Our teacher is very well informed.

Author: What are you going to prepare, then?

The boy: We're asked to prepare narration on a group event and on a personal event. Many of my classmates have found very good examples. They'd use the essays after changing the names of places and the leading roles...

Author: Sometimes this kind of game will be seen through. You think your classmates will get away with it? How are you preparing for it?

The boy: I've also got a model essay and I'm going to use it... If they do it, why shouldn't I? If we all do so, it must be hard to see who did which essay and who copied it...

(Author's interview)

We may say, at least children still know how to copy other pupils' essays: indeed, except for textbooks they may know little of other things, as a schoolteacher says:

In the present school curriculum, at the junior secondary level, the concern is how to get the pupils into the senior secondary, and in the senior secondary, how to get them into university. So in every subject, the contents are set to be difficult from the first year in the junior secondary, and they are not very practical; there is little about what is actually going on now in society, about the local culture or geography, how to get along with people, general knowledge of laws and regulations, and so on. For those 13- or 14-year-olds, these kinds of tips are perhaps more useful than complicated formulas. In my school, I often see some junior final year pupils not even knowing how to cross the road! (Author's interview)

There are other factors contributing to the distortion in teaching and learning. The aspiration of many parents is that their children go on to regular academic education and then on to higher education. For example, in the author's field study, the keypoint regular (academic) senior secondary school is the most popular among junior secondary graduates and their parents. This is supported by the comparison of categories of schools (Table 18.3), or by the

Table 18.3 *The comparison of categories of schools*

		Parents				
		Father			**Mother**	
		Ordinary	Ordinary		Ordinary	Ordinary
Desire	Keypoint	Class 2	Class 3	Keypoint	Class 2	Class 3
Regular school:						
keypoint	39	17	22	39	18	24
ordinary		1	7		1	4
Technical			5			5
Vocational						
Specialized		1	2			2
Other choice		1				2
Total	39	20	36	39	19	37
Regular school:						
keypoint	23	2	3	15	10	6
ordinary			5			6
Technical		6	2			3
Vocational					1	1
Specialized			3			3
Other choice						2
Total	23	8	13	15	11	21

- The parents are associated with the type of secondary schools by way of the schools their children are in. This applies to the following tables as well, except when their own education level is discussed.
- For each sub-table, the rows indicate the choices preferred by the respondent, and the columns under each type of respondent indicate the school they/their children are in.
- Regular secondary schools are officially classified as key-point and non-keypoint schools. But better conditioned ordinary schools are quite often seen as class 2 schools, and those ordinary schools with poorer conditions are seen as class 3 schools.

Source: Author's investigations in Beijing

level of education of parents (Table 18.4). This has created problems in two aspects. On the one hand, there is more pressure on teachers and schools. On the other, there is a sharp contrast between parental aspirations and a severe situation in educational provision, particularly the extremely limited places in the regular senior secondary schools and universities (Table 18.5).

Table 18.4   *Parents' aspirations by educational background*

| | **Father** | | **Mother** | |
Aspirations	Higher Education	Secondary Education or Lower	Higher Education	Secondary Education or Lower
Regular school				
Keypoint	61	17	58	23
Ordinary	1	6	1	3
Technical	1	4		5
Specialized		3		2
Other choices		1		2
Total	63	31	59	35

Source: Author's investigation in three schools in Beijing

Table 18.5   *Numbers of enrolment to and application for senior secondary schools in Beijing, 1995*

Types of school	Applicants	Enrolment	Applicant:Enrolment
Regular secondary	51,948	36,393	1.43:1.00
Keypoint	31,024	10,675	2.91:1.00
Ordinary	20,924	25,718	1.00:1.23
Specialized secondary	51,511	17,923	2.87:1.00
Technical schools	7,476	36,663	1.00:2.86
All	123,757	112,432	1.10:1.00

Source: Calculated from the figures published in *Beijing Evening News*, June 1995

High parental pressure on children to succeed may arise from different factors. For example, the 'one-child' policy since the early 1980s has led to parents putting all their hopes upon one child. There is also the influence of the traditional values of parenting. In China, the Confucian idea has been prevalent. For a long time, opinions like 'a scholar is over and above all other trades' and 'a good scholar will make an official' have had a strong influence on child upbringing. Research in Shanghai city, among 807 parents from the 194 families sampled, found that two-thirds of the parents expected their children to complete at least undergraduate study, and a further 8 per cent wished their children to go beyond undergraduate study; in career choice, the majority of parents want their children to do mental work (Liu *et al*, 1987).

Could there be alternative measures?

Although in policy there is emphasis on being all-round, in practice, teaching and learning in schools is quite against all-round education. A basic measure of the state is to reduce the subjects to be examined. The idea seems to be that, once selection and pressure have been reduced, pupils would have more free time and opportunities to receive training in wider aspects (Liu, 1993). However, research shows that once some subjects have been excluded from examination, these subjects will not be interesting, and great attention will soon turn to those subjects to be examined (Wu, 1995).

Another measure of the state is to set up more and more parental schools. It is believed that such schools would help to change the education values of parents and, especially, lead them to care not only about the academic learning of their children but other non-academic aspects of child development (Zhao, 1993). This seems to be putting all the responsibility and pressure upon families. This policy is very unrealistic, because what is mostly taught in parents' schools is not about how parents can get their children into better schools – a problem about which parents care deeply.

Could there be alternative measures? There have been continuous efforts in academic research to search for ways in which the power of external exams to affect curriculum can be reduced. Dore (1976) put forward his suggestions. Two of his ideas are:

- Earlier selection into jobs – later selection for promotion or further training by the employer or the market; and
- Abolition of educational qualifications – selection for jobs through aptitude tests. (Summarized in Little, 1984)

Earlier selection for employment, with extended opportunities for on-the-job training and qualification upgrading, would lead to much closer links between learning and work. But labour costs for employers would be higher, and the reform would meet resistance from stakeholders in the present system of higher-secondary and post-secondary education.

Aptitude tests are far from immune to the effects of instruction. When verbal reasoning, numerical reasoning, or other aptitude-type questions are included in high-stake examinations, teachers nearly always devote considerable attention to training their students in how to tackle them. Contrary to common opinion, 'aptitude' tests do not measure innate capacities or underdeveloped potential (Little, 1984).

Somerset discussed various possibilities, and the problems of internal assessment (in Little and Wolf, 1996). What is suggested is to transfer some of the responsibility for assessing school leavers to the schools themselves. Internal assessment has been introduced in a number of countries, most often to complement, but in a few cases to replace altogether, external assessment through an examination.

Internal assessment has some obvious advantages. Because measurements can be made over an extended period rather than on a single occasion, the high levels of anxiety often provided by external examinations are largely avoided. For the same reason, a more rounded view of each pupil's strengths and weaknesses could be built up. Trends in performance can be identified and allowances can be made if performance at a particular time is affected by ill-health, personal or family stress, or bad luck.

Internal assessment would also help to promote an 'educational assessment' which:

1. deals with the individual's achievement relative to himself rather than to others;
2. seeks to test for competence rather than for intelligence;
3. takes place in relatively uncontrolled conditions and so does not produce 'well-behaved' data;
4. looks for 'best' rather than 'typical' performances;
5. is most effective when rules and regulations characteristic of standardized testing are relaxed;
6. embodies a constructive outlook on assessment where the aim is to help rather than sentence the individual (Gipps in Little and Wolf, 1996).

Nevertheless, internal assessment would have its problems. First, the quality of teacher-made tests needs to be ensured. The accuracy and fairness of assessment systems very much depend on the quality of the instruments used. The question papers set for external examinations show many weaknesses, such as: they depend too heavily on recall, particularly on the recall of fragmented factual material; they pay too little attention to information-processing and problem-solving skills; they tend to focus on abstract and specialized topics rather than on topics with practical application. But equally, teacher-made tests would suffer from the same weaknesses, and maybe to an even more marked degree. Second, how much can the judgement of teachers be trusted? This question may be of particular importance to many Third World countries, where trust based on the teachers' work and examinations still needs to be built up. Third, competent and committed teachers can rank the pupils in their charge with considerable accuracy, but with the best will in the world, if teachers want to judge how their pupils compare with pupils in other schools, they need to build up regular contact with other teachers in other schools, or to find similar measures. This issue also touches upon the problem of teachers' training; as educational spending is already very high in many developing countries, how much more could be spent on training teachers so as to make the school examinations be of a satisfactory standard?

Somerset also puts forward an idea of using examinations backwash. He thinks that examinations are harmful only if they are of inadequate quality (Little and Wolf, 1996).

But how to use the impact of examinations and ensure quality in the curriculum? Little (1984) stresses fundamental examination reform. A radical examination reform would help to improve the balance of skills taught and examined, and promote the teaching, learning and assessing of problem-solving skills of relevance.

This idea of a fundamental reform in the school assessment system seems to be very attractive. What is assessed always influences what and how teachers teach, how pupils learn and how their parents manage (Ekstein and Noah, 1993). If examinations cover broad aspects and do not examine book knowledge alone, then pupils, teachers, students and parents themselves would consciously have a wider focus in learning, in teaching as well as parenting.

Notes

1. In the late 1970s, this saying of Deng Xiao-ping appeared in newspaper articles.
2. Pan Zhongming and her associates have conducted surveys on school teaching/learning in many provinces in China. Their research is continuing. The findings of their research between 1989 and 1991 in the sampled schools in nine provinces have been reported in Pan *et al*, 1991; in this research, their surveys cover 7,837 pupils and 7,788 teachers.

The author carried out fieldwork in 1995 in Beijing in five different secondary schools, including two keypoint schools and three ordinary schools. A total of 96 pupils answered questionnaires and 16 pupils from different schools were interviewed.

References

Deng, X (1985) Deng Xiao-ping's speech at the National Conference on Education, *People's Daily,* Beijing, 20 May

Dore, R (1976) *The Diploma Disease: Education, qualification and development*, Allen & Unwin, London

Eckstein, M A and Noah, H J (1993) *Secondary School Examinations: International perspectives on policies and practice*, Yale University Press, Yale

Little, A (1984) Combating Diploma Disease, in *Education versus qualification*, ed J Oxenham, Allen & Unwin, London

Little, A and Wolf, A (eds) (1996) *Assessment in Transition*, Pergamon, Oxford

Liu, B (1993) There must be a fundamental transition of our educational values, in *How do we bring up our children today?*, The People's Daily Press, Beijing

Liu, Y et al (1987) *A Study on the Chinese Marriage and Family*, Social Science Documents Press

National Institute of Educational Science, *National Programme for Education Development 1992–2000*. A photocopy distributed by National Institute of Educational Science, Beijing

Pan Z et al (1991) *A Research Report of Surveys in the Schools in 9 Provinces*, Central Institute for Education Research Report, Beijing

Wang, G (1996) Educational Assessment in China, *Assessment in Education*, **3** (1)

Wu, F Z (1995) An investigation and meditation on school assessments, in *ZhuiQiu* ('Pursuit', a journal), 21 July, Beijing

Zhao, Y L (1993) Parents must learn, and society must help, in *How do we bring up our children today?*, The People's Daily Press, Beijing

Chapter 19

Valuing Studies of Society and Environment

Gavin Faichney

Introduction

> In Studies of Society and Environment (SOSE), the emerging area of civics and
> citizenship will support students in becoming active and informed citizens
> with the ability to exercise judgement and responsibility in matters of morality,
> ethics, the law and social justice. (Ministry of Education, P-10 Progress, Au-
> gust, 1998: 3)

While the last decade of the 20th century in Australia has been characterized
by changes to the political makeup of parliaments (in the case of five of the
seven parliaments, a swing to conservatism), at the same time, Australians are
considering aspects of reform. Such reform interests include a desire for constitutional change towards a republic, a recognition for the most part of social
and cultural diversity, uncertainty over economic directions resulting from
changing international and domestic markets, an acceptance of the development of organization and representation by minority and ethnic groups within
our society, and an anxiety over the perceived breakdown of traditional community values among the young. To an external observer such a confused state
of affairs may well imply a nation that has no sense of direction. Politically at
least, however, Australia has historically been the most stable democratic entity
in the region. From a social perspective, Australia's reputation for reform over
the 20th century continues to be reflected in the debates over issues, like those
outlined above, and ensures the development of a society that reflects a belief in
its ability to maintain a 'fair go for all'.

In view of these circumstances, and without the benefit of an established religion, Bill of Rights or other 'official guideline for acceptable social behaviour', social educators are constantly seeking an acceptable basis for the incorporation of values education into curriculum programmes.

This discussion will analyse the place of values education in the development of young people's understanding of society and environment and their role and responsibility, developed through such understandings as outlined in the implementation of curriculum in the education system of the State of Victoria. This case study will focus on Victoria's attempts to develop values education for its diverse population.

The Australian system of government is based on a federation of six states and two territories, each with their own form of representative government. The Constitution, which is actually an act of the British Parliament, established a federal government in 1901 with specific powers, with the remaining responsibilities continuing to be the province of the State governments. Such a situation has ensured that federal/state tensions have developed and remain an integral part of political life. A clear example of this is the manner in which education is delivered. The Federal Government is the main source of funding for the implementation of educational policy. The various State governments however, are constitutionally responsible for the school systems that deliver education. Having seven different authorities responsible for policy has led to a diversity in education systems, structures and curriculum across the country.

Since the 1970s the development of the curriculum in Victorian schools has been the responsibility of the individual schools – school-based curriculum development. The Ministry/Department of Education has supplied frameworks and curriculum guidelines; however, because of a philosophy that a centralized, mandated curriculum would not adequately cater for the differing needs of students from a variety of social and cultural backgrounds, schools have been encouraged to either adopt, adapt or develop their own curriculum, within the frameworks provided by the State, to meet the needs of the students in their own particular school setting.

Curriculum change has become a recurrent factor within the educational systems of Australia and particularly in the State of Victoria over the last decade. Between 1987 and the year 2000 three major reorganizations of curriculum, specifically for the compulsory years of schooling – Preparatory year to Year 10, have taken place:

1987–88   Development of the Frameworks of Education
           Preparatory Year to Year 10 (compulsory years of schooling) (P-10)
1993–95   The Curriculum & Standards Frameworks
1998–99   The Curriculum & Standards Framework 2000

Throughout this period the Key Learning Area (KLA) of Social Education has consistently held as its main goal the preparation of young people to enable them to fulfil their role as members of society:

> [a] major goal of social education is to enable students to participate effectively in society. This requires more than being well-informed... knowing about their own society...; it requires a range of skills, a developed and defensible system of values – including a commitment to democratic values – habits of reflection and critical analysis, and practical knowledge and experience of social and political action. (Social Education Framework P-10, 1987: 8)

and again:

> Studies in the SOSE learning area allow students to develop knowledge, skills and values that enable them to participate as active and informed citizens in a democratic society and in the global community. (Curriculum and Standards Framework (CSF) Studies of Society and Environment, 1995: 9)

Whilst the current review (1999) of the Curriculum and Standards Framework (CSF) retains this aspiration, one of the foci for the Studies of Society and Environment (SOSE) review committee has been the development of a more meaningful approach to values education:

> The revised Common and Agreed Goals for Schooling provide a foundation for the intellectual, physical, social, spiritual, moral and aesthetic development of young Australians. (P-10 Progress, August, 1998: 3)

In these years of curriculum revision, a constant factor within the social education learning area has been the concern that the main goal of social education is to prepare young people to take their place as citizens within our society.

School education in Australia (the driest continent in the world) crossed a watershed in 1989. In April, the 60th annual meeting of the Australian Education Council was held in Hobart, the capital of our smallest state. There, a non-partisan agreement was reached when the Australian Education Council – consisting of the State and Federal Ministers responsible for education[1] – produced The Hobart Declaration on Schooling. This incorporated the Common and Agreed Goals for Schooling in Australia (Appendix 1). This agreement was to set the agenda for the various curriculum developments that occurred throughout Australia during the early to mid-1990s.

As this writer has noted previously (1994(a)), with regard to the KLA 'Studies of Society and Environment', of the ten goals agreed to, five would seem to have direct implication for this learning area: Goals 1, 2, 4, 7 and 8 as well as at least three of the points under Goal 6 outline goals (Appendix 1) that relate to the content, skills and values inherent in that learning area.

As outlined by the writer (1994b), together with the UK, The Netherlands and the United States, the national curriculum developments in and around Australia were all undertaken as a result of political and legislative initiatives. Following the adoption of the Common and Agreed Goals, the Australian Education Council (AEC) established a new national curriculum agency – the Curriculum Corporation of Australia. The mission statement of this agency defines its role as:

> facilitating collaboration among government and non-government schools and school systems and education authorities in curriculum development. (reported by Piper, 1991: 2)

At its meeting in April 1991, The Australian Education Council approved eight areas of learning which were to become the focus of the development of the national curriculum. These areas are:

English
Mathematics
Science
Technology
Studies of Society and Environment
Health (Incorporating Physical Education and Personal Development)
Languages other than English (LOTE)
The Arts

Under the auspices of the Curriculum Corporation, national curriculum mapping exercises were undertaken in 1990. The purpose of these exercises was to determine both the nature and the level of implementation of the different types of curriculum in all school systems across the various states and territories of Australia. By the end of 1991, this was completed and the findings of the mapping groups were collated to provide a national perspective for each of the eight learning areas:

> This platform of commonality formed the basis for collaboration among the systems to determine a set of common curriculum principles to meet the needs of all students. (Beazley, 1992: 26)

The collaborative nature of this curriculum development was illustrated by the manner in which the various national curriculum projects were undertaken. Using the curriculum maps as a basis, briefs were prepared for each of the eight learning areas and project teams established with each of the six states taking on the responsibility for the development of at least one of these areas.

The changing nature of Australian society made it advisable that its multi-cultural composition be taken into account as these 'new' curriculum developments were being designed. This reflected both the growing confidence and significance of ethnic groups within the community and the impact that this was having within the political arena. At the same time, increasing concern was being expressed, also reflected within political circles, through demands from the community and commercial interests for the education system to be more accountable.

The development of 'national statements' reinforced this notion with the adoption by the Australian Education Council (AEC) of Languages other than English as one of the eight learning areas. Such languages, taught across our school systems, now incorporate a range of Asian, Slavic, European, Arab, Indic, African and more recently Koori (Aboriginal) languages. Other organizational and curriculum influences are also evident. The recognition of, allowance for and learning about different customs, values and beliefs as both content within, and factors that need to be considered when teaching a socially comprehensive curriculum (see Goals 1, 2, and 3 of the Agreed Goals for Schooling, Appendix 1), were apparently more widely accepted and adopted. In this respect, multiculturalism within Australia became both a part of the curriculum and a strategy for implementing it.

In a more specific sense, within the national statement Studies of Society and Environment, the multicultural nature of Australian society was addressed through both the 'Essential Learning about Australia', where three of the 15 listed aspects of 'essential knowledge about Australia' are:

- ways of life of various groups in Australia's past and present, changes over time in their roles in Australian society and their contribution to Australia today;
- demographic and location patterns in Australia;
- aspects of the cultures of Aboriginal and Torres Strait Islander Australians. (Studies of Society and Environment, 1994: 4).

In this sense the Curriculum perspectives are 'those issues... common to some or all learning' (Curriculum and Assessment (CURRASS) Guidelines Papers, 1994: 3). In the Studies of Society and Environment statement both Aboriginal and Torres Strait Islander and Multicultural perspectives are identified as being significant. It was felt by the writers that the 'statement' ought to reflect first:

the achievements of Aboriginal and Torres Strait Islander cultures in Australian society. Students [should] gain an accurate knowledge of... Torres Strait

> Islander... and Aboriginal societies, learning of their diverse and complex cultures... gain a respect for... Australia's indigenous peoples and recognize the importance of this heritage in developing a unique Australian identity. (Studies of Society and Environment, 1994: 6)

and second with regard to multicultural perspectives:

> Students develop an understanding of Australia's cultural and linguistic diversity, both past and present. Students learn about the achievements of individuals and groups of various ethnic and cultural backgrounds and their contribution to Australia's social, cultural and economic development. They explore the history of migration to Australia and recognize that peoples of many cultures have come together as one nation. (Studies of Society and Environment, 1994: 7)

Fundamentally then, the multicultural nature of Australian society has influenced both the organization of schooling within the various systems and the nature of the curriculum that is implemented within those systems. The changing sources of immigration to this country has meant that differing sets of needs and values have had to be accommodated, as the variety of cultural groups has increased.

As indicated above, the development of these statements has been achieved through a policy of 'national collaborative curriculum development'. Part of the tension that arises from such policies, however, is the constitutional responsibility for education in Australia. Whilst the major funding for education is supplied by the Federal Government, the responsibility for the organization and staffing of the school systems and for the development and implementation of education programmes remains in the hands of the State and Territory Governments. The strategy of focusing the efforts of curriculum development through the AEC and the Curriculum Corporation was a deliberate attempt to defuse the problem of 'state rights'. The involvement of the state curriculum divisions as writers of the 'national statements' in a strategy of 'collaboration' was intended to create and maintain the concept of ownership of the curriculum process through use of the existing state resources and expertise. This was achieved with mixed success as the proposed 'national curriculum' was only partially adopted.

In 1993, at the request of the 'new' Victorian Minister for Education, the State Board of Studies evaluated the 'national statements'. It was felt that these statements and the profiles for student assessment were inadequate and difficult to administer in the prevailing school climate. As a result, KLA Committees were established to develop Curriculum and Standards Frameworks based on the eight learning areas identified by the AEC that would be flexible enough to enable schools to develop their own school-based curriculum.

It needs to be recognized in the first instance however, that what constitutes a learning outcome at the Curriculum and Standards Framework level often does not translate into practice at the school level. It will be the responsibility of the school to develop, implement and evaluate appropriate curriculum programs for students. (Major Directions in Curriculum in 1994, Education News, Apr 21, 1994)

The initial development of the Curriculum & Standards Frameworks for each of the eight KLAs in the Victorian school systems in 1995 heralded an intense period of change in the development and implementation of curriculum at both the school and classroom level. This writer has elsewhere documented a case study of one school's attempt to initiate curriculum, based on the CSF model (Faichney, 1995). In each of these KLAs, the focus shifted to the development and attainment of Learning Outcomes by the students.

The State of Victoria in 1995 produced the Curriculum & Standards Framework based around the eight KLAs agreed to nationally. The Curriculum & Standards Framework Studies of Society and Environment is the KLA with responsibility for the implementation of social education. In an Analysis of the SOSE Component of the Curriculum and Standards Framework, undertaken for the SOSE review committee in September 1998, Gilbert commented that:

> The Victorian SOSE CSF makes very little reference to values. Brief mention is made in the outline of the nature of the learning area, but this is not carried through to the statement of goals. While opportunities for values education occur in the outcome statements which refer to evaluation, these are very few in number, and there appears to be no systematic consideration of the implications of values for the outcomes, or the development through the levels. (Gilbert, 1998: 24)

Thus, in the Victorian state system, values education is without a definitive role in the programmes of Studies of Society and Environment. An overview of the 103 Learning Outcomes – across the five Conceptual Strands of SOSE – listed in the seven levels for reporting student achievement indicate that only nine of them are concerned with aspects of valuing. Of these, 50 per cent occur in Level 7, which is the extension level for Year 10 students. The immediate conclusion of this observation confirms Gilbert's statement.

A closer examination of the document, however, reveals that while values outcomes are not very explicit, the indicators for each outcome often reveal opportunities for values education if teachers use these indicators to evaluate students' performance of the Learning Outcomes. For the 103 Learning Outcomes, there are 385 indicators listed, with an average of 3.5 indicators for each Learning Outcome. In all, 50 of the Indicators focus on values, and these are spread across the various Conceptual Strands and the levels of achievement.

Some examples from the CSF SOSE document may help to clarify the possibility for values education in this KLA. Level one, the first year of schooling, does not really identify any Learning Outcomes with a focus on values.

At level 2 (Years 1 & 2) the Conceptual Strand of Time, Continuity and Change lists the Learning Outcome:

> Describes aspects of the local community and family ways of life that have endured or changed.

While this does not directly imply any value orientation, the Indicator for this Learning outcome suggests that it will be evident when students:

> describe ways of life valued and preserved in the family or local community.

If the product of the student's investigation of a topic related to the examination of Family Life and Tradition results in such a description, in either written or oral form, then it would be possible for his/her teacher to demonstrate student achievement of an aspect of values education.

A more mature example might be from the Conceptual Strand Place and Space, level 4 (Years 5 and 6), where a Learning Outcome is:

> Explain different views of individuals and groups about issues related to the care of places.

The value orientation is more obvious here, and would probably find differing expression among students from different communities. The Indicator suggests that its achievement will be evident when a student:

> discusses and assesses the viewpoints of individuals on land use issues (coastal development, logging, urban renewal).

This example highlights the dilemma for teachers. To what extent, particularly in light of the lack of any clearly defined guidelines, can a teacher encourage his/her students to examine and question policies and interests of government and local employees, without transgressing the trust placed in him/her with regard to the education of the young people of a local community? Recent research (Prior, 1999) indicates how the values aspirations in social education of the major players in school communities – teachers, parents, students – are convergent rather than, as often anticipated, divergent.

Finally, an example from level 6 (Years 9 and 10) in the Conceptual Strand Culture. One of the three Learning Outcomes for this level is:

Explore the core values of Australian society.

At this level it is anticipated that the student will exhibit the following Indicators as evidence of achieving this Learning Outcome:

Analyses the core values of an Australian religious group, political party, environmental group or social group;
compares Australian core values with those of an Asian or Pacific Islander society;
explains the functions and interactions of language, literature, the arts, traditions, beliefs, values, and behaviour patterns to demonstrate an understanding of culture as an integrated whole.

As can be seen from this example, it is anticipated that there is a range of achievement in the Indicators. While this is reflected in all the Learning Outcomes, it is not anticipated that all students will necessarily achieve the full range. This of course raises another issue, particularly in those secondary colleges where this KLA is an elective study. How can teachers plan and implement programmes which will provide students with the opportunity to become educated citizens if they are not going to experience studies that will allow them to develop the range of the Learning Outcomes or in extreme cases have no experience with them at all?

In an extension of the previously mentioned policy of 'school-based curriculum' and as a basis for their triennial funding, The Department of Education requires state schools to prepare a School Charter which, among other things, addresses issues relating to codes of conduct for teachers and students, student welfare and discipline practices. Each of these components of the School Charter, together with the School Mission Statement, articulates the values position of individual schools:

The nature of values and education means that values are a public matter on which schools must take a positive position (Gilbert and Hoepper, 1996: 59).

Meeting the requirement to prepare such documents, however, does not necessarily result in a values education programme within the curriculum. It does ensure that teachers have a basis for establishing an accepted value position within that school. Gilbert and Hoepper (1996) have suggested that there are five possible approaches to the implementation of a values education within the SOSE curriculum – Inculcation, Values Analysis, Values Clarification, Critical Rationalism and Approaches from Human Rights. Whilst each of these approaches may have a role to play in a values education programme, Gilbert and Hoepper (1996: 70) suggest that the latter two are most appropriate.

To implement any of these approaches of course presupposes that the curriculum of the school (since it is the school's responsibility to develop its own curriculum) will in fact incorporate 'content' that will allow for such approaches. A review of schools' curriculum across the state – undertaken in 1997 – indicated that many schools were unhappy with the lack of direction provided by the CSFs. With regard to SOSE, many secondary colleges did not feel confident with the integrated approach of the five conceptual strands – Time, Continuity and Change; Place and Space; Culture; Resources; and Natural and Social Systems. Teachers of the traditional disciplines of History, Geography, Commerce and Politics found it difficult to relate to curriculum frameworks designed around conceptual strands outside their field of expertise.

To determine the extent to which the CSF SOSE was assisting schools in developing their curriculum offerings, the SOSE committee distributed a questionnaire to both primary schools and secondary colleges in April 1998. A representative selection of the responses are indicated below. In summary, the CSF SOSE was seen as being too broad and inclusive, lacking in direction and specificity and setting a range of Learning Outcomes of which available teaching time did not permit adequate coverage.

> The amalgam of SOSE poses time problems and the generalization of methodologies to 'social studies' (away from Geography and History)… We would like to take the document outcomes into more depth than the CSF suggests (Commerce). Our subject area does not fit comfortably into SOSE. (St Paul's Anglican Grammar School)

> Change the names of the Strands. Reduce from five Strands to three or four. Fewer and more focused Learning Outcomes. Essential Learning/Core Subjects to include Australian Studies, Asian Studies, Civics and Citizenship. (Mt Erin Secondary College)

In primary schools where teachers are expected to implement all of the eight KLAs there was a more general level of concern. Time management seemed to be a major factor.

> Too many strands at the junior primary level. Number of Strands within KLAs need to be varied at different stages of schooling. Each KLA to be allotted a certain number of hours per week. Identification of essential learning or core content in each KLA. (Fountain Gate Primary School)

> A stronger recognition of an integrated curriculum as not only an educationally sound methodology, but also as a time-effective way of covering the curriculum. This is particularly valuable in primary schools. (Hamlyn Banks Primary School)

The non-prescriptive nature of the curriculum documents, particularly with regard to 'values education', allows teachers, who feel themselves under pressure to cover content, to ignore this element of their teaching. As well, without specific directions and strategies, teachers feel uncomfortable teaching 'values'. The task to be addressed by the present SOSE CSF Review Committee is to work within the directions of the Advisory Committee and with the suggestions from teachers, schools and subject associations, to produce a CSF 2000 which will further enhance the delivery of the KLA within schools. The rationale for the CSF II Studies of Society and Environment states in part:

> The Study of Society aspect recognizes that humans organize themselves into communities and nation states to form complex, culturally based institutions and systems. The establishment of such communities enables citizens to develop behaviours based on societal values such as concern for justice, truth, responsibility, morality, freedom and respect for all community members, whilst accepting the democratic processes of society. (CSF II Studies of Society and Environment, 1999: 1)

The responsibility of this committee is to develop a curriculum framework that will not only enable, but also assist, teachers to implement a social education programme in their school to allow students to develop as knowledgeable young people who can takes their place as citizens of the 21st century. To achieve this, more explicit Values Learning Outcomes are required.

Historically, the articulation of specific values in social education curriculum documents has been avoided in Australia for fear of either infringing individuals' rights to freedoms or, in contemporary terms, of being considered politically incorrect. Departments of Education and their agencies are more inclined to make strong statements about the need for the inclusion of values in curriculum, and then rely on the schools to implement these given the school's responsibility for its curriculum development. The current posturing for more explicit and specific values statements may well translate into statements within the 'new' frameworks. It will then remain to be seen how or if teachers will embrace these recommendations. If the statements are prescriptive, it is more likely that teachers will adopt and implement the resultant Learning Outcomes. If the framework lacks such direction, it would appear that very little will change with regard to 'values education' in the state of Victoria.

Note

1. Both the Federal and the six State governments of Australia are based on the parliamentary system. The Australian Education Council consists of the seven Ministers of Education and their Heads of Department who meet annually to review educational policy.

Appendix 1: Common and Agreed Goals for Schooling in Australia (1989)

1. To provide an excellent education for all young people, one which develops their talents and capacities to full potential, and is relevant to the social, cultural and economic needs of the nation.
2. To enable all students to achieve high standards of learning and to develop self-confidence, optimism, high self-esteem, respect for others, and achievement of personal excellence.
3. To promote equality of educational opportunities, and to provide for groups with special learning requirements.
4. To respond to the current and emerging economic and social needs of the nation, and to provide those skills which will allow students maximum flexibility and adaptability in their future employment and other aspects of life.
5. To provide a foundation for further education and training, in terms of knowledge and skills, respect for learning and positive attitudes for life-long education.
6. To develop in students:

   - the skills of English literacy, including skills in listening, speaking, reading and writing;
   - skills of numeracy, and other mathematical skills;
   - skills of analysis and problem solving;
   - skills of information processing and computing;
   - an understanding of the role of science and technology in society, together with scientific and technological skills;
   - a knowledge and appreciation of Australia's historical and geographical context;
   - a knowledge of languages other than English;
   - an appreciation and understanding of, and confidence to participate in, the creative arts;
   - an understanding of, and concern for, balanced development and the global environment; and
   - a capacity to exercise judgements in matters of morality, ethics and social justice.

7. To develop knowledge, skills, attitudes and values which will enable students to participate as active and informed citizens in our democratic Australian society within an international context.
8. To provide students with an understanding and respect for our cultural heritage including the particular cultural background of Aboriginal and ethnic groups.

9. To provide for the physical development and personal health and fitness of students, and for the creative use of leisure time.
10. To provide appropriate career education and knowledge of the world of work, including an understanding of the nature and place of work in our society.

Providing a sound basis for a collaborative effort to enhance Australian Schooling, the agreed national goals will be reviewed from time to time, in response to the changing needs of Australian society.

Appendix 2: Australia's Common and Agreed National Goals for Schooling in the 21st Century (1998)

In the information age the greatest challenge will be to invest wisely in the intellectual and technological knowledge, skill and understanding of our young people. Successful nations will be those which accept the opportunities that globalization presents to schooling.

Australians in the 21st century will be active and informed citizens of complex and rapidly changing local and global communities. They will be enterprising, adaptable and socially responsible contributors to our democratic, cohesive, culturally rich and diverse Australian society.

Schools will be learning communities of students, families and teachers. They will be committed to pursuing excellence and equity, and to exploring and advancing individual, group and societal development.

Our world class school education, based on agreed national goals, will provide the foundation for young Australians' intellectual, physical, social, spiritual, moral and aesthetic development. It will give them the knowledge, skills, attitudes and values relevant to present and emerging social, cultural and economic needs in local, national and international settings.

The achievement of Australia's common and agreed national goals for schooling establishes the pathway for lifelong learning, from the foundations established in the early years through to senior secondary education including vocational education and linking to employment and continuing education and training.

Schooling should develop fully the talents and capacities of every student. In particular, when students leave school they should:

- have skills in analysis and problem solving and the ability to become confident and technologically competent members of 21st century society;
- have qualities of self-confidence, optimism, high self-esteem, and a commitment to personal excellence as a basis for their potential life roles as

family, community and workforce members;

- be active and informed citizens with the ability to exercise judgement and responsibility in matters of morality, ethics and social justice; and the capacity to make sense of their world, to think about how things got to be the way they are, to make rational and informed decisions about their own lives and to collaborate with others;
- have a foundation for, and positive attitudes towards, vocational education and training, further education, employment and lifelong learning.

In terms of curriculum, students should have:

- attained high standards of knowledge, skills and understanding through a comprehensive and balanced curriculum encompassing the agreed eight key learning areas and the interrelationships between them:
  - the arts
  - English
  - health and physical education
  - languages other than English
  - mathematics
  - science
  - studies of society and environment
  - technology;
- attained the skills of numeracy and English literacy; in particular, every child leaving primary school should be numerate, able to read, write, spell and communicate at an appropriate level;
- been encouraged to be enterprising and to acquire those skills which will allow them maximum flexibility and adaptability in the future.

In addition, schooling should be socially just, and should ensure that:

- outcomes for educationally disadvantaged students improve and match more closely those of other students;
- Aboriginal and Torres Strait Islander students have equitable access, participation and outcomes;
- all students have understanding of and respect for Aboriginal cultures, and Torres Strait Islander cultures to achieve reconciliation between indigenous and non-indigenous Australians;
- all students have the knowledge, cultural understanding and skills which respect individuals' freedom to celebrate languages and cultures within a socially cohesive framework of shared values.

The National Goals for Schooling provide a basis for State and Territory school education systems, non-government school authorities and the Commonwealth to work together to:

- promote productive learning partnerships among students, parents, educators, business, industry and the wider community;
- provide safe, supportive learning and working environments;
- strengthen the status and quality of the teaching profession; and
- identify specific national targets, plans and strategies.

References

Beazley, K (1992) National Curriculum: Commonwealth perspectives, *Unicorn*, **18** (3), September

Board of Studies (1995) *Curriculum & Standards Framework: Studies of society and environment*, Board of Studies, Carlton, Victoria

Curriculum Corporation (1994) *CURRASS Guidelines Papers*, Curriculum Corporation, Carlton, Victoria

Faichney, G W (1994a) Social educators: where are you? It's time to stand up and be counted, *The Social Educator*, **12** (1), April

Faichney, G W (1994b) *Comparative Curriculum Standards*, Paper presented at 74th NCSS Annual Conference, Phoenix AZ, November

Faichney, G W (1995) *Localizing National Curriculum to Meet School/Students' Needs: Some Strategies from Downunder*, Paper presented at 2nd International Assembly of Social Educators, in conjunction with the 75th Annual Meeting of the National Council for the Social Studies, Chicago IL, 9 November

Gilbert, R (1998) *Analysis of the SOSE Component of the Curriculum and Standards Framework*, Board of Studies, Carlton

Gilbert, R and Hoepper, B (1996) The place of values, in *Studying Society and Environment*, ed R Gilbert, Macmillan Education Australia, Melbourne

Ministry of Education (1987) *The Social Education Framework P-10*, Ministry of Education (Schools Division), Victoria

Ministry of Education (1988) *The Social Education Framework, P-10 Progress*, Ministry of Education (Schools Division), Victoria

Ministry of Education (1989) *CSF II Studies of Society and Enivornment*, Ministry of Education (Schools Division), Victoria

Piper, K (1991) National Curriculum two years on: an undelivered paper, *Curriculum Perspectives*, **11** (3), September

Prior, W (1999) Perspectives of citizenship: teachers, students and their parents talk about what it means to be a good citizen in Australia, *Theory and Research in Social Education*, **27** (2), Spring

Chapter 20

In Search of a Vision of the Good: Values Education and the Postmodern Condition[1]

Hanan Alexander

Introduction

Our modern way of life is a product of two revolutions, the Enlightenment and the Emancipation. The Enlightenment challenged medieval conceptions of the good rooted in scripture, replacing them with a life based on science and technology. The Emancipation is the political programme of the Enlightenment. It enabled people to abandon the corporate identities of medieval life for citizenship in nations conceived to protect individual rights and economic interests. As a result of these revolutions, moral theory replaced examination of the good with justification of the right and political theory shifted from asking about who should rule to preserving one's right to choose a conception of the good life.[2]

Values education was transformed by these developments.[3] Rather than initiation into faith communities with prescribed ways of life, its task became socialization to the norms of society (Durkheim, 1986), or clarification of personal values (Simon and Kirschenbaum, 1992), or advancement on a scale of cognitive-moral development (Kohlberg, 1981; Munsey, 1980). However, during the past quarter-century there has been disenchantment with the 'Enlightenment project'. Feminists have critiqued rational, rule-bound ethics and advanced a conception of education rooted in the ideal of a caring effect (Gilligan, 1993; Noddings, 1986). Communitarians have argued that we can only make sense of the individual self in the context of a communal vision of the good (Green, 1999; Taylor, 1989, 1991). Post-moderns and critical pedagogues have challenged economic instrumentalism and asserted that the preference for individual rights has underprivileged large classes of oppressed peoples (Mc Laren, 1997; Aronowitz and Giroux, 1991).

In critiquing the impact of Enlightenment moral theory on values education, there has been a tendency to ignore the achievements of its political counterpart, the Emancipation. The purpose of this chapter is to chart a course for values education that acknowledges the moral failings of the Enlightenment without abandoning the political accomplishments of the Emancipation.

Enlightenment and its discontents

The Enlightenment emerged in the 17th century as a critique of both the scholastic synthesis of medieval rationalists and the simple faith of the non-rationalists. Moral theory shifted at this juncture from advancing a comprehensive account of how to live based on scripture to the justification of individual rights. Immanuel Kant, for example, offered an analysis of moral behaviour as the exercise of one's rational duty to treat each person as an end rather than a means (Kant, 1990,1997a). John Stuart Mill argued that conduct was to be justified according to its consequences. Among the alternative courses of action available, the most ethical would be the one that resulted in the greatest good for the greatest number of people (Mill, 1993). John Locke held that the morality of a behaviour was to be judged on the basis of a social contract to which one implicitly agrees when one enjoys the benefits of a society guaranteed by such a covenant (Locke, 1988).

If Enlightenment moral theory analysed right action, modern religious thought dissected the nature of correct belief. Kant proposed a 'religion of reason' based on the duty to treat others solely as ends (Kant, 1960, 1997b). His rationalist followers contended that our most sacred beliefs could be grounded in a rational ideal that lay beyond our full comprehension, but that all scientific thought strove to understand and all moral practice sought to emulate (Cohen, 1995). The pragmatic descendants of Mill, such as William James, claimed that religious faith should be embraced because it leads to the consequence of more meaningful, purposeful lives (James, 1995). Covenant theologians argued that Jews and Christians are bound by faith commitments contracted with God long ago (vide Varner, 1996; Holwerda, 1994; Borowitz, 1991).

Since no agreement could be reached on the correct rationale for either moral behaviour or religious belief, romantic alternatives stepped in that attributed moral and religious intuitions not to reasons, but to feelings.

Emotivism in moral philosophy suggested that there are no rational bases to ethical intuitions; rather they are the result of purely subjective emotions (Moore, 1994). Friedrich Schleiermacher argued that religion is not related to rational ideals at all, but is rather an expression of non-rational feelings (1996). Soren Kierkegaard claimed that religious commitments cannot be adduced by logical argument. They require a leap of faith that supersedes rationality. The moral claims of religion are above rationality and call for acceptance on the basis of faith rather than reason (Kierkegaard, 1986a,b).

Given the contestability of moral and religious commitments, it is no wonder that 20th-century conceptions of education deal, not with what way of life is best, but rather with what sort of scientific knowledge and technical skill will best prepare youngsters for adulthood.

The rise of instrumentalism

The extraordinary success of technology at enhancing our lives has led some to equate scientific thinking with higher values. From the easing of daily chores, to increases in leisure time, to advances in health care and medical science, to transformations in communication, travel and entertainment, we have been enriched, enhanced and empowered by advances in science and technology. But to view these advances as sources of higher value is to misconceive *describing* the way the world is or can be with *prescribing* how it ought to be.

One consequence of this misconception has been to view either critical or instrumental reasoning as the ultimate moral ideal. Critical reasoning teaches us to identify good and bad reasons so that we can criticize or defend an idea. Instrumental reasoning involves identifying the means needed to achieve desired ends (*vide* Siegel, 1988). But, critical or instrumental reasoning cannot be our ultimate moral ideals; rather, they are tools for achieving those ideals.

Charles Taylor points out that the rationalization and instrumentalization of values leads to a centring on the self that results in choices that are increasingly vacuous. Consequently, our choices become less distinct from each other and we have fewer of them. With fewer moral choices to make, we become less practised and proficient at making them. Rationalization and instrumentalization of values, therefore, flatten our horizons of significance by severely limiting the choices at our disposal and our ability to make choices. Idealizing reasons and techniques rather than the values they justify and engender leads to a problem on another score. It restricts the degree to which people will be willing or able to reach beyond the confines of their own instrumental self-interests to forge ties with others in communities of shared values and memory (Taylor, 1991).

The culture of narcissism

We have, consequently, become unsure about the ideals with which we should identify. Without a sense of the ideals to emulate, it has become unclear whether we should affiliate with any groups outside of those that share our most narrow self-serving interests. Our sense of moral conduct has become greatly diminished because there seem to be no ideals to serve outside of ourselves. We have come to discover meaning not in values that emanate from history, or tradition, or God, but from momentary and fleeting sensations that 'feel good'. Christopher Lasch calls this centring on the self the 'culture of narcissism' (Lasch, 1991).

But moral ideals cannot be found in the confines of the self alone. The very concept of an ideal suggests an appeal to something beyond the self, something higher, more lofty, more elevated. To say that something is an ideal assumes that something else is not. To say that something is valuable, or meaningful, or preferable means that something else is not valuable, or meaningful, or desirable. Ethical terms must convey distinctions between better and worse, otherwise they convey no content whatsoever. To make these distinctions, there must be a dividing line that distinguishes good from bad, right from wrong, better from worse. The very idea of pursuing a moral life means appealing to standards by which to measure the worth of that life. It is the absent standards of value that have sent people searching for a vision of the good life. Modernism, they have come to realize, leads to a radical individualism that worships the self, and this turns out to be the worship of nothing at all.

Rationalism and romanticism

The feminist reaction to rationalism, the post-modern critique of instrumentalism, and the communitarian quest for community, are not entirely new. At each stage in the development of modernity, a non- and sometimes anti-rational reaction occurred that is often called romanticism. In the 17th century, the Enlightenment generated the foundations of modern mathematics and science and the basis for a neutral liberal society. A romantic response emerged that criticized the lack of feeling and emotion in the new rationality, and complained of its emphasis on the universal over the individual. Then, in the 18th century, the scientific revolution translated to technology and a reaction against the pervasiveness of instrumental reason developed. At the same time, the lack of community in the newly industrialized world was bemoaned.

As the emergence of logical analysis became the model for studying behaviour and the basis for social policy in the 20th century, the Western world became more secular and urban. Concern was voiced about the penchant of logicians for analysing the formal relations between ideas while ignoring their content. It was also noted that behavioural analysis paid too much attention to the mechanics of mind and the structure of society, and not enough to personal feelings and communal yearnings. Anti-formalism emerged, along with organic thinking that used biological metaphors to describe human life in terms of integrated wholes rather than disconnected parts. Conservative politicians and anti-liberal religious leaders began to speak nostalgically about the more cohesive community of yesterday in which people were less logical and analytical.

Most recently, we have witnessed dramatic changes in the physical sciences. Quantum physics relativized our assumptions about the relations between time, space and matter. The sands began to shift under that which appeared to the early modern empiricists and to most regular modern folk as fixed and 'objective'. If external reality – matter – is not fixed in space and time, then perhaps related assumptions about the nature of knowledge and inquiry should also be questioned. This led critics to doubt whether logic is a given of consciousness rather than a creation of culture, whether knowledge is 'objective' rather than constructed, and whether the natural and social sciences are governed by reason rather than by individual and cultural bias.

Many Enlightenment critics echo, and trace their origins to, earlier romantic revivals. Some even claim to shut down the debate, proclaiming the end of modernity and the victory of their own forms of neo-romanticism.[4] However, the way out of the morass of instrumentalism and narcissism is not to be found in the victory of romanticism over rationalism, but rather in the recognition that both inclinations are necessary to conceiving and living a good life.

The concept of a good life

The problem with relying solely on the rational and the scientific is that they offer no understanding of the higher values on which to base morality, religion and education. Suppose Kant is right that our ethical duty is to conform our behaviour to a rational ideal. Whose rationality are we to follow? Kant believed that reason was part of the structure of consciousness, built into the very possibility of thinking. But suppose consciousness does not come in a single package, but is influenced by culture and gender and genes. How can we make sense of our rational duty when the very idea of there being a single account of pure reason is called to question (*vide* Alexander, 1996)? Alternatively, suppose we accept the utilitarian principle – 'the greatest good for the greatest number'. How are we to determine what counts as a good to be measured against the greatest number? Similarly, if we agree to abide by a social contract, which contract are we to follow? These problems persist within modern religious thought as well. According to which rationality, whose conception of meaningful, or what religious covenant am I to conform my belief and practice? (MacIntyre, 1989).

Romantic solutions alone are no better at resolving the dilemmas of instrumentalism and narcissism. In the extreme, they transform ethical and religious doctrines into matters that are so personal that they defy intelligent discourse altogether. In order to account for which rationality, or what measure of utility, or whose social contract, we require not an analysis or justification of moral conduct but a synthesis of the ethical whole, a vision of what life at its best can be. Yet, it is precisely such a comprehensive vision that is missing from Enlightenment discourse.

What does it mean to have such a concept? The concept of goodness can be conceived in terms of four criteria: 1) it is an ethical concept; 2) it is holistic; 3) it is pragmatic; and 4) it is synthetic. 'Goodness', like the concept of 'right', is an **ethical** concept in that it enables us to distinguish positive from negative value (Lamore, 1996: 19–40). However, unlike the 'right', which is a tool for analysis and justification of conduct, 'the good' is **holistic**, envisaging the whole rather than analysing the parts. It is also **pragmatic**; it is expressed in terms of concrete examples of excellence or virtues to be practised, rather than in abstract rules or principles to be applied.

Finally, goodness is synthetic. There are many different ethical traditions in the world. To say that a tradition is ethical means that, however it differs from others, it embraces certain basic assumptions without which the concept of ethics would make no sense. These are the conditions of moral agency adumbrated below. To say that goodness is synthetic means that it integrates the values of a particular tradition with those required of other traditions that wish to refer to themselves meaningfully as ethical. It is this holistic, pragmatic, synthetic sort of ethics that is missing from Enlightenment morality.

The achievements of emancipation

If the Enlightenment failed to provide comprehensive ethical vision, it nonetheless conceived the political conditions necessary for ethical discourse. These include the limitation of power through checks and balances, the centrality of open inquiry, and the moral agency of citizens. Karl Popper (1966) referred to societies that preserve these conditions as 'open'. Others call them liberal or democratic societies.

Checks and balances

Popper contrasted his approach to Plato's influential political theory. In *The Republic*, Plato addressed the question: 'Who should rule in a just society, the majority or the best and the brightest?' The problem with the first option is that majorities sometimes elect tyrants who curtail freedom and deny the right to rule. Citizens should not be enfranchised, therefore, because they may not understand these dangers. Plato held that only those who understand the ideal of justice – the best and the brightest – should govern (Plato, 1979).

Popper objected that reasonable people may differ over the meaning of political and ethical ideals, and even when they do not, their rulers can misunderstand and misapply those ideals. People – even talented people – make mistakes. We err not only in what we believe, but also in how we transform our beliefs into policy and practice. To place unchecked authority in the hands of an elite is to put at risk the rights and freedoms of the many by ignoring the fallibility of the few.

Plato assumed that someone would have unchecked power, the only issue being who. This resulted in the 'theory of unchecked sovereignty'. Popper claimed that the question for political theory should be not, 'who should rule?' but rather, 'how can society be organized to protect against the mistakes of those in power?' The politics that emerges from this question seeks to constrain power. Popper called this a 'theory of checks and balances' (Popper, 1966).

The centrality of inquiry

Cartesian scepticism lies at the heart of a society built around checks and balances. Such a society empowers its citizens to question the authority of those in power in order to seek a better way. It challenges accepted dogma and requires beliefs and behaviours to withstand criticism. The assumption that I have the truth in my pocket is stultifying. It assumes that the beliefs that we hold and the lives that we lead are as good as they can be. This shuts down hope of improvement and stifles the possibility of progress. Open society is founded on our capacity to recognize that accepted answers may be mistaken, and to learn from those mistakes. It is because of this capacity to learn from mistakes that we can be moral agents.

Moral agency

Societies rooted in the doctrines of checks and balances and free inquiry require citizens who are intelligent, free and fallible. Intelligent people have the capacity to inquire. Free agents can be held accountable for their actions. And fallible citizens can be mistaken, so that intelligence and freedom can be employed in charting a new course. Those who meet these conditions are 'moral agents' (Taylor, 1988: 15–44; 1989: 25–52).

To engage in a meaningful moral conversation we must first have the capacity to understand the difference between good and bad, right and wrong, better and worse. If we cannot understand the difference between positive and negative values, then our choices will be arbitrary. There will be no material difference between intentional choices and caprice. Our choices must be informed by a moral understanding based on our ability to discern positive from negative value. To be a moral being, in other words, entails intelligence.

Free will is another prerequisite for moral agency. The point of ethics is to establish standards of behaviour. This assumes that I can take charge of my actions and behave according to the ethic I decide to endorse. If my behaviour is not controlled by my choices, but determined by such external forces as history, society, chemistry, or the gods, then there is no point to ethical discourse. To influence my behaviour we would need to alter the course of history, or change society, or modify my chemistry, or manipulate the gods.

One consequence of these assumptions is that I can misunderstand and make incorrect choices. I can be wrong, both in what I believe and in how I act. In a word, I am fallible. Human beliefs and behaviours are fallible because they are contingent; they could always be otherwise. This is the third condition of moral agency.

If, as we have seen, moral vision cannot emanate from the self alone, then a society of moral agents must be more than a community of individuals. It must be a community of communities, each espousing a distinct moral teaching, but also sharing in common with other ethical traditions a commitment to 'preserve, protect, and defend' the status of all human beings as intelligent, empowered, and fallible moral agents. It is such a society, and the very notion of moral agency that it protects, that makes possible the search for a good life. For without the conditions of moral agency, the very idea of ethical vision makes no sense.

The challenges of values education

Enlightenment moral theory requires reassessment because it has failed to provide a spiritual vision of the good life. But this does not mean that all vestiges of the Enlightenment should be abandoned. The Enlightenment critical traditions that gave rise to political pluralism and intellectual freedom must be preserved. They protect our right to challenge even our most fundamental assumptions and provide the tools to do so.

The problem is how to offer a compelling moral vision while preserving the Enlightenment principles and values that are crucial to democracy. How is it possible in open society to re-examine and adopt higher ideals, given the Enlightenment's privatization of good (*vide* Nozick, 1981: 8). This calls us to break out of the Enlightenment dialectic that views reasoning and feeling as dichotomous in order to understand them as complementary. We require not new modes of thinking and feeling that are disengaged from one another, but renewed ways of feeling intelligently, thinking morally and living thoughtfully. The concept of a good life as conceived here offers the possibility of this sort of integrated existence. The challenge of values education in an emancipated, post-modern age is to promote only those putative ethical visions that embrace the conditions of moral agency and that are, therefore, at home in open societies.

Notes

1. This argument is developed more completely by the author in a forthcoming volume entitled *Intelligent Spirituality: Education and the renewal of goodness*.
2. The shift from the priority of the right to the priority of the good is central to the communitarian critique of liberal moral philosophy. See Stephen Mulhall and Adam Swift (1992) *Liberals and Communitarians*, Blackwell, Oxford, and Charles Lamore (1996) The right and the good, in *The Morals of Modernity*, Cambridge University Press, Cambridge and New York.
3. In this chapter I use the terms 'values', 'moral', and 'ethical' education interchangeably, even though 'values' connotes personal preference, 'morals' suggests individual obligation, and 'ethical' indicates collective purpose. For a discussion of differences between the moral and ethical, see Bernard Williams (1985) *Ethics and the Limits of Philosophy*, Harvard University Press, Cambridge, pp 6–7; and for origins of the concept of 'values', see Thomas Green (1999) *Voices: The educational formation of conscience*, University of Notre Dame Press, pp 122–47.
4. Some critics of modern thought argue that the shift from the priority of the right to that of the good is not a sufficiently dramatic departure from Lockean and Kantian metaphysics and epistemology. For example, Douglas Sloan (1993) *Insight-Imagination: The emancipation of thought and the modern world*, Greenwood, Westport, CT.

References

Alexander, H A (1996) Rationality and redemption: ideology, indoctrination and learning communities, in *Philosophy of Education Yearbook 1996*, The Philosophy of Education Society, Champaign, IL

Aronowitz, S and Giroux, H (1991) *Postmodern Education: Politics, culture and social criticism*, University of Minnesota Press, Minneapolis

Borowitz, E B (1991) *Renewing the Covenant: A theology for the postmodern Jew*, The Jewish Publication Society, Philadelphia

Cohen, H (1995) *The Religion of Reason Out of the Sources of Judaism*, Scholars Press, Atlanta, GA

Durkheim, E (1986) *Moral Education: A study in the theory and application of the sociology of education*, Free Press, New York

Gilligan, C (1993) *In a Different Voice: Psychological theory and women's development*, Harvard University Press, Cambridge

Green, T (1999) *Voices: The educational formation of conscience*, University of Notre Dame Press, Notre Dame, IN

Gregor, M (ed) (1996) *The Metaphysics of Morals*, Cambridge University Press, Cambridge and New York

Holwerda, D (1994) *Jesus and Israel: One covenant or two?*, Eerdmans Publishing, Grand Rapids, MI

James, W (1995) The will to believe, in *The Will to Believe and Other Writings by William James*, Doubleday, New York

Kant, I (1960) *Religion Within the Limits of Reason Alone*, tr G Hatfeld, HarperCollins, New York

Kant, I (1997a) *Critique of Practical Reason*, ed M Gregor, Cambridge University Press, Cambridge and New York

Kant, I (1997b) *Prolegomena to any Future Metaphysics*, tr G Hatfeld, Cambridge University Press, Cambridge and New York

Kierkegaard, S (1986a) *Fear and Trembling*, Viking Press, New York

Kierkegaard, S (1986b) *Either/Or: A fragment of life*, ed V Armita, Viking Press, New York

Kohlberg, L (1981) *The Meaning and Measurement of Moral Development*, Clark University, Heinz Werner Institute for Developmental Analysis, Clark University, MA

Lamore, C (1996) The right and the good, in *The Morals of Modernity*, Cambridge University Press, Cambridge and New York, pp 19–40

Lasch, C (1991) *The Culture of Narcissism: American life in an age of diminishing expectations,* W W Norton, New York

Locke, J (1988) *Two Treatises on Government*, ed P Last, Cambridge University Press, Cambridge and New York

MacIntyre, A (1989) *Whose Justice, Which Rationality?*, University of Notre Dame Press, Notre Dame, IN

McLaren, P (1997) *Life in Schools: An introduction to critical pedagogy in the foundations of education*, Addison-Wesley, New York

Mill, J S (1993) *On Liberty and Utilitarianism*, Bantam Books, New York

Moore, G E (1994) *Principa Ethica*, ed T Baldwin, Cambridge University Press, Cambridge and New York

Mulhall, S and Swift, A (1992) *Liberals and Communitarians*, Blackwell, Oxford

Munsey, B (ed) (1980) *Moral Development, Moral Education, and Kohlberg*, Religious Education, Birmingham

Noddings, N (1986) *Caring: A feminine approach to ethics and moral education*, University of California Press, Berkeley

Nozick, R (1981) *Philosophical Explanations*, Harvard University Press, Cambridge

Plato (tr 1979) *The Republic*, tr D Lee, Viking Press, Penguin Classic, Cambridge

Popper, K R (1966) *The Open Society and its Enemies, Volume 1: The Spell of Plato*, Princeton University Press, Princeton

Schleiermacher, F (1996) *On Religion: Speeches to its cultured despisers*, tr R Crouter, Cambridge University Press, Cambridge

Siegel, H (1988) *Educating Reason: Rationality, critical thinking, and education*, Routledge, New York

Simon, S and Kirschenbaum, H (1992) *Values Clarification*, Hart, New York

Sloan, D (1993) *Insight-Imagination: The emancipation of thought and the modern world*, Greenwood, Westport, CT

Taylor, C (1988) What is human agency?, in *Human Agency and Language*, Cambridge University Press, Cambridge and New York

Taylor, C (1989) *Sources of the Self: The making of modern identity*, Harvard University Press, Cambridge

Taylor, C (1991) *The Ethics of Authenticity*, Harvard University Press, Cambridge

Varner, K (1996) *Whose Right It Is: A handbook of covenant theology*, Destiny Image, Shippensburg, PA

Williams, B (1985) *Ethics and the Limit of Philosophy*, Harvard University Press, Cambridge

In Search of Common Values: Ethnic Schema, Ethnic Conflict and National Reconciliation in Fiji

Steven Ratuva

Introduction

Values, the ethical ideals and beliefs of society, help to shape and define the parameters for individual and group perceptions and relationships.[1] Within sociological theory, the nature, purpose and origins of values have been the subject of debate for years. Functionalists regard *value consensus* to be fundamental to social integration.[2] Exponents of the plural society thesis argue that ethnic conflict naturally arises from irreconcilable differences of values between ethnic groups.[3] Certain developmental sociologists and psychologists who subscribe to the Modernizationist school attempt to categorize 'primitive' and 'advanced' societies along a developmental continuum in relation to their moral and social characteristics.[4] A central aspect of this argument is that certain societies are more 'advanced' than others by virtue of their 'superior' values, such as their competitiveness and so-called 'need to achieve', and thus are more likely to develop faster along the capitalist path.[5] The Marxian paradigm takes the view that *dominant values* are reproduced by institutions that represent the interests of dominant classes.[6]

I do not intend to critique these various sociological approaches, but to focus specifically on conflict arising out of differences in ethnic values. Contrary to what the plural society thesis exponents contend, I argue that ethnic conflict does not result from mere 'differences' in cultural values, but from how these 'differences' (whether real or perceived) are stereotyped, politicized and used as means of political mobilization. Ethnicity becomes problematic when it is officially legitimized and institutionalized. Ethnic values are not unchangeable and primordial but are constantly being reinvented and reproduced by communities to suit changing circumstances.[7]

Different ethnic groups evolve values that largely reflect the complex sociological and psychological process of their identity creation. Ethnic identification involves a dialectical process of 'internal' identification by the 'in-group' itself and 'external' identification of the 'in-group' by the 'out-group'. There is usually a tendency to mobilize collective consciousness in relation to certain 'primordial' characteristics in the form of myths of common ancestry or identifiable common cultural traits. These are reproduced as abstract or 'tangible' symbols of common ethnic identity.[8] Thus ethnic values are collective forms of consciousness, perception and behaviour (sometimes institutionalized and sometimes informal) which define relationship within and with other ethnic groups.

The articulation of ethnic values in everyday life could be broadly defined within three major forms of relationship: first is *ethnic hegemony* – the control of the power structures by an ethnic group and the hegemonic imposition of its values on other communities; second is *ethnic segregation* – the tendency to keep ethnic communities apart; and third, *integration* – the desire to integrate various communities into a harmonious whole. This chapter briefly examines these three tendencies in the context of Fiji, where ethnicity is systematically deployed as the basis for daily organization and perception. It will briefly examine the historical background to ethnic diversity, and then look at how ethnic values had been reproduced and mobilized and how these erupted into racial violence and military coup. The chapter then looks at some of the contributions by civil society to the process of national reconciliation in Fiji.

Fiji, with about 800 islands, is a group of South Pacific Archipelago, located between 15 and 22 degrees South latitude and 177 degrees West and 175 degrees East longitude. It has a land area of 18,272 square kilometres and a total Exclusive Economic Zone (EEZ) area of 1,260,000 square kilometres. The total population is about 800,000: about 51.1 per cent are Fijians; 43.6 per cent are Indians; and 5.3 per cent consists of Europeans, Part-Europeans, Chinese and Pacific Islanders. This ethnic diversity has been the basis for much of Fiji's political problems in its recent and past history.

Constructing separate identities

Before European contact, the Fijian society consisted of autonomous polities engaged in trade, inter-marriage and conflict over resources and territories. Upon British colonial rule in 1874, these independent entities were integrated under a centralized colonial state.

Early relations between Fijians and the British were defined by a set of leg-islation and institutions collectively referred to as the Native Policy. The Na-tive Policy included: the incorporation of traditional chiefs into the hierarchy of the colonial administration to administer over native affairs[9]; the prohibi-tion of further land alienation and vesting the remaining land under the Fijian community; the imposition of native tax; and the restriction of use of native labour. Although these were justified under philanthropic guises, Sir Arthur Gordon, the first governor, did not want to risk a major anti-colonial rebel-lion such as in New Zealand by making sure that no further land was to be alienated and that use of Fijian labour on European sugar plantations was to be restricted. While pacifying Fijians through cooption and patronization of the chiefs, the Native Policy also provided revenue for the colonial govern-ment through native taxation.[10]

A fundamental aspect of the Native Policy was the reinvention of a system of land tenure and socio-political structure by the British, to settle once and for all the 'problem' of controlling the 'natives' under a centralized author-ity.[11] This helped to reshape Fijian identity. Fijians came to see themselves as a homogeneous community, relative to Europeans who, because they con-trolled the state machinery and new technology, were seen as 'superior'. Conversely, Europeans saw Fijians as child-like 'savages' whose place at the bottom of the social hierarchy was divinely ordained.[12] The ethnic relations in Fiji became more complex as a result of the recruitment of Indian labour-ers to Fiji in the late 1870s.

The new Indian identity

The recruitment of the Indian indentured labourers to work on the sugar plantations added a new dimension to the class and ethnic character of the colonial economy. The Fijians were 'saved' from being used *en masse* as cheap sugar cane plantation labourers, which otherwise would have led to destruc-tive changes in the Fijian society, and possibly large-scale anti-colonial rebel-lion. Between May 1879 and November 1916, a total of 60,553 Indians were recruited under the Indentured System. Of the total, 16.1 per cent were High Caste Brahmins, 31.3 per cent Agriculturalists, 6.7 per cent Artisans, 31.2 per cent Low Castes, 14.6 per cent Muslims and 0.1 per cent Christians.[13]

The common dehumanizing experience of the plantation labour under-mined the class, religious, caste and ethnic heterogeneity of the Indian mi-grants, and created a common bond and identity, which became the psychological force behind their future political solidarity and demands. The near-slavery conditions of plantation life created the environment for common identification and mobilization, despite their social heterogeneity. 'Indianness', as a collective ethnic identity, became a historical construction that evolved out of the conditions of colonial capitalism.

Ethnic separation: A way of life

The social space created by the colonial economy not only generated the separate development of ethnic identities, it also reinforced these antagonistic identities. Part of the antagonistic features of identity creation was the reproduction of stereotypes. Fijians stereotyped Indians as 'cunning', 'selfish' and 'scheming', while Indians stereotyped Fijians as 'lazy', 'stupid' and 'savage.' Again these perceptions reflected the socioeconomic division of the colonial economy; Indians indulged in rigorous plantation life and Fijians were kept in the 'relaxed' subsistence economy.

Over the years, ethnic consciousness was reproduced by various institutions – the state and political system, education and religion, to mention the main ones. The political system since 1874, when Fiji became a British colony, was based on ethnic representation in parliament. Fijians were ruled separately under the Native Administration while Indians remained unrepresented until 1929 when they were granted political representation. At this point the Fijians were still 'represented' by chiefs, acting as 'comprador' for the colonial state, through nominations. The various constitutions such as the 1937 Constitution, 1961 Constitution (which provided partial franchise to Fijians), 1964 Constitution and 1965 Constitution all entrenched separate ethnic representation. Since the 1940s the Indian population had overtaken the Fijian population and this led to fear amongst Fijians of their possible political subordination. Thus, at independence in 1970, the new political system attempted to provide a compromise that was meant to allay Fijian fear of being politically marginalized and also to ensure Indian political security. This 'compromise' was made by elites of the two major ethnic groups. But this did little to undermine future political tension, which culminated in the 1987 military coup (we will look at the coup later).

The important thing to remember is that the ethnicization of politics helped to create political identities that were antagonistic. Fijians perceived Indians as power-hungry and political conspirators bent on destroying Fijian culture and taking away their land. Indians on the other hand saw Fijians as colonial collaborators who were too stupid to make decisions for themselves and who were too lazy to utilize their land fully and contribute to economic development. These perceptions were exaggerated in many cases and were used by extremist Fijian nationalists to justify their call for the repatriation of Indians to India in the 1970s and also as justification for the widespread anti-Indian nationalist euphoria during the 1987 military coup.

The preponderance of Indians in the business sector provided Fijians with 'evidence' of their 'conspiracy' to 'take over' Fiji. This perception was flawed because, although Indians dominated retailing, jewellery and the like, the major industries such as tourism, sugar, manufacturing and wholesaling were still controlled by TNCs and the government.

The ethnicist schema also prevailed in civil society institutions such as sports, religion and education. In sports for instance, rugby was the exclusive domain of Fijians while Indians have been mostly associated with soccer and hockey with Europeans and part-Europeans.

Religion and education have played prominent roles in reproducing ethnicist values and consciousness. Christianity was the main Fijian religion and Hinduism and Islam were the main religions for Indians. Christianity was more than just a guardian of faith, it was also the means by which Fijians defined their culture and identity and also a mobilizational and justificatory mechanism for nationalism. During the 1987 military coup, for instance, Colonel Rabuka the coup-maker and his supporters justified the coup as a 'will of God'. They argued that the coup was an attempt to stop the 'heathen races' from taking over political power in Fiji. The military junta imposed a Sunday ban in response to demands by Methodists (the largest Christian denomination). Methodist youths went amok, fire bombing and desecrating Hindu temples. Religious bigotry and racism were justified as ordained by the Christian God.

The school system largely reflected the ethnic and class character of the Fiji society. School classification and the curriculum taught were based on ethnicity. In 1938, of the 442 schools, 16 were exclusively for children of European and Part-European origins, 346 were for Fijians, and 80 for Indians. Of the 16 Europeans schools, 4 were government run, 5 were run by the Colonial Sugar Refinery (CSR) which controlled the sugar industry, 4 were run by Christian missionaries, and 3 by local European communities.[14]

The apartheid-like ethnic separation of schools helped to legitimize the structural inequality and ethnicist values of the colonial order. By being educated separately, children of different ethnic groups grew up to accept ethnic separateness as a natural condition of life. Other ethnic categories were perceived negatively, and this helped reinforce the ethnic stereotypes about each other.

Although there was a central education department, the emphasis in what was being taught differed considerably. Fijian schools in the 1930s, 40s and 50s were geared towards enabling Fijian children to acquire just enough to be able to read the bible and religious instructions to become good children of God or be reliable 'literate' workers.[15] Meanwhile, for Indians, education was seen as a means of escaping from the bondage of plantation life and a lifeline to a prosperous future. Like Fijians, education amongst Indians was conducted in an atmosphere of ethnic isolation. In Indian schools, apart from the academic subjects, emphasis was on learning their own languages and aspects of their traditional culture. While maintenance of pride in a collective identity, through study of 'traditional culture', was sentimentally comforting for both Fijians and Indians, its effect on reinforcing ethnic parochialism and separation, both at the personal and political levels of interaction, had been significant.

Apart from reinforcing and reproducing divergent ethnic consciousness, cultural education for Fijians and Indians also locked them into a subordinate level of cultural hierarchy. Teaching of vernacular languages and aspects of local culture were considered secondary; in fact, token modes of pedagogy. The primary mode of instruction was, and still is, English. It was, and still is, the only compulsory subject in the Fiji school system. English was not only a language, but a mode of articulation and reasoning. It was a total cultural mould, an instrument of cultural hegemony. One's degree of 'civilization' and status in the community was determined by one's proficiency in the English language and familiarity with English middle class cultural values. High chiefs, especially the educated ones, were usually considered to be the most 'civilized' because of their near-perfect imitation of British 'Oxford' English and English high-class cultural values. Some of these chiefs were educated at Oxford and were specially groomed by the colonial state to run Fiji and continue to perpetuate the British political values after independence.

The curriculum taught over the years, until now, revolved around the Eurocentric world-view which presented everything European as superior. History, for instance, reinforced the myths about 'great' British kings and heroes. School textbooks still talk about Pacific Islands being 'discovered' by Abel Tasman, Captain James Cook, etc. Colonial and post-colonial education had two mutually reinforcing latent effects: the reproduction of European cultural hegemony, and reproduction of ethnic segregation.

As ethnicity became perpetually reproduced, politicized and crystallized, it also became objectified as a legitimate social construct and representation on its own, around which other realms of social existence were to be defined.[16] Moreover, the political and ideological tension built up over the years exploded into a military coup on 14 May 1987, a month after the Indian-dominated Fiji Labour Party-National Federation Party Coalition won over the Fijian-dominated Alliance Party in a general election a month before.

Ethnic explosion: the 1987 military coup

The military coup took place on 14 May 1987 after the defeated Alliance

Party, fearing losing control of its established political and economic interests, mobilized nationalist passion, with the support of the military, to overthrow the new multi-racial Coalition. The intervention of the predominantly Fijian military was justified as protecting Fijian interests from being usurped by 'foreign races'.

Following the coup were widespread arrests, torture and intimidation of many Indians and Fijian opponents of the coup. There were riots in the capital city against Indians, with their shops and vehicles destroyed, and there was widespread arson. The strategy was to make life as miserable as possible for the Indians and force them to leave Fiji. The Methodist Church was strongly supportive of the coup and even suggested that, now that the 'heathens' were overthrown from political power, Christianity was to be the state religion. For five years, until 1992, Fiji was ruled by decree, imposed by a series of post-coup 'governments'. The 1992 election was carried out under what has been described as the 'racist' 1990 Constitution, promulgated by decree by the post-coup junta. The 1990 Constitution attempted to reassert Fijian political ascendancy and marginalized the political rights of Indians and other ethnic groups.

The coup brought into focus a number of important concerns. Firstly, it brought into question the value of democratic participation in an ethnically divided society. In the case of Fiji, although democracy (or liberal democracy to be more precise) through the 1970 Constitution was generally considered to be 'the' solution to Fiji's ethnic problems, this proved not to be the case. Lurking below the facade of democracy was collective ethnic animosity and intolerance, reproduced through political, religious and educational institutions, which were easily mobilized by nationalists to serve particular political ends. Formal democracy became unworkable when nationalist agitation on a large scale, supported by a highly politicized Fijian-dominated military controlled political centre stage. Secondly, the imposition of dominant ethnic values involved the use of coercion to subjugate various ethnic groups and their values. The coup for instance attempted to suppress the Hindu religion and promote Christianity as the dominant religion through violent means, using biblical texts as moral justification. Thirdly, the coup intensified the Indians' sense of insecurity as they felt culturally persecuted. Although they considered Fiji as their home, the coup reminded them of the fragility and insecurity of their Diaspora position. Fourthly, the coup increased the sense of distrust between the two major races. Friends suddenly became 'enemies' and families were separated as migration, especially amongst Indians, increased. In 1987 alone about 13,445 people migrated overseas, compared to a mere 3,691 in 1986.[17] Lastly, a major irony was that the coup forced the different communities to reassess and redefine their relations with each other. 'Multi-racialism', the dominant political slogan of the 1970s and 80s, was no longer to be taken for granted. Fiji had seen the worst and there was a feeling of 'ethnic fatigue', as there was realization that preoccupation with ethnicity hindered harmonious relations and was a barrier to economic development. This was the atmosphere within which a new national reconciliatory process took place. Civil society organizations and a number of liberal political organizations and leaders began campaigning for a new reconciliatory constitution which would represent the collective aspirations and values of all ethnic groups in Fiji.

Promoting multi-ethnic values: The role of civil society

Two big tasks which faced civil society in Fiji were, first, the attempt to come to terms with the dominance of ethnicized values which led to social fragmentation at all levels of society; and secondly, the search for common values to enable the ethnically fragmented society to come to terms with their antagonistic history and to collectively embrace a national spirit based on national reconciliation. A number of important civil society initiatives were made towards these ideals.

One of the generally agreed solutions was that it was important to reform the 1990 Constitution which institutionalized racial discrimination. It was on this basis that the Fiji Constitution Review Commission (CRC) was appointed by the president in March 1995, to review the constitution and make recommendations based on nation-wide consultation with civil society organizations and individuals. Thus the new 1997 Constitution, which provided for a framework for national reconciliation, was largely the result of this democratic consultation. The new constitution provided for a multi-party, multi-ethnic government and a series of concessions that appealed to various ethnic groups.

In addition to the constitutional changes, a number of civil society organizations such as the Fiji-I-Care, Inter-Faith and the Fiji Citizens Constitutional Forum (CCF) have been involved in facilitating multi-ethnic agendas through various programmes.[18] The Fiji-I-Care's role was to promote goodwill through more inter-ethnic interaction while the Inter-Faith brought together all the various beliefs – including the various Christian denominations, Islam, Hinduism, Buddhism and Sikhism – to worship together under a common roof. The CCF was a more political, although non-partisan group, which campaigned for constitutional reforms that reflected the multi-ethnic character of the nation, human rights and good governance.

Amongst the achievements of the CCF campaign were the incorporation of multicultural studies in the school curriculum and the setting up of the Human Rights Commission, amongst others. The introduction of multicultural studies in schools was significant because it attempted to negate the hidden curriculum that encouraged ethnic consciousness throughout the century. The intention was to socialize students with multi-ethnic values at an early age and in a more formal way.

Fiji's future political stability would depend to a great extent on how ethnic tolerance is institutionalized, not only politically in the constitution, but also psychologically and socially in relation to how multi-ethnic values are articulated in everyday relationships.

Conclusion

Ethnic values result from the way ethnic groups define the normative parameters of their collective identity. In multi-ethnic societies these values define the extent and character of interaction with other ethnic groups. More often than not, these interactions take antagonistic forms which would have dramatic consequences on society generally. In Fiji, the separate reproduction of ethnic identities and values from the colonial to the post-colonial periods, and official encouragement of this by the state, provided the social and political environment for ethnic antagonism, culminating in the 1987 military coup. Deployment of ethnic values as instruments for political mobilization and justification for various political and economic interests is potentially volatile and could lead to disastrous consequences. The role of civil society in creating an environment for multi-ethnic harmony, using political, religious and educational mechanisms, has been crucial in Fiji. Creating a collective national identity became an important national priority – a collective identity which synthesized diversity in a deliberate and almost social engineering way. Thus the 1997 Constitution, amongst other things, officially declared that everyone in Fiji, despite their ethnicity, was to be called a 'Fiji Islander'.

Notes

1. See Haralambos, M and Holborn, M (1995) *Sociology: Themes and perspectives*, Collins Educational, London.
2. See Parsons, T (1964) *Social Structure and Personality*, Free Press, New York.
3. See for instance Furnivall, J S (1948) *Colonial Policy and Practice*, Cambridge University Press, Cambridge.
4. For instance see Black, C (1966) Change as a condition of modern life, in *Modernization: Dynamics of growth*, ed M Weiner, VAO, Washington.
5. This premise is based on the Social Darwinian assumption about the 'superiority' of some societies over others. It became the philosophical basis for 'scientific racism'. See for instance McClelland, D (1961) *The Achieving Society*, van Nostrand, Princetown.

6. This view has influenced neo-Marxian and non-Marxian perspectives alike. Gramsci (a neo-Marxian) argues that hegemony arises from control over cultural and ideological institutions in society by dominant classes (see Gramsci, 1971). A similar argument is made by Bourdieu (who regards himself as a 'non-Marxist'), who argues that dominant classes impose dominant values and declare them legitimate. Because cultural values are merely impositions by the powerful, they are 'arbitrary' thus the term *cultural arbitrary* (see Bourdieu, 1994).

7. Values are social constructs that evolve in relation to the dynamics of specific social conditions. Although there are some acknowledged universal values – such as honesty or freedom, for example – how they are articulated in everyday human relationships would depend on the moral system and political interests of the concerned society or group. For instance, in the name of 'freedom' not only are they interpreted differently, they are also used as convenient means to justify certain practices. They are not necessarily consensual in a given socio-historical situation. Values are only meaningful in relation to the political and social context from which they emerge. As societies change, so too do their values. As societies increasingly become integrated through globalization, values – whether they relate to human rights, sustainability, equality, freedom, liberty, etc – also become globalized, and become part of a global 'ethical system'.

8. See, for instance, Brown, D (1994) *The State and Ethnic Politics in Southeast Asia*, Routledge, London; also Stavenhagen, R (1996) *Ethnic Conflicts and the Nation-State*, Macmillan, London.

9. This powerful chiefly elite and the legitimizing ideology of 'tradition' had been nurtured and incorporated into the political power structure of Fiji's political system, and became a permanent component of Fiji's political system. During the colonial and post-colonial periods, this dominant traditional elite was used as the translator and guardian of Fijian 'tradition'. It embodied a mutual synthesis of despotic and nepotic rule over ethnic Fijians; despotic because chiefly rule, legitimized by Christianity and traditional myths, was considered an unquestioned divine right, and nepotic because most high chiefs were related by blood and they reproduced their dominance through endogamy and monopoly of key roles and positions in political leadership, civil life and the military.

10. Narayan (1984), pp 33–34.

11. The ideological justification for the Native Policy was derived from the anthropological Social Darwinist stereotyping that 'lower races' needed to be allowed to develop separately at their own pace, because they could not compete with the 'superior races' (survival of the fittest). Within this racist discourse was created a relationship of dependency (on British paternalism), a system of 'traditional' despotism by chiefs to rule on behalf of the Fijians.

12. The Native Policy provided the fertile ground for the construction and reproduction of a 'primordial' ethnic identity of the ethnic Fijians. Previously, ethnic Fijians lived in autonomous social units. The colonial discourse reconstructed an identity, based on ethnic Fijians as a primordial grouping, with common origins and an unbroken connection with a mythical past. The politically charged distinctions between the concepts of *taukei* (owner) versus *vulagi* (foreigner) discourse had its origin in this process of social reconstruction, and became a

permanent part of the ethnic Fijian definition of political space. The Native Policy also legitimized and crystallized the dominance of a reconstructed chiefly system. Independent chiefdoms and local polities were centralized under preferred paramount chiefs, acting as comprador for the colonial state. Certain chiefdoms were marginalized and others propped up to ensure a system of streamlined authority under a single structure.

13. Gillion (1962), p 209.
14. Narayan (1984), pp 72–75.
15. There was a lot of emphasis put on becoming 'good Christians', and being subservient to 'divinely ordained' worldly authorities, and being a 'good Fijian', by being respectful to one's chief. Both had the effect of neutralizing critical thinking and independent consciousness, and breeding unquestioning consent. Education was not seen as a vehicle for social mobility and social reflection, but a tool of domestication, and of one's acceptance of one's subaltern position in the social hierarchy. The reproduction of values based on ethnic and class differentiation reproduced a pattern of political behaviour consistent with the dominant hegemonic order.
16. An unfortunate consequence has been that political discourse which is not based on ethnic logic is considered marginal and illegitimate. The political divide is defined by the politicization of ethnicity as the dominant factor, around which a complex interplay of religious, tribal and other historically determined forms of loyalty revolve. The military coup of 1987 merely intensified the ethnic antagonism, and despite this, there have been serious efforts to search for common values that will deconstruct the dominant ethnicist values, and empower the civil society.
17. See Fiji Bureau of Statistics (1992).
18. The Fiji-I-Care and the Inter-Faith are fundamentally religious in orientation, and have been actively involved in mobilizing people of different ethnicity and faith to worship together and come to terms with each other's values. The central focus is on moral enlightenment as a counter to political fragmentation and contradiction. The members of the Fiji-I-Care and Inter-Faith are closely aligned to the CCF, a much more broadly based civil society network which has been campaigning for constitutional reform.

References

Black, C (1966) Change as a condition of modern life, in *Modernization: Dynamics of growth*, ed M Weiner, VAO, Washington

Bourdieu, P (1994) *Reproduction in Education, Society and Culture*, Sage, London

Brown, D (1994) *The State and Ethnic Politics in Southeast Asia*, Routledge, London

Fiji Bureau of Statistics (1992) *Population Statistics*, Fiji Government, Suva

Fiji Constitution Review Commission (1996) *The Fiji Islands, Towards a United Future: Report of the Fiji Constitutional Review Commission*, Fiji Government, Suva

Furnivall, J S (1948) *Colonial Policy and Practice*, Cambridge University Press, Cambridge

Gillion, K L (1962) *Fiji's Indian Migrants: A history to the end of the indenture*, Oxford University Press, Oxford

Gramsci, A (1971) *Selections from Prison Notebooks*, New Left Books, New York

Haralambos, M and Holborn, M (1995) *Sociology: Themes and perspectives*, Collins Educational, London

Lal, B (1988) *Power and Prejudice: The making of the Fiji crisis*, New Zealand Institute of International Affairs, Wellington

McClelland, D (1961) *The Achieving Society*, van Nostrand, Princetown

Narayan, J (1984) *The Political Economy of Fiji*, South Pacific Review Press, Suva

Parsons, T (1964) *Social Structure and Personality*, Free Press, New York

Premdas, R (1982) Constitutional challenges: the rise of Fijian nationalism, *Pacific Perspective*, **10** (2)

Stavenhagen, R (1996) *Ethnic Conflict and the Nation-State*, Macmillan, London

Chapter 22

A Canadian Experience: Transcending Pluralism

Donald Santor

Introduction: historical foundation

Moral education has been a significant part of public schooling in Canada from the beginning of the 19th century. In the Province of Ontario,[1] as in most other parts of Canada, public schooling was erected on the twin pillars of moral education and religious education. Values education was a little-known term in the 19th century; instead, the emphasis was placed on moral education – education that taught children appropriate behaviour, education that taught them right from wrong.

Throughout the 19th century, educators never wavered in their commitment to teaching morality. It was enshrined in law and in the regulations that governed public schooling, and without a break this commitment continued into the 20th century. By 1900 teachers in training were exposed to moral education handbooks (Waldegrave, 1906) in the Normal Schools (teacher training institution). These handbooks, largely expository in nature, were based on sound principles:

> Moral lessons without an ethical atmosphere and discipline in the school would be worse than useless. On the other hand, discipline misses its aim if, under its control, the power of intelligent self-government, and the idea of devotion to the social good, are not developed. (Waldegrave, 1906: 7)

The emphasis was on demonstrating how to teach morality as well as inculcate the traditional virtues that would enable children to become good citizens and employees. Teacher handbooks were soon supplemented with curriculum materials that integrated moral teaching with the subject content. The most common expression of this approach was to integrate morality with literature. For example, a series of widely used readers, subtitled *A Series Embodying a Graded System of Moral Instruction*,[2] included stories, poems, myths, religious texts and aphorisms that were selected for their moral content. Themes that were repeatedly placed before the students, among others, included industry, temperance, courage, charity, purity, righteousness and heroism. Though a little outdated, this approach has never completely fallen into disfavour. This prescriptive approach received full support from the parents because they believed it affirmed what they were doing at home, and that it was consistent with the ethical standards of Christianity.

The clearest and most complete direction given to teachers appeared in the revised Education Act[3] of 1944. Revised once again in 1998, the direction to teach morality remained virtually unchanged:

> It is the duty of a teacher... to inculcate by precept and example respect for religion, the principles of Judaeo-Christian morality and the highest regard for truth, justice, loyalty, love of country, humanity, benevolence, sobriety, industry, frugality, purity, temperance and all other virtues.[4]

The Ministry of Education continuously believed that teaching values were necessary for the education of children, but it did not indicate how it was to be done. There was, however, general agreement that the values inculcated or taught should be consistent with the Judaeo-Christian tradition. Consequently, moral education was often integrated with teaching non-doctrinal Christianity in the public schools and doctrinal Christianity in the Roman Catholic separate schools.

By the 1960s many Jewish, Muslim and secular parents expressed their opposition to the exclusive teaching of Christianity in the public schools, even though it included a moral dimension. Their opposition was based largely on the fact that Canadian society included a broad range of religious traditions, and it would be inappropriate to either expose or impose Christianity alone on Jewish, Hindu, Buddhist, Muslim or Aboriginal children and ignore these other faiths. This opposition reflected the fact that Canada had become a multicultural society,[5] and that it was no longer acceptable to fuse the teaching of morality with religion in the public schools. Parents still wanted moral education, but many of them wanted it to be disentangled from religious instruction. To accommodate their concern, provincial governments established a number of commissions to investigate the problem and make recommendations. Two main recommendations emerged from their re-

ports: firstly, that children should receive a systematic programn
education, and secondly, that religious education should include e
the world's major religious traditions (Ontario Department of I ....aion,
1969). In spite of what appeared to be a reasonable approach to the moral education of children, considerable opposition was mounted by parental groups
all over Canada.

Opposition to moral values education

Parental opposition to values education stemmed from a variety of sources.
Many parents questioned why the schools were taking on something new
when already they had an overloaded curriculum. Instead, some parents
urged the schools to concentrate on the basics – the three R's – and leave the
teaching of values, and especially moral values, to the home and to the religious community. Value educators conducted numerous 'home and school'[6]
information sessions to explain that the teaching of values and morality had
always been part of the curriculum and that it was nothing new. In addition
parents had to be reassured that both the home and school had a joint responsibility for engaging in the moral education of the children and that it was not
the exclusive domain of either.

Led by some Christian churches, opposition from religious communities
advanced and reinforced parental concerns. These churches stated that what
the children needed to know was laid down in scripture. There was a strong
tendency to treat Biblical morality as absolute: teachers should simply concentrate on inculcating the rules and norms of behaviour that were found in
the Bible. The non-Christian communities were somewhat fearful of this approach – it might perpetuate the Christian imperialism that they had suffered
under for so many years. Resistance from the churches moderated slightly
when they realized that the initiative for moral values education emanated
from the Christian community in the 19th century, and that the school's
mandate was essentially consistent with their own. Resistance from the other
world faith traditions declined when parents realized there was considerable
agreement on the moral values that should be inculcated or nurtured. But the
central question, whether moral values education could exist apart from religious education or from a religious tradition, would continue to be a source of
contention. The conventional wisdom was that since the various religious
traditions had different values and ethical standards, it would be very difficult, if not impossible, to develop a values education programme that could
transcend multi-faith pluralism.

By the late 1960s Canada openly acknowledged that it had become a multicultural society, and this reality was reflected in a change in both attitude and

policy.[7] Visible minorities were now a significant component of the population; immigrants from Africa, Asia and Latin America were easily distinguishable from the dominant population, and they seemed to embrace different values. As the number of immigrants increased, they found their voice and sought to have their values expressed in the education system. The multicultural policy of the late 1960s was enshrined in the *Canadian Charter of Rights and Freedoms* (1982) and gave their concerns legal standing:

> 15. (1) Every individual is equal before and under the law and has the right to equal protection and equal benefit of the law without discrimination and, in particular, without discrimination based on race, national or ethnic origin, colour, religion, sex, age, or mental or physical disability.

The concerns of ethnic minorities, now legitimized by the Charter, sharpened the questions that were raised concerning values education. Whose values will the school teach? Will the values of the visible ethnic minorities be included? Can a values education programme transcend a multitude of ethnic and religious communities? Should ethnic/religious minorities be entitled to their own schools funded from the public purse? While the different ethnic and religious communities did not flatly oppose values education, they did compel educators to think more seriously about establishing a broadly based foundation.

One of the most justifiable sources of opposition to values education arose from the methodology used in the early projects. Some projects, for example, were based heavily on Kohlberg's theory of moral development. Students were often engaged in discussing moral dilemmas that had little to do with their lives. Although Kohlberg's theory had much to offer, many teachers, parents and religious leaders were troubled by a taxonomy of reasoning that appeared to rely on genetic structuralism. In spite of the considerable criticism of Kohlberg's moral development theory, children were often subjected to simplistic measurement devices that classified them by 'stage', or assigned them to a stage of moral reasoning based on their age.

Projects that drew heavily on 'values clarification' theory (Raths *et al*, 1978) brought justifiable charges of moral relativism, invasion of privacy and engaging in therapy without proper training. Students in a classroom setting might be asked what they would most like to improve: 'your looks, the way you use your time, or your social life' (Simon *et al*, 1972). While many of the exercises were harmless and fun to do, the ones that probed students' insecurities or exposed some of their most private thoughts received considerable attention. Articles in the daily press about the 'Lifeboat Dilemma' or the 'Stranded on the Moon Dilemma' aggravated the situation. Public discussion and controversy reached such a point that in 1981 the Ontario Minister of Education issued a memorandum proscribing approaches in values education that were based on therapeutic psychology or that invaded the privacy of the child. The memorandum asserted that privacy of both the child and the home is one of the fundamental tenets of a democratic society. Consequently, *educational* models were acceptable, *therapeutic* models were not.

Resolution of the major issues

Universality of values education

A major step forward in the development of a values education programme that could transcend different cultural communities was the eventual acceptance by parents that education about values was taking place all the time and was taking place everywhere, in spite of any efforts to impede or promote it. Children, regardless of their ethnic roots and religious traditions, were learning values in virtually every activity they engaged in: playing in the street, attending mid-week activities, going to church, synagogue or mosque, playing on athletic teams, listening to music, or going to school. Within the school setting, values were implicitly and explicitly taught through the adherence to rules, through the selection of course content, through the pedagogical techniques employed by the teacher, and through the everyday communication that occurred when teachers and students were talking with each other. The fundamental point to emerge from this observation was that the teaching of values could not be stopped, even if parents, teachers and government tried. Therefore it made sense for home and school to co-operate, since they shared the same child, and to identify more clearly what should be done, and how, and then to get on with it.

Policy position

Before teachers and schools could systematically approach moral values education, it was necessary to develop a policy position that could transcend ethnic and religious minorities and assure them that such a programme was not a threat to their cultural identity. In 1980, for example, the Ontario Ministry of Education included values in the 13 fundamental goals for education:

> The goals of education, therefore, consist of helping each student develop:
>
> - Esteem for the customs, cultures, and beliefs of a wide variety of societal groups (10);
> - Respect for the environment and a commitment to the wise use of resources (12);

● Values related to personal ethical or religious beliefs and to the common welfare of society (13). (Ministry of Education, Toronto, 1980)

Conspicuous by its absence is the specific suggestion that there could be a
critical reflection on values or value positions that were detrimental to the
well-being of society. In recommending that students develop 'esteem for the
customs, cultures, and beliefs of a wide variety of societal groups', schools
might inadvertently condone practices that are injurious to the well-being of
the individual or of the society. For instance, a cultural or religious minority
(as well as the dominant society for that matter) could advocate discrimination against women or against another cultural or religious group; taken to
the extreme, this goal might even condone female genital mutilation. Surely
teachers and students should not be expected to respect these kinds of customs or values. Teachers would soon discover, however, that students would
inevitably be drawn into a critique of values and customs, regardless of their
origin, that were detrimental to human well-being.

Foundational values

The most pressing question asked by parents when they were first exposed to
values education was: Whose values will you teach? There was an intuitive
assumption that schools or teachers would inculcate or indoctrinate only
their own values, if not the predominant societal values. Parents from minority groups concluded that their own unique cultural and religious values
might be ignored or suppressed. Provincial and local jurisdictions engaged
parents in dialogue, and it soon became apparent that there was a set of foun-
dational values on which all could agree. To allay parental and teacher concerns, lists of values were included in the education programmes. Values
common to many programmes were:

compassion	patience
co-operation	peace
courage	respect for the environment
courtesy	respect for life
freedom	respect for others
generosity	respect for self
honesty	responsibility
justice	self-discipline
loyalty	sensitivity
moderation	tolerance.

(Ministry of Education, Toronto, 1983: 6)

Listing values solved one problem: assuring parents that the schools stood for something, and that there was a foundation for the values education programme. The list of values resolved a political problem, but left unanswered several underlying philosophical, ethical and theological questions: What do these values mean? Are they absolute? Where did these values come from? Can, or do they exist apart from a religious tradition? What value(s), if any, has priority? What kind of action or behaviour do these values require of the individual? How do we resolve a conflict between values? For example, does 'respect for life' and 'respect for others' endorse or condemn capital punishment? It was obvious that not all cultural or religious communities answered these questions the same way; but it was also obvious that there was considerable disagreement within an ethnic, cultural or religious community. Religious communities were divided among and within themselves on a myriad of issues: for example, homosexuality, abortion, birth control, euthanasia, corporal punishment, toleration of other faith traditions, and the role and status of women. Reluctantly, parents in all cultural communities realized they would have to wrestle with these questions as they engaged in the moral growth of their children.

There is still no complete agreement on whether there are universal values that can transcend a pluralistic society (Fleischer, 1994; Holm and Bowker, 1994). Regardless, there is a social reality that had to be addressed: children from a variety of cultural/ethnic/religious traditions sit in the same classroom, live in the same neighbourhood and play in the same street, and they will live and work in the same pluralistic society for the rest of their lives. Therefore the fundamental question that the schools must address is: What can the schools do to better prepare children for this reality? The choices are few: do nothing; separate them and educate them in cultural/religious enclaves; or engage them in a values education programme that embraces the pluralistic reality. Not to adopt the last option is to abdicate responsibility.

Aims and objectives

While the Ministries of Education developed general policy positions, it was left to local boards of education to write specific objectives that could help classroom teachers implement the general policy. Once again there was a need to assure parents that their particular culture or religious tradition would not be threatened. Specific objectives that appeared in board of education value programmes included:

Students will have the opportunity:

- to become aware of the values of self, home, school and community;
- to clarify personal and societal values;

- to reflect on individual and societal values;
- to become sensitive to the values of others;
- to consider the consequences of one's values for self and others;
- to become aware of the importance of one's values to an individual and to society;
- to recognize a value conflict;
- to facilitate the development of moral reasoning;
- to develop methods for resolving value conflicts; and
- to promote the development of morally autonomous individuals who live and act with regard for the rights, life and dignity of all persons.
(London (Ontario) Board of Education, 1983)

Most parents, regardless of their cultural origin, could support these objectives: they reflected and confirmed their life experience. If children were to become responsible citizens, both the home and the school, as well as the religious community, would have to devote considerable effort in helping children internalize and act on these objectives. Collectively considered, these objectives would help children make the transition from moral conformity to responsible moral autonomy, and would increasingly urge them to consider and act upon the well-being of the common good.

During the 1980s objectives were rewritten as outcomes; for example, instead of stating that students 'will have the opportunity to become sensitive to the values of others' it was now stated that students 'will be sensitive to others'. Educators soon recognized that it was impossible to guarantee that value outcomes such as these could be realized, and in the 1990s 'outcomes' were rewritten as 'expectations'. Few parents, regardless of their ethnic or religious roots, could disagree with objectives, outcomes or expectations that addressed the needs of the individual as well as the needs of society.

Classroom methodology

While most parents could be convinced that values education was good for children and that it was very much a part of what teachers did on a regular basis, parents still wanted to be assured that the methods used by the teachers would be supportive of them and would not invade the privacy of either the student or the home. Consequently, teachers had to re-examine the approaches they were using and find a way to incorporate the values that would nurture pro-social behaviour. Instead of concentrating on moral autonomy in the early years, teachers would emphasize discussion and reflection on those values that would advance the well-being of the individual and of the society – in short the values that would promote human well-being. As the child matured the emphasis would change (Figure 22.1), but the nurturing of pro-social values would always be a major part of the programme. It was necessary to nurture pro-social behaviour during the early years, but to work towards developing socially responsible citizens who would be capable of making autonomous decisions appropriate for a democracy. The degree of control exercised in the primary grades would be greatly relaxed during the adolescent years, even though the achievement of social responsibility and moral autonomy varied with the individual.

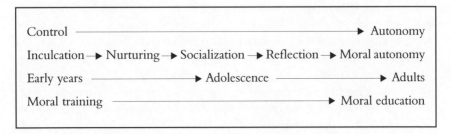

Figure 22.1   *Multiple perspectives on values education*

One of the pedagogical approaches that helped advance this perspective was developed by Clive Beck (1980) and his associates. The Reflective Approach to Values Education required children to consider the values that contributed to social well-being, namely honesty, kindness, co-operation, sharing and helpfulness, but they were also required to reflect on these values. For example, the mini-unit entitled *Helping* (Beck, 1980) included the following sequence of activities: Give examples of helping. Why do people help each other? Why is helping important? Can people help others too much?, etc. Parents from most cultural and ethnic communities found this approach acceptable because it coincided with responsible and effective parenting. Parents certainly wanted their children to understand and act on the value of helping, and on reflection they realized that too much help is detrimental to the child – it could stifle the development of independence and initiative, values that are essential to maturity and citizenship.

Organic fusion with the existing curriculum

Educators used a variety of approaches for implementing a values education programme in the classroom: some schools established separate courses in values education; some designed discrete units within established courses, and some favoured what became known as 'organic fusion' with the existing curriculum. Parents were not entirely supportive of the separate course approach because it aggravated the problems of an already crowded curriculum. There was little support for a new programme that deprived students of time spent on core subjects. The discrete unit approach worked well as long as the topics chosen fitted the curriculum. Beck's mini-unit on *Helping* for Grade 1 children fitted nicely into the study of the family and school community. Few parents could object that this was not supportive.

The 'organic fusion' approach integrated the teaching of values with the existing curriculum. Topics and units, already part of the curriculum, were used as vehicles for moral values discussion. After students had studied the relevant database and the associated concepts, the stage was set for values analysis and reflection. Teachers usually combined the best features of moral reasoning[8] and alternatives reasoning (Fraenkel, 1980) (Figure 22.2) to explore the topic, to clarify the issues and to examine the alternatives through which there might be resolution. Almost every topic in the curriculum had a values dimension, but some more than others explicitly included relevant value conflicts: citizenship education, human rights, animal rights, social welfare, resource utilization, capital punishment, use and testing of nuclear weapons, free trade, abortion, civil disobedience, same sex marriage and benefits etc. Ignoring these topics and the inherent value conflicts would ill prepare students for living in a complex world.

Vision for values education

In spite of a century-long commitment to values education, parents and educators have had considerable difficulty articulating a vision that could transcend their diverse concerns and goals. At first the vision was expressed in utilitarian language with a focus on the student – to produce good citizens, to help children act justly, or to engage in character formation. Later the vision expanded and took on a societal focus – to develop a just society, to promote the well-being of the common good, or to advance human well-being. While none of the visions caused great alarm, none was universally adopted. Embedded within each of them was a recognition of various philosophical, theological or psychological ideas. The vision that prevails at any time seems to reflect the needs of society and the political philosophy that holds office.

Conclusion

In spite of the widespread acceptance for values education, there remains some opposition to the idea of a programme that is a significant component of the curriculum.

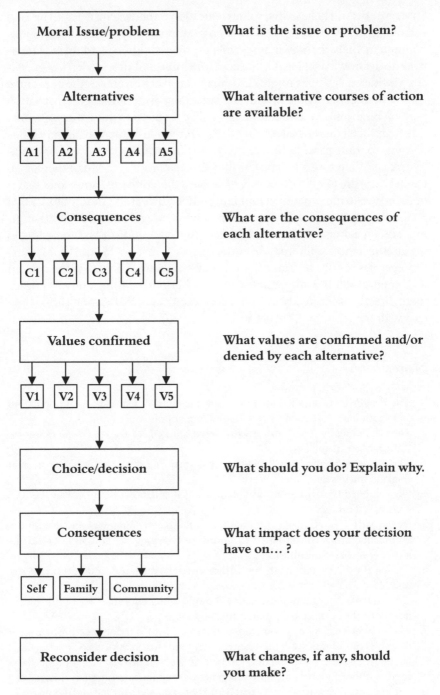

Figure 22.2 *Alternatives reasoning approach*

Some parents still believe that values education is their exclusive domain, and still others believe that only a values programme that is rooted in a religious tradition, namely their own, is suitable for their children. And there is resistance to acknowledge, let alone accept, the impact of postmodernity on values: the idea that values might be human constructions raises the combined spectre of uncertainty, relativism and situation ethics. To suggest that values may not be absolute and that students will be required to think through some value conflicts, thereby advancing their own moral autonomy, is very troublesome to some parents. Situation ethics is frequently viewed as moral relativism, and therefore a betrayal of the Christian tradition. Moral theologian Daniel Maguire (1978) effectively deals with this concern: 'Any ethics that is not sensitive to the situation it is judging is not ethics at all. And any ethics that is closed to the situation is closed to creativity.' Maguire reinforces his argument by appealing to Aquinas: 'Human actions are good or bad according to the circumstances' (Thomas Aquinas, *Summa Theologica* I II q. 18 a.3).

Regardless of this resistance, values education just won't go away, nor can it be suppressed. It is impossible to teach children anything and not engage them directly or indirectly in values education: values education simply 'comes with the territory' (Purpel and Ryan, 1976).

Notes

1. The Province of Ontario contains about one-third of Canada's total population and about half of Canada's English-speaking population.
2. *The Fourth Golden Rule Book: A series embodying a graded system of moral instruction* (1916), Macmillan, Toronto.
3. The revised Education Act of 1944 was patterned after the Education Act passed in England during the Second World War.
4. Consolidated Ontario Education Statues and Regulations 1998, pp 188–89, Carswell, Toronto.
5. By the early 1800s Canada was a multicultural society, but it was possible for the dominant cultural communities to ignore both the presence and rights of the minority ethnic communities.
6. During the 1970s and 1980s the author conducted several hundred home and school workshops and information sessions for parents and teachers. The collective result was the gradual acceptance of moral values education as a rightful component of the educational programme.
7. The Province of Ontario alone can identify well over 100 distinct ethnic/cultural/religious communities; but this reality is not unique to Ontario – it is Canada-wide.
8. Lawrence Kohlberg's moral development model can be easily used in the classroom without adopting the inherent genetic structuralism. Emphasis instead can be placed on a growth paradigm that began with a concern for self and would eventually include a concern for others and ultimately a concern for the rights of all.

References

Beck, C, McCoy, N and Bradley-Cameron, J (1980) *Reflecting on Values: Learning materials for grades 1–6*, Ontario Institute for Studies in Education, Toronto

Fleischer, S (1994) Limits of universalism, in *The Ethics of Culture*, Chapter 1, Cornell University Press, Ithaca, NY

Fraenkel, J (1980) *Helping Students Think and Value: Strategies for teaching the social studies*, 2nd edn, Prentice-Hall, Englewood Cliffs, NJ

Government of Canada (1982) *Canadian Charter of Rights and Freedoms*, Queen's Printer, Ottawa, Section 15:1

Holm, J and Bowker, J (eds) (1994) *Making Moral Decisions: Themes in religious studies*, Pinter, London

London Board of Education (1983) *Moral Education Manual*, Ontario, London

Maguire, D C (1978) *The Moral Choice*, Doubleday, New York

Ministry of Education, Toronto (1980) *Issues and Directions: The response to the Final Report of the Commission on Declining School Enrolments in Ontario*, pp 6–7, Toronto

Ministry of Education, Toronto (1983) *Personal and Societal Values: A resource guide for the primary and junior divisions*, p 6, Toronto

Ontario Department of Education (1969) *Religious Information and Moral Development: The Report of the Committee on Religious Education in the Public Schools of the Province of Ontario*, Toronto

Purpel, D and Ryan, K (eds) (1976) *Moral Education:…It comes with the territory*, McCutcheon Publishing, Berkeley, CA

Raths, L E, Harmin, M and Simon, S B (1978) *Values and Teaching: Working with values in the classroom*, 2nd edn, Merrill Books, Ohio

Simon, S B, Howe, L W and Kirschenbaum, H (1972) *Values Clarification: A handbook of practical strategies for teachers and students*, Hart Publishing, New York

Waldegrave, A J (c 1906) *A Teacher's Handbook of Moral Lessons*, Thomas Nelson and Sons, London

Index

Alexander, H.   2
Annette, J.   1, 3, 4
Apple, M.   161
Aquinas, T.   334
Archer, M.   212–14
Arendt, H.   224
Aristotle   68, 69, 74
Armstrong, P.   219–20, 222, 224, 226
Arnot, M. *et al*   4, 112
Aron, R.   46
Aronowitz, S.   301
Asia   257–70
Australia   285–99
autonomy   149
Ayer, A.J.   204

Balfour, R.   254
Ball, S.J.   86, 87, 89, 90–92, 103
Barber, B.   110, 115–16, 118
Barber, M.   89–90, 93
Barnett, R.   115
Bates, R.   17
Battistoni, R. *et al*   118
Beazley, K.   288
Becher, T.   115
Beck, C.   331–32
Beck, L.   138
Bender T. *et al*   115
Benhabib, S.   134
Berger, P.L. *et al*   80, 218, 226
Bernstein, B.   215, 227, 253
Bhaskar, R.   204, 207–08, 211
Blackman, S.   86
Bogdan, R.   230
Boswell, J.   134

Bourdieu, P.   81
Boyatzis, R.   159
Brennan, J.   117
Brentano, F.   135
Brown, P. *et al*   84, 85
Bryk, A.S.   20, 21
Buckingham-Hatfield, S.   119
bullying   73

Cairns, J.   3, 6 ff
Callaghan, J.   82
Callan, E.   112
Canada   323–334
Carr, D.   19, 41, 72
Charter   88   110
China   273–   83
choice   90–91, 103–4
Christie, P.   252
Citizen's Charter   110
citizenship   4, 6–22, 109–20, 249–55,
      285–99
Clark, D.   93–4
Claxton, G. *et al*   93
Cohen, H.   301
Cole, M.   165
Coleman, J.   144
Collins, M.   161
Comer, J.P.   17
Commission for Racial Equality
      (CRE)   176–77, 179–80
communitarianism   110, 120, 300
community   52ff, 119–20
community service learning   4, 109–120
Community Service Volunteers
      (CSV)   113, 119

competence   159–63
Corbett, J.   107
Costello, P.   112
Crewe, I. *et al*   109
Crick, B.   109, 112–13, 177
Crick report,   109, 113
Cummings, W.K.   261, 263
Curren, C.   135

Daggar, R.   111
Dahrendorf, R.   134
Dearden, R.,   167
Dearing, R.   1, 4, 112–14, 116–17, 119
Delpit, L.   253–254
De Maria, W.   162
democracy   8
Deng, Xiao-Ping   273–74, 277
Denzin, N.   206
Department for Education and
     Employment (DfEE)   6, 102,
     127, 158, 173, 176
Dewey, J.   55, 117, 259
differentiation   98–9
Dionne, E.J.   109
Dore, R.P.   80, 277, 281
Drew, S.   116
Durkheim, E.   79, 223, 300

Education Action Zones   9
Education Acts
   1944   6, 82
   1988   6, 7, 83
   1997   103
educational research   203–17, 218–27,
     230–44
   cross-cultural   257–70
Edwards, J.   112
Edwards, T.   83, 90
Eliot, T.S.   189
Elliott, J.   19, 118
Elshtain, J.B.   111
Ely, M.   231
empathy   64
Erickson, J.   113
Etzioni, A.   110, 130

Fiji   311–321
Finger, M.   221
Fisher, R.   50–56
Fogelman, K.   112
Foucault, M.   13, 44, 86, 209–14,
     209–13, 214
Fraenkel, J.   332
Frankena, W.K.   159–162
freedom   134–35
Freire, P. *et al*   13, 251–52

Gadamer, H.G.   5, 214–15
Gardner, H.   14
General Teaching Council   133, 169–71
Giddens, A.   80, 84, 110, 207, 209
Gilbert, R.   291, 293
Gillborn, D.   164
Gilligan, C.   31 , 117, 300
Gipps, C.   282
Glaser, B.D.   231
golden rule   28, 134
Goodson, I.   139
Gorham, E.   119
Gouldner, A.V.   219
Grace, G.   131
Gray, J.   109, 140
Greider, W.   109
Griffiths, M.   71
Guarasci, R. *et al*   118

Habermas, J.   35, 55–56, 221
Hahn, C.   113
Hale, T.   220, 227
Halsey, A.H.   114
Halstead, J.M. *et al*   19,
Hare, R.   28, 33
Hargreaves, A.   10
Harvey, L.   117
Haydon, G.   2.
Hegel, F.   53
Hill, D.   102
HM Inspectors of Schools (HMI)   12
     see also OFSTED
Hoar, M.   220
Hodgkinson, P.   161

Hogan, P.   137, 142
Hopkins, D.   194–99
Hughes, M.   90
Hyland, T.   47, 160

individual educational plans
      (IEPs)   106
Institute of Education, University of
      London   7
Issit, M.   162–63

Jackson, R.   236
Jacoby, B.   118
James, W.   301
Janks, H.   250, 252
Jarvis, P.   221
John, G.   12, 13, 14, 176
Jones, E.B.   112

Kant, I.   35, 63, 301
Kennedy, K.   113
Kerr, D.   113
Kierkegaard, S.   302
Kluckholm, F.   258, 266, 269, 270
Knowledge   7, 8, 15, 16, 86, 88, 209–14
Kohlberg, L.   28, 31 , 44, 56, 58, 63,
      117, 259, 266, 300, 334
Kolakowski, L.   203–4
Kolb, D.   117
Kumar, K.   84, 85
Kymlicka, W.   111

Lasch, C.   130–31, 140–41, 143, 303
Lash, S.   84
Lave, J. et al   11, 12
Lawton, D.   8, 10, 11, 20
Lewis, H.   138
life histories   218–27
Lipman, M.   55
Lipson, L.   132
Little, A.   281, 282, 283
Little, B.   117
Liu, B.   276
Liu, Y.   281
Locke, J.   301

Lonner, W.   260
Lyon, D.   142

McAninch, A.R.   140
MacBeath, J.   13
McCormick, J.   119
MacIntyre, A.   50, 132, 139, 191–92,
      205, 212, 215, 250, 255, 305
Mackie, J.L.   69
McLaughlin, M. et al   21
Macmurray, J.   133
McPhail, P.   259
Macpherson, W.   177–81
Maguire, D.C.   334
Marsh, M.   10
Martin, D.   139
Matthews, T.   59
Mead, G.   63
Merttens, R.   133
Midgley, M.   128–29, 144
Mill, J.S.   301
Miller, N.   222
modernisation   14
Mohan, J.   119
Moore, G.   302
moral education   38–49, 51, 79–93,
      323–34
moral reasoning   27–36, 71
Morley, L. et al   7
Morrow, W.   250–51
Mortimore, P.   12
Mulhall, S.   111, 120

national curriculum   7, 8, 9, 79, 87,
      89, 96–100, 187
National Curriculum Council
      (NCC)   6, 111–12, 216
National Values Forum   2, 18, 51, 72,
      157
National Vocational Qualifications
      (NVQs)   88, 105, 189
Newfield, D.   254–55
New York State Council on
      Curriculum and Assessment   20
Nietzsche, F.   30

Nonaka, I. *et al* 6
Norwich, B. 3, 107
Nottingham Values Group 194–200
Nussbaum, M. 137

Oakley, F. 114
Oakshott, M. 81, 82, 116
OECD 90
OFSTED 5, 8, 105, 108, 128, 164,
  173, 178, 216
O'Hagan, K. 159
Oldfield, A. 111
Oliver, D. 110
Ormell, C. 140
Oser, F.K. 267–68, 270

pancasila 264
pedagogy 136–38
Perkins, D.N. 56–57
personal, social and health education,
  (PSHE) 8, 18, 111–12
Peters, R.S. 190
Petit, P. 111
philosophy for children 50–66
Piaget, J. 58, 259, 270
Plato 58, 68, 69, 306
Poole, R. 69
Popper, K. 305–06
Porter, A. 112
positivism 203–05
Potter, J. 113
Priestley, J. 19
Pring, R. 15, 81, 82, 83, 87, 88, 89,
  129, 190, 193
Prior, D. 110
Prior, W. 292
professionalism 127–44, 147–57, 165–66
Purpel, D. 1, 334
Putnam, R. 110

Qualifications and Curriculum
  Authority (QCA) 8, 17, 18,
  106, 177, 190

Ramsay, J. 162
Randall, P. 73

Ranson, S. 11
Raths, L.E. 326
Raz, J. 131
Reason, P. 224–25
Reddy, S. 251, 253
Reeher, G. *et al*, 118
relativism 30, 36, 326
Riddell, S. 103
Rieff, P. 130
Rigsby, L. *et al* 17
Rimmerman, C. 118
Robertson, R. 84
Rokeach, M. 258, 266, 269
Rose, M. 13
Royal Society of Arts (RSA) 14, 15
Rudduck, J. *et al* 10
Rutter, M. *et al* 10

Sacks, J. 130 , 134
Santor, D. 1
Schluter, M. 133–34
School Curriculum and Assessment
  Authority (SCAA) 2, 18, 43, 45,
  47, 51, 72, 74, 79, 106, 157 –58, 171
Scotland 168–70, 174–76
Scott, D. 5
Scott, P. 114
Scruton, R. 134
Sedgwick, F. 111
Selbourne, D. 143
self-interest 67–75
Shafir, G. 111
Sherman, A. 131
Shilling, C. 88
Simon, S.B. 326
Skilbeck, M. 87
Skinner, B.F. 250
Smith, R. 71
Sockett, H. 132
Socrates 53
South Africa 249–55
Speaker's Commission on
  Citizenship 110, 112
special educational needs 9, 96–07
Spens report 82
Stoll, L. *et al* 13, 20, 92

Stones, E.   193–94
Storkey, E.   133
Stout, J.   132, 141
Straughan, R.   34, 44, 71
Structuration   80
Studies of Society and Environment
      (SOSE)   285–99
Sutherland, S.   6, 21

targets   105
Tate, N.   112, 158, 161, 171
Taylor, C.   111, 302, 307
Taylor, M.   19
teacher education   4, 127–42, 186–200
Teacher Training Agency (TTA)   19,
      89, 106, 128, 158–82, 189–90
Terchek, R.   111
Thayer-Bacon, B.J.   135
Thomas, E.   2
Thompson, M.   136
Tomlinson, J.   2 , 4, 136, 138, 142
Tomlinson, S.   112
Tonnes, F.   54–55
Torrance, H.   87
transcendence   64
Triandis, H.C.   260
Turner, B.S.   14, 111

Universities Council for the Education
      of Teachers (UCET)   147–57

UNESCO   21, 262
Ungoed-Thomas, J.   190–93

values clarification   326–27
Vattimo, G.   130
Verwoerd, H.F.   250
vocationalism   81

Waldman, S.   119
Wang, G.   276
Warnock, M.   35
Wasserman, S.   140
Watson, D. et al   118
Weber, M.   14, 46, 84, 144
Weil, S.W. et al   117
White, J.   17, 34, 71
Williams, R.   86
Wilson, J.   4, 35, 44, 70, 75, 142, 259,
      270
Wittgenstein, L.   141–42
Wolin, S.   111
Wolfe, A.   134
Woodruffe, C.   159
Wringe, C.   2
Wu, F.Z.   281
Wuthnow, R.   110

Young, M.   7, 12

Zhao, Y.L.   281